GUATE ᴍᴀᴌᴀ

Adventures in Nature

Second Edition

Richard Mahler

JOHN MUIR PUBLICATIONS
SANTA FE, NEW MEXICO

John Muir Publications, P.O. Box 613, Santa Fe, New Mexico 87504

Printed in the United States of America.

Second edition. First printing May 1999.

Portions of this book were previously published as *Guatemala: A Natural Destination*
© 1993, 1995 by Richard Mahler.

Library of Congress Cataloging-in-Publication Data
Mahler, Richard.
    Guatemala: adventures in nature / Richard Mahler.—2nd ed.
       p. cm.
    Includes index.
    ISBN 1-56261-430-4
    1. Guatemala—Guidebooks. 2. Natural history—Guatemala—Guidebooks.
    3. Outdoor recreation—Guatemala—Guidebooks.
    I. Title
    F1463.6.M35   1999
    917.28104'53—dc21   00-18064
                                        CIP

Editors: Dianna Delling
Graphics Editor: Heather Pool
Production: Marie J.T. Vigil
Design: Janine Lehmann
Cover design: Janine Lehmann
Typesetting: Marcie Pottern
Maps: Kathleen Sparkes—White Hart Design
Printer: Publishers Press

Title page photo: INGUAT—Woman weaving with back-strap loom
Large Front Cover: © Unicorn Stock, Photos/A. Romy—Temple I at Tikal
Small Front Cover: © Byron Jorjarion—Butterfly
Large Back Cover: © Index Stock Photography, Inc—Dock on Lake Atitlán
Small Back Cover: © Phillip M. Zito—Woman at village market

Distributed to the book trade by
Publishers Group West
Berkeley, California

CONTENTS

CONTENTS

ACKNOWLEDGMENTS

The author wishes to acknowledge the many people—too numerous to name—who generously provided the insight and assistance that made *Guatemala: Adventures in Nature* possible. Particular thanks go to new acquaintances and friends who, often on short notice and with no compensation, went out of the way to help me. For this edition, the list includes Carla Molina, Carlos Crowe, Ken Johnson, Tammy Ridenour, Elizabeth Bell, David and Susie Grenville, Liza Fourré, Scott Davis, Steve Kalminson, Kate Droney, Cathy Lopez-Sandler, Ron Mader, Magda Lopez, Peter Eltringham, Riki Stevens, Ginger Johnson, Andrew Fleckner, Carole Trombetta, Ramiro Tejada, Sandra Orieste, Carol Meyer, John Burnett, John Biskovich, Terry Kovick, Jeff Salz, Mary Dell Lucas, Steele Wotkyns, and Rony Ruíz.

Special thanks go to my talented photographers—Kevin Schafer, Bob Mahler, Tony Rath, Don Usner, Jim Smith, and Elizabeth Bell—as well as the equally skilled editors and graphic artists at John Muir Publications. The Guatemala Tourist Commission (INGUAT) provided valuable assistance in addition to fine maps and photographs.

As always, my greatest appreciation goes to the wise, warm, and wonderful *Guatemaltecos* who always make sure that my days and nights in their lovely country are never to be forgotten.

Gulf of Mexico

Yucatán

CAMPECHE

Quintana Roo

Yucatán

Campeche

Peninsula

MEXICO

BELIZE

BELIZE CITY

Chiapas

Petén

Tikal National Park

BELMOPAN

Lago Petén Itzá
FLORES

13

5

13

MAYA MOUNTAINS

Barrier Reef

Gulf of Honduras

Rio Dulce

PUERTO BARRIOS

GUATEMALA

Verapaces

Lago de Izabal

SIERRA DE LOS CUCHUMATANES

CA 1

SAN PEDRO SULA

Western Highlands

SANTA CRUZ DEL QUICHÉ

CA 14

SIERRA DE LAS MINAS

CA 9

QUETZALTENANGO

Lago de Atitlán

Atitlán N.P.

ANTIGUA

GUATEMALA CITY

JALAPA

CA 10

HONDURAS

9S

CA 2

8

19

12

SANTA ANA

Pacific Ocean

2

EL SALVADOR

N

0 SCALE   115 KILOMETERS   115 MILES   ▨ NATIONAL PARK

▬ • ▬ • ▬ INTERNATIONAL BOUNDARY

1

GUATEMALA: AN ADVENTURE AWAITS

Guatemala has been called—with every justification—the travel bargain of the Americas. Many experienced travelers say it's like Mexico was two decades ago. Today's Guatemala is easily accessible, spectacularly beautiful, friendly, cultured, intriguing, and very inexpensive, while providing high-quality services and values.

Yet none of these attributes, taken alone or together, adequately communicates what makes this a special place. Certainly other countries can be described using the same string of adjectives. Like a delicious salad or a lively dinner party, what makes Guatemala unique is no single ingredient or characteristic but the sum of its many parts.

And what parts it has! From the scalding black-sand beaches of the Pacific to the frigid peaks of 33 volcanoes, from cactus-studded deserts to grassy savannas, Guatemala is one of the most ecologically diverse countries in the world. Its name, in fact, means "land of many trees." Within an area the size of Tennessee, visitors will find tropical jungles, highland pine forests, white-water rivers, crystalline lakes, offshore coral reefs, and musty limestone caverns as well as modern skyscrapers, Spanish colonial cathedrals, and ancient Maya ruins. Guatemala also boasts a pleasant spring-like climate, a modern international airport, and a substantial tourism infrastructure of good roads, hotels, restaurants, and services.

Still, a visitor's strongest impressions are derived not from Guatemala's magnificent natural beauty, awesome archaeological

1

About the Facts and Figures in this Book

Prior to 1996, political unrest in Guatemala discouraged many foreigners from visiting. Since the signing of peace treaties ended the country's civil war, rapid changes have been underway. One result is a slow but steady rise in prices as more and more travelers discover Guatemala. Therefore, please use the prices in this book as a guideline, as they are apt to have changed by the time you read them. (Note that all prices are in U.S. dollars except as indicated.) Every effort has been made to provide accurate information (as of early 1999), including phone numbers and e-mail addresses that can help you verify details on your own. If you find numbers (of any kind) have changed, the author would love to hear from you. Particularly welcome are comments from expatriates living in Guatemala, citizens of Guatemala, and eco-adventurers. Please address your comments to Richard Mahler, c/o John Muir Publications, Box 613, Santa Fe, NM 87504.

monuments, or considerable creature comforts, but rather from the country's 11 million warmhearted people and their indomitable spirit. Whether practicing Spanish verb conjugations with a middle-class family in Antigua or discussing proper *plátano* preparation with a peasant farmer in the Huehuetenango market, travelers are almost always treated with the most gracious charm.

THE MAYA CULTURE

About half of the Guatemalan people are descended directly from the ancient Maya whose sophisticated civilization flourished here for more than a thousand years. Millions of *indígena* (indigenous) Guatemalans dress, speak, work, and worship much as their ancestors did when the Spanish conquistadors marched in from Mexico nearly five centuries ago. In today's Guatemala you can witness the living Maya culture, complete

Don Usner

The traditional backstrap loom is ubiquitous in highland Guatemala.

with ceremonial sacrifices, elaborate timekeeping rituals, and the cultivation of sacred crops.

THE LADINO CULTURE

The most Indian of Central American nations, Guatemala is also the birthplace of Spanish colonialism along the Mesoamerican isthmus. More than 40 percent of its citizens now identify themselves as *Ladinos* (westernized indígena or those of mixed Indian-European descent), and their heritage is reflected in the remnants of Spain's 16th-century conquest, including the massive churches and ornate public buildings of Antigua. Visitors stumble upon colonial Guatemala in the country's rain forest, where the red-brick fort of San Felipe hunkers over the Río Dulce, and on the temperate slopes of Sierra Madre volcanoes, where the elegant mansions of the *patrones* preside over vast coffee and sugarcane plantations. It is the presence of these two vital and often clashing cultures, along with those of the Caribbean-coast Garifuna and other ethnic minorities, that enrich and enliven Guatemala and also curse it with poverty, hunger, and civil unrest.

There is a small but significant minority of Guatemalan citizens who are Caucasian, directly descended from European or North American ancestors. Guatemalans of German heritage, in particular, are found in

3

the coffee industry, while many of U.S. and Canadian descent are employed in tourism and crafts export.

THE POLITICAL SITUATION

Coming to Guatemala means bearing witness to it all, for it is impossible to travel here without confronting the best and worst that this remarkable country has to offer. They exist side by side for everyone to see; socioeconomic problems are not neatly shunted aside or covered up as they are in many countries that might consider themselves more advanced.

Every traveler planning a trip to Guatemala will almost certainly be asked at least once—if not many times—some variation of this central question: "Aren't you concerned, what with all the political repression and civil unrest down there?" This is a fair inquiry, given Guatemala's appalling human rights record and its history of horrific political repression. Fortunately, the level of political violence has been sharply reduced in recent years. In 1996, sweeping peace accords were signed that formally ended 36 years of civil war. In 1997, a period of reconciliation and reconstruction began as the military downsized and guerrillas disbanded.

SAFETY CONCERNS

Guatemala is not as dangerous as is often assumed by foreigners, particularly among those who have never been there. Yet there is enough risk to warrant concern. The best way to minimize your risk is simply by using common sense. For example, it's inadvisable to use illegal drugs such as marijuana or cocaine in Guatemala, or to make remarks and engage in behavior that might be offensive to local people. Above all, it is imprudent to flash signs of wealth—including fancy watches or camera equipment, expensive jewelry or purses—in public places. Don't travel at night unless you've inquired locally about criminal activity in the areas you'll be passing through. If you plan to tour an isolated or rural area, consider hiring a trustworthy local guide to show you around. Inform yourself before you become vulnerable.

It's important to point out that individuals have followed all of these precautions and still been robbed—or worse—in Guatemala in recent years. People have been held-up or burglarized in the middle of Tikal's main plaza and in the finest hotel of Guatemala City. Even members of the police force and military have been robbed, while on duty and in uniform!

Yet it's equally important to note that the vast majority of Guatemalans are friendly, helpful, and honest people, who are often happy to go out of their way to help foreign visitors. As elsewhere in the world, including the U.S., the negative actions of a handful of desperados can overshadow the good deeds of thousands.

In 1999, conditions in Guatemala were in a state of flux. As this book went to press, for example, the slopes of the previously risky Pacaya volcano were heavily patrolled by the National Police and considered safe. Yet Guatemala City had been experiencing a wave of robberies and kidnappings. If the past is any indicator, such conditions may have changed dramatically by the time you read this. In the end, you must weigh the pros and cons of visiting a country that is very much in transition. This guidebook tries to present Guatemala as fairly and as accur-ately as possible, so that you can make an informed decision about visiting this fascinating (and challenging) country.

HISTORY

By far the best known of the several pre-Columbian civilizations of Guate-mala is that of the Maya, believed to have begun evolving in the region as an agricultural society around 1,500 B.C., perhaps as an offshoot of south-ern Mexico's Olmec culture, which flourished until about 400 B.C.

Discoveries at Nakbé, in the Petén jungle of northern Guatemala, suggest that the first Maya city may have been founded at that site sometime between 800 and 600 B.C. The ancestors of these people, however, arrived much earlier. Stone tools have been found in Guatemala's central mountains dating back to 9,000 B.C., and worked chips found in neighboring Belize were made as early as 20,000 B.C., an estimated 5,000 years after the first waves of nomadic hunters entered Central America from the north.

No one knows exactly where the earliest Maya predecessors came from, although they seem to have shared many fundamental beliefs with some of the early Chinese and East Indian people, and it is possible that ancient Maya and Asians had a shared cultural history. Both groups explored human links to nature through divination and shamanism as well as intellectual and moral control. The Maya, for example, believed that the first human beings were created from corn, originally a wild highland grass that the Maya began domesticating many centuries ago.

In creating these bridges between heaven and earth, humankind assumed the burden of maintaining specific ceremonies as a kind of ritual theater for observing, celebrating, and retaining the order of the natural universe. The Maya chose to explore the cosmos—and their relation to it—through a preoccupation with the mathematics of eternal time and the solidarity of the basic elements of our universe. These beliefs are manifested in solstice and equinox markers, for example, as well as enor-mous astronomical observatories and the precise projection of their "long count" calendar as far as 142 nonillion years into the future. Such under-lying cosmic concepts of social order are radically different from those that forged the human-centered European civilizations of the Greeks, Romans, and, later, the Spanish.

The Classic Maya

During the height of what archaeologists call the Classic period, roughly A.D. 250 to 900, the Maya flourished throughout most of Guatemala and Belize, as well as northern Honduras, northwestern El Salvador, and the southern Mexican states of Chiapas, Campeche, Yucatán, and Quintana Roo. Research suggests that the Maya world drew its strength from a clearly defined ideological backbone that enabled the few to dominate the many. Not only did this allow a ruling hereditary elite of priest-kings to emerge, but it also made feasible enormous construction projects ranging from complex reservoirs and raised-bed irrigation schemes to elaborately decorated temples and burial crypts.

Throughout the Classic period, the Maya civilization was composed of independent and frequently antagonistic city-states, in many respects like those of the early Greek civilization. Although these city-states had many ceremonial and religious elements, they were seldom peaceful, particularly from A.D. 500 to 800. The most powerful members of society, a tiny caste of priestly royalty, spent considerable energy planning attacks on their neighbors or, in turn, defending themselves from the marauding armies of their enemies. Nevertheless, they found the time and resources to supervise construction of large, ornate ceremonial structures such as the pyramids of El Mirador—which, until relatively recently, were the tallest buildings in the Western Hemisphere.

The Maya were master builders and talented artisans, despite the fact that wheels (other than those used in toys), metal tools, and beasts of burden were unknown to them. Their ceramics, weavings, friezes, and jewelry were carefully and beautifully made. Clever farmers, the Maya built elaborate aqueducts, causeways, and ponds to capture rainwater and irrigate their fields of maize, squash, and other crops. They drained swamps and built terraced gardens fertilized by compost and partially shaded by tall trees. Their jungle discoveries gave us chocolate, beans, avocados, tomatoes, pineapples, and rubber. Shrewd and aggressive traders, they exchanged seeds, tools, and other valuable objects with such faraway groups as the ancestral Puebloans of the American Southwest, the Aztec of central Mexico, and the Inca of Peru.

The Collapse of the Maya

As the various Maya city-states waxed and waned in power and influence, some sites fell into ruin or were abandoned. Only a handful of communities were occupied for many centuries at a stretch. Most flour-

Don Usner

The main plaza in Tikal

ished for 100 or 200 years before being eclipsed by a sister city or rival.

No one is certain why the Maya civilization began rapidly deteriorating around A.D. 800. One theory suggests an angry peasant revolt toppled the governing theocracy. Some experts believe the Maya over-exploited the forests, farms, and water supplies that sustained them, perhaps at the behest of greedy emperors. Another possible explanation is that severe drought and famine undermined and fatally weakened the culture's infrastructure. Substantial proof of a long draught has been described by paleoclimatologists. Yet another theory speculates that non-Maya invaders, such as southern Mexico's Toltecs, invaded the territory and seized power by force.

Only remnants of the civilization remained when the first Spanish explorers arrived early in the 16th century. Many of the Classic Maya city-states had been abandoned for centuries by the time Europeans first stumbled upon them. The Maya had fractionalized into warring tribes, although they maintained many common cultural traditions.

The Living Maya

Today, about 8 million Maya still occupy much of their original homeland. They are the direct descendants of the indigenous people of the region, and

7

many of them maintain the mythological and chronological order that the Spanish tried for centuries to disrupt, discredit, and replace.

Many who have observed modern Guatemala argue that the spiritual conquest of the Maya by outsiders has never taken place. In fact, a majority of the country's people are still full-blooded indígena (the preferred term in Guatemala for Indians or Native Americans) who not only speak their own languages but also participate in timeless religious ceremonies that take place far away from the prying eyes of "foreigners."

Much of both ancient and contemporary Maya culture remains unknown to us, in large measure because the conquering Spanish went out of their way to kill holy men and destroy their sacred writings and temples. In 1562, for example, Bishop Diego de Landa declared 27 hieroglyphic panels to be the devil's work and tossed them into the flames. When the Spanish monarchy learned of de Landa's action, the bishop was so severely riprimanded that he convinced an indígena to "tell him" the Maya alphabet. This information has helped solve the riddle of Mayan script. It is largely through painstaking archaeology and anthropology that we have been able to piece together what little we know about the ancient Maya.

The Colonial Period

The first European to appear anywhere near Guatemala was Christopher Columbus, who cruised its eastern coastline during his fourth trip to the New World in 1502. Shortly thereafter, the first conquistadors arrived on orders of the Spanish crown. Under a directive from the ruthless Hernán Cortés, conqueror of the Aztecs, Pedro de Alvarado was sent south from Mexico City in 1523.

Alvarado's band of several hundred Spanish soldiers was allied with Aztec and Tlaxcalan indígena mercenaries in their goal of seizing Guatemala by force. By deceitfully playing off one ethnic group against another, Alvarado quickly and easily took control of the western highlands, although skirmishes continued for many years. He immediately established a Spanish base near the Maya city of Iximché and, after moving his capital further east, Alvarado was given autocratic command of a new political jurisdiction stretching from Chiapas to Panama. He ruled this so-called Kingdom of Guatemala until his death in 1541.

Under Alvarado, the traditional indígena way of life was completely disrupted. Farmers who had worked the same land for generations were uprooted from their rural homes and forced to live in new towns and villages laid out in a grid pattern by the Spanish. The conquerors forced the indígena to give up many of their customs, religious ceremonies, even their names, under penalty of incarceration, torture, or execution. Many were either enslaved or forced to work as indentured servants.

INGUAT

Masked participants in the Dance of the Conquerors

The ceremonies of the indigenous Maya were preserved largely through oral traditions and secrecy. Today, Maya shamanism is experiencing a revival and many indígena communities have a much-revered shaman performing rituals in their midst. For a lively and informative discussion of this tradition, see any of the books written by the late University of Texas archaeologist, Linda Schele.

In 1543 a volcanic eruption and subsequent flood destroyed the Guatemalan capital. Alvarado's widow, who had officially succeeded him as head of the colonial administration for only 36 hours, was killed in the disaster. Survivors moved the capital from Ciudad Vieja to what is now the city of La Antigua Guatemala (simply called Antigua), located in the picturesque Panchoy Valley beneath the Agua, Fuego, and Acatenango volcanoes. The new settlement, purposely designed to manifest all of Spain's presumed institutional values, quickly grew to become the third-largest European community in the New World, after Lima and Mexico City.

Although the early Spanish colonials were disappointed to find little gold or silver in Guatemala, they soon realized that indígena labor could be used in large-scale production of indigo and cochineal (natural blue

9

dyes and red dyes, respectively) as well as other agricultural exports. A wealthy landed aristocracy joined the Catholic Church's local hierarchy in maintaining a firm grip on the country's levers of power and privilege. By the middle 1700s, these groups had established a comfortable, sophisticated enclave for themselves.

In 1773, a series of severe earthquakes caused the capital to be moved once again, this time to its present location in the broad plain that has become Guatemala City. Antigua was never abandoned, however, and it remains the spiritual heart of the country's Ladino (Spanish-descended) culture. The city was declared a national cultural monument in 1944 and a United Nations World Heritage Site in 1979.

Guatemalan Independence

Guatemala, like most of Latin America, became free from Spain in 1821 but was claimed by Mexico under threat of force until 1823. The department of Chiapas was occupied by the Mexican Army and permanently severed from Guatemala.

After declaring its independence a second time, what remained of Guatemala became part of a loose, semi-autonomous federation called the United Provinces of Central America, which dissolved in late 1838. Political infighting among the region's would-be leaders kept Guatemala under the rule of a Honduran dictator for another nine years.

Even after its official founding as an independent republic on September 15, 1847, Guatemala continued to suffer political troubles and chaotic government. The small Ladino ruling class immediately split into two opposing factions: conservatives who defended the concentration of power among wealthy landowners and the Catholic Church, versus liberals (mostly merchants and businessmen) who favored gradual dismantling of the church's enormous material empire and a reform of the legal system. Battles between these two groups continued, figuratively and literally, for the next hundred years.

Guatemala's founding president, the staunch conservative Rafael Carrera, remained in office until 1865, after which his aggressively status-quo policies were pursued by a handpicked successor, Vicente Cerna. In 1871, liberals usurped the long-ruling conservatives in a coup led by Miguel García Granados, who was replaced in the presidency by activist liberal Rufino Barrios in 1873.

The Barrios Era

President Barrios launched an ambitious reform program that included the establishment of a national bank system and a public school system, the construction of railroads and power-generating networks, and the improvement of highways. He ordered the confiscation of a great deal of church property and abolished the land tenure tradition that had permitted the indígena to farm their own property without holding legal deeds. Barrios also implemented a forced-labor system that allowed Ladino plantation owners to exploit indígena workers for a specified period of time each year. This controversial edict remained on the books until 1944, and the wealthiest families of Guatemala built empires for themselves in the interim. Conscripted labor also enriched hundreds of new immigrants from Germany who, lured by President Barrios with offers of virtually free land and plant stock, began developing coffee into the country's number-one industry. Barrios' expansionist policies led in 1885 to an unsuccessful Guatemalan invasion of El Salvador, where he was killed in battle.

The Barrios administration ended amid sharp questioning by social critics about political incompetence, repression, greed, and corruption. Such charges would only escalate through the 1880s and 1890s, as dictators shamelessly courted foreign investors and encouraged the military to play an increasingly powerful role in enforcing the presumed rights of the wealthy.

During this period the United Fruit Company, a giant multinational corporation based in the United States, made sweetheart deals with the Guatemalan government and military. These concessions gave the company effective control of the Caribbean railway and direct ownership of huge banana plantations. For the next 50 years, the company would exert tremendous influence on how the country was run.

20th-Century Guatemala

In 1898, Manuel Estrada Cabrera took over as president and ruled over Guatemala's affairs by force until 1920, when he was declared legally insane. During Cabrera's regime the government went completely bankrupt, and social unrest threatened to erupt into open revolt. He kept the opposition at bay through the purchased loyalty of iron-fisted generals and ruthless secret police. It was not until 1931, after a series of short-lived administrations failed to restore order and bolster the wracked economy, that some measure of socioeconomic stability returned to Guatemala, under the strongman rule of Jorge Ubico.

Reform-minded Ubico canceled the indígena debt of servitude instituted by Barrios but immediately introduced new laws that obliged peasants to work on plantations for insignificant wages. United Fruit, meanwhile, was granted an exemption from all property taxes and import duties. Ubico developed a network of spies whose information was used by roving death squads to murder dissenters. Mass rioting against Ubico's dictatorship forced him to resign in July 1944, and a progressive schoolteacher named Juan José Arévalo was elected to succeed him the following December in the first (relatively) free and fair balloting in Guatemala's history.

During his six-year term, Arévalo started a national welfare program, built new schools, rewrote the labor code, unharnessed the news media, and redistributed power back to local governments. These policies of "spiritual socialism" were intensified in the early 1950s by President Jacobo Arbenz, who, after another generally untainted election, came up with a controversial reform plan that would allow small farmers to take over unused public land and cultivate new private parcels carved out of idle tracts held by large private plantations. Wealthy landowners, notably United Fruit, were violently opposed to any kind of land redistribution and sought help from the U.S. government in toppling Arbenz. The U.S. Central Intelligence Agency (CIA) orchestrated a successful 1954 coup, which led to the forced replacement of Arbenz by yet another ultra-conservative dictator. Since the overthrow of Arbenz, Guatemala has been ruled either directly or indirectly by the military, although a nominally civilian government was reestablished in 1986 after the military was guaranteed amnesty from prosecution for criminal activity of any kind.

Civil War

Repression of political dissent, particularly any that espoused liberal or socialistic reform, became routine after the CIA coup but was never completely unchallenged by the Guatemalan people, who refer to the period's ongoing civil war as *El Conflicto*. Violence involving anti-government guerrillas, the Guatemalan military, and paramilitary forces escalated throughout the 1950s and 1960s, culminating in the August 1968 assassination of U.S. Ambassador John Gordon Mein.

In 1977, the Carter administration's human rights campaign targeted Central America, and relations between the United States and Guatemala soured. Military aid was sharply reduced, then suspended as Guatemala suffered an almost complete breakdown in social order between 1978 and 1984. The economy went into a tailspin as a series of fraudulent elections and military coups wracked the government.

An aggressive, reform-minded guerrilla movement and powerful right-wing death squads plunged Guatemala into open civil war throughout the late 1970s and early 1980s. According to estimates by the Roman Catholic Church, more than 150,000 people were killed, 50,000 "disappeared," and 300,000 wounded over the course of the 36-year civil war.

The Guatemalan military's scorched-earth campaign was so violent that some 440 villages were completely destroyed. More than 1 million

Guatemalans (one in eight) were internally displaced, and an estimated 300,000 escaped to Mexico, Belize, the U.S., and Canada.

In 1985, Guatemala's national constitution was rewritten and its first free election in more than 30 years was held. Vinicio Cerezo, a moderate Christian Democrat whose party had been a frequent death-squad target, was elected president for a five-year term. His cautious improvements reduced the level of political violence to about a thousand deaths a year and gave the sagging economy a shot in the arm without seriously jeopardizing the privileges of the wealthy elite.

Cerezo's successor was Jorge Serrano, who made headlines by promising to investigate human rights abuses, root out institutional corruption, and normalize relations with neighboring Belize (claimed by Guatemala since 1859). Faced with possible impeachment over alleged bribery and corruption charges, President Serrano tried in 1993 to assume dictatorial powers in a self-engineered coup. The attempt failed, however, and within two weeks he was replaced by Ramiro de León Carpio, Guatemala's former ombudsman for human rights.

Peace Arrives

In early 1996, Alvaro Arzú took office after a relatively peaceful election. Arzú carried out a purge of top officers in the Guatemalan military and dismissed more than a hundred police officers for corruption. On December 29, 1996, the president's representatives signed peace accords with guerrilla leaders that formally ended 36 years of fighting. Civil unrest continues in Guatemala but now generally relates to drug trafficking and other criminal activity.

Relations with many foreign governments dramatically improved in 1997 because of Guatemala's new peace accords and its stated commitment to affirm human rights. Criticism continues, however, over the government's alleged failure to aggressively prosecute military and security officials suspected of involvement (with the admitted complicity of the CIA) in the murders of a number of foreign nationals, including at least four U.S. citizens. The Guatemalan judicial system is still largely ineffective, and the president and legislature are under constant pressure from a small but powerful cadre of constituents who are happy with a system that makes them the "haves" and millions of others the "have-nots."

The consensus among many U.S. government officials, business executives, and human rights activists is that although Guatemala's political situation is improving, the nation is a long way from truly representative democracy and needs to feel continual pressure if it is to change significantly. It can be argued that tourists, simply through their presence and influence, exert some of that pressure and, by spending money at locally owned businesses and espousing democratic ideals, can be a force for alleviating poverty and encouraging political reform. At the very least, the decisions by visitors on how they will spend their time and money in Guatemala will go a long way in determining how tourism develops in the post–civil war era.

ECONOMY

Historically, the Guatemalan export economy has been based on agricultural commodities, mainly coffee, sugar, bananas, rubber, vegetables, and spices. About two-thirds of all exports are still farm-related, employing about the same ratio of the Guatemalan work force.

Today tourism is variously listed as Guatemala's largest or second-largest industry, with about 550,000 foreign visitors projected to generate about $400 million in 1999.

In third place among industries is the "non-traditional" sector, including vegetables, flowers, ceramics, jewelry, and furniture. With the largest industrial base in Central America, Guatemala is also an important manufacturer of pharmaceuticals, chemicals, clothing, wood, and food products. Thanks to lenient tax laws, a number of overseas-financed factories and assembly plants, known as *maquiladoras*, have opened during recent years in Guatemala City and Antigua. The country is a modest producer of petroleum, beef, and fish. Its gross domestic product was valued at $14 billion in 1998.

Despite some positive signs, the Guatemalan economy is still troubled. Commodity prices and tourism are subject to dramatic fluctuations due to a variety of reasons. Guatemala is still a net importer of food, and industrial diversification has been slow. Like other Latin American countries, Guatemala pays substantial interest on its foreign debt and has great difficulty persuading its wealthiest citizens to invest their money in the domestic economy. Many rich families prefer to send their capital and take their holidays abroad.

In contrast, the vast majority of Guatemalans live in dire poverty. The minimum wage is pegged at about $3.00 a day, although many workers earn even less. The average income of a Guatemalan is one-third of a Mexican and one-sixteenth of someone living in the U.S. Bear in mind that the average Guatemalan indígena earns less than half the income of a Guatemalan Ladino (also called a *Guatemalteco*). The country's average annual household income is about $1,600.

Guatemala's economy would be in much worse shape if not for the large amount of cash flowing into the country from illegal drug production and transshipment. There is no official estimate of the amount of revenue involved, but U.S. officials confirm that Guatemala is an important transfer point for cocaine and heroin being shipped from Mexico, Asia, and South America to the United States and Europe. Marijuana and opium poppies are also grown in remote areas of the country (the climate is not suited for the coca plants that produce cocaine).

RELIGION

Freedom of religion has been guaranteed by Guatemala's national constitution since the late 19th century, and there is a wide range of religious expression. In much of the country the Catholicism introduced by Spanish missionaries nearly 500 years ago has melded with indigenous beliefs and practices that originated with the ancient Maya. This "folk Catholicism" manifests itself in many ways. For example, when the early Spanish priests ordered indígena to stop worshiping their traditional gods—representing corn, rain, the sun, and so on—the Maya response was to give the gods the names of Christian saints and continue with their prayers. Similarly, the indígena often transferred their ceremonial rituals, such as incense-burning, animal sacrifice, and street celebration, to activities sanctioned by the church. In short, they changed the form of their religious expression but not its substance.

The Día de Difuntos celebration is among the most sacred days on the Maya calendar.

Some Catholic officials have been more receptive to this process than others. In Chichicastenango, Santiago Atitlán, Cobán, Zunil, Momostenango, and San Pedro Carchá, indígena languages and rituals have become an integral part of Catholic ceremonies with the blessing and encouragement of local priests. In the Petén, for example, the local bishop takes part in a ceremony in which the indígena dance around a sacred stone monument inside a circle of pine needles. And on the venerated steps of the Church of Santo Tomás in Chichicastenango, visitors can see Quiché worshipers cross themselves while standing before the doorway, then burn rum and copal incense before speaking aloud to their ancient gods. Inside the church, sand and feather designs are laid out in front of a Christian altar to honor departed relatives in the customary Maya way. In Ladino-dominated areas, such as Guatemala City, more conservative and traditional forms of Catholic worship are the norm.

Since the 1960s, other Christian denominations have made considerable inroads in Guatemala, and an estimated 38 percent of the population now identifies itself as evangelical Protestant. Over the last 20 years many Guatemalan towns and villages have converted, seemingly in their entirety, to the very conservative forms of Protestantism that are being promoted throughout Central America by churches based primarily in the southern United States. In most instances folk religions are completely abandoned after conversion. Evangelicals often preach vehemently against any use of alcohol, which has been intimately involved in indígena fiestas and religious rituals for thousands of years. The missionaries also decry the practices of *curanderos*, or folk healers, and the ritual brotherhoods known as *cofradías*, which manage indígena governments and organize the elaborate festivals that are a major form of public worship. Evangelicals now control much of the electronic media in Guatemala, broadcasting religious messages on radio and television 24 hours a day. Nevertheless, there is an ongoing revival of shamanism and ritual in the traditional Maya villages of Guatemala.

POPULATION PATTERNS AND MODERNIZATION

As of early 1999, the estimated population of Guatemala was about 11 million. This is a dramatic increase from the roughly 3 million counted in 1950 and the 4 million of 1964. At its current annual growth rate of 2.5 percent a year, Guatemala is one of the fastest-growing nations on earth, which has put a severe strain on the nation's ability to provide its citizens with adequate housing, food, water, electricity, health care, education, transportation, employment, and other basic services. An estimated 1 million to 1.5 million Guatemalans now live in the United States.

About 55 percent of today's Guatemalans belong to one of 22 distinct

Mayan ethnolinguistic groups, and nearly all of the others are of mixed Maya and European descent, referred to in Guatemala as Ladinos (as are "Westernized" indígena). A small number of Guatemalans are of African, Asian, European, or East Indian heritage, and there are several thousand Garifuna (African-Native American) people on the Caribbean coast. Most Guatemalans refer to visitors from the U.S., Canada, Europe, and other Western countries as *gringos*, a term interchangeable with "tourist" and rarely regarded as an insult.

What is perhaps most significant about Guatemala's demographic profile is its high percentage of full-blooded indígena, surpassed only by Bolivia and a few parts of South America's Andean plateau. Nevertheless, centuries of Spanish and Ladino presence have yet to break down the strong cultural, economic, and linguistic barriers between indígena and non-indígena groups.

As a result of its long-standing racial divisions, Guatemala appears more resistant to social change and modernization than almost any nation in the Western Hemisphere. Except in a few Guatemalan communities, the indígena are neither invited nor encouraged to exercise any significant degree of economic or political power. Only a small percentage of elected officials, military officers, ordained priests, and ministers are indígena. Instead, most contemporary Maya remain farmers, laborers, artisans, and proprietors of small shops. Historically, many Guatemalan Ladinos have looked down on the indígena as inferior, and, in turn, many Indians cast eyes of mistrust and suspicion on Ladinos. No meaningful move toward modernization can be expected until serious steps are taken to change this unfortunate reality.

Since the signing of peace accords in late 1996, political participation by indigenous Guatemalans has increased and there are a growing number of indígena representatives (including women) in the national congress. Others, such as Nobel Prize winner Rigoberta Menchú and environmentalist Aura Marina Otzoy, are working with grassroots organizations outside of electoral politics to accomplish their goals. Nevertheless, an estimated 60 percent of private land in Guatemala is still owned by 2 percent of population and only 45 percent of the modern Maya are able to read and write. It's easy to see why social, political, and economic reform is still a priority.

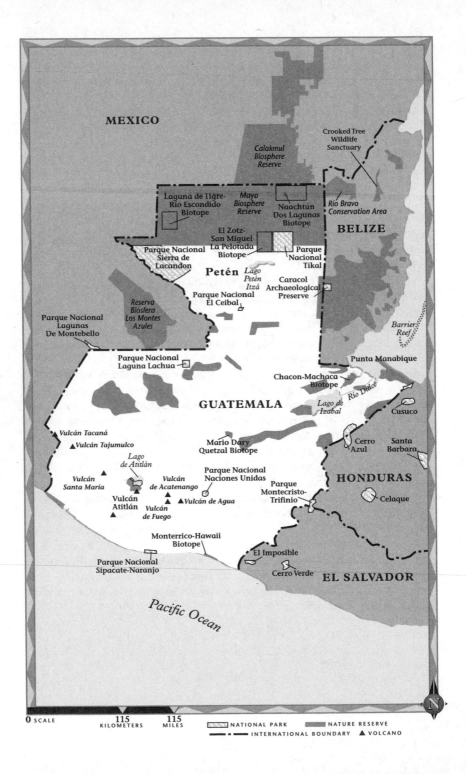

MEXICO

Calakmul
Biosphere
Reserve

Crooked Tree
Wildlife
Sanctuary

Laguna de Tigre-
Río Escondido
Biotope

Maya
Biosphere
Reserve

Naachtún
Dos Lagunas
Biotope

Río Bravo
Conservation Area

BELIZE

El Zotz-
San Miguel
La Pelotada
Biotope

Parque Nacional
Sierra de
Lacandon

Parque
Nacional
Tikal

Petén

Lago
Petén
Itzá

Caracol
Archaeological
Preserve

Parque Nacional
El Ceibal

Reserva
Biósfera
Los Montes
Azules

Parque Nacional
Lagunas
De Montebello

Barrier
Reef

Parque Nacional
Laguna Lachua

Punta Manabique

Chacon-Machaca
Biotope

Río Dulce

GUATEMALA

Lago de
Izabal

Cusuco

Vulcán Tacaná

Vulcán Tajumulco

Mario Dary
Quetzal Biotope

Cerro
Azul

Santa
Barbara

Lago
de Atitlán

Vulcán
Santa María

Vulcán
de Acatenango

Parque Nacional
Naciones Unidas

HONDURAS

Parque
Montecristo-
Trifinio

Celaque

Vulcán
Atitlán

Vulcán
de Fuego

Vulcán de Agua

Monterrico-Hawaii
Biotope

El Imposible

Parque Nacional
Sipacate-Naranjo

Cerro Verde

EL SALVADOR

Pacific Ocean

0 SCALE

115
KILOMETERS

115
MILES

NATIONAL PARK

NATURE RESERVE

INTERNATIONAL BOUNDARY ▲ VOLCANO

N

2

CONSERVATION
AND RESPONSIBLE
TOURISM

The quetzal, a brilliantly colored bird with a long swooping tail, is a fitting symbol for the ongoing campaign to protect Guatemala's rich and unusual natural environment. It is a rare creature, independent in spirit and resplendent in form. Quetzals have been prized and revered since ancient times, when the Maya collected and traded their bright feathers like money. Despite repeated attempts, modern zoologists have seldom been able to keep the quetzal alive in captivity and human destruction of its mountain cloud-forest habitat threatens the bird's survival in the wild. Its range in Guatemala, once over 20,000 square miles, is now less than 3 percent of that original territory. In contrast to the hundreds of thousands of quetzals that probably flitted among the Maya during ancient times, today there are only an estimated 40,000 Guatemalan birds, mostly in the rugged Sierra de las Minas and Cuchumatanes Mountains. This despite a law that since 1895 has prohibited killing the animal.

In the paradoxical case of the quetzal, people profess one set of values but act out another. Guatemalans clearly love their national bird yet nevertheless continue to cut down the dense foliage that provides its nesting sites and sustenance.

So it is with the complicated, often contradictory, conservation movement of Guatemala. The words from political leaders, industrialists, researchers, and bureaucrats sound good—professing a firm commitment to protection of the environment—yet much destructive activity is occurring each day, often in direct violation of laws and policies already on the books.

HISTORICAL CONTEXT

Anthropologists suspect that a primary reason for the Maya civilization's decline was widespread degradation of the environment in the latter years of this pre-Columbian empire. This apparently occurred through over-harvesting, nutrient depletion, deforestation, and misappropriation of scarce water resources. For many previous centuries the Maya had lived in balance and harmony with their surroundings, managing their natural resources creatively and wisely. Farmland was composted and fertilized, allowed to lie fallow, and cultivated with diverse crops that complemented one another. Swamps were drained and terraced gardens were watered with ingenious irrigation systems.

By the late eighth century the Maya population apparently had grown to the point that it was consuming resources at a rate faster than nature could replace them. Archaeological evidence suggests that during this time the Maya experienced drought, soil erosion, and malnutrition. Entire cities were abandoned. As a result, nearly all that physically remains of a complex and impressive society has been reclaimed by a forest whose balances, processes, and rhythms were apparently violated or ignored.

The people of Guatemala are again at a crossroads. The country's population could double from 1999's estimated 11 million by 2025. As one foreign aid official put it, "Trying to solve environmental problems here without addressing population growth is like trying to mop up a flooded kitchen without first turning off the faucet." As a direct result of this unchecked growth, forests, wetlands, and other vital ecosystems are being destroyed at an alarming rate. Pollution of the nation's air, land, and water is almost completely unregulated. Fortunately, there are signs that the rate of ecological destruction and exploitation may some day be checked.

According to scientists, Guatemala may have been the first place in the world where corn, avocados, guava, yucca, runner beans, and chocolate were domesticated as food plants. Tomatoes, squash, chile, and other plants appear to have been brought here thousands of years ago from other parts of the Americas. Around many archaeological sites, the descendants of fruit and nut trees planted centuries are still productive sources of nutritious food for local residents as well as animals and birds. But 20th-century Guatemala is not like the Classic Maya world.

Plant and Timber Extraction

The modern world's seemingly insatiable appetite for tropical lumber has had a terrible impact on Guatemala's lush, beautiful forests. As early as

Deforestation in the Sierra Chamá of Alta Verapaz

1935, a reforestation law was passed to help restore clear-cut areas. Unfortunately, most of the trees that were planted were non-native species, such as fast-growing eucalyptus.

No one knows exactly how much timber is being harvested in the Petén, the nation's largest remaining wilderness, but estimates are around 90,000 acres a year. Experts predict that if the present rate of destruction continues, there will be virtually no forest left in this Ohio-sized ecosystem by the year 2020. An estimated 45 percent of the Petén's forest cover has been lost since 1940 because of the ceaseless slashing of chainsaws and machetes.

SUBSISTENCE FARMING

The nation, it seems, is stymied by a web of conflicting interests and traditions. The centuries-old practice of slash-and-burn *milpa* agriculture demands that forest be cut down for its timber, then replaced with such favored subsistence crops as corn, squash, and beans, which exhaust the thin topsoil within three or four years. After the earth lies fallow for another seven years, a new crop is traditionally planted. Farmers sometimes choose to grow plantation crops using obsolete techniques that are often unsuited for the specialized growing conditions of the Petén.

Government encouragement of the migration and resettlement of landless Guatemalan peasants in the Petén is a policy that relieves pressure for

21

land reform in other parts of the nation but puts increased demand on the fragile ecosystem. As long as officials consider agrarian reform in the south and west to be subversive, this trend is likely to continue.

CATTLE RAISING

The new push toward cattle production as a source of export income is another important factor in changing Guatemala's land-use priorities. More than 60 percent of the country's beef is shipped overseas, primarily to fast-food chains in the U.S. Typically, cattle ranchers move in when farmers move out, after nutrient exhaustion, ground compaction, and weed growth have made cultivating those lands difficult.

Even areas that have been granted some degree of official environmental protection, such as the Maya Biosphere Reserve, are suffering from unauthorized agriculture and cash extraction businesses. Satellite photos show that in some "special protection" areas more than half of all forest has been illegally removed during the past decade, replaced with cows and farms.

ENVIRONMENTAL DEGRADATION

The construction of roads by loggers, game poachers, and oil explorers through freshly cut swaths of jungle inevitably brings a new wave of settlers,

This sign urges Guatemalan farmers to use reforestation techniques in managing their land.

many of them poorly educated peasants whose hunting, timbering, and farming practices are environmentally wasteful and scientifically unsound. Some of these homesteaders become chainsaw-toting "pirates" who cut and sell illegally harvested trees to unscrupulous timber companies.

The capture and export of wild parrots, monkeys, and other exotic wildlife is a huge business in Guatemala, with many more animals captured than nature can quickly replace. While a limited number of economic activities are legal in the buffer zones surrounding Guatemala's parks, there is insufficient law enforcement and bribery is endemic.

CONSERVATION AND RESPONSIBLE TOURISM

An increase in ecotourism was contemplated in the December 1996 peace accords. However, since their signing the government of Guatemala has appeared to be more interested in corporate exploitation of the country's natural resources than in protecting them for future generations of tourists and Guatemalans.

Although there is verbal support for conservation, the government seems eager to exploit its natural resources. Since 1996, for example, many concessions for oil exploration and timber extraction have been granted in the western portions of the Maya Biosphere Reserve, an ecologically significant tract of the Petén tropical forest that had previously been off-limits to such development. Affected areas include the relatively pristine Sierra Lacandón National Park and Laguna del Tigre. Organizations fighting these inroads include Conservation International, ProPetén, and Madre Selva, a particularly assertive group directed by Magali Rosa in Guatemala City.

As an integral part of the peace process that ended Guatemala's civil war, the country's poor were promised access to unoccupied land. Unwilling to wait for government action, thousands of squatters have invaded national parks and protected areas. These individuals are cutting trees, killing animals, and fouling waterways as they create their new homesteads. Because the government has neither a coherent environmental policy nor the political will to enforce its environmental laws, the squatters are homesteading with impunity.

In some areas illegal homesteading is accompanied by acts of apparent terrorism. In 1997, for example, a brand-new biological research station near the village of San Lorenzo Marmol was destroyed by unidentified vandals who poured gasoline around the base of the structure and set it on fire. The station was a joint project of the World Wildlife Federation and Defensores de la Naturaleza, a Guatemalan environmental group.

The environmental movement in Guatemala is fragmented and has so far failed to convince the majority of Guatemalans that their natural environment is threatened by human activities. Local environmentalists blame this in part on their own squabbling and competition for scarce funds, as well as poor communication with their fellow citizens.

According to Carla Molina, a Guatemalan environmentalist active in ecotourism, positive signs in the fight for improving environmental controls include the imposition of an auto emissions testing system by the government agency CONAMA, which may help cut the severe air pollution in Guatemala City and other urban areas.

Rural air pollution is harder to control. Thousands of fires burned in forests throughout the region in spring 1998, spreading smoke as far north as Chicago. Such fires are lit every year by peasants as a way of clearing land, but a prolonged drought caused many of the blazes to spread beyond control. Other fires were caused by careless motorists who threw burning cigarettes out of their car windows. In a pattern of weather extremes that is becoming more common throughout the world, the regional drought was followed in fall 1998 by some of the heaviest rains and worst floods in decades.

Ecotourism is no cure-all for environmental problems, of course. In recent years, the label has been applied to everything from simple nature walks to huge resorts that offer rides in dolphin-chasing speedboats.

"The devil is in the details," Steve Schwartzmann, senior scientist at the Environmental Defense Fund, told a Knight-Ridder reporter in a 1998 interview. "Ecotourism can be a great way to generate income for preservation, but it can also be a perfectly good way to stimulate the degradation of isolated places."

SOCIAL AND ECONOMIC ISSUES

In the final analysis, Guatemala's environmental dilemmas cannot be resolved until issues involving basic social, political, economic, land tenure, and human rights questions are addressed as well.

Guatemalan policymakers have many problems in common with developing nations throughout the world, but there are several factors that make their country's current situation unique from an environmentalist's point of view:

• About one-third of all land cover is already eroded or seriously degraded, some of it irretrievably. This is especially significant because much of the soil is composed of unconsolidated volcanic ash that is highly susceptible to erosion when exposed to the elements. Erosion—often from slash-and-burn agriculture, timber harvesting, and mining—leads to rapid silting of rivers and lakes, contaminating water supplies, killing fish, disrupting the ecosystem, increasing the likelihood of flooding, and threatening irrigation systems.

A volcano looms over the highland valleys of Guatemala.

• Oil exploration and drilling threaten the Petén, coastal lowlands, and several wilderness areas, as do proposed hydroelectric projects that would flood agricultural areas, displace residents (and wildlife), and increase evaporative water loss. Road building related to army maneuvers and military-related timber extraction, as well as dam building, destroys forest habitat and encourages migration of homesteaders into what were once wilderness areas.

• With the encouragement, cooperation, and partial funding of the U.S. Drug Enforcement Agency and U.S. State Department, many rural areas in Guatemala have been sprayed with Round-Up, malathion, paraquat, and other powerful herbicides designed to defoliate plantations of marijuana and opium poppies. Too often the long-term result is contaminated land, non-drug-related crop losses, and illness among humans, poultry, livestock, and other animals.

• The continued use of powerful agricultural fertilizers and pesticides in Guatemala has done untold damage over the years, polluting ground water, fouling streams, and jeopardizing plant and animal life. When fruits and vegetables produced in Guatemala exceed pesticide levels set by the U.S. and Europe, they are usually distributed on the local market. The cumulative result, according to one estimate, is that Guatemalans have more DDT in their body fat than any other people in the world.

*Enjoying one of the many soothing
waterfalls of the Alta Verapaz region*

Richard Mahler

• The uncontrolled growth of Guatemala City—from fewer than 300,000 residents only four decades ago to over 2 million today—has created an environmental catastrophe. The capital is running out of clean water, clean air, and cheap energy. Its streets reach gridlock during morning and evening commute times. Factories and garbage dumps disperse tons of toxic material into the sky around the clock. Diesel fumes choke the downtown area, and dense smog settles in the valleys on calm days and overnight, escalating the risk of heart disease, asthma, lead poisoning, and cancer for all residents. Without a liquid waste treatment system, Guatemala City's sewers have turned one of the country's largest waterways, the Motagua, into a dead river full of solvents, heavy metals, and human excrement. Here, as in the rest of Guatemala, thousands of residents have no sanitary facilities whatsoever.

• Several of Guatemala's many wild rivers are in danger of being dammed for generation of hydroelectric power, flood control, drinking water, and agricultural irrigation. About 15 percent of the country's electricity now comes from a massive hydroelectric generator on the Río Chixoy, high in the Sierra de Chamá of Alta Verapaz. Poor construction, a lack of spare parts, and fluctuating water levels have forced this plant to operate far below its planned capacity, and engineers are once again eyeing the Río Cahabón farther east and the scenic Río Usumacinta to the north as possible sites for new hydroelectric projects, despite the presence of earthquake faults in the Cahabón area and priceless archaeological treasures along the Usumacinta. Below the Chixoy dam, meanwhile, siltation has fouled much of that river's large and important watershed.

The challenging and competing demands of a rapidly growing population, lackluster economy, and threatened environment have placed Guatemala's policymakers in an unenviable position. The difficult decisions they are being forced to make are unlikely to satisfy any single constituency, including environmentalists.

"We and the U.S. want to save our forests," former Guatemalan government official Jorge Cabrera told *U.S. News & World Report* in an interview, "but for us it is not just an ethical problem. We are not talking about quality of life for our people . . . We are talking about our survival."

SEEDS OF CHANGE

Despite the rapid pace of deforestation and environmental pollution, there is cause for cautious optimism in Guatemala. More and more logging companies seem to be complying with permit restrictions limiting the number and species of trees that may be removed from a specific area over a given period of time. These businesses are also becoming more involved in reforestation, having made the happy discovery that certain commercially valuable softwoods can be grown quicker and more easily in the fragile jungle soil. Timber cutters are also more willing to select faster-growing "secondary" trees like rosewood, rather than such prized but slow-growing hardwoods as mahogany. Lumber is a multimillion-dollar business in Guatemala and loggers are eager to find new sources of profits. It should be noted that a shift to plantation-style forestry may make sense in areas that have already been cut, but the approach does not replicate the diverse ecosystem that originally existed.

More rural residents are turning toward sustainable harvesting of indigenous forest products, including chicle, rattan, rubber, allspice, xate (an ornamental palm used by florists), wild nuts, and wild fruits. Conservation International and other groups are following a model pioneered by the nonprofit organization Cultural Survival in Brazil, where rain forest products are being used in producing natural oils, carvings, sponges, bowls, gourds, and foodstuffs sold both domestically and overseas. Working with government and industry, environmentalists are finding ways to increase local wages and manage selective timber harvesting. Some protected scenic areas—known as *biotopos*—are now overseen by Guatemala's national university in cooperation with the government tourism agency.

Guatemalans have also become aware that the tourist trade is at stake. Tens of thousands of nature lovers come to the jungle each year to see exotic birds and animals, marvel at orchids, float rivers, and explore Maya ruins—spending much-needed dollars and creating many jobs in the process (more than the timber industry, in fact). Nobody comes to this part of the world to see a desert, as residents of the dry wastelands of Jalapa and El Progreso are well aware.

ENVIRONMENTAL ACTIVISM

During the 1980s and '90s, a strong environmental movement has emerged among Guatemalan students, educators, and professionals, and its ideas

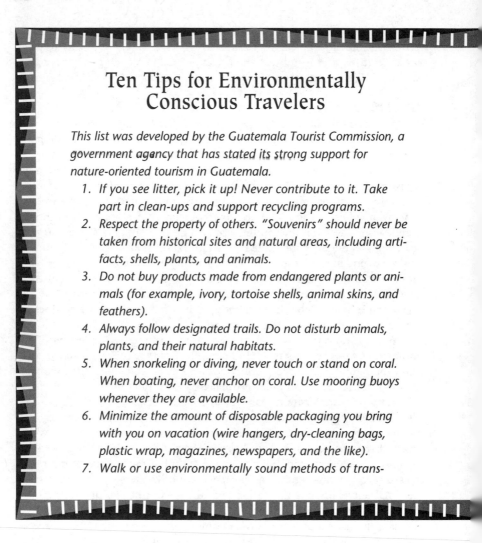

Ten Tips for Environmentally Conscious Travelers

This list was developed by the Guatemala Tourist Commission, a government agency that has stated its strong support for nature-oriented tourism in Guatemala.

1. *If you see litter, pick it up! Never contribute to it. Take part in clean-ups and support recycling programs.*
2. *Respect the property of others. "Souvenirs" should never be taken from historical sites and natural areas, including artifacts, shells, plants, and animals.*
3. *Do not buy products made from endangered plants or animals (for example, ivory, tortoise shells, animal skins, and feathers).*
4. *Always follow designated trails. Do not disturb animals, plants, and their natural habitats.*
5. *When snorkeling or diving, never touch or stand on coral. When boating, never anchor on coral. Use mooring buoys whenever they are available.*
6. *Minimize the amount of disposable packaging you bring with you on vacation (wire hangers, dry-cleaning bags, plastic wrap, magazines, newspapers, and the like).*
7. *Walk or use environmentally sound methods of trans-*

have become more and more popular among all classes, ages, and ethnic groups. During the Cerezo administration (1985–1990), the National Commission for the Environment (CONAMA) was created, and it immediately began working to slow deforestation and to set up large, biologically significant nature reserves. Following in this effort under Presidents Jorge Serrano and Ramiro de León Carpio (1990–1995) were several non-governmental organizations dedicated to conservation and environmental education. Foremost among the latter is Defenders of Nature, a private nonprofit *portation whenever possible. Encourage the drivers of public vehicles to stop engines when parked.*

8. *Encourage hotels, airlines, resorts, cruise lines, tour operators, and merchants that you patronize to be environmentally conscious. Consider their impacts on energy consumption, water, air, trash generation, noise levels, and local culture.*

9. *Respect the privacy of others. Inquire before photographing people and their activities. Learn about lifestyles, customs, manners, and cultures of the regions you visit.*

10. *Remember that you are a guest! Respect another's community, culture, and environment. Learn about and support local efforts to preserve these entities.*

A supplement to this list is offered by Horizontes Nature Tours, which advises its clients to: (in the forest) ". . . stay on trails, keep very quiet, never feed wildlife, take garbage with you, and never buy souvenirs made from wildlife products; and (in a new culture) learn what is and isn't socially acceptable, use your camera with courtesy and discretion, never buy authentic archaeological artifacts, support local conservation projects, and seek ways to help local communities."

group that has been working closely with Conservation International as well as other U.S. and European environmental groups. The U.S. Agency for International Development has provided much support for projects that promote wise use of the country's natural resources.

More and more decision-makers in the Guatemalan government and industry seem to be paying attention to what the country's environmental activists are saying and doing. One indication of this is the growing commitment by the Guatemala Tourist Commission to *ecoturismo*—tourism that promotes a respectful appreciation of nature, indigenous cultures, and archaeological sites. In 1997, the government launched an aggressive anti-littering campaign, driven home by the posting throughout the country of this blunt slogan: *NO SEA COCHE* (DON'T BE A PIG)! By actively supporting such efforts, today's tourist can actually be a part of the solution to the problem of environmental and cultural degradation.

SUSTAINABLE USE OF NATURAL RESOURCES

For *Peteneros* like Adrián Velásquez, the jungle is both home and workplace. Every few months, he and his neighbors set off through the forest in search of the bright green leaves of the xate palm, a low-growing species recognizable by its many long fronds. Velásquez and his fellow *xateros* (xate cutters) hack off a few of the fronds and carry them back to their village in a plastic bucket or burlap sack. Their proper cutting does not injure the xate.

The harvested fronds are sent to San Benito, near Flores, where they are sorted and packaged for export to florists throughout Europe and the U.S. The palm leaves are prized for their long-lasting color and are used in formal flower arrangements with lilies, tulips, roses, and other blossoms.

Xate collecting is part of a trend toward "sustainable development" of Guatemala's forests, whereby industries that thrive on non-threatening use of natural resources are encouraged. Men like Velásquez earn twice as much money collecting xate as they would growing corn. Taken as a whole, their efforts annually contribute an estimated $7.5 million in foreign exchange to the Guatemalan economy.

More than 3,100 square miles of the northern Petén have been designated an "extractive reserve" by the Guatemalan government. There Velásquez and members of some 8,000 other families are allowed to make their living from nondestructive exploitation of the Maya Biosphere's natural treasures. It is hoped that the forest gatherers will eventually organize themselves into cooperatives that can train and license members, cracking down on individuals who overcut xate palms, overtap chicle, or chop down allspice trees to get at a few choice berries in the uppermost branches.

Along the shores of Lake Petén Itzá local residents from the village of San José have established their own nature reserve—BioItzá—as a way of protecting their natural heritage for future generations.

The U.S. government had poured millions of taxpayer dollars into the Petén in an effort to save its tropical forest. One project, the brainchild of Centro Maya, attempts to teach local farmers the sustainable agricultural techniques used by the ancient Maya. The premise is that since modern farming is unable to adequately feed the Petén's current population of some 360,000, there must be some value to practices that fed an estimated 2.5 million Maya over a period of 600 years.

"People who live in the forest will use it one way or another," explained tropical ecologist Jim Nations of Conservation International in an interview with *Buzzworm* magazine. "If they are forced to use it in a bad way because of policies that encourage its destruction, then that's exactly what they'll do. But if they are encouraged to use it in a way that lets the forest survive, then that's good for them and the forest."

Sustainable harvests of wild forest products in Guatemala include allspice, peppercorn, rattan, hearts of palm, xate palm, rubber, and chicle. The latter is tapped from the chicozapote tree (also called sapodilla or chicle tree) for use as a chewing-gum base. The market for chicle declined with the introduction of synthetics in the 1940s but was revived in the 1990s as gum manufacturers in Japan and other countries have reverted to natural formulas. Other valuable extractives that can be cultivated and harvested without damaging the ecosystem include vanilla, sarsaparilla, camphor, cinnamon, bamboo, cacao, honey, and quinine (an antimalarial compound from the chinchona tree).

Red-eyed tree frog

3

FLORA AND FAUNA OF GUATEMALA

Guatemala is situated at subtropic latitudes and stretches across the isthmus of Central America from the Pacific Ocean to the Caribbean Sea. Guatemala's longest land border (598 miles) is with Mexico, followed by Belize (165 miles), Honduras (159 miles), and El Salvador (126 miles).

Because much of its 42,042 square miles is mountainous, following a chain of 33 volcanoes and the non-volcanic Cuchumatanes range, the country's climate and ecology are astonishingly varied. Fourteen distinct life zones are found at elevations ranging from sea level to more than 13,000 feet, each with its own flora and fauna.

Much of the highlands has a temperate climate similar to that of Southern California, with oak, maple, and pine forests. The Petén's tropical lowland forest is much like those of South America, yet it also displays uniquely North American characteristics. In contrast, the highest peaks are sometimes dusted with snow during the coldest months of winter.

As the northernmost link in the isthmus bridge between North and South America, Guatemala is a place of incredible biodiversity. Its habitats support an estimated 1,600 species of vertebrate fauna and many thousands of invertebrate species. Some botanists believe the country is home to the most diverse flora in Central America, hosting an estimated 9,000 species of vascular plants, 700 kinds of trees, and more than 600 types of orchids (nearly 200 of which are unique to the region).

Ocellated turkeys are frequently seen in Tikal National Park.

Richard Mahler

Guatemala even has 48 known species of cacti! At last count, there were 738 known bird species (including about 200 species of migrants), 251 species of mammals, 214 species of reptiles, 112 species of amphibians, and 220 species of fresh-water fish. The number of individual insect species runs into the thousands.

As of 1999, an estimated 35 percent of Guatemala was covered by forests, 16 percent by seasonal farmland, 13 percent by meadows and pastures, 4 percent by permanent crops, and 32 percent by cities, deserts, and other features. Amazingly, large sections of Guatemala remain uninventoried by biologists. It is not unheard of for an expert working in a remote area to find a plant or animal species that was previously unknown to science.

Guatemala is home to Central America's deepest lake (1,019-foot Atitlán), highest mountain (13,846-foot Tajumulco), driest desert (the Motagua Valley), and, until recently, largest expanse of wilderness (the Petén). This is one of the few places in the world where a single day's drive can take you from a steamy coastal banana plantation, past a coffee finca, through an apple orchard and highland wheat field, to a windswept sheep pasture overshadowed by an icy alpine peak. You can snorkel in the aquamarine Caribbean in the morning, hike through dank caves and misty cloud forests in the afternoon, and relax in one of nature's soothing hot springs on a cool mountainside that same night.

Because of Guatemala's privileged geographic position, diverse climate, and rich soil, many species that are typically North American reach their southern limit here (the Guatemalan fir tree, for instance) and, conversely, many South American species reach their northern limit (for example, the giant anteater). The greatest threat to this species and habitat diversity is human population growth—expected to grow to nearly 22 million by 2025. Of these residents, an estimated 62 percent will live in rural areas, putting continual pressure on wildlife, soil, water, and other natural resources. A word to the wise should be sufficient: See Guatemala now!

For detailed information about the flora and fauna of the region, see *Belize and Northern Guatemala: The Ecotravellers' Wildlife Guide*, by Les Beletsky (Academic Press, 1998).

BIRDS

Petén Turkey
One of the unusual indigenous birds of Guatemala is the Petén turkey (*pavo dorado*), also known as the ocellated or golden turkey, found only in the northeast Petén. It is a common—almost tame—bird at Tikal National Park, but has become locally extinct in much of its former range because it is easy to hunt and delicious to eat. It is one of only two species of wild turkeys in the world (the other is found in the United States).

Horned Guan
Another large native fowl is the horned guan (*pavo de cacho*), extant on the slopes of the Tajumulco, Tolimán, Tecpán, Fuego, and Zunil volcanoes. Known locally as the *pavón*, this surprisingly graceful bird is distinguished by its black-and-white plumage and a 2-inch scarlet horn on the top of its head. The guan prefers dense vegetation, where it survives on a diet of green leaves, fruit, and insects. It is more frequently heard than seen, muttering a low mooing sound and clacking its yellow beak when alarmed. The biggest threat to the horned guan is the market for its meat, considered a local delicacy despite the fact that fewer than a thousand birds remain in the wild.

Quetzal
Although somewhat less endangered than the guan, the quetzal has become increasingly scarce in Guatemala and could become locally extinct within the next 10 or 15 years. In pre-Columbian times, the regal plumage of this bird was used in the headdresses of Aztec and Maya royalty and its elegant feathers were traded like currency. From the stelae of the Classic Maya to

the *huipiles* (woven blouses) of the contemporary Maya, the image of this bird is often found in Guatemalan artwork. In real life, the markings of a male quetzal are unmistakable: brilliant green and blue wings, iridescent red breast, and a 2- to 4-foot tail that curls up at the end like an inverted question mark. Although it has long been illegal to capture or kill the quetzal, live specimens are rarely seen—and mostly in the highest cloud forests of the departments of Verapaz, where it often feeds on the fruit of wild avocado trees. Attempts to breed the bird in captivity are rarely successful, which is why it is often stuffed and mounted when on display, and why it has become a symbol for freedom among Guatemalans. Your best chance for seeing a live quetzal is at the Biotopo de Quetzal, near Cobán, or in the Sierra de las Minas cloud forest.

Adult quetzals feed mainly on fruit, while the nestlings also eat lizards, frogs, and insects. Sadly, only about 20 percent of the young become fledglings and another 20 percent will die before reaching maturity. Increasing human encroachment of the birds' cloud forest and mountain-slope habitat remains the quetzals' biggest threat, as more land is converted to field and pasture. The areas with the highest concentrations of quetzals are the Guaxac, Cacquipec, and Yakijux mountains of Alta Verapaz.

The ancient Maya valued quetzal feathers more than gold, and killing the bird brought a death sentence. Feathers were plucked from live quetzals, which were released to grow new ones.

The birds are solitary outside of the spring nesting season, when males fly up and down 100-foot trees, circling in song as his elaborate tail trails behind like a streamer. Females lack the male's bright plumage, with dun-colored heads and only a splotch of red on their chests.

Azacuán

Another winged creature of special significance to the ancient Maya was the *azacuán*, the Spanish name for Swainson's hawk. These birds fly as far as Canada during April and May, returning after the rainy season in November. From this migratory pattern, the Maya concluded that the gods had given the azacuán the responsibility for opening and closing the celestial springs from which rain is derived.

Atitlán Grebe

One of the saddest chapters in Guatemalan ecological history concerns the Atitlán grebe, a flightless waterbird that was until relatively recently found nowhere else on the planet except along a few patches of the Lake Atitlán shoreline. Today it is extinct, a victim of several factors that conspired against its continued existence. Perhaps the fatal blow was the introduction of non-native bass to the lake during the 1950s and '60s, in a bid to promote

sportfishing. The aggressive bass ate
most of the fledgling grebes, and by
1965 there were only 80 birds left.
Destruction of the grebe's habitat by
local residents, who prized the reeds
they lived in, finished them off in
the late 1980s, after declining water
levels (apparently caused by a 1976
earthquake) made their survival
increasingly precarious. You will
still find an Atitlán grebe sanctuary
near the village of Santiago Atitlán,
but it harbors a more common form
of grebe and other water birds.

Keel-billed toucan and Garifuna friend

Keel-Billed Toucan

The brilliantly colored keel-billed
toucan is probably better known in
the U.S. as "the Fruit Loops™
bird" because of its association with that popular breakfast cereal. The
toucan is fairly common in the lowland tropical forests of Guatemala and
prefers to live in tall trees, particularly those that bear nuts or fruit. The
bird tends to swoop low as it flies, owing to the weight of its canoe-shaped
bill. The toucan's stubby wings seem undersized for such a big load. The
red-tipped beak is apple green with a triangle of orange on top and a
streak of powder blue below. The toucan has green around its eyes, yellow
on its collar, red under its tail, and its legs and feet are bright blue. No
wonder this bird is a favorite subject for school children to draw!

Jabiru Stork

The jabiru is the largest flying bird in the Western Hemisphere, standing up to 5 feet tall and with a wingspan reaching up to 10 feet or more.
It is also one of the rarest birds in Central America, and Guatemala is
fortunate to harbor a few of these magnificent animals. Besides its size,
the jabiru can be identified by its massive black bill, which turns up
slightly, and its bare black head, which has a wide, inflatable crimson
band at the base of the neck. Jabirus return from Mexico around November to make their nests, usually at the tops of tall, secluded trees. Breeding continues until early April, when the birds begin migrating back to
Mexico for the summer. The Pacific Coast and northwestern Petén wetlands are a favorite breeding ground of this enormous bird. The jabiru
feeds on fish, snails, frogs, and snakes.

Parrots, Parakeets, and Macaws

All members of the same genus, seven species of parrots, one species of parakeet, and one species of macaw make Guatemala their home. Parrots have few enemies in the jungle except for larger predators, who tend to eliminate the weakest or most vulnerable birds. A far bigger threat is posed by humans, who continue to destroy the parrot's forest habitat, capture the animal for commercial purposes, or even kill it for food. The capture of young parrots usually does considerable damage to the environment, since nesting trees are often cut down in the hope that chicks will somehow survive the fall.

The species captured in greatest numbers in Guatemala is the yellow-headed parrot, prized in North America as a fluent and easily trained "talker." Other vocal members of the same family are the Aztec (or olive-throated) parakeet and mealy (or blue-crowned) parrot. The mealy parrot mates for life and almost always flies in a two-by-two formation with its partner. These species are quite social and like to live near others of their kind.

The common names of parrots are inspired by easily identifiable head markings ("lore" refers to the area between eyes and beak, "crown" is the top of the head, and "front" is the forehead, while "hood" and "head" are self-explanatory). The less gregarious parrots found in Guatemala are the brown-hooded, red-lored, yellow-lored, yellow-headed, white-fronted, and white-crowned. Only sharp-eyed birders are usually able to tell the latter two species apart. Like many tropical animals (and people), parrots usually nap during the heat of the day and are most often seen during later afternoon and early morning feeding periods. The birds roost overnight.

One of the rarest birds in Guatemala is the scarlet macaw, the third-largest of the world's 16 surviving macaw species. It is one of eight such species in danger of extinction throughout much of its range, which extends from subtropical Mexico south to Bolivia.

INGUAT

The scarlet macaw is indigenous to the lowland forests of Guatemala.

38

A macaw sighting is an unforgettable experience. Mature birds are over 2 feet tall and have brilliant plumage, particularly bright red wing feathers speckled with dabs of yellow, orange, and blue. Humans pose the greatest threat to this magnificent bird, through the destruction of its forest habitat, nest-robbing for the wild bird trade, and killing for meat and feathers.

There are believed to be only about 300 pairs of macaws left in Guatemala and recent threats to the species include poaching of nests and deliberate destruction of feeding sites. One of the few efforts to reverse the trend is underway at the community of Laureles, on the Usumacinta River near Ixcoche Lagoon. Here a Guatemala City–based tourist company, Ecotourism & Adventure Travel Specialists, is working with would-be poachers to preserve macaws as an attraction for nature-oriented travelers. Other areas where macaws still live include the Sierra Lacandón and Laguna del Tigre national parks, as well as Laguna Lachua.

Blue-Crowned Motmot

The beautiful and relatively large blue-crowned motmot is easily identified by its deep-throated *hoot-hoot* call (usually heard at dawn or dusk). It is also distinguished by its indigo head feathers and long tail. The latter acquires an oddly pointed shape through removal of central feathers by preening and wear.

While the blue-crowned motmot is fairly common, its cousin, the keel-billed motmot, is one of the rarest birds in Central America, and only a few sightings have been documented. The latter bird is believed to be extinct in Mexico and there have been only two confirmed recent sightings in Guatemala.

MAMMALS

Caribbean Manatee

The Caribbean (or West Indian) manatee was once common in Lake Izabal and along the Río Dulce. The manatee has a body like a large seal, a head like a tuskless walrus, and skin like an elephant. This enormous, gentle vegetarian (also called a sea cow) was an important food source of the ancient coastal Maya and is still hunted throughout its diminishing range, although the animals are now protected within the Chocón Machacas Preserve near Lívingston.

Because the manatee spends most of its time under water, munching on grasses, you'll be very lucky to see one. They do surface to breathe, however, and you can sometimes see their whiskered noses and beady eyes poking skyward from the water. The manatee is one of at least 30 animal species in Guatemala listed as endangered.

Jaguar

The jaguar, regarded as the most sacred of all beasts by the lowland Maya (who revered it as a primeval symbol of darkness and of nature), is fighting for its survival in the country's forests and wetlands, where it is often regarded as a destructive predator by cattle-ranchers. Along the Pacific slope, cattlemen pay bounties of $600 or more for jaguar carcasses—equivalent to a peasant's entire annual salary. Called *tigre* by locals, the jaguar was once found from northern New Mexico through southern Argentina, but its need for large tracts of uninhabited land makes the jaguar's future uncertain. Up to 6 feet long and weighing as much as 250 pounds, this nocturnal predator feeds primarily on peccary, paca, fish, or deer, along with an occasional bird, lizard, or turtle. Contrary to local belief, jaguars will not attack humans unless provoked and usually do not kill livestock unless their habitat has been destroyed and their natural prey replaced by cattle. Jaguars are very territorial, ranging over vast areas of forest and savanna. The male, a solitary creature who partners with one female at a time, marks the boundaries of his kingdom with tree scratches and ground scrapings.

Thankfully, enough undisturbed habitat remains to sustain relatively healthy populations of four other species of cat in the jungles of the Petén and Verapaz: the puma (also called mountain lion), ocelot, margay, and jaguarundi.

Monkeys

Monkeys are another family of large mammals that has been hard-hit by poaching and habitat destruction in addition to such infectious diseases as yellow fever. Spider and black howler monkeys have become locally extinct in much of their former territory (lowland forests) and are still killed by rural Maya for food. However, successful reintroduction of these primates has been achieved in some areas, including Tikal National Park, where you're most apt to see a spider monkey swinging through the trees. These fruit-eaters can travel at very high speeds through the forest canopy, using their long tails to grasp and swing from overhanging limbs. In lowland areas near the Río Dulce and the Honduras border you may also encounter the white-faced capuchin monkey, a small primate at the northernmost limit of its range. The howler is so named for its distinctive (and harmless) growl, caused by a bone in the throat that can scrape against its vocal chords. Howlers use this vocalization to warn off intruders and to establish male dominance.

REPTILES AND AMPHIBIANS

Morelet's Crocodile

The Morelet's crocodile is another top-of-the-food-chain species whose presence in patches of Guatemalan wilderness is a healthy ecological sign. Like its smaller relative, the cayman, the crocodile (which can grow up to 13 feet long here) is often killed for its meat and skin. When their natural habitat is encroached upon, these animals also have a tendency to eat dogs, pigs, and other livestock, which means they don't usually last long around farms and cattle ranches.

Basilisk

One of the oddest reptiles in Guatemala is the basilisk lizard, a type of iguana. This prehistoric-looking animal moves with great speed—often on its hind legs—through its riverside habitat, often so fast that it seems to be able to skim right across the surface of a river without sinking. (This is why, in Belize, basilisks are popularly called "Jesus Christ lizards.") Researchers have determined that the basilisk actually forms a bubble of air beneath its feet; extra flaps of skin across the toes of its enlarged rear feet make this water-walking trick possible.

While these omnivorous reptiles appear fierce—like miniature Tyrannosaurus rex—they prefer to munch on leaves, flowers, and fruit in their favorite trees (often a giant ficus), in addition to the occasional insect and bird. They can be distinguished by their ridged backs, ranging in color from yellow-brown to muted gray, and (among males) reddish throat sacs. Local people love to eat the raw eggs of the female basilisk, and the creatures are becoming scarce in areas where pesticides are used. Predatory birds also are another enemy. The dominant males are very territorial and can be seen perched on high tree limbs from which they can survey their domains along inland waterways.

Fer-de-lance and Tropical Rattlesnake

Known in Guatemala as *barba amarilla* or *tres minutos*, the fer-de-lance is a much-feared nocturnal pit viper related to the water moccasin and tropical rattlesnake. Because of its fast-acting venom, the fer-de-lance is considered to be among the world's deadliest snakes. However, unless it's provoked or you are very unlucky, the vipers will generally avoid you and stick to smaller game, such as birds and rats. The fer-de-lance is at home in tropical forests and savannas of Guatemala. Adults can reach 8 feet in length, enabling the snake to strike from a coiled position. Its two retractable fangs are the largest of any snake in proportion to size. Keen awareness of smell and temperature enables the fer-de-lance to accurately pinpoint warm bodies in the dark, when it is most likely to be active. It is easily identified by its arrow-shaped head, diamond-patterned back, and thick-set body. If you are bitten, seek medical help at once. The best prevention is wearing high-top boots, however, since most fer-de-lance bites are in the feet and ankles.

If you hear a rattle as you approach an unfamiliar snake, it is probably not a fer-de-lance but a tropical rattlesnake (or *cascabel*), the only rattlesnake species in Guatemala. Inhabiting the same territory as the fer-de-lance, it is the most poisonous of all rattlers and can grow up to 7 feet in length.

Sea Turtles

The beaches of Guatemala's eastern and western seacoasts have long been nesting sites for sea turtles, and if you are very lucky you will see a pregnant female hauling herself out of the water to deposit eggs in the warm sand. Loggerheads, hawksbills, and green ridleys have historically used the Caribbean beaches, while olive ridleys and leatherbacks prefer the Pacific coast. Some of these turtles, such as the mature leatherbacks, can grow to more than 6 feet in length and a weight of over 1,200 pounds. Although the situation is changing, many turtles are still hunted by humans for their flesh, eggs, and shells. Increasingly, sea turtles are being kept from their traditional nesting areas by fences, buildings, people, pets, bright lights, and loud noises. For these reasons, three species found in Guatemala have been declared endangered.

Remarkably, sea turtles have been on Earth for about 150 million years (outlasting dinosaurs) yet little is known about their lives in the wild. We do know that they can stay underwater for several hours, returning to the surface to breathe for only a few minutes before diving again. Due to unrestricted hunting and other human-related threats in much of the world (including Guatemala), there are probably half as many sea turtles today as in the 1970s. Seven of our planet's known sea turtle species are considered endangered.

FLOWERING PLANTS AND TREES

White Nun Orchid

Guatemala's national flower is the *monja blanca*, or white nun, which grows wild in the cloud forests of Alta Verapaz and is now seldom seen anywhere else. This rare, beautiful flower, believed to be the only immaculately white orchid in the world, derives its name from its six large white petals and stamen, which are shaped like a nun's habit. Like many orchids, air plants, and bromeliads, the monja blanca prefers cool, high altitudes where dense vegetation restricts the amount of direct sunlight

INGUAT

The white nun orchid, Guatemala's national flower

penetrating the forest canopy. Orchids evolve so rapidly that a species may be found in the limbs of a single jungle tree and nowhere else on the planet. Such plants are of great interest to scientists because they may contain unique compounds that may be useful in treating human diseases or chronic medical conditions.

Sapodilla Tree

The tropical forests of Guatemala contain many useful plants, including the sapodilla tree, from which a sticky substance is tapped that formed the original base of chewing gum. Chicle was a major export of the Petén jungle during the first half of the 20th century but has largely been replaced by synthetics. A few countries, mainly in Japan, still import chicle, which, in turn, provides a source of income for those *chicleros* living in or near the forest. Like the rubber tree, which also grows wild in the Petén, the sapodilla must be tapped carefully to insure that it will remain alive to provide chicle over a period of many years.

Strangler Fig

A much less "friendly" tropical tree is the strangler fig, a member of the ficus family that, in turn, has many species in Guatemalan forests. The strangler fig is so named because its seeds (dropped by birds) are germinated in the high branches of a host tree, which the newcomer proceeds slowly to engulf with its bark, roots, and branches until death occurs. The strangler fig eventually makes its way to the ground, anchoring the tree when its unfortunate host rots and crumbles beneath its deadly grasp.

Mahogany

A less common tropic tree is the mahogany, a prized hardwood used to make fine furniture and that takes up to 80 years to mature. Its height (100 feet or more) and shallow root structure prompt the mahogany to grow large supporting buttresses at its base, spanning up to 20 feet across the forest floor. Never numerous, this tree has become very scarce due to its harvesting for export and slow propagation. The mahogany has small whitish flowers and dark, pear-shaped seed pods. When the ripe fruits fall and become scattered by animals, the rich mulch of the forest floor allows them to germinate and sprout, beginning a new cycle of life.

Ceiba

The national tree of Guatemala is the ceiba, also known as the kapok or silk cotton tree. A tall, stately tree that spreads its limbs at the top of the forest canopy, its downy fibers are used to this day to stuff pillows and cushions. The ceiba's most important role in many Guatemalan communities, however, is to shade the main plaza with its leafy, long-reaching branches. This traditions goes back many centuries, to the days when the ancient Maya cultivated ceibas in the plazas of their cities. In some of Guatemala's famous Mayan ruins, these trees (or their descendants) still tower as high as 100 feet or more over what is left of these long-abandoned communities. A ceiba is an ecosystem in itself, since its clefts and branches (up to 150 feet across) are populated by many species of orchid, fern, cacti, and bromeliad. Iguanas and other reptiles like to bask in the sun in its highest reaches.

Palm Trees

The cohune palm, widespread throughout the lowlands of Guatemala, is one of the forest community's most useful members. Its fronds are used as thatch in roofs, and a valuable cooking oil can be extracted from its fruit. Husks from the tree's palm nuts make excellent fuel, and the nut meat can be pounded into a flour that will store many weeks without spoiling. The nuts are very hard and can be carved into clothing buttons and even jewelry. The cohune was highly regarded by the ancient Maya, who considered it a symbol of fertility. Because of the palm's many practical uses, it is almost always spared when forests are cut down for subsistence agriculture.

Dominant in low-lying marshes and along riverbanks are palmetto palms, which can grow to great heights and provide fronds used for walls and roofs in traditional house construction.

Coconut palms are not native to the region but were introduced on Guatemala's coasts in the late 18th and early 19th centuries as a commercial crop. A few coconuts are still harvested for their oil, meat, and husks (an excellent fuel for making charcoal), but the industry has pretty much died out.

Mangrove roots

Mangroves

Much of the Caribbean and part of the Pacific coastlines of Guatemala are covered by dense stands of black, white, and red mangrove. Different types of mangroves are adapted to varying degrees of salinity, and you will notice them changing as you go away from sources of salt water. A good place to observe this is along the waterways of the Monterrico biotope, south of Guatemala City. The ancient Maya made extensive use of the mangrove wetlands as hunting grounds, as evidenced by the use of crocodile and manatee images in their artwork. Although these tangled thickets have traditionally been despised by settlers, who often cleared them as quickly as possible, they protect shorelines from erosion during storms and provide an irreplaceable nursery for small fish and crustaceans. Above the waterline, birders can see egrets, herons, ibises, roseate spoonbills, pelicans, frigate birds, raptors, and boobies amid the tangled roots and branches. Coatimundis, crocodiles, anteaters, jaguars, raccoons, and boa constrictors are also found in these wetland areas.

The San Pedro volcano looms over Lake Atitlán.

4

SPECIAL
INTERESTS
AND ACTIVITIES

Some travelers love to shop, while others want to take in cultural or historical attractions. Still others are eager to experience outdoor adventures. Many like to sample a little of everything when they travel. Fortunately, Guatemala has something to offer almost every range of interest, including traditional cultures, Maya archaeology, natural history, water sports, hiking, birding, caving, fishing, and, yes, even shopping. This chapter presents highlights for each of these categories, including a rundown of practical information on companies and individuals providing relevant specialized services for the discriminating traveler. Note that many outfitters offer tours and assistance in more than one category.

NATIVE CRAFTS AND ARTS

Guatemala has a long, colorful native handicraft tradition that continues to be an extremely important part of the country's economy. This is particularly true in the highland villages, where there is localized specialization in designs and art forms from one community to the next. These crafts are popularly known by the collective (and interchangeable) terms *artesanía* or *típica*.

Handwoven textiles are probably the most popular craft purchase in Guatemala. These items display brilliant colors and intricate designs that relate to their specific place, ethnic group, tribe, or family of origin. The weavings can be purchased in the form of raw cloth or finished

The Bargaining Tradition

Buying in public markets gives a visitor access to the very heart of Guatemala's indigenous culture, since the buying and selling of artesanía predates the arrival of the Spanish and is still often carried out in hushed tones, although the younger generations are becoming increasingly aggressive. Bargaining is a vital part of this tradition, and foreigners are expected to participate. In fact, sellers may feel puzzled or even offended if you do not engage in this friendly ritualistic game.

Experienced bargainers usually start by offering about 40 or 50 percent of the first price that is quoted, then working their way toward a middle-ground compromise that will likely be about two-thirds or three-fourths of the original price. Remember to look around and compare prices before starting any serious negotiating. And do not start bargaining unless you intend to purchase the item for a price you propose. It offends Guatemalans if you offer to buy something for a stated amount and then walk away empty-handed.

Bargaining is not allowed in most "fixed price" shops or where price tags have been attached to merchandise. In smaller shops you can ask if there are any "discounts" (for example, if you buy more than one item at a time). Check local English-language tourist publications such as The Siglo News *and* The Revue *for up-to-date information about retail stores selling artesanía.*

garments, including everything from trousers *(pantalones)* to skirts *(faldas)* to hats *(sombreros)*. Most popular is the woven and often embroidered blouse worn by indigenous women, called the *huipil* (pronounced wee-PEEL), which may be worn over skirts or pants, stretched on a frame, or displayed on a wall. These weavings—in untailored lengths called *corte*—usually contain cotton fiber, with wool or silk threads sometimes mixed in. Acrylic fibers are becoming more common. Quality, availability, and prices vary considerably for these and other handmade items, depending on where you are. Such goods are generally less expensive in remote rural villages and more costly in urban, touristy areas. The exception is Panajachel, where the sheer volume of trade yields good prices for the persistent shopper.

While textiles are by far the most common artesanía purchase, bargains can also be found on high-quality wood carvings, leather goods, straw hats, ceramics, baskets, mats, furniture, and jewelry. Many of the oldest and most valuable items have already found their way into museum and gallery collections, but there are still plenty of well-made goods. Inexpensive souvenir items include wrist and hair bands, earrings, and embroidered coin purses.

As a rule, prices are much lower in public markets than they are in shops. Lower prices are also more likely the farther you get from the main tourist towns—Antigua and Chichicastenango—and the closer you get to the article's place of manufacture. Your best bet is almost always to buy an item from the person who made it.

Crafts

The native craftwork of Guatemala is among the most varied and interesting in the world, a natural result of the country's rich pre-Columbian and Spanish colonial traditions. Few of the artisans producing these objects have any formal training, relying instead on techniques and designs passed down to them through many generations. The materials used in their creations, such as vegetable dyes and natural fibers, are often obtained locally. Much of the thread used in Guatemalan textiles (*tejidos*) is still spun and colored by hand, and ceramics (*cerámica*) are frequently produced with local clays and wood-burning kilns.

Marketplaces dot the countryside, and almost every village sets aside at least one day each week for the buying and selling of a dizzying array of handicrafts and foodstuffs. These markets are the gathering places where indígena not only bargain for, trade, and purchase the daily necessities of life but also gossip, strengthen family ties, and reaffirm social traditions that date back centuries.

Many stores, galleries, and workshops sell handcrafted items directly to the public. Look for signs containing the words *artesanía* or *confecciónes típicas*. Other hints: A *taller artesanál* is an artist's studio, and a *cooperativa de tejidos* is a textile cooperative.

Traditional fiestas, filled with dancing, drinking, music, parades, and merrymaking, commemorate the patron saints of each town and major

Market in Panajachel

Richard Mahler

events of historical or religious significance. On any given day, a fiesta is being held somewhere in one of Guatemala's more than 4,000 towns and villages.

A good place to get an overview of Guatemalan crafts is the **Mercado de Artesanía** located near the national museum complex on Calzada del Aeropuerto in Guatemala City's La Aurora Park, a few blocks from the international airport terminal in Zone 13. The market is dedicated exclusively to handcrafted típica that reflects the country's traditions and cultural heritage. It is open daily from 9:30 a.m. to 6:00 p.m. except on Sunday, when it closes at 2:00 p.m.

Those interested in buying mail-order products directly from indigenous people may wish to contact **Mayan Crafts** (845 N. Lincoln St., Arlington, VA 22201; 703/527-5067), **Shawcross Aid Programme** (R.D. 4, Box 10, 4043 State Route 39, Shelby, OH 44875; 419/347-2937), **Pueblo to People** (P.O. Box 2545, Houston, TX 77252; 800/843-5257), **Adopt-A-Village** (206 Sixth St., Bonita Springs, FL 33923; 813/495-7222), or **Trade Wind** (P.O. Box 380, Summertown, TN 38483; 800/445-1991). These progressive (and in some cases nonprofit) organizations work with the Guatemalan Maya on craft projects as well as human rights, economic development, and literacy programs. An excellent source of information about these and similar projects around the world is nonprofit

Weekly Market Days

Here are some weekly market days in communities most often frequented by tourists:

- Chimaltenango—*Monday, Thursday*
- Sacapulas, Nebaj, Chichicastenango—*Thursday, Sunday*
- Todos Santos, Senahú, Santa Clara la Laguna—*Saturday*
- Esquipulas, Rabinal, Tactic, Salamá—*Sunday*
- Palín—*Wednesday, Friday*
- Sololá—*Tuesday, Friday*
- Zunil, Tucurú—*Monday*
- Aguacatán, San Francisco el Alto, San Marcos, Santiago Atitlán—*Friday*
- Momostenango—*Wednesday, Sunday*
- Totonicapán, Santa Cruz del Quiché—*Thursday, Saturday*
- Antigua—*Monday, Thursday, Saturday*
- Huehuetenango, Quetzaltenango, Panajachel, Lívingston, Cobán, Guatemala City—*every day*

Cultural Survival and its quarterly magazine of the same name (53-A Church Street, Cambridge, MA 02138; 617/495-2562). There are retail outlets for some Guatemalan artisans' cooperatives in Antigua, Quetzaltenango, and Guatemala City.

Textiles and Clothing

The traditional *traje*, or clothing, of the indigenous Guatemalan people is admired around the world for its fine quality and colorful embroidery. The intricate designs, which vary dramatically from one village to the next, are carefully made using pre-Columbian techniques on backstrap (also called stick) looms or, less commonly, foot-powered treadle looms introduced by the Spanish. Men traditionally have done much of the crochet work, although women have now assumed

51

much of this responsibility in order to meet tourist demand. Textiles are mostly woven with wool, silk, acrylic, or cotton thread, depending on the region. You will also see some jaspe (resist or tie-dye) design that is similar to the ikat styling of Indonesia.

It is estimated that there are at least 325 major patterns reflected in the traditional dress still worn by the indígena residents of about 2,000 Guatemalan villages. Each costume reflects some aspect of its own geography, family structure, patron saint, or history, in some cases even incorporating Spanish colonial dress. Dress may also be altered depending on the wearer's sex, age, tribal affiliation, and social rank.

A woman often has a minimum of four different ceremonial costumes, their designs and symbols varying for each occasion. Men, who have been less loyal to the customs of traditional dress, usually have only one or two outfits. In many villages men have adapted completely to Western clothing styles. Most women, however, continue to wear more traditional garb.

Some of the more popular textile markets are in **Santiago Atitlán** (noted for its animal and geometric designs), **Panajachel** (vibrant combinations of red and purple, along with animals), **San Juan Chamelco**

Traditional Highland Maya Attire

Despite the many ceremonial and regional differences, the typical dress of Guatemalan Indigena women usually includes a huipil *(untailored smock-style blouse),* corte *or* refajo *(skirt),* faja *(woman's belt),* tzute *(scarf or headdress), and* rebozo *(shawl). The word "huipil," incidentally, is derived from an Aztec phrase meaning "my covering" (in Spanish,* mi tapado*).*

Traditional men's attire includes pantalones *(trousers),* cincho *(man's belt),* camisa *(shirt),* chaleco *or* capixay *(tunic or vest),* cotón *or* chaqueta *(jacket),* banda *(sash),* sombrero *or* gorra *(hat or cap), and a shoulder-bag, often crocheted, called a* morral.

(braided work), **Chichicastenango** (traditional-looking clothes in North American sizes), **San Francisco El Alto** (*huipiles*), and **San Antonio Aguas Calientes** (high-quality designs and dyes). In many textile centers, foreigners can easily obtain personalized weaving instruction from some of the most talented practitioners. See Chapter 7: Western Highlands for more detailed discussions of these communities, their weavers, and their markets.

Spanish words for popular non-clothing textile items include *cartera* (clutch bag), *monedero* (coin purse), *tzute grande* (wall hanging), *mantel* (tablecloth), *tapate* (coaster), *servilleta* or *serviette* (napkin), and *funda de almohada* (pillow case).

Blankets

In the western mountains of Guatemala, the town of **Momostenango** is famous for its woolen *ponchos momostecos* ("blankets from Momo"). These are made on foot-operated looms by local Quiché Maya men and sold at the town's Sunday market. The women are in charge of washing, carding, and spinning the wool, which is sheared from sheep grazed in nearby upland meadows. The finished blankets are washed in a local hot spring before being sold. Although the best selection and prices are found at the Momostenango public market, you can find these distinctive blankets in stores and *mercados* through the highlands.

Leather

From traditional sandals to leather portfolios and cigarette cases, leather has always been a major resource for Guatemalan crafters. A *talabartería* sign indicates a saddlery, leather goods store, or leather studio.

Jewelry

Since the Maya epoch, Guatemalan jade has been one of the main stones used in jewelry making. The craft has been revived in **Antigua** over the past two decades with the production of traditional and modern designs of bracelets, earrings, necklaces, and other pieces of jewelry. High-quality and multicolored jade quarried in ancient and recently rediscovered mines of the Sierra de las Minas range of southeast Guatemala is used. (Note that although jade is spelled the same in Spanish and in English, its Spanish pronunciation is HAH-day.)

The town of **Tactic**, in Alta Verapaz, is known for its silver jewelry, and filigree is the specialty of craftspeople in nearby **San Pedro Carchá**. There are gold- and silver-workers in other parts of the country who specialize in religious artifacts for churches and homes. Tin is also crafted in various Guatemalan communities into cages, candleholders, and other decorative objects. If you are interested in these kinds of craftwork, be on the lookout for stores marked *joyería* (jewelry).

In **Lívingston**, on the Caribbean coast, seeds of the wild guiscoyol plant are used to make rings and earrings. You can also see jewelry made out of black coral and turtle shells, although it is now illegal for visitors to take these items out of the country. The government believes that commercial use of these items threatens their continuing presence in the marine ecosystem.

Cane and Palm

Woven palm hats are popular throughout Guatemala. Some of the most attractive and colorful are made in **Todos Santos Cuchumatán** and **Santa Cruz del Quiché**. It is not accurate to call these "Panama" hats, since the slender reeds used to make Panamas are found exclusively in Ecuador.

From **San Raimundo, Iztapa, Lake Atitlán**, and **San Juan Sacatepéquez** come the large variety of mats and baskets made with different types of cane and reed as well as fibers from the maguey cactus. Small straw baskets are mostly made in **Tecpán**, near Chimaltenango.

Wood

Wood-crafted Guatemalan products (*productos de madera*) include vivid folkloric masks (*máscaras*), delicately carved squash gourds, brightly colored chests (*cajas*), colonial doors, rattan chairs, musical instruments, wooden fruit, and bentwood boxes. The villages of the wooded area of **southwestern Totonicapán** are particularly noted for their carved toys (*juguetes*), varnished fruit, and furniture (*muebles*). The town of **Palín** is noted for its fine masks, and **Antigua** is a major producer of colonial-style doors and furniture, much of it exported to the U.S. **Francisco Márquez** and the **Juárez** brothers of Antigua are famous for their woodwork, and their studios are open to the public.

Ceramics

A great variety of ceramic objects (*cerámica*) are produced in Guatemala, reflecting two primary traditions: pre-Columbian and Spanish colonial. Examples range from the glazed pottery of **Jalapa, Huehuetenango**, and **Totonicapán** (made with techniques introduced during the colonial era) to the unglazed animal-shaped clay creations of **Chiantla** and **San Luis Jilotepeque**. The latter are produced using open-air bonfires rather than kilns, just as they were in prehistoric times by the Pokomán Maya. **Rabinal**, in Baja Verapaz, is one of the few places where a combination of indígena and European techniques is applied to figures, toys, and other objects, using *nij*, an unusual dye derived from insects.

Hand-carved masks are among the many souvenirs for sale in highland markets.

Some artists, such as the brothers **Federico and Andrés Tuymax** of Totonicapán, have established national reputations for the quality of their ceramic work. As with weavers, indígena potters often use designs and materials whose origins are lost in antiquity. In **Santa Apolonia**, for example, the red ceramic ware draws heavily on Cakchiquel Maya techniques, yielding balloon-shaped bowls and flat cooking pans called *comales.*

It is primarily the women who have carried on the pre-Columbian ceramic traditions, molding clay by hand and using natural clays and dyes. Their products are mainly utilitarian, and decorative motifs are simple: plants, animals, and human forms, such as the *mengalas* (maidservants) and *chichiguas* (nursemaids) of the 19th century.

The Spanish introduced potters' wheels, oxide glazes, mineral enamels, and painted crockery to Guatemala. The main producer of colonial-style white earthenware (*majólica*) is **Antigua**, where **Francisco Montiel** and his family are recognized as perhaps the foremost practitioners (Subidita a San Felipe 20). Other renowned craftsmen in Antigua include **Cruz and Guillermo España** (Calle Real de San Felipe 83), for his ceramic pigeons and other birds, and members of the **Rodenas family** (Calle de Chajón 24), for their painted miniatures, including tiny dishware, butterflies, and *nacimientos* (nativity scenes). Also recommended is **Marcelino C. Monroy** (Calle de los Pasos 28). In nearby **Jocotenango**, the **Barrios family** (Camino a San Felipe 3-26) and **José Gerardo López Pérez** (Colonia Clarita 6) are famous for their wood, ceramic, and bronze work.

Other centers of European-type ceramics are **Jalapa, Totonicapán**, and **San Cristóbal**. The many workshops of **Totonicapán**, between Quetzaltenango and Santa Cruz del Quiché, are worth visiting, particularly during the annual fiesta of the Archangel (September 14 to 30), Semana Santa (Holy Week), and the village's Tuesday and Saturday markets.

Dance

The traditional *danzas* (dances) of Guatemala are often a kind of musical play recreating a specific historic event through the use of unvarying ritualized scripts and masks. Some danzas are performed in only one community, while others, like the famous Dance of the Spanish Conquest, are part of the annual fiestas in many towns and villages. **Rabinal** presents portions of its extended dance drama, the Rabinal Achí, during its January 25 to 29 fiesta, along with an elaborate ceremony calling for a bountiful harvest. In **Lívingston**, the unique traditions of the Garifuna people are celebrated in dance celebrations several times a year, particularly during the May 13 to 15 commemoration of the arrival of their ancestors from Honduras and Belize.

The most dependable times of year to see dances are during a town's patron saint celebration, the Christmas season (December 7 through January 6), and *Semana Santa* (the week preceding Easter).

Typically, dances are only one small part of a community-wide fiesta that includes much drinking and carousing. This is why many dancers are often so drunk that they can barely stand up, particularly if the danza is scheduled toward the end of the day. Besides *aguardiente* (sugarcane liquor) and *atol* (a hot corn beverage), large quantities of food are consumed, including such special-occasion treats as *buñuelos* (honey-coated fried pastries), *jocón* (a chicken dish), *torrejas* (similar to French toast), stuffed peppers (*chile rellenos*), and *plátanos en gloria* (plantains fried in sweet sauce).

An excellent resource for those interested in seeing Guatemalan dances is the **Directory of Fiestas** (*Directorio de Fiestas*) published and distributed free of charge by INGUAT, the government tourist commission. It contains a detailed description of festivals throughout the country, indexed by date and location.

Music

The marimba is Guatemala's national musical instrument. It is a large wooden xylophone set on a waist-high stand, which some believe to be of

West African origin. Others think its roots are in the ancient cultures of Central America, citing ancient Maya drawings that show a marimba-like instrument being played.

It is believed that the marimba originally consisted of a single row of wooden bars placed over hollowed gourds set on the ground. It eventually evolved to its current appearance, where the bars are arranged in piano-like fashion. Each slab of wood vibrates in a specific major or minor key when struck with a rubber-wrapped-with-yarn mallet heads. Today's marimbas can be as large as five octaves in sound range. In Guatemala, as many as seven musicians hammer away at their modern double-keyboard marimbas in large dance bands, accompanied by drums, guitars, flutes, trumpets, saxophones, rhythm instruments, and even banjos.

During religious processions and fiestas, a traditional Maya *chirimía* (a recorder-like flute that sounds like an oboe) often plays a prominent role. In ancient times wind instruments were sometimes made out of conch or snail shells (*caracoles*), and other times out of a piece of bone. The sacred Maya book called the Popol Vuh makes several references to flutes brought from the legendary homeland of Tulán during the great migration of indígena into Guatemala. Many of the melodies that have been handed down through the generations bear a striking resemblance to bird songs, particularly that of the *cenzontle*, or "bird of a thousand voices."

Traditional Maya percussion instruments include the box-shaped *cajita* and skin-covered *tun* (similar to a conga drum). With the arrival of the Spanish, the violin, tuba, and guitar also became common members of rural ensembles.

Cassette tapes and compact discs of Guatemalan music are sold for about $7 each by **INGUAT** through its offices. Another excellent source is **Casa K'ojom**, a private museum of indigenous music in Antigua (at Calle Recoletos 55).

Maya Arts, Culture, and Archaeology Tours

In Guatemala

AmeriSpan Guatemala, 6 a. Avenida 40, Antigua; 832-0164, fax 832-1896, amerispan@guate.net. Tours of highland village, with emphasis on indigenous culture. Also arranges Spanish-language instruction and home-stays in Antigua and Quetzaltenango. Office in Antigua (see Chapter 6).

Maya Tours, Edificio Valsari, Nivel 3, Oficina 304; 6a. Calle 1-36, Zone 10; Guatemala City; 440-3712. Adventure, culture, and archaeology tours.

Ney's Viajes y Turismo, 13a. Calle 0-56, Zone 10; 333-5441, fax 333-5411. Traditional tours of highlands, cities, and Tikal, with emphasis on cultural sights and archaeology.

Panorama Guatemala Cultural, 5a. Avenida 8-57, Zone 9; Guatemala City; 331-4174. Tours specializing in archaeology, textiles, crafts, history, and folklore.

SCDRYS, Diagonal 117-17, Zone 1; Quetzaltenango; 763-0409; fax 761-6873. Nonprofit social service group offering tours and homestays in Maya villages.

Tropical Tours, 4a. Calle 2-51, Zone 10; Guatemala City; 339-3662, fax 332-3748. Adventure and archaeological tours of Tikal and other Petén sites.

Viajes Nuevo Mundo, Edificio Plaza Viva, Oficina 20-3; 6a. Avenida y 10a. Calle, Zone 1; Guatemala City; 250-8759. Cultural and religious tours.

In the U.S. and Canada
Art Workshops in Antigua, 4758 Lyndale Ave. S.; Minneapolis, MN 55409; (612) 825-0747, fax 825-6637, info@artguat.org; in Antigua 832-3584. Classes in weaving, writing, photography, painting, gardening, and crafts; based in Antigua. Highly recommended.

Earthwatch, 680 Mt. Auburn Street; Watertown, MA 02272; (617) 926-8200. Archaeological fieldwork and tours.

Explorations, Inc., 27655 Kent Rd.; Bonita Springs, FL 33923; (800) 446-9660. Tours highlighting the archaeology and living history of the Maya, including highland villages and markets as well as ancient archaeological sites.

Far Horizons Archaeological & Cultural Trips, P.O. Box 91900; Albuquerque, NM 87199; (800) 552-4575, journey@farhorizon.com, www.farhorizon.com. Expeditions emphasizing culture and archaeology, usually limited to 15 participants; founder is an archaeologist and most trips are led by an archaeologist; other options include contemporary Maya festivals and Guatemalan natural history. Highly recommended.

Foundation for Field Research, P.O. Box 2010; Alpine, CA 91903; (619) 445-9264. Archaeological (and nature) field research and study trips. Send for free copy of *Explorer News*, the FFR catalog.

Guatemala Travel Representatives, 720 Worthshire; Houston, TX 77008; (800) 451-8017; in Texas (713) 688-1985; fax (713) 869-2540. Travel to highlands, Petén, and Guatemala City, specializing in culture, history, nature, and archaeology.

Recursos de Santa Fe, 826 Camino del Monte Rey, Santa Fe, NM 87505; (505) 982-9301, recursos@aol.com. Mayan Back Roads guided tour to ancient Maya sites as well as seldom-visited towns, parks, and markets. Includes sites in Belize and Yucatán.

Maya Seminars, 968 Corona Street; Denver, CO 80218; (303) 467-7112. History and archaeology of the Maya world; will customize trips for groups of four or more.

School of American Research, 660 García; Santa Fe, NM 87501; (505) 982-2919. Education and study trips to Mayan sites.

The Sierra Club, 730 Polk Street; San Francisco, CA 94109; (415) 776-2211. Education and study trips to Maya sites and nature reserves of Central America.

Smithsonian Odyssey Tours & Research Expeditions, Smithsonian Institution; 1100 Jefferson Drive SW; Washington, DC 20560; (202) 357-1350 or (800) 524-4125. Archaeology, anthropology, and nature-related study tours and fieldwork trips.

VOLCANO CLIMBING

The backbone of Guatemala's interior is a range of volcanic mountains that runs the entire length of the country diagonally from Mexico to El Salvador. There are at least 33 volcanoes, although some have been dormant for so many decades that they technically have been removed from this classification. Only five are considered currently active.

The list of volcanoes below is in descending order of accessibility from Guatemala City, with Pacaya the easiest and Tajumulco the most difficult to reach from the capital. Check bulletin boards, travel agents, and local newspapers in Antigua and Panajachel for volcano-trekking guides serving those areas. Local INGUAT offices can provide suggestions. Prices for guided trips start at about $10 per person for the easiest treks. You'll pay at least 50 percent more if you require a horse.

For those who read Spanish, *La Guía de los Volcanes de Guatemala* (The Guide to the Volcanoes of Guatemala) by Carlos E. Prahl Redondo, a member of the nation's largest mountaineering club, is

INGUAT

Most volcano climbing requires no special equipment, but climbers should be in good physical condition.

highly recommended. It provides detailed trail maps and specific climbing recommendations for each of Guatemala's volcanoes as well as for other important mountains.

A good map is a must when climbing a volcano. Guatemala's Military Geographic Institute puts out the best series, updated in 1992. You can buy them directly from the government or at the Casa Andinista bookstore in Antigua. In the U.S., try MapLink, 25 East Mason St., Santa Barbara, CA 93101 (805/965-4402, fax 805/962-0884).

When volcano climbing be sure to bring a hat, sunglasses, sunscreen, and plenty of water. Comfortable shoes with plenty of tread are essential. For most volcanoes, a jacket and a rain poncho are also advised, since the peaks are almost always cool, damp, and windy.

Pacaya

In recent years the slopes of this volcano have been the scene of many bloody shoot-outs between bandits, tourists, and security guards hired to protect tourists. In early 1997, five people were shot (and three killed) on excursions here. In 1998 there was a major eruption atop Pacaya. The situation may have changed by the time you read this, but be sure to check locally before considering a hike up this volcano. The author's suggestion is to gaze from afar unless you are willing to accept the considerable risk of being attacked by armed thieves on the mountainside.

Visitors who do reach the 8,420-foot summit of Pacaya can enjoy the spectacle of an active volcano spewing steam, ash, and lava. One can stand near the lower crater (the higher one is dormant) and watch a bubbling cauldron of hot liquids, sludge, and molten rock. Allow about an hour and 45 minutes for the ascent from the village of San Vicente de Pacaya and about an hour to descend the well-marked trail. Four accessible peaks of varying difficulty await at the top of the volcano.

Public transportation to this area is limited: You can take a bus from the capital's Zone 4 terminal to San Vicente, leaving at or before 7:00 a.m. and returning on the last bus at 4:00 p.m. Several tour companies, of varying reliability and ethics, arrange guided trips to the top of Pacaya from Antigua and Guatemala City.

Agua

From almost any point in the city of Antigua, the Agua volcano dominates the southern horizon. Ascent of the 12,356-foot mountain takes anywhere from 3 to 5 hours, depending on your physical condition and whether your trek begins at the cemetery outside the village of Santa María de Jesús or at the end of the access road that goes partway up the volcano's north peak. The descent is from 2 to 3 hours. Santa María is a 45-minute bus ride from Antigua, a good base for climbers. The first bus leaves Antigua about 5 a.m. Guides and horses are available in both Santa María and Antigua.

A good place to gather information or arrange a guide is in Antigua at either the Club Andinista at 6a. Avenida Norte 34 or Casa Andinista at 4a. Calle Oriente 5A. Several travel agencies in Antigua also provide information and guide services. There is a small *pensión* in Santa María, with meals available. The hike is not particularly arduous and can be made without much difficulty by a reasonably fit person.

The first part of the climb is through cornfields and coffee plantations, punctuated by patches of dense vegetation that includes wild geraniums, orchids, and begonias. Near the summit, the broadleaf jungle gives way to pine forest and grasslands.

The awesome view from the top sweeps from the Pacific Ocean to tropical lowlands, plus smoggy Guatemala City to the south. A scar on the volcano's north slope gives mute testimony to the 1541 earthquake, which loosened a natural dam on the peak and sent millions of gallons of mud and water smashing into Ciudad Vieja, destroying what was then the Guatemalan capital. The city was relocated and the volcano rechristened Agua.

Today there are communications antennae near the top of Agua. Because there have also been robberies and violent attacks on foreign visitors climbing the volcano, it is strongly recommended that you inquire locally about conditions before heading up Agua. If you decide to go, hire an experienced guide and try to hike in a group, especially if you are attempting a full-moon trek. As always in Guatemala, carry a photocopy of your passport identification and as few valuables as possible.

San Pedro

Perhaps the most photographed volcano in Guatemala, San Pedro looms above the western shoreline of Lake Atitlán to a height of 9,908 feet. Its almost perfectly shaped cone rises between the villages of San Pedro la Laguna and Santiago Atitlán. The lake itself is 5,210 feet above sea level.

Thick forests obscure the view during much of the ascent, which is steep but not especially arduous. Bring water, however, because there is none to be found on this hike. The trail begins behind the village of San Pedro, where guides can easily be secured: Check at local restaurants and hotels. This is the only one of the three Atitlán-area volcanoes that can be hiked in a single day. Athletic climbers will reach the top in 2 or 3 hours and return in 1 or 1½ hours. Others may need 4 or 5 hours to get up and 2 hours to come down.

By special arrangement you can take a boat from Santiago Atitlán and climb the volcano from its west side, then come down the east slope into San Pedro. Inquire at the Posada de Santiago in Santiago Atitlán to arrange an experienced guide and transport across the water. At the same hotel you can hire guides for nature treks into wilderness areas behind San Pedro, including Cerro Cabeza del Burro, and El Mirador (see Chapter 7: Western Highlands).

Atitlán and Tolimán

Atitlán is one of the twin peaks that hover over the south side of Lake Atitlán. At 11,604 feet, this is the higher of the two. Both are recommended as two-day trips, although it's possible to climb each peak in one very long day. Atitlán is considered a more difficult climb, primarily because of the many deep ravines that cut into its slopes and the lack of any natural water source. Allow 8 hours for the ascent and 5 hours for the hike down.

Tolimán is 10,360 feet high and still vents steam and noxious gas from its twin craters. Climbing Tolimán is time-consuming, but a small waterfall near the summit provides a welcome respite and is frequented by wild animals; if you sit still amid the trees you might see them. Allow 7 or 8 hours to reach the top, 4 or 5 hours to descend. There are several routes for climbing each of the volcanoes, but the most popular one starts with a common trail that begins at the town of San Lucas Tolimán.

Fuego

The cone of this active volcano, north of Antigua, was destroyed by a 1949 eruption, and smoke, steam, and lava spews from the new crater on a fairly regular basis. Excursions to the 12,346-foot peak can be made in a single day, although it is better to allot two days to climb Fuego and/or nearby Acatenango. The most popular ascent follows a rough trail from the village of Alotenango, east of the peak, reached in about an hour by bus, private car, or taxi from Antigua. Allow 8 to 10 hours going up and 6 to 8 hours coming down. Inquire locally about Fuego's level of volcanic activity before making any climbing plans: The fumes it emits can be toxic. This is a strenuous climb and the services of an experienced guide are strongly advised.

Acatenango
The two peaks of this 13,042-foot volcano near Antigua, have not erupted since the mid-1920s, but experts will tell you that's a geological eyeblink. There are three routes of ascent, each taking between 6 and 8 hours. Descent time is 3 to 4 hours. The easiest way up is the trail that starts at the coffee plantation called La Soledad, an easy drive from Antigua via the villages of Yepocapa or Acatenango. Public buses run daily from Antigua to San Miguel Dueñas and La Finca Concepción Calderas, both within walking distance of La Soledad. Many climbers prefer to camp halfway up the volcano and stay at a rustic shelter on a plateau called La Mesita. Snow sometimes dusts this peak during January.

Tecuamburro
The twin peaks of this forest-covered volcano provide one of the easier climbs in Guatemala. The ascent can be made in under 2 hours from the trailhead on Route 16 in the Río los Esclavos valley north of Chiquimulilla, off the Pacific Coastal Highway (CA-2). The descent takes about 1 hour. There are many coffee plantations on the mountain's slopes, but the summit itself is heavily forested. Tecuamburro's lateral saddle contains a sulphurous lake called Ixpaco, filled with milky-white water that gives off a strong odor and, on full-moon nights, an eerie luminescence. Lago Ixpaco, surrounded by tall eucalyptus trees, is also accessible by road.

Santa María
This is a hard climb through luxuriant and beautiful forests, but the view from the top is breathtaking. Santa María has been very active during the past 200 years, devastating nearby villages and farms with its lava and ash as recently as the 1920s. Allow 5 hours for the climb up its conical 12,376-foot peak and 3 hours for the return. The easiest trail begins outside the village of Llanos de Pinal, about 5 miles west of Quetzaltenango. You can climb partway up the slope and get a good view of the Santiaguito crater below, where there is often an impressive show of volcanic fireworks.

Santiaguito
Still very active (since 1902), this peak lies just below Santa María, not far from Quetzaltenango. It can be climbed from the villages of La Isla or

Llanos de Pinal in about 2 hours. The return trip from the summit (about 9,000 feet) takes about the same length of time. Inquire locally before heading out. The continued volcanic activity has created a forbidding moonscape around the base of Santiaguito known as the Valley of Desolation. Several outfitters (inquire at Rincón de los Antojitos) organize trips up the volcano from nearby Quetzaltenango. Landslides and poisonous gases pose real danger on Santiaguito: Five climbers have died here in recent years.

Tacaná

Guatemala's second-highest peak, 13,429-foot Tacaná is a grueling climb from the village of Sabinal, near the Mexican border. This volcano has a majestic cone that was formed in 1855 during its last eruption. Guides and horses can be hired in Sabinal or the nearby village of Tacaná, which is 50 miles (3 hours) by four-wheel-drive vehicle from the town of San Marcos. There is bus service several times a day from San Pedro to Tacaná (5 hours), with a minibus continuing to Sabinal.

The usual route involves a 3-hour hike to La Haciendita, where you'll find water and a campsite, continuing the following day for another 6 or 7 hours to the summit. The descent takes about 10 hours. It is also possible to ascend Tacaná from the Mexican side of the border, leaving from the village of Unión Juárez.

Tajumulco

The highest mountain in Guatemala, 13,846-foot Tajumulco commands a sweeping view of the Cuchumatanes Mountains and the department of San Marcos. The climb is not especially difficult, but the altitude can cause dizziness and fatigue, or even heart problems for those with cardiac conditions. The ascent takes about 5 hours from the village of Tuichán (on the road that ends at Tacaná). Most climbers travel by horseback to the hamlet of Horqueta, at about 13,000 feet, and spend the night there before beginning the final climb. Descent time is about 3 hours.

The old crater, about 230 feet below the newer summit, is still used by Maya shamans for centuries-old rituals and ceremonies. On the climb up this and nearby peaks you may catch a glimpse of the elusive quetzal in the Cuchumatanes cloud forest, one of the bird's few remaining intact Guatemalan habitats.

Unless you have made prior arrangements, the best way to secure a guide and transportation for the climb is to stop by the office of the *alcalde* (mayor) in one of the villages around the base of the volcano. During the rainy season, the top of Tajumulco is often obscured by clouds, and there is sometimes ice and snow at its higher elevations.

Volcano Climbing Outfitters

Asociación Andinismo Chicag, 6a. Avenida Norte 34; Antigua; 832-3343. Mountaineering club that arranges volcano climbs and rents equipment; good information resource.

Ecotourism and Adventure Specialists, Avenida Reforma 8-60, Zone 9, #105; Guatemala City; 361-3104, fax 334-0453, ecoadventure@ mail2.guate.net. Recommended.

Expedición Panamundo, 6a. Avenida 14-75, Zone 9; Guatemala City; 331-7588, fax 331-7565. Specializes in archaeology, nature, volcano climbing, trekking, rafting, bird-watching, and botany trips, with particular emphasis on remote Mayan sites in the Petén, Belize, Mexico, and Honduras. Recommended.

Natán Hardeman, c/o Inter-American School; Quetzaltenango; IAS@uvg.edu.gt. Specialist in volcano climbs in the Quetzaltenango area.

Maya Expeditions, 15a. Calle 1-91, Zone 10; Guatemala City; 363-4965, fax 337-4666, mayaexp@guate.net. Custom volcano climbs and other outdoor adventures. Recommended.

El Rincón de los Antojitos, 15a. Avenida at 5a. Calle, Zone 1; Quetzaltenango. Information clearinghouse for volcano climbs in Quetzaltenango area; also a friendly and recommended restaurant.

Viva Tours, Avenida de la Reforma 12-81, Zona 10; Guatemala City; 368-0677. Specializes in volcano and fishing tours as well as the traditional circuit of popular destinations.

CAVING

Cave exploration, a relatively new sport also called caving, is rapidly becoming popular in Guatemala as new underground passages are discovered almost every year. Only a few caves are set up to accommodate inexperienced visitors, however, with such conveniences as electric lighting, ladders, and guardrails. Most are not easily accessible, and some are closed entirely to visitors without government permits.

The caves of Guatemala, with few exceptions, are formed from the erosive and corrosive impact of slightly acidic rainwater on soft, porous limestone. Since these caves are often directly linked to active underground aquifers or aboveground rivers, caution should be exercised when visiting them. It is possible for water levels inside the caves to rise rapidly during periods of heavy rain, even when there is no storm in the immediate vicinity of the cave entrance. Due to high moisture levels in the caves, ceilings and walls are often unstable. Use an experienced guide whenever possible.

Caves were considered sacred gateways to the underworld by the ancient Maya, and some are still used by their modern descendants for religious purposes. Please do not disturb any altars, drawings, pottery, or other artifacts that you come across. If you believe you have made a new discovery of scientific value, contact officials at Guatemala's Department of Archaeology, History, and Ethnography as soon as possible (253-1570 or 232-5571 in Guatemala City).

The following is a brief summary of Guatemala's most accessible caves. Each is described in greater detail in the chapter corresponding to its specific geographic location.

Naj Tunich

Located in the Maya Mountains near Poptún, in Petén, this cave was sacred to the Maya, who decorated its walls with elaborate carbon frescoes and hieroglyphics in about 800 B.C. It holds spectacular geological formations as well. In 1997, archaeological work was done here to preserve and record these rare drawings. Access to Naj Tunich has been restricted in recent years because of vandalism, so check locally before making any plans. Smaller limestone caves in the same area should still be open. The operators of Finca Ixabel (927-7363), a lodge and farm south of Poptún, have organized two-day trips to the cave in the past and are a good source of current information. Also try the Castellanos family at Villa de los Castellanos (927-7541) in nearby Machaquilá.

Aktun Kan

This "cave of the serpent," near Santa Elena in the Petén, is filled with strangely shaped stalactites and stalagmites that reflect iridescent light. Electric lights have been installed in the main passages and there is no need to hire a guide. The cave is maintained as a park and there is a small admission fee. Local legend holds that an enormous snake once lived here.

Jobitzinaj

The western outlet of the Aktun Kan system south of Lake Petén Itzá, this complex includes several caves totaling a mile or so in length. Like Aktun Kan, it is within walking distance of the town of Santa Elena. Bring candles or, better yet, flashlights, as well as good hiking shoes.

Lanquín

Rock formations here appear in the shape of cones, crests, and small crystallized designs. This is the source of the Río Lanquín, which gushes dramatically from the cave's mouth into a steep-sided jungle canyon. The cave is a national park in Alta Verapaz, about a 2-hour drive northeast of Cobán. You'll pay a small admission fee, after which the caretaker will turn on a set of electric lights (arrange fee in advance). No guide or special equipment is needed, though a flashlight in a cave is always a prudent idea. There's a primitive camping/hammock-hanging area near the cave's entrance and a moderately-priced lodge/restaurant nearby. At dusk you'll see a cloud of bats emerge from the cave's recesses.

Candelaria

A large, four-part underground network said to encompass more than 200 individual caves and exceeding 15 miles in length, Candelaria is located about 7 miles west of Raxrúja in the department of Alta Verapaz, north of Cobán. The Río Candelaria flows from the mouth of the main cave, which was highly revered by the ancient Maya. Because the passages are usually flooded, tours are often conducted on kayaks or rubber rafts; during some months they are impassable. Most of the cave entrances are on private land and it's very unlikely that you'll get to go inside if you simply show up. Instead you will need to book a guided excursion through Maya Expeditions (Guatemala City) or U and I Tours (952-1547 in Cobán). A French expatriate named Daniel Dreux has built a dorm/bungalow lodge here, Complex Cultural de Candelaria, but this is often booked in advance by French tour groups. Dreux can be contacted through Servicios Turísticos de Petén at the number above.

San Pedro Mártir

Located near Palín, about 45 miles south of Guatemala City on the road to Escuintla, this cave system is noted for its magnificent underground emerald-colored river and waterfall, which seem to be flowing and falling upside down. This phenomenon is apparently due to the unusual conchshell shape of the chambers. Inquire locally about access.

San Juan Chamelco

In Alta Verapaz, not far from Lanquín but more extensive in size, these caves are full of underground canals and rivers that twist and turn through large galleries and passageways. Located about 7 miles south of Cobán, just outside the village of San Juan Chamelco. Contact U and I Tours (952-1547) in Cobán.

Caving Outfitters

Ecotourism and Adventure Specialists, Avenida Reforma 8-60, Zone 9, #105; Guatemala City; 361-3104, fax 334-0453, ecoadventure @mail2.guate.net. Recommended.

Finca Ixobel, Poptún; 927-7363. Arranges tours of caves in the Poptún Highlands. Recommended.

Hotel El Recreo Lanquín, Lanquín; 951-2160, fax 951-2333. Tours of Lanquín Cave and others in the greater Cobán area.

Maya Expeditions, 15a. Calle 1-91, Zone 10; Guatemala City; 363-4965, fax 337-4666, mayaexp@guate.net. Offers float trips through the Candelaria cave complex of Alta Verapaz. Recommended.

U and I Tours, Hostel D'Acuña; 4a. Calle 3-11; Cobán; 952-1547. Candelaria cave–complex tours, outdoor adventure outfitter for the Verapaz and Petén areas. Recommended.

Villa de los Castellanos, Machaquilá; 927-7541, petenq@#inforia. com.gt. Cave tours in the Poptún highlands.

WATER RECREATION

Guatemala is one of the least-known destinations in Central America for water sports, which is unfortunate. While most people are familiar with the country's archaeological ruins and indigenous cultures, few potential visitors think much about Guatemala's magnificent white-water rivers, fresh-water lakes, and long stretches of Caribbean and Pacific coastline.

Several local tour operators and outfitters specializing in water recreation and adventure travel are excellent resources for those interested in this kind of recreation. They provide regularly scheduled package tours and can arrange customized trips as well. Only a handful of U.S.-based travel companies organize trips to Guatemala that are specifically designed around rafting or other kinds of water sports.

Sailing and Boating

Sailboats and other small craft can be chartered (with or without a skipper and crew) at many locations. There are also a number of marinas where private boats entering Guatemalan waters can be berthed, mainly on the Río Dulce and at the Pacific port of San José. Inquire locally for information.

The main destinations for sailboat and power-boat recreation in Guatemala are, in roughly descending order of popularity, Lake Atitlán,

INGUAT

Sailing on the Río Dulce

Lake Amatitlán, Lake Izabal, Lake Petén Itzá, and Lake Petexbatún. The Pacific and Caribbean coasts offer ocean boating opportunities, and the Caribbean coast is particularly well suited for sailors and yachtspeople. The Río Dulce and Lake Izabal make safe and attractive anchorages during hurricanes and tropical storms. For more details, see chapters relating to these destinations geographically, or inquire at local travel agencies.

English-language newspapers in Antigua and Guatemala City sometimes carry advertisements for sailboats available for charter on the country's lakes and coastlines. Recommended is Aventuras Vacacionales, in Antigua, which offers excursions of three or six days each on the 46-foot catamaran *Polynesian* on Lake Izabal, Río Dulce, and up the Bay of Honduras as far as Belize.

The most detailed English-language compendium of sailing information pertaining to Guatemala's east coast and the Río Dulce is Captain Freya Rauscher's *Cruising Guide to Belize and Mexico's Caribbean Coast, including Guatemala's Río Dulce* (Wescott Cove Press), which has many helpful charts and diagrams.

Fishing

Boats are fairly easy to rent on Guatemala's largest fresh-water lakes but fishing tackle is much harder to find: Most locals use simple hooks or nets and get their own bait. You will need to inquire among hotels and travel agencies in order to find gear. The most popular fishing lake is Izabal, which has several sportfishing resorts along Río Dulce at the eastern mouth of the lake. Popular gamefish here include snook, tarpon, and bass.

The Pacific coast of Guatemala boasts some of the world's best billfish opportunities, including marlin, sawfish, mackerel, sailfish, and dolphinfish (mahi-mahi). For deep-sea Pacific fishing, contact American-owned Guatemala Sport Fishing (202-4942), which offers one- to three-day packages on a 31-foot yacht, specializing in sailfish, or Guatemala Offshore

Fishing, based in one of the country's only tackle shops: Kurican (231-7222, 5a. Avenida 11-63, Zone 9, Guatemala City). In Puerto San Jose, try Hotel Turicentro Martita (881-1504), a full-service hotel on the beach.

Kayaking and Canoeing

Kayaking and canoeing are increasingly popular in Guatemala, but access is limited for the foreign visitor due to a shortage of local services and equipment. Your best bets for rentals are the major hotels (such as Hotel Visión Azul) and marinas of Lake Atitlán (try Lake Recreation Services) in the western highlands and Lake Amatitlán south of Guatemala City. You can also rent kayaks and canoes along the Chiquimulilla Canal (which runs parallel to the Pacific), the Monterrico nature reserve southeast of San José, as well as the marinas of the Río Dulce. Several local operators, such as Ecotourism & Adventure Specialists and Excursiónes Spross, will arrange sea-kayaking expeditions through the southern cayes of Belize.

Water levels of mountain rivers fluctuate dramatically, depending on local rainfall. For this reason it's best to make your arrangements for white-water trips well in advance. The best rivers for kayak and canoe trips include the San Pedro, Sauce, Polochic, Chixoy, Panamá, Matanzas, Coyolate, Lanquín, de los Esclavos, and Pasión, as well as the country's various lakes and wetlands. Area Verde Expeditions in Antigua (and Salida, Colo.) is a specialist in arranging such trips, as is Maya Expeditions in Guatemala City. Ask your airline in advance about the best way to pack and transport kayaks and other water-sports gear.

White-Water Rafting

Since the late 1980s, Maya Expeditions, Area Verde Expeditions, and members of the Guatemala Kayaking Club have been exploring the country's principal rivers to determine their suitability for white-water rafting, kayaking, and canoe trips. Maya's knowledgeable American owner Tammy Ridenour and her experienced Guatemalan guides use only top-notch equipment for their many float trips down the Cahabón, Pasión, Mopán, Chiquibul, Naranjo, and upper Motagua Rivers. Maya's services, which also include bungee jumping and excursions to remote archaeological sites and volcanic peaks, are highly recommended.

In the past, Servicios Turísticos del Petén, Aventuras sin Límites, Ecotourism & Adventure Specialists, Maya Expeditions, and Expedición Panamundo have offered river trips on the Río Usumacinta, which forms the middle third of Guatemala's northwestern border with Mexico, and its Guatemalan tributary, the Río de la Pasión. Maya's trips are presented in cooperation with a Brigham Young University team that is conducting the first archaeological fieldwork at Piedras Negras since the

Richard Mahler

Class III and IV rapids challenge white-water rafters.

1930s. Most trips have been suspended below Yaxchilán for safety reasons (see Chapter 11).

The Usumacinta, known as "the river of the sacred monkey," was (and still is) an important Maya trade route, linking the lowlands of Mexico and the Petén with the Guatemalan highlands through such navigable tributaries as the Río Chixoy. This river system is the best way of seeing the region, particularly such remote archaeological sites as Yaxchilán, El Cayo, and Piedras Negras. Wildlife is abundant, particularly near the campsites of Desempeño (Cayo Island) and Piedras Negras.

The Usumacinta is a large and fairly slow-moving jungle river, with only a few Class I and II rapids. Archaeology and nature are its main attractions. The upper reaches of the Pasión are narrower, with more white water. Trips from Sayaxché to Palenque, Mexico, usually take nine days and eight nights but can be broken up into segments as short as one day each. Separate boat trips can be arranged to the several Maya ruins along the shoreline of Lake Petexbatún.

Among Guatemala's best white-water rivers (Classes III and IV) is the Cahabón, which is a one- to five-day trip from the Sierra de Chamá of Alta Verapaz to a pull-out point near Lake Izabal at Cahaboncito. Attractions along the way include a natural thermal hot spring, several large waterfalls, and large, seldom-visited caves. There is abundant bird and animal life along the lower reaches of this river, which are inhabited only by a few Kekchí Maya. Area Verde Expeditions (Salida, Colorado) and Maya Expeditions (Guatemala City) are among the recommended outfitters on the Cahabón. Area Verde also does one-day rafting and kayaking trips on the upper stretch of the river from a Lanquín base camp. (Note that Area Verde Expeditions is not associated with the Area Verde Foundation, a nonprofit Guatemalan philanthropic organization established and supported by Maya Expeditions.)

Most outfitters operating on the Cahabón also take excursions to the nearby quetzal reserve, Lanquín Cave, and Semuc Champey pools. There is sometimes a stop at the Quiriguá ruins on the return trip to Guatemala City.

Area Verde also offers white-water raft and kayak trips on the upper Río Chixoy, with Class III and IV rapids through a steep canyon, from Sacapulas all the way to the hydroelectric reservoir.

Class II and III rapids are run by several operators on the Río Naranjo, along the Pacific slope, during the wet season, with side trips to nearby Olmec and Maya sites, plus natural hot springs. This is a one- to five-day trip.

The Río de los Esclavos, less than 2 hours from Guatemala City on the Pacific coast, provides Class III and IV rapids from July through October. You'll see magnificent scenery on this full-day trip through a deep gorge in the shadow of the Jumaytepeque volcano. Other white-water opportunities include the upper Río Motagua, northwest of Guatemala City, which combines a day of Class II and III rapids with a visit to the Mixco Viejo ruins and geologically rich side streams. The Río Coyolate is a Class I and II Pacific Coast river and an easy day trip from Antigua or Guatemala City, runnable from June through October. Both Maya and Area Verde can arrange trips to all floatable Pacific slope and Western Highlands rivers.

Maya Expeditions also offers a five-day "caves and rivers" trip down the Class II Río Chiquibul in northeast Petén that includes a tour of the Tikal and seldom-visited Nakum, Yaxhá, and Topoxte ruins, as well as sacred Mayan caves (with burial chambers and ceramic pots still intact after 1,100 years). These trips, through lush tropical forest, are coordinated with nonprofit Conservation International, which is working in the area to involve villagers in low-impact tourism projects.

Perhaps Guatemala's most unusual river trip involves the Río Candelaria, north of Cobán in Alta Verapaz. On a three- or four-day excursion, visitors can explore much of the Candelaria cave network on an underground rafting expedition. The river eventually flows outside the cavern network and continues through dense jungle to join the Río Chixoy. The float is best attempted March–August, as high water during the rainy season can make the caves impassable.

Several slow and wide jungle rivers in Guatemala also can be navigated, such as the Sarstún along the southern Belize border, and the Chiquibul and upper Mopán in the Petén. Ask locally about access and guides.

Discussed at length in Chapter 10 is the Río Dulce, the slow but scenic jungle river that connects Lake Izabal and El Golfete with the Caribbean. Visitors can book passage on the twice-weekly mail boat along the river or hire a motorized private launch for a trip that includes stops at a hot spring and a manatee reserve.

Just across the border in Honduras, Go Native Adventure Tours (Copán Ruínas, Honduras) arranges Class III and Class IV white-water trips down the Río Copán as far as Santa Rita.

Guatemala City's Maya Expeditions has been offering custom itineraries, from three days to three weeks, since 1987. Such trips are offered year-round and range from budget to luxury excursions. Options include hiking, rafting, deep-sea fishing, archaeology, mountain biking, birding, volcano climbing, horseback riding, bungee jumping, paragliding, parachute free jumps, and art/culture tours.

If you're planning a trip on a Guatemalan river, be sure to ask your outfitter or guide in advance what you should bring. Some operators provide tents and sleeping gear; others do not. Your personal effects should include strong sunscreen, sunglasses (with safety cord), hat, insect repellent, swimming suit, tight-fitting shoes that can get wet, and personal identification. A flashlight is also helpful. Waterproof boxes and duffel bags are usually provided to stow your gear. Children under 12 are sometimes barred from river trips for safety and insurance reasons. Finally, it's important to recognize that white-water rafting involves some risk. Travelers are occasionally injured or even killed on Guatemalan trips through accidents that are no fault of either the operator or the traveler.

Windsurfing

Windsurfing is an increasingly popular sport on Guatemala's Lake Atitlán, Lake Izabal, and Río Dulce. The ideal season is October through May, with strongest winds prevailing from October through early January. Lake Atitlán's average wind speed throughout the year is 15 knots per hour, increasing to 25 knots during November and December. Conditions are similar on Izabal and the Río Dulce, with the highest average wind speeds (20 to 25 knots) between November and January. About 300 local windsurfers belong to La Ráfaga (Gust of Wind), Guatemala's national windsurfing club, which hosts regattas and excursions at various times of the year. There are several stores and tour operators in Guatemala City catering to windsurfers; inquire locally as to names, addresses, and phone numbers. Your best resource in Panajachel is Lake Recreation Services, on the public beach, which rents kayaks, windsurfers, and other water sports gear. Remember to do your Lake Atitlán windsurfing (as well as kayaking and sailing) in the morning: a strong and unpredictable afternoon wind, *el xocomil*, can make navigating difficult.

Diving

Scuba diving and snorkeling have limited popularity in Guatemala, owing to the relative lack of sites for engaging in these activities. Lake Atitlán is increasingly popular, however, as is the short stretch of Caribbean coastline along Guatemala's east coast and the nearby cayes of Belize. In contrast, waters off the Pacific Coast are deep and treacherous. Outfitters include Pro Diver in Guatemala City (6a. Avenida 7-61, Zone 9, 332-3296), Ecotourism and Adventure Travel Specialists (361-3104 in Guatemala City), and Posada de Iguana Perdida on Lake Atitlán (Santa Cruz de la Laguna, fax 762-1196). All offer PADI scuba certification courses. In Antigua, Rainbow Travel Center (7a. Avenida Sur #8, 832-4202) arranges diving tours to the Bay Islands of Honduras, starting at about $200 plus airfare, while Adventure Travel Center Viareal (4a. Calle Oriente 14, 832-0162) sets up dive/snorkel trips to Honduras and Belize.

Water Recreation Outfitters

In Guatemala

Area Verde Foundation, 15a. Calle 1-91, Zone 10; Guatemala City; 237-4666. Not to be confused with the Colorado-based company of the same name, this nonprofit Guatemalan company specializes in whitewater and nature-oriented trips. Recommended.

Aventuras sin Límites, 11a. Avenida 9-30, Zone 1; Guatemala City; 232-8452, fax 594-7293; 4a. Calle 8-15; Santa Elena; 926-5196. Emphasis on archaeology, birding, photography, canoeing, trekking, white-water rafting, and fishing. Petén specialists.

Aventuras Vacacionales, 1a. Avenida Sur 11B; Antigua; 832-3352, in U.S. fax (702) 255-3641. Sailing trips on 33-foot and 55-foot yachts on the Río Dulce, Lago Izabal, and to the Belize cayes. Up to six days.

Ecotourism & Adventure Specialists, Avenida Reforma 8-60, Zone 9, Guatemala City; 361-3104, fax 334-0453, ecoadventure@mail2.guate .net. River trips on the Pasión and Usumacinta. Recommended.

Expedición Panamundo, 6a. Avenida 14-75, Zone 9; Guatemala City;

331-7621, fax 331-7565. Specializes in archaeology, nature, volcano climbing, trekking, rafting, birding, and botany trips, with particular emphasis on remote Maya sites in the Petén, Belize, Mexico, and Honduras. Recommended.

Lake Recreation Services, Panajachel (on the public beach). Outfitter providing kayaks, windsurfers, canoes, and other water recreation services for Lake Atitlán. Recommended.

Maya Expeditions, 15a. Calle 1-91, Zone 10; Guatemala City; 337-4666, fax 363-4965, mayaexp@guate.net. Specializes in white-water rafting, volcano climbing, bungee jumping, birding, treks to remote archaeological sites, caves, and other "natural" destinations. Custom trips arranged for travel by boat, foot, or horseback. Highly recommended.

Monja Blanca Expeditions Travel Agency, 4a. Avenida Sur 8; Antigua; 832-3863. Trips to the Highlands, Río Dulce, Copán, and other runs. White-water rafting and kayaking. Shuttle service between Panajachel, Antigua, and Guatemala City.

Servicios Turísticos del Petén, 2a. Avenida 7-78, Zona 10; Guatemala City; 334-6235, fax 334-6237. Archaeology, nature, rafting, and trekking, with special emphasis on Maya sites of the Petén. Candelaria Cave trips.

Travel International, Avenida de la Reforma 6-30, Zone 4; Guatemala City; 331-0016. Río Dulce, Belize, and Lake Izabal fishing and boating trips; booking agent for Catamaran Island Hotel.

In the U.S. and Canada
Area Verde Expeditions; Box 476, Salida, CO 81201; (719) 539-7102, heesaker@areaverde.com. White-water trips down Río Cahabón and other rivers; nature and culture excursions.

Castle Rock Center for Environmental Adventures, 412 Road 6NS; Cody, WY 82414; (800) 356-9965.White-water rafting, mountain biking, sea kayaking, sailing, mountain climbing, and windsurfing.

Ceiba Adventures, P.O. Box 2274; Flagstaff, AZ 86003; (520) 527-0171, fax (520) 527-8127; ceiba@prime.net.com; www.primenet.com/~ceiba. River trips on the Usumacinta, white-water and caving trips in Chiapas and Belize, excursions to Maya sites in the Petén and Chiapas, as well as to Lacandón Indian villages. Highly recommended.

ConoAndes Expeditions, 3712 75th Street; Queens, NY 11372; (800) 242-5554; in New York (718) 446-8577.Canoe, kayak, and adventure trips.

Guatemala Unlimited, P.O. Box 786; Berkeley, CA 94701; (800) 733-3350 or (415) 661-5364; Guatemala1@aol.com; or 337-4666 in Guatemala City. Specialist in budget and independent travel; arranges tours to ruins and highland villages; assists with weaving classes, rafting, mountain biking, Spanish schools, and deep-sea fishing. Recommended.

Mountain Travel-Sobek Expeditions, 6420 Fairmount Avenue; El Cerrito, CA 94530; (800) 227-2384, fax (510) 525-7710. Fiestas and markets in highlands. River trips on the Río Usumacinta, ecological adventures, and explorations of Maya ruins.

Remarkable Journeys, Box 31855; Houston, TX 77231-1855; (800) 856-1993, fax (713) 728-8334; cooltrips@remjourneys.com. Offers ten-day "river of ruins" white-water float down the Río Usumacinta, guided by a seasoned river guide and Mayanist. Recommended.

BIRDING, HIKING, HORSEBACK RIDING, AND NATURE TOURS

Birding

With about 600 native species and over 200 migrants, Guatemala is a terrific place for a birder. As you would expect, the best locations for watching birds are the parks and reserves discussed throughout the book, which incorporate a wide variety of relatively undisturbed natural habitats. Maya ruins are also often excellent observation posts, due to the dense vegetation that remains around most sites. The lowland ruin of Quiriguá, for example, is completely surrounded by an enormous banana plantation, yet its high tropical forest canopy is a favorite hangout for many species. Tikal is an even better location for birding, with the added advantage of an outstanding and widely available field guide: *The Birds of Tikal.*

Not far to the west of Tikal, in the Maya Biosphere Reserve, a route called the Scarlet Macaw (Guacamayo) Trail has been developed by local residents under the auspices of ProPetén-Conservation International. Not a trail in the traditional sense, this route winds through the Petén's thick tropical forest from Lake Petén Itzá as far as the Río San Pedro, and is best traveled by a combination of public bus or four-wheel-drive vehicle, power-boat, horseback, and foot. Trips can be arranged through U and I Travel

(Cobán), Monkey
(Guatemala City/E
450-foot cliff that i
hosts and guides a
villages of El Cruc
Besides hundreds
monkeys, tapirs, c

Other import
zal Reserve, Mont
Birding tour speci
Aventuras sin Lím

Two of the r
Guides' well-illus
tions in the Yucat
(Dennis Rogers,
Birds of Mexico a
Sophie Webb, O

spend a few days at Tikal National Park
several well-maintained nature trails
tackle the rugged Sierra de las Mi
the highlands, or Las Victorias
Cobán that is gradually reve
New Forests Project,
offers unusual "environ
forest-trekking with
sites, modern Ma
see solar ovens
to pay $1,60
An e
Trail T
or Ji
ta

Horseback Riding

Equestrians will find the largest number of outfitters in Antigua, the Petén, and the villages around Lake Atitlán. Keep in mind that Guatemalan horses tend to be smaller than North American horses, but they are well-adapted to rugged countryside and heavy loads.

One of the country's best outfitters is Aventura en Atitlán, which provides guided horseback (and hiking) tours in the Lake Atitlán area. Operated by U.S. expatriates Jim and Nancy Matison at a coffee *finca* about six miles from Santiago Atitlán, Aventura specializes in nature-oriented excursions accompanied by fine meals (dinner rides include wine and cocktails). Destinations range from coffee plantations and a quetzal reserve to El Mirador (a ridge-top viewpoint) and the cloud forests of local volcanos. Prices range from $40 to $50 per person ($22 to $35 for hiking tours). The Matisons also offer a luxurious two-room suite (Luna de Miel) for overnight visitors ($250, double occupancy) that includes all meals and unlimited access to hiking/horseback trips. Contact Aventura en Atitlán at 201-5527 or write c/o 13591 Nogales Dr., Del Mar, CA 92014.

Hiking and Nature Tours

Outfitters specializing in the outdoors, including many that also arrange birding and rafting trips, also arrange natural history and nature-oriented trekking tours into the wilds of Guatemala, including the Petén and the highland cloud forests. Another good way to see the flora and fauna of the country is to arrange a guided volcano climb (see previous section) or to

, which has abundant wildlife and
The more adventurous may want to
as Biosphere, on the eastern edge of
National Park, a former coffee finca near
ting to wilderness.

based in Washington, D.C. (202/547-3800),
mental tours" of Guatemala that combine rain
visits to successful reforestation projects, ancient Maya
a families, and biointensive permaculture gardens. You'll
cooperatively run farms, and sustainable tree farms. Expect
(plus airfare) for the two-week excursions.

cellent nature-oriented travel specialist is Leif Ness, at Green
ours in Guatemala City (332-3540). In Panajachel, try Lee Valenti
and Nancy Matison through Panajachel Tourist Services, Calle San-
der (762-2333). The Matisons specialize in guided horseback tours
of the Lake Atitlán region. Across the lake, inquire at Posada de Santiago in Santiago Atitlán to arrange excellent back-country treks on foot
guided by experienced and reliable locals. For overall nature-oriented
travel assistance, contact Guatemala Unlimited, based in Guatemala
City and Berkeley, California; Monkey Eco Tours in the Flores area;
and Ecotourism & Adventure Speicalists in Guatemala City.

Birding, Hiking, Horseback Riding, and Nature Tour Outfitters

Caribbean Internacional de Viajes, 9a. Avenida 13-58, Zone 1;
Guatemala City; 251-4952. Adventure travel in the Petén, Alta Verapaz,
Caribbean coast, and Lake Izabal areas.

Ecogua, 6a. Calle 5-33, Zone 1; Guatemala City; 238-0381, ext. 22.
Nature and cultural tours.

Ecotourism & Adventure speicalists, Avenida Reforma 8-60, #105,
Zone 9; Guatemala City; 361-3104, fax 334-0453, ecoadventure@
mail2.guate.net. Ecotourism and adventure travel; specializing in trips to
Tikal, the Petén, and Punta Manabique. Highly recommended.

Green Trails Cultural and Ecological Tours, 9a. Calle 4-10, Zone 10;
Guatemala City; 332-3540. Emphasis on natural history and Maya sites,
particularly in Alta Verapaz and the Petén. Recommended.

Jungle Flying Tours, Avenida Hincapié y 18a. Calle, Zone 13;
Guatemala City; 360-4920, fax 331-4995. Nature, archaeology, and cul-

tural tours, including overnight camping expeditions and trips by private charter aircraft. Also offers boat trips on Lake Petén Itzá and Río de la Pasión. Flies regularly to Copán.

Monkey Eco Tours, Ni'tún Ecolodge, San Andrés, Petén; 204-8826 or 361-3104. Recommended trips to remote Maya ruins and natural history destinations in association with Ecotourism & Adventure Specialists.

Outdoors Life/Excursiones Calypso, 3a. Calle 7-15, Zone 9; Guatemala City. Wilderness treks in Guatemala, beach camping trips to Belize cayes. Store at this location sells camping and mountaineering equipment.

U and I Tours, c/o Hostal de Acuña; 4a. Calle 3-11, Zone 2; Cobán, Alta Verapaz; 952-1547, fax 952-1268. Operated by Marcio and Ashley Acuña, two of the area's top environmentalists; tours of Candelaria Caves, Semuc Champey, and other natural attractions. Recommended.

In the U.S. and Canada
Above the Clouds Trekking, P.O. Box 398; Worcester, MA 01062; (800) 233-4499. Nature-oriented adventure travel.

Adventure Center, 1311 63rd Street, Suite 200; Emeryville, CA 94608; (800) 227-8747, in California (510) 654-1879. Adventure travel with small groups and expert guides. Send for the current catalog.

Forum Travel, 91 Gregory Lane #21; Pleasant Hill, CA 94523; (510) 671-2900. Individually crafted eco-adventures.

Fourth Dimension Tours, 1150 NW 72nd Avenue, Suite 250; Miami, FL 33126; (800) 343-0020; in Florida (305) 477-1525, fax (305) 477-0731. Nature, adventure, and cultural tours.

Global Adventures, P.O. Box 1897; Boulder, CO 80306; (303) 440-6911 or (800) 322-6911. Nature-oriented adventure travel.

Guatemala Unlimited, Box 786; Berkeley, CA 94701; (800) 733-3350, fax (415) 661-6149, Guatemala1@aol.com. Full-service, nature-oriented outfitter, affiliated with Maya Expeditions. Recommended.

Holbrook Travel, 3540 NW 13th St., Gainesville, FL 32609; (800) 451-7111, fax (352) 371-3710. Guided natural history tours; Christmas and Easter cultural tours; photographic and Maya ruin tours.

International Expeditions, One Environs Park; Helena, AL 35080; (800) 633-4734; in Alabama (205) 428-1700, fax 428-1714. Natural history and archaeology-oriented soft adventure trips to Tikal, Copán, and Belize. Recommended.

New Forests Project Tours, 731 Eighth Street SE; Washington, DC 20003; (202) 547-3800; fax (202) 546-4784, ic-nfp@clark.net. Enviromental tours that visit sustainable development projects, the Petén rain forest, biointensive gardening, Maya ruins, and other destinations.

Ocean Connection, 16734 El Camino Real; Houston, TX 77062; (713) 486-6993. Adventure travel with emphasis on nature, Mayan sites, water recreation, birds, and excursions throughout Belize.

Outback Expeditions, Box 16343; Seattle, WA 98116; (206) 932-7012; fax (206) 935-1213. Wildlife, hiking, photography, and kayaking tours, with options to Belize and Mexico.

Mark Smith Nature Tours/Full Circle Tours, 2421 Quimby NW; Portland, OR 97210; (503) 223-7716. Birding, natural history specialist.

Wilderness Travel, 1102 Ninth Street; Berkeley, CA 94710; (800) 368-2794; info@wildernesstravel.com. "Ruta May" 12-day trips to Maya sites and more.

BICYCLING

Guatemala is a very good place to ride a bicycle. The distances between villages and towns, particularly in the highlands, are short, and there is a fairly comprehensive road network. Drivers are used to people on bicycles and generally treat them with courtesy. In remote Maya villages, local residents are using bikes more and more as a handy way to get around. Because of the hot climate and more limited services, few cyclists attempt major trips in the Petén or coastal lowlands.

Mountain bikes will have an easier time of it in rural areas, where roads are unpaved and full of potholes. Racing and street bicycles are fairly popular among urban Guatemalans, many of whom can be seen on the Pan American Highway and other paved thoroughfares every dry weekend. The twisting mountain road between Antigua and the capital seems to be a perennial favorite.

Guatemala City has several large bicycle clubs and some well-equipped specialty stores. In fact, almost any town in the country has at least one place where you can change a tire, fix a gearshift, or buy spare parts. As anywhere, it is prudent to carry a spare tire and emergency tools at all times. If your problem cannot be repaired on the spot, second-class buses will carry bikes on their roofs for an additional fee (a dollar or less). There are many places to rent bicycles in Guatemala City, Quetzaltenango, Antigua, and Panajachel. Rates are quoted for hourly, daily, weekly, or monthly rentals. The widest selection seems to be in Antigua, where many Spanish students use bicycles while in language school.

Antigua is also the home of what is perhaps Guatemala's best bike-based tour company, Antigua Mountain Bike (El Rosario 9, 5a. Avenida Sur 36). Arturo Rosales and his American wife, Susan, have 15 bicycles available for rent, some equipped with child carriers. The couple can be hired as guides for up to five-day tours of such highland destinations as Lake Atitlán and the Agua volcano. Day trips are made to indigenous villages near Antigua, including the textile center of San Antonio Aguas Calientes, and nearby coffee, macadamia nut, and rose plantations.

Similar tours of the region are offered by Maya Mountain Tours (1a Avenida Sur 15; 832-3383). Escley Rent-A-Bike (Avenida Norte 4-C), rents mountain bikes by the hour, day, or week.

In Panajachel, another ideal place for cycling, bicycles can be rented from Moto Servicio Quiché (which also has motorbikes) and Bicicletas Gaby, near the beach off Avenida Santander. You can also check at the larger hotels (try Hotel del Lago) and at Los Geranios Turicentro on Avenida Rancho Grande. In Quetzaltenango, try VRISA, near the main plaza, and the Guatemala Unlimited travel agency (not to be confused with the U.S.-based outfitter). Paradise Bicycle Tours puts together long-distance bike tours of both Guatemala and Belize.

Be sure to inspect and road-test your bicycle—and agree on payment terms—before completing the rental transaction.

Bicycling Outfitters

Antigua Mountain Bike, El Rosario 9, 5a. Avenida Sur 36, Antigua. Bicycle rentals and tours of the Antigua area.

Caiman Expeditions, 2901 East Speedway; Tucson, AZ 85716; (800) 365-2383; in Arizona (602) 299-1047. Diving, rafting, sea kayaking, archaeology, climbing, and mountain biking.

Maya Mountain Bike, 1a. Avenida Sur 15, Antigua; 832-3383. Recommended.

Paradise Bicycle Tours, P.O. Box 1726; Evergreen, CO 80439; (800) 626-8271. For riders of all abilities; tours of Belize, Guatemala, and Africa.

Tour de Caña, P.O. Box 7293; Philadelphia, PA 19101; (215) 222-1253. Bicycle tours throughout Guatemala and Central America.

VRISA Bicycle Rental,15a. Avenida 0-67; Quetzaltenango; 761-3862. Offers maps and bicycles for local touring.

CAMPING AND YOUTH HOSTELS

Camping is not popular among Guatemalans, and there are few campgrounds. Formal campgrounds are limited to Tikal and a few parks, lakes, beaches, and nature reserves. There are exceptions, of course, and one recommendation is El Gringo Perdido, near Tikal National Park (which also has a decent but relatively expensive campsite).

The moderately priced, family-oriented Las Hamacas, on the outskirts of Guatemala City at Km. 32 on the highway to Lake Amatitlán, allows a maximum of two children per couple. There is no charge for kids up to 2 years of age and a 25 percent discount for those 12 and under.

If you have a recreational vehicle or travel trailer, some of the larger hotels will allow you to "camp" in their parking lots—or at least store your vehicle if you stay in one of their rooms. Trailer/RV parks in the Amatitlán area south of Guatemala City include Auto Mariscos and Le Red, both at Km. 33 on the main highway. Expect to pay about $2 to $6 per night, with minimal hook-ups and services.

Youth hostels do not exist in Guatemala as such, probably because hotel prices are already so low that nobody sees any advantage in starting one. Some of the budget hotels, such as Cobán's Hostal de Acuña, have borrowed the term to indicate low-cost, dorm-style accommodations.

SPANISH AND OTHER INSTRUCTION

Teaching (and studying) Spanish is a booming industry in Guatemala and an important source of income for the many people who now rent rooms, prepare meals, or teach classes. Those who run the many businesses frequented by foreign visitors also benefit from the scores of private schools in Guatemala offering various levels of instruction in the speaking, reading, and writing of Spanish. Some of these are very specialized, catering exclusively to a Japanese-speaking or Chinese-speaking, for example. Some are designed for entry-level students, while others can help the middle- or advanced-level Spanish speaker become more fluent.

As of 1999, more than 50 language schools were registered in Antigua alone, enrolling up to 1,000 students each month. Quetzaltenango is also emerging as a center for instruction, and there are Spanish schools in Huehuetenango, Panajachel, San Andrés, Lívingston, Todos Santos, and Guatemala City as well. The government of Guatemala occasionally

Se Hable Español

Studying Spanish in Guatemala is a bargain in several respects. The costs of instruction and lodging are low, the quality of instruction is generally high, classes are usually small, and the experience provides an excellent means of learning about the country's people, history, and attractions. There are programs to suit every level of ability, from absolute beginner to advanced. Switching schools is a common practice, so you might want to pay for only one week at a time. Ask fellow students how they feel about the instruction they're receiving in other schools and feel free to change at week's end.

Wherever you go, it's a terrific idea to stay with a Guatemalan family. Daily life will be more authentic and you'll get wonderful exposure to informal conversation. If you can afford it, one-on-one instruction is recommended for the serious student. And when you get back home, try to set up an ongoing system of study and practice with friends. If available, watch Spanish-language TV and read Spanish-language magazines or newspapers.

updates its list of school names, addresses, and phone numbers. This Spanish-school roster, prepared by INGUAT, can be obtained free of charge by writing your nearest Guatemalan embassy, consulate, or tourism office.

If you have only a short amount of time, you may be better off studying in an outlying area, such as Quetzaltenango. English is widely spoken in Antigua—because many foreigners live or visit there—and students often find it too easy to speak anything but Spanish after hours of practicing the language. Be aware that most families take in more than one student, so you are likely to share quarters with another English-speaker.

Longevity is one positive characteristic of a Spanish school. Of the dozens of schools to choose from in Antigua, for example, only a handful have been in business for a decade or more. The best schools offer one-to-one, immersion-style instruction by motivated, knowledgeable instructors. Besides academic excellence, teacher qualifications, and the endorsement of former students, another factor in choosing a school may be the distribution of its profits. Some institutions now devote a certain percentage of their income to charitable causes, such as orphanages and indígena development programs. If this is an important criterion to you, be sure to make inquiries. You may also wish to check a school's membership in professional associations, since some have little or no accreditation.

The schools' fees vary substantially, although all are very reasonable by U.S. standards. Expect to pay about $150 to $200 a week for room and board plus 4 to 8 hours of daily instruction. Instruction alone can be arranged for about $85 to $135 a week. Considering how much you would pay for a hotel or apartment, and to eat meals in restaurants, this is a very good value. Note that most schools do not accept credit cards.

Antigua: A long-time favorite language school in Antigua is **Proyecto Linguistico Francisco Marroquín** (7a. Calle Poniente 31, 832-2886; in U.S. 800/552-2051), which has a record of excellence under the direction of its British dean, Pamela Hirst-Prins. It is also the largest, and contributes in many ways to the community. Other recommended schools include **Academía de Español Guatemala** (3a. Avenida Sur 15, 832-0344), **San José el Viejo** (1a. Calle Poniente 24, 832-3028), **Centro Linguistico Maya** (5a. Calle Poniente 20, 832-0656), **Academía Cristiana de Español** (832-3922), and **Tecún Umán** (6a. Calle Poniente 34, 832-2792).

If you'd like help finding an appropriate school, **AmeriSpan** at 6a. Avenida Norte 40 (832-0164) is highly recommended as a source of impartial and reliable information.

Quetzaltenango: Spanish schools in Quetzaltenango include **Guatemalensis** (19 Avenida 2-14, Zona 1, in U.S. 415/387-7812); **La Escuela Minerva** (24 Avenida 4-39, Zone 3, fax 767-4427, alternativas@guate.net); and **Proyecto Lingüístico Quetzalteco de Español** (5a. Calle 2-40, Zone 1; plq@c.net.gt; or in U.S. 800/963-9889); **Proyecto Lingüístico Xelaju** (1a. Calle 16-87, Zone 1, 761-2631); **Centro Maya de Idiomas** (21 Avenida 5-69, Zone 3; info@centromaya.org); **International Spanish-Language School of Central America** (212/734-3949; isl@quicklink.com); and **La Hermanidad Educativa** (with schools in both Quetzaltenango and Todos Santos; in the U.S. write 915 Cole Street #363; San Francisco, CA 94117; 800/963-9889).

Huehuetenango: Here schools include **Fundación Veintitres** (6a. Avenida 6-126, Zona 1, 764-1478) and **Xinabajul** (6a. Avenida 0-69, Zona 1, 764-1518).

Cobán: The language school is **Instituto Cobán Internacional** (952-1727, 2a. Calle 1-23), which offers full board, 20 hours of teaching, and two excursions per week for about $135.

Lívingston: The **Escuela Tropical de Idiomas** (948-1544) arranges instruction (4 to 6 hours a day), housing (with meals), and recreational activities. Instructors are from local Garífuna, Kekchí, Asian, and Ladino cultures.

Chimaltenango: Spanish & Mayan Language School of Chimaltenango, 9a. Calle Final, Zone 1; 839-1492; geotours@gua.net. Former Peace Corps workers involved in ecotourism and in the support of needy families.

San Andrés: In San Andrés, near Flores, the conservation group ProPetén co-sponsors the recommended **Eco-Escuela de Español.**

Guatemala City: The main language schools include **Instituto Guatemalteco Americano** (331-0022, Ruta 1 4-05, Zona 4), **Easy** (337-3970, Blvd. Los Próceres 9-67, Zone 10), **Centro de Aprendizaje de Lenguas** (476-7208, Avenida Reforma 0-63, Zone 10), and **Instituto Centro América** (361-6786, 1a. Calle 16-93, Zone 1; in U.S. 214/699-0935).

Panajachel: Try **Jabel Cotzij** on Callejón Londres off Calle Santander (762-1378), or **Escuela de Español Panajachel** (762-2637) on Calle 14 de Febrero off Santander.

Todo Santos: The main language school is **Proyecto Lingüístico,** 5a. Calle 2-40, Zone 1, Quetzaltenango (U.S. tel. 718/965-8522).

Perhaps the most unusual approach to Spanish-language schooling is that offered by **Backroads International** (800/227-7889 or 504/522-7888, backroadsinternational@cmq.com), which provides instruction during 16-day tours (maximum of 16 students) of Guatemala that include visits to Tikal and Lake Atitlán. Instructors are native Guatemalans with a minimum of ten years teaching experience and 100 hours of education training. The Guatemala connection for Backroads is Olga Pokorny of **Viajes Exclusivos** in Guatemala City (Edificio Villa Vistana 1103, Avenida las Américas 34-42, Zone 13; tel. 333-3456; www.backroadsinternational.com).

Art Workshops in Guatemala, based in Antigua and Minneapolis, offers workshops Spanish language study, workshops are offered in weaving, painting, gardening, jewelry, writing, theater, and photography. Contact Liza Fourré, director, (612) 825-0747 or info@artguat.org. In Antigua, call 832-3584.

For an online directory of Spanish-language schools here and elsewhere, check out www2.planeta.com/mader/ecotravel/schools.

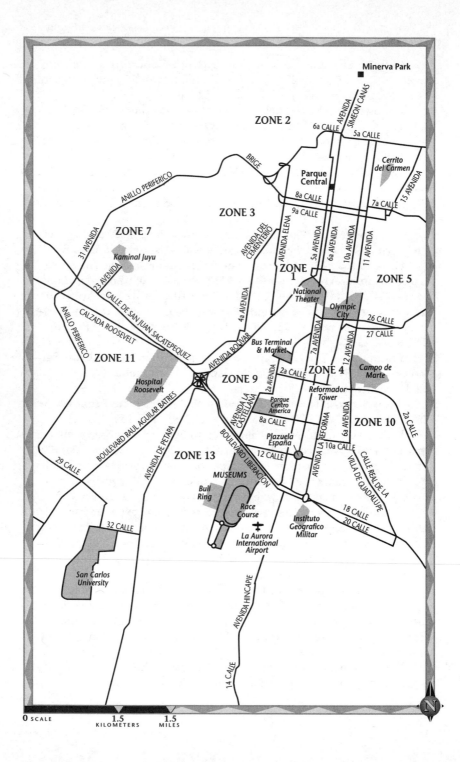

5

GUATEMALA CITY AND VICINITY

Guatemala City is the hub of the most industrialized and heavily populated part of the nation. Home to one-third of Guatemala's citizens, this
place is the first glimpse of the country for hundreds of thousands of
incoming visitors each year, yet it is everything the rest of Guatemala is
not. Referred to as "Guate" or "El Capital" by locals, it is ugly, crowded,
noisy, and polluted.

Guatemala City's 2-million-plus residents inhabit a high plateau—
about 4,500 feet above sea level—that drops off into plunging canyons
and is ringed by volcanoes. Little planning has gone into the development
of the sprawling capital and it now faces serious shortages of electricity,
water, public transportation, police protection, housing, parks, and jobs.

Yet despite its drawbacks, Guatemala City does have a significant
range of worthwhile attractions and hidden charms. With its broad
avenues, high-rise buildings, and cosmopolitan restaurants, the capital
can be a pleasant place to get acclimated, run errands, and learn about
the country's history, culture, and natural resources. A visit to the
archaeology museum in Aurora Park, for example, is a helpful prereq-
uisite for a trip to Tikal, since the museum holds many of that ancient
city's finest artifacts and displays a scale-model replica of Tikal at its
height. You can also examine stelae, friezes, and carvings brought here
from other major Maya ruins.

Guatemala City is the place to visit government offices, embassies,
and corporate headquarters, along with some of the country's best tour

operators, public markets, cathedrals, libraries, and galleries. If you need to extend your visa, set up an excursion, mail a package, or buy some last-minute *típica*, you've come to the right place.

Guatemala City is also home to symphonies, theater companies, and nightclubs. The climate is pleasing, the accommodations are comfortable, and the people are relatively friendly. There are restaurants, attractions, and services (including Spanish schools) suited to fit the needs and budget of every traveler.

The contrast of rich and poor is dramatic here. Wealthier Ladino residents have withdrawn to the shady suburbs, where they are hidden behind high walls and barbed-wire fences. The noisy inner city is left to the modest, box-like homes of the middle class and the shanties of the largely indígena peasantry.

HISTORY

Hemmed into the broad Valley of the Hermitage, surrounded by the lush green hills and smoldering volcanoes of the Sierra Madre, Nueva Guatemala de Asunción was founded as the nation's third capital on the first day of 1776, after the original Spanish colonial capital at Santiago (officially renamed La Antigua Guatemala but now simply called Antigua) was leveled in a series of terrible earthquakes. The Valley of the Hermitage was mostly empty at the time, home to a few farmers and the

Guatemala City is the largest metropolis in Central America.

ancient ruins of Kaminal Juyú. Guatemala City was laid out in the classic colonial grid pattern around a central plaza.

The new site has not been immune to earthquakes of its own: Guatemala City has been devastated by major temblors in 1917, 1918, and 1976. The last one killed more than 25,000 people throughout the country and destroyed most of the few colonial buildings in the capital that had not been knocked down 58 years earlier.

Thanks to generous international contributions and characteristic Guatemalan resolve, the city has been completely rebuilt. Modern hotels, restaurants, apartment houses, office towers, and shopping centers seem to be everywhere. Unfortunately, these are of uninspired design. Unlike Antigua and Quetzaltenango, where a deliberate effort has been made to rebuild in conformity with traditional styles, Guatemala City's architecture has precious little appeal.

GETTING AROUND

Orientation
Like nearly all Guatemalan cities, the capital is divided into geographic zones, comparable to U.S. zip codes. There are 21 such zones, but only five of these are of much interest to travelers. The oldest part of the city, surrounding the Parque Central, is Zone 1, an engaging collection of historic buildings and busy markets. But the locus of commerce has moved south to Zone 4's high-tech civic center and financial headquarters as well as to the wide avenues of Zones 9 and 10. Around the perimeter are the factories, warehouses, and manufacturing centers that employ many Guatemala City residents, whose own modest neighborhoods are spread flat and low across the smoggy horizon.

Each of Guatemala City's geographic zones (*zonas*) has its own numbered grid pattern. Numbered avenues (*avenidas*) run from north to south and numbered streets (*calles*) run east to west. As in other Spanish-speaking countries, the house number generally follows the street name. Thus an address of 6a. Avenida 8-22, Zona 1, is on Sixth Avenue, between Eighth and Ninth Streets at building number 22, in Zone 1. The lowercase "a" appearing immediately after the number of a street or avenue is merely the Spanish abbreviation for the street's proper name. For instance, 7a. Avenida is the contraction for Séptima Avenida (Seventh Avenue).

It is important to remember that the same address often exists in several different zones, therefore, knowing the zone number is essential. The situation is aggravated by the fact that many intersections are poorly marked; and that some roads in the older parts of town are also still identified by their original colonial names, since replaced on most maps by the

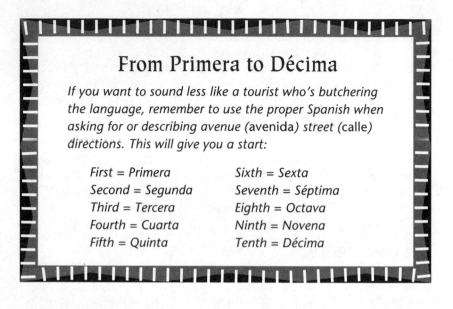

From Primera a Décima

If you want to sound less like a tourist who's butchering the language, remember to use the proper Spanish when asking for or describing avenue (avenida) street (calle) directions. This will give you a start:

First = Primera	Sixth = Sexta
Second = Segunda	Seventh = Séptima
Third = Tercera	Eighth = Octava
Fourth = Cuarta	Ninth = Novena
Fifth = Quinta	Tenth = Décima

numbers-only system. Note that many thoroughfares have one-way traffic or are divided by wide traffic medians. A first-time visitor's confusion may be intensified by the fact that two parallel streets or avenues sometimes have the *same* number. In these instances the second street or avenue, which is usually narrow or shorter, is identified by a capital letter "A." For example, 13a. Calle "A" is a small street that runs parallel between 13a. Calle and 14a. Calle.

Zones 1 and 4 in Guatemala City's downtown area, along with 9, 10, and 13 in the upscale business district, are the districts of most interest to foreign visitors, since they contain the majority of hotels, restaurants, offices, museums, and other amenities. The broad, tree-lined Avenida de la Reforma bisects Zones 9 and 10, connecting the urban center with La Aurora International Airport. An extension of Avenida de la Reforma, 7a. Avenida, is likewise one of the main thoroughfares of Zones 1 and 4.

The official Guatemala Tourist Map (*Mapa Turistico*), available from any INGUAT office, includes an excellent, detailed map of the capital as well as Antigua and other cities. You would do well to carry a copy of this map with you while memorizing landmarks and orienting yourself. After a day or two, Guatemala City's pragmatic layout will begin to make sense.

Pedestrians need to be extremely wary in the capital. There are virtually no crosswalks, and traffic does not yield to those on foot. Be careful

The Bus to Antigua

Buses leave roughly every hour during the day for Antigua (the cost is about 75¢, and often an extra fee for large luggage) from 15a. Calle in Zone 1, between 3a. and 4a. Avenida, stopping along 18a. Calle to pick up fares en route. You may be accosted by touts on board who wish to enroll you in a Spanish school. It's best to resist these high-pressure tactics and check out the schools when you arrive (if you haven't already done so). An INGUAT (tourist commission) representative often meets arriving buses in Antigua and can provide a list of government-recommended schools, as well as answer other questions. Unless you know where you're going, it's important to stay on the Antigua-bound bus until the last stop, which is the municipal bus terminal near the center of town. Shuttle buses to Antigua provide direct service for $10 to $15. Call Atitrans at. 832-0644.

and look both ways when crossing any intersection: Speeding and flaunting traffic laws are common pastimes in this macho, seatbelt-free culture.

Buses

Unfortunately, Guatemala City has no single central bus station. Instead, it has several public terminals, plus a number of private stations operated by individual bus companies exclusively for the convenience of their own passengers. Most of these are spread around Zone 1, in the older part of the city, although one large public bus terminal is located in the adjacent Zone 4. The latter is generally referred to as Terminal de Buses (or Muelle Central) and is on 4a. Avenida near 1a. Calle.

Because arrival and departure points (and schedules) for the various bus lines change frequently, you may want to check locally when planning trips in or out of Guatemala City. Most Salvadoran, eastern, and coastal destinations (including Monterrico) are served by the frenzied

Terminal de Buses in Zone 4; most highland towns are reached by buses leaving from the terminal at 18a. Calle and 5a. Avenida in Zone 1; and most Caribbean and Petén destinations are served by the terminals at 9a. Avenida and 19a. Calle in Zone 1 (also known as the FEGUA, or *Tren,* Terminal). Passengers pay their fares on board, although first-class bus tickets can be purchased in advance. International companies provide service to Mexico and the rest of Central America.

Guatemala City's local bus system is inexpensive and extensive, serving virtually all of the capital. The ramshackle buses are invariably crowded, however, and the sheer number of routes and schedules can be intimidating at first. Also, the final destination of a bus, identified by a placard in the front window, is sometimes reached by such a long and painfully slow route that you are better off taking a taxi or even walking.

Buses shuttle up and down Avenida de la Reforma between Zones 1, 2, 4, 9, and 10 along the busiest routes. Since schedules quickly become outdated, you will do best to make local inquiries before using the municipal bus lines. Few of the drivers speak English, but most hotel personnel and cab drivers have good working knowledge of the system.

Taxis

Guatemala City taxis are plentiful and relatively cheap, although they become noticeably scarcer and more expensive at night, when they are mostly replaced by jitneys, a sort of collective taxi. But even during the day, taxis tend to congregate near hotels and bus stations rather than circulate in search of passengers.

A registered taxi always bears a license plate that begins with the capital letter A. Those meeting the standards of the tourist commission will bear the INGUAT emblem. Most taxis are unmetered, so always settle on the amount you are going to pay before setting out and be prepared to bargain. Moderately priced yellow cabs can be called at 1-801-332-1515 (tollfree); they're fast and reliable.

Auto Rental

Several major car rental agencies operate in Guatemala City, offering everything from four-wheel-drive Land Rovers to luxury limos. You will find agency offices at the airport, in major hotels, and along Avenida de la Reforma. Renting a car in Guatemala is relatively expensive, with rates similar to those you pay in the United States or Europe. A driver's license and credit card are usually required.

Make sure you understand your insurance coverage before signing any contracts, as liability varies dramatically from one rental company to the next. Some companies, for example, do not provide insurance covering accident damage or towing. You can obtain the names of several reputable agencies that sell comprehensive insurance policies for drivers in Guatemala and Central America from Hertz, Avis, Dollar, and other major car rental chains that have good reputations in the region (see Appendix B for a complete list). Local agencies, which are generally cheaper, include Tabarini, Tally, Tikal, and Optima.

Drive defensively in Guatemala City: The locals are aggressive behind the wheel and frequently ignore signs, signals, and even sirens. Stoplights are often turned off at night, and avenida traffic is then given the right of way over calles. Fill your tank before heading out of Guatemala City; gas stations are rare in the countryside and an INGUAT gas station map is helpful. Park your car in a garage or guarded lot (marked *parqueo* or *estacionamiento*) and remove your valuables, especially at night. Young boys will invariably offer to look after your car when you park in a public place, and refusing their services may be an invitation to vandalism or theft. The prudent course is to appoint one youth to remain on guard and reward him with a modest tip. Auto theft and break-ins are a serious problem in Guatemala.

VISITOR INFORMATION

Tourism Offices
The main office of **INGUAT** (the Guatemala Tourist Commission) is in Zone 4 at 7a. Avenida 1-17, near the Civic Center (331-1333, fax 331-8893). INGUAT distributes low-cost and free brochures from 8:30 a.m. to 5:00 p.m. Monday through Friday, and from 8:00 a.m. to noon Saturday. Questions are answered in Spanish or English (and sometimes other languages) at the information desk on the ground floor.

The **Military Geographic Institute** (Instituto Geográfico Militar) at Avenida las Américas 5-76 in Zone 13 sells good road maps as well as provincial and topographic maps. Most of the more detailed maps are not for sale but can be inspected at the institute's offices. Photocopies of some are also sold in a few bookstores around the country, notably Casa Andinista in Antigua.

Banking
Some of the more efficient full-service banks in the capital are the **Banco de Guatemala** (Centro Cívico, 7a. Avenida, Zone 4), **Lloyds Bank** (8a. Avenida 10-67, Zone 1), **Banco Industrial** (7a. Avenida 11-20, Zone 1), and the **Banco de Guatemala** airport branch, which is usually open on Sundays and holidays. Hours for other banks are generally 8:00 a.m. to 2:30 p.m., although some offices are open later on weekdays and on

Saturday mornings. Because Zone 4 is Guatemala City's financial center, banks along its main thoroughfares are fairly efficient in changing foreign currency and similar transactions.

Major credit cards, traveler's checks, and small-denomination U.S. currency are widely accepted in Guatemala City. A fee is often charged for converting traveler's checks or processing credit cards. There is an **American Express** office and mail center at the Banco del Café, Avenida de la Reforma 9-00, Zone 9 (331-1311). You can draw cash against a credit card there or at **Credomatic**, 4th floor, 7a. Avenida 6-22, in Zone 9 (331-7436). Automatic teller machines for Visa dispense cash at various locations, particularly in Zones 4, 9, and 10. Cash services for other credit cards are relatively uncommon in Guatemala.

Telephone, Post Office, and Internet Access

Public telephones are hard to find in Guatemala City, as in the rest of the country. They accept 10- and 25-centavo coins. For long-distance and international calls, try the office of the national phone monopoly, **Telgua**, which provides more than a dozen phones for walk-in use. Telgua's main office is at 7a. Avenida and 12a. Calle in Zone 1. International telegrams can be sent from the same location. Collect calls can be made overseas from public phones in the lobbies of the Camino Real, El Dorado, and Conquistador hotels as well as at the airport.

The main post office is at 7a. Avenida and 12a. Calle in Zone 1. Domestic telegrams are also sent from there. Hours are 9:00 a.m. to 5:30 p.m. weekdays; 8:00 a.m. to 3:00 p.m. Saturdays. This is the most efficient post office in the country when it comes to sending and receiving overseas packages; look for the English-language "parcel post" sign in the back on the ground floor. Remember that packages sent to foreign countries must be inspected before they are sealed. Stamp collectors can buy packets of Guatemalan stamps at the *Filatelica* window in the main post office. Guatemala's postal and telephone systems became privately managed in 1998, which has created many improvements.

Outgoing mail may be sent from a few public postal boxes (look for the *buzón correo*) and most hotel reception desks. Several private shipping services in Guatemala City will ship packages overseas, including Federal Express, UPS, and DHL. Recommended are **U.S. Postal** (334-5880) at 2a. Avenida 7-16, Zone 10, which also has a public fax and post office boxes, or **Express Network** (15a. Calle 6-38, Zone 10), which specializes in mail shipment.

E-mail and Internet services are available through **Café InterNet** (333-4549: 5a. Avenida at 16-11, Zone 10; www.centramerica.com/ cafe_internet), which also serves food. **Guatemala Online/Prodata**

(334-7490; 11a. Calle 3-23, Zone 9; www.pronet.net.gt) provides Central American hotel, auto rental, and flight information. E-mail is increasingly common among Guatemalan hotels and outfitters, as are various Cybermania Internet Centers.

Fiestas and Holidays

The more colorful festivals are held outside the capital, but Guatemala City celebrates the days leading up to **Christmas** and **Easter** with a great deal of pageantry and celebration. Because Easter falls during the height of the Guatemalan summer, many outdoor fairs are held in the public parks at this time of year. Schools are closed and many businesses shut down during **Semana Santa** (Holy Week), which sometimes makes it difficult to obtain reservations in hotels, at restaurants, and on buses and airplanes.

The capital's annual **feast days** honoring the Virgen de la Asunción occur August 14 to 16, with most events scheduled in the city's churches, Hipódromo del Norte, and Jocotenango neighborhood. As you would expect, there are parades, fireworks, and speeches on the various anniversaries of national independence and revolution.

THINGS TO SEE AND DO IN ZONE 1

This is the oldest, busiest, and loudest neighborhood in the capital. It is also the most crowded: Its cramped streets and narrow sidewalks are jammed with vehicles and pedestrians, particularly during weekday rush hours and weekend nights. The two main, parallel shopping streets, 6a. and 7a. Avenidas, are lined with stores and restaurants of every description, although most upscale businesses have relocated to the relative calm of Zone 9 or 10.

A good orientation point is the main plaza, **Parque Central**, which many residents would say is the true heart of their city. The plaza is surrounded by the main cathedral and government buildings, and crisscrossed by 5a. and 6a. Avenidas and 6a. and 8a. Calles. Once the site of a huge public market, the plaza is now a wide and pleasant expanse of grass and monuments above an underground parking lot. The northern side is dominated by the **National Palace**, an imposing gray-green neoclassic building faced with imitation stone, completed in 1943 to house the offices of the president and executive branch of government. The upper-floor reception halls and a small, rather unimpressive archaeological museum in the basement are open to the public, as are several inner courtyards and patios. The interior stained-glass and painted murals that tell the story of Guatemalan history are especially memorable. Security at the National Palace is tight, as one would expect, but tourists are welcome (though you must pass through a metal detector

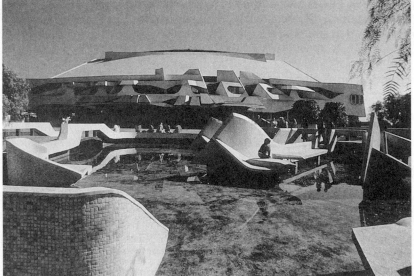

The modern Metropolitan Theater is in the heart of Guatemala City.

and may be searched). The National Palace is open from 8:00 a.m. to 4:30 p.m. Monday through Friday and until noon on Saturday.

On the eastern boundary of the park is Guatemala City's main cathedral, **Catedral Metropolitana**, one of the few colonial structures in the city not destroyed by earthquakes and well worth a visit. Built between 1782 and 1868, the cathedral blends baroque and neoclassical elements in its regal façade. The interior of the church contains many old paintings and elaborate gold-covered altars, some brought from Antigua when the capital was moved here. Next door is another colonial-era structure, the **Archbishop's Palace**, noted for its enormous wooden doors. On the opposite side of the plaza from the cathedral is the **National Library**, a modern structure housing important documents relating to the history of Guatemala and Central America.

Immediately behind the cathedral on 8a. Calle (between 7a. and 9a. Avenidas) is the **Central Market**, moved into a new concrete structure after the 1976 quake. The block-square building has three levels: The top is a parking lot, the middle section a handicraft market, and the basement a food, flower, and general merchandise pavilion. Prices are reasonable, especially for shrewd bargainers. You can buy fine textiles and crafts from all over Guatemala without much competition from other tourists, since they routinely overlook this festive place. The bottom floor holds a number of inexpensive restaurants and several nearby stores sell bolts of Guatemalan cloth. A number of other sources of handicrafts exist in Zone 1, including **Mujer de Esperanza** (15a. Calle 10-29) and **La Momosteca** (7a. Avenida 14-48).

Northeast of the market are two of the most impressive churches in Guatemala City. **La Merced** (11a. Avenida and 5a. Calle) is of baroque design and was completed in 1813. It houses a beautiful collection of religious artifacts retrieved from the ruins of colonial Antigua. At the top of a small hill on 11a. Avenida, near 1a. Calle, five blocks east and north of Parque Central, is **La Ermita del Carmen**, a church and hermitage rebuilt to conform to its 17th-century design after the devastating 1917 earthquake. This landmark, perched atop a steep hill called El Cerrito del Carmen, was originally built in 1620—the first church in the valley—and is known for its classic architecture, ornate gold and mahogany altar, lovely gardens, and sweeping view of the city, especially appealing at sunset.

South of Parque Central, in the heart of the smoggy and claustro-phobic 6a. Avenida shopping district at the corner of 13a. Calle, is the glass-domed **Iglesia de San Francisco**. Parts of this church have survived intact since 1780, and the interior is known for its large wood carving of the Sacred Heart. This, along with some paintings and statues, was salvaged from the 1773 earthquakes in Antigua. One block south of San Francisco is the police headquarters, in a medieval-looking castle with fake battlements.

The **National History Museum** (9a. Calle 9-70) houses a small collection of colonial furniture, firearms, paintings, and other artifacts, as well as changing exhibits of old photos and other items. This and other national museums are open from 9:00 a.m. to noon and 2:00 p.m. to 4:00 p.m. daily, except Monday, for a token admission fee of about 50 cents. Nearby, at 9a. Calle 6-65 (in the basement), is **Librería Arnel**, one of Guatemala's best bookstores, although its hours are frustratingly irregular.

Near the boundary with Zone 4 is the **Civic Center**, a high-rise complex of government ministries and banks dominated by City Hall, known for its famous interior mural entitled *The Mestizo Race of Guatemala*, painted by Carlos Mérida. This a bold portrayal of the country's Ladino history by one of its finest artists.

Overlooking the Centro Cívico is the **Fortress of San José**, an old Spanish battlement containing a small military museum. The fort has been converted into a park, dominated by the strikingly modernistic blue-and-white **National Theater** building. Guatemala's National Symphony, Chamber Orchestra, and two ballet companies (one classic, the other folkloric/contemporary) perform here occasionally in one of three

The neo-Gothic Yurrita Chapel in Guatemala City

auditoriums. A small hill on the theater grounds offers a good view of the city. Unfortunately, this park is locked much of the time, apparently for security reasons.

THINGS TO SEE AND DO IN ZONE 2

A small, older neighborhood that is rather sedate and overlooked, Zone 2 has little to offer the casual visitor except shady **Minerva Park**, situated on the edge of a deep ravine that marks the official northern boundary of the capital. Here you can see an enormous three-dimensional relief map (**Mapa en Relieve**) of Guatemala, renovated in 1997. The outdoor map has topographically exaggerated mountain ranges, volcanoes, and real water designating the nation's lakes and rivers. Underground plumbing fills oceans and lakes, and makes the rivers run. If you are the sort of person who gets oriented by looking at maps, this may be a helpful place to begin your Guatemalan visit.

Built in 1905, this unusual attraction covers nearly 8,000 square feet and uses a dual scale: $1/2,000$ for height; $1/10,000$ for land area. A national historic monument, the relief map documents some features (like extensive railroads) that no longer exist. The park is open from 8:00 a.m. to 5:00 p.m. daily. Fairs are also held periodically in Minerva Park, which has two public swimming pools and is at the end of Avenida Simeón Cañas. Buses 1, 45, and 46 have routes that go past the park.

THINGS TO SEE AND DO IN ZONE 4

Acting as a bridge between Guatemala City's "old" and "new," Zone 4 is a mostly commercial area with lots of office buildings, high-rise hotels, modern shopping centers, and only a couple of worthwhile attractions. Foremost among these is **La Capilla Yurrita** (Ruta 6 at 1a. Calle), a small chapel that looks more like a miniature Russian Orthodox cathedral than the Roman Catholic church that it is. A rich eccentric built this ornate, rust-red structure as his private place of worship in 1928 and it was later opened to the public, although hours have always been irregular. The exterior is a mass of fancy grillwork, soaring turrets, and twisting pillars. The inside is like something out of Eastern Europe, with lots of carved woodwork, stained glass, and gilded altars. Sitting inside this neo-Gothic chapel, you would never guess you were in Central America.

Just down the street from La Yurrita (also called Nuestra Señora de las Angustias), Ruta 6 runs into 7a. Avenida, one of Guatemala City's busiest north-south thoroughfares. There are several skyscrapers along this road, notably **Edificio El Tríangulo** (home of Clark Tours) and the **Conquistador Sheraton Hotel**. A few blocks north is the headquarters of Guatemala's tourist commission, INGUAT, at 7a. Avenida 1-17. Across the street is the **Olympic City** recreation center, where you can sometimes take in a lively soccer match. Most of these sports facilities are closed to non-members, however.

A few blocks in the opposite direction, at the corner of 4a. Avenida and 9a. Calle, is Guatemala City's largest bus terminal and the adjacent **Terminal Market**. Both are pretty disorganized, and you will likely have to ask for help to find what you want. Fortunately, most buses to destinations of touristic interest leave from other locations. The market, however, offers some real bargains for those who can put up with the chaotic atmosphere. Sadly, you may also see parrots, turtles, monkeys, and other exotic wildlife being sold illegally, as is the case in large markets throughout Guatemala.

Spanish is taught at the **Instituto Guatemateco Americano**, Ruta 1, 4-05; 331-0022.

THINGS TO SEE AND DO IN ZONE 7

This nondescript neighborhood on the outskirts of Guatemala is justly overlooked by most visitors. Yet it harbors one of the oldest archaeological sites in Central America.

Located on a broad plain in Zone 7, a few miles west of downtown, **Kaminal Juyú** was inhabited about 2,300 years ago by a little-known indigenous people called the Miraflores, who, like the Maya, were apparently ruled by a powerful religious royalty. The Miraflores tribe was conquered by the pre-Classic era Teotihuacán of central Mexico, who themselves became dominated by the highland Maya. The city was abandoned, rebuilt, destroyed, and again abandoned about A.D. 900. It was first excavated in 1899. Since then some 200 mounds have been found, containing temple pyramids, altars, stelae, and various other structures. An estimated 3,000 to 5,000 people lived here during the Miraflores period, many of them probably supported by the trading of cacao beans collected in lowland forests.

Excavation work continues here intermittently, and the site (reached by bus, car, or taxi) may now be toured only with prior permission from the **Instituto de Antropología e Historia** (Institute of Anthropology and History), headquartered in Zone 1 at 12a. Avenida 11-65 (253-1570). Officials will ask why you wish to visit Kaminal Juyú, and it is usually sufficient to explain that you are a foreign visitor with an interest in the region's archaeology. After issuing a permit, the institute will arrange to have the gates to the site unlocked and may provide an escort.

Kaminal Juyú is unlike the ruins most visitors are accustomed to and is best-suited to those with a deep interest in ancient civilizations. The above-ground site looks like unconsolidated heaps of clay and limestone rubble covered with large expanses of galvanized steel designed to ward off the elements. Only some statuary and a few stelae are recognizable as ancient artifacts. Underneath the site, however, is a maze of passageways leading into dark burial tombs and temple chambers adorned with hieroglyphics and sacrificial altars. (Be sure to bring candles or a flashlight.) The skeletal remains of an adult and a child can still be seen in one subterranean location, although the jade jewelry, sculpture, and ceramic artifacts for which Kaminal Juyú is best known have been removed by archaeologists for far-flung museums or crushed by construction equipment. Looters have absconded with much of the rest.

The ruins are just west of the intersection of Diagonal 24 and 24a. Avenida in the northwest quadrant of the city. The 16-BC/Kaminal Juyú bus goes directly past the site. You can board a bus at 6a. Avenida and 6a. Calle for the 20-minute trip.

THINGS TO SEE AND DO IN ZONE 9

If Zone 4 is the place where wealthy Guatemalans work and run errands, Zone 9 is where they shop and socialize. The boundary between the two is marked by the **Tower of the Reformer**, at 7a. Avenida and 2a. Calle. Erected by strongman President Rufino Barrios to commemorate the coup of 1871 (and his subsequent activist dictatorship), this imitation Eiffel Tower is capped by a large bell, rung every June 30 (Army Day) to mark the revolution's anniversary. At the southern end of Zone 9 is a monument to Guatemalan independence called **El Obelisco**, rising high above the busy intersection of Boulevard Independencia and Avenida de la Reforma.

Of the capital's several main thoroughfares, Reforma is the most scenic. Running parallel to and one block east of 7a. Avenida, it is a wide, tree-lined avenue flanked by embassies, luxury apartment buildings, plush restaurants, and deluxe hotels. For strollers, this is the most pleasant boulevard in Guatemala City, although the constant traffic is very noisy at rush hour.

On the top floor of one of the office buildings lining Avenida de la Reforma (at 8-16) is the **Popol Vuh Museum of Archaeology**, which contains a large collection of exquisite pre-Columbian jewelry and artifacts as well as fine colonial art and antiques. A private collector obtained most items in the museum, which is operated in association with Francisco Marroquín University and highly recommended. The impressive and beautifully displayed holdings include Maya jade masks and carved stelae, colonial ceramics and religious paintings, figurines, and a wide variety of other priceless treasures. There are also a small but well-stocked gift shop and a library on the premises. The displays are not very well marked, so you may wish to buy an inexpensive guidebook in addition to paying the admission fee of about $1.50. Open from 9:00 a.m. to 4:30 p.m. daily except Sunday. Look for the museum's sign (next to a carved Olmec head) on the ground level facing Avenida de la Reforma.

A few blocks farther south, between 10a. and 15a. Calle on either side of Reforma, is an area called **La Zona Viva**, "the lively zone" (sometimes called **La Zona Rosa**). The most fashionable stores, restaurants, discos, and nightclubs in Guatemala City are here, under the shadow of the tall Camino Real, one of the capital's most prestigious five-star hotels. It is in La Zona Viva that you are most likely to encounter members of the Guatemalan and expatriate elite. Some of their more popular hangouts are **Las Sillas, Mostachon,** and **Lum's**. Several fine stores sell overpriced but tasteful artesanía in Zone 9; **Sombol** at Avenida de la Reforma 14-14 is particularly recommended.

THINGS TO SEE AND DO IN ZONE 10

Avenida de la Reforma serves as the boundary between Zones 9 and 10, with the latter extending into the fashionable neighborhoods on the east side of this broad, shady thoroughfare.

The **Botanical Garden** (Avenida de la Reforma at 1a. Calle) is an island of calm in the city's hustle and bustle. It is also an excellent place to see hundreds of labeled trees, shrubs, and flowers native to Guatemala. Try to stop by before you head for Tikal. The collection is by no means exhaustive, but it provides a good overview of the nation's amazingly diverse flora. Specimens are identified by their Spanish and Latin names only. Open Monday through Friday from 8:00 a.m. to noon and 2:00 p.m. to 6:00 p.m., Saturdays 8:30 a.m. to 12:30 p.m., closed December 1 to January 15. Enter on Reforma.

Adjacent to the garden is the small **Natural History Museum**, also operated by the University of San Carlos, open the same hours as the garden. It contains some dusty old stuffed birds and other animals indigenous to Guatemala. Admission to both attractions is free.

Another museum in Zone 10 very much worth visiting is **Museo Ixchel de Traje Indígena** (331-3638, on the campus of Francisco Marroquín University at 6a. Calle Final), featuring an excellent collection of thousands of samples of handmade textiles and *traje* (clothing) from throughout Guatemala, including a number of unusual and fascinating ceremonial costumes. Some fine paintings of Maya in their native dress and impressive pieces of jewelry are on display as well as contemporary art exhibitions. The history and techniques involved in Guatemala's weaving traditions are explained in illustrations captioned in English and Spanish: Don't miss the 15-minute video that brings these traditions to life, explaining the important links between traje and language group. Open from 8:00 a.m. to 4:50 p.m. weekdays, and 9:00 a.m. to 12:50 p.m. Saturdays. There is a $2 fee to enter the museum. Handicrafts and souvenirs are sold in a gift shop downstairs and a small café sells gourmet coffee and pastries. The nonprofit group that runs Museo Ixchel also funds research on indigenous Guatemalan culture and maintains a small library on the subject.

Books and weavings are on sale and, as at Museo Popol Vuh, there are sometimes seminars and slide-shows held here. Outdoor signage is poor, however: The museum is the first large building on your left as you enter the campus, which lies at the bottom of a deep ravine.

For those interested in Maya archaeology, informative lectures are sometimes given in English by visiting scholars at the larger hotels along Avenida de la Reforma, notably the Camino Real at the intersection of 14a. Calle.

As you travel along Reforma you may notice a compound that looks like a poor man's version of a European castle. This is the officers' training school for the Guatemalan military. A few blocks south, also heavily fortified, is the **United States Embassy**.

Among the better Guatemalan handicraft stores in this district are **Bizarro** (1a. Avenida 13-68) and **Colección** 21 (13a. Calle 2-75). Other well-stocked gift shops are along 14a. Calle between Avenida de Reforma and 7a. Avenida.

THINGS TO SEE AND DO IN ZONE 13

This zone incorporates the airport neighborhood of Guatemala City, immediately south of Zones 9 and 10. The constant takeoffs and landings of jet aircraft make this an extremely noisy area but one worth visiting to take in the several national museums located in **Aurora Park**, just across 11a. Avenida from the international terminal.

The **Museum of Archaeology and Ethnography** has a very good collection of Maya artifacts, including a scale model of Tikal and a vast collection of stelae, jade, and incense burners discovered at various ruins around the country. A visit to this museum, renovated in 1997, is highly recommended before you head for Guatemala's numerous archaeological sites. It also offers an interesting display of indígena culture that includes many traditional masks and costumes. Unfortunately, as in most Guatemalan museums, the exhibits are not well marked and the little information presented is mostly in Spanish. If you can read only English, you may get more out of a visit by going with a knowledgeable tour guide, available in the museum lobby or through a local travel agency or one of the larger hotels. The museum has a 20 cent admission fee and is open Tuesday through Friday from 9:00 a.m. to 4:30 p.m., Saturdays and Sundays from 9:00 a.m. to noon and 2:00 to 4:30 p.m.

Directly across the street from the archaeology museum is the **Museum of Modern Art**. Despite its name, the museum's collection includes paintings and other artwork produced by Guatemalans over the past two centuries. Except for some large murals, not much here is particularly memorable. The art collection has the same hours as the Museum of Archaeology and Ethnology, with an equally minuscule admission charge.

The third state institution in the Aurora complex is the **Natural History Museum**, offering a limited assortment of preserved birds and animals as well as some crystals and other stones. The hours and admission fee are as listed above.

Also in Aurora Park, at the intersection of 6a. Calle and Boulevard Aeropuerto, is the **Artisans' Market** (Mercado de Artesanos), which displays and sells folk art and craftwork from all areas of the country. You can get a good overview of what is available in the rest of Guatemala, although prices tend to be higher than at other public markets and the merchandise tends to be touristy. There is a cafeteria here, and outdoor marimba concerts are held daily. Open 9:00 a.m. to 6:00 p.m. Monday through Saturday, 9:00 a.m. to noon on Sunday.

At the far end of the park is the relatively pleasant **Guatemala Zoological Garden**. Unlike those in many zoos, the birds and animals here seem well cared for, and their cages are fairly large. There are lots of shade trees and snack vendors, plus rides for the kids. On weekends the zoo and the rest of Aurora Park is often crowded with families taking in the sights, having picnics, and generally enjoying each other's company. It's a great place to view a slice of middle-class Guatemalan life. Admission is about a dollar.

Getting There

The international airport in the center of the city has daily flights to many U.S. and Central American cities as well as to the Tikal airport (in Santa

Elena). The Pan American Highway passes through the city from north to south. Guatemala City has a wide range of bus services and car rental agencies.

Where to Stay in Guatemala City
Note: All hotel prices here and elsewhere in this book are for double-occupancy and in U.S. dollars, based on 1999 research.

Zone 1
Chalet Suizo, 14a. Calle 6-82; $25 with bath, $19 without; 251-3786. Deservedly in high favor among travelers on a budget. Friendly, Swiss-run, its clean, spacious rooms overlook interior courtyards. Modest restaurant and efficient travel/tour agency on site; baggage storage and safe-deposit boxes available.

Hotel Centenario, 6a. Calle 5-33; $43, with cable TV and phone in each room; 238-0381, fax 238-2039. Slightly out of the way; clean, with an eco-travel agency on site.

Hotel Colonial, 7a. Avenida 14-19; $35 with private bath, $25 without; 232-6722, fax 232-8671. Comfortable, centrally located, 42 rooms. Rather sterile and unfriendly. A good restaurant is on the first floor.

Hotel Pan American, one block west of Parque Central at 9a. Calle 5-63; $50–$75; 232-6807, fax 232-6402. Elegant, 58-room, older hotel with an excellent restaurant that is open to the public (you will be served by waiters in Quiché Maya costumes). Regrettably, noise in this busy commercial neighborhood—and anywhere else in Zone 1—can be a real problem for light sleepers (another reason to pack earplugs). Recommended.

Hotel Spring, 8a. Avenida 12-65; $18 and up; 232-6637. Choice of shared or private bath. Interior courtyard and restaurant; most rooms offer cable TV. Excellent value; a favorite of the U.S. Peace Corps.

La Posada Belén, 13a. Calle A 10-30; $40–$55; 232-9226, fax 251-3478, pbelen@guatemalaweb.com. Ten rooms in an old colonial home on a quiet side street. Helpful owner, Francesca Sanchinelli, speaks fluent English and some French. Meals available to guests in a dining room lined with antiques and artifacts. A good value, highly recommended.

Ritz Continental, 6a. Avenida A 10-13; $60 and up; 238-1671, fax

232-8431, in the U.S. (402) 498-4300. Luxurious, 202-room facility with pool, TV, a/c, and two restaurants on the premises.

Zone 4
Conquistador Ramada, Via 5, 4-68; $60 and up; 331-2223, fax 334-7245. This two-tower, steel-and-glass structure offers first-class rooms with TV, a/c, balconies, and, in some cases, complete kitchens. Ground floor is a huge atrium with several restaurants, bars, a disco, and a gift shop.

Plaza Hotel, Via 7, 6-17; $58 and up; 332-7626, fax 331-6824. Modern but low-key hotel with a full range of services, 60 plush guest rooms, a pool, and meeting facilities.

Zone 9
Camino Real Westin, Avenida la Reforma at 14a. Calle; $100 and up; 448-4633, fax 337-4313. TV, a/c, pool, bar, shopping arcade, fitness center, and restaurants.

Cortija Reforma, Avenida de la Reforma 2-18; $100 and up; 331-8876. Modern 150-room hotel with well-appointed three-room suites, each with TV, refrigerator, and balcony. Shops, restaurant, and lounge (but no pool).

El Dorado Marriott, 7a. Avenida 15-45; $100 and up; 331-7777, fax 332-1877. Luxury high-rise hotel, spacious rooms with TV, a/c, and other amenities. Pool, bar, gift shops, gym, restaurants.

Hotel Princesa Reforma, 13a. Calle 7-65; $95 and up; 334-1414, fax 334-4546, princgua@guate.net. Luxury business travelers' hotel (with Internet access, fax/modem facilities, and two-line phones). Sauna, gym, pool, tennis court.

Hotel Villa Española, 2a. Calle 7-51; $85 and up; 331-8503, fax 332-2515. Small, Mediterranean-style hotel with courtyard, restaurant, and bar.

Residencial Carrillón, 5a. Avenida 11-25; $65 and up; 334-4036, fax 332-4267. Modern yet small hotel some distance from the Zona Viva.

Zone 10
Alameda Guest House, 4a. Avenida 14-10; $45 and up; 360-0152. A

remodeled old home, with seven charming rooms that share baths. Recommended.

Guatemala Fiesta, 1a. Avenida 13-22; $100 and up; 332-2555, fax 332-2569. Quieter than the nearby Camino Real and costs about the same. Besides the usual bar, pool, and disco, there's a large conference center.

Residencial Reforma/La Casa Grande, Avenida de la Reforma 7-67; $70; 332-0914, fax 336-7911. Elegant, Moorish-looking mansion near U.S. Embassy that offers good food and roomy quarters. Recommended.

Zone 13
El Aeropuerto Guest House, 15a. Calle "A" 7-32; $39; 332-3086, fax 362-1264, hotairpt@guate.net. Under same management as Hincapie (see below) and with similar amenities. Five-minute walk to airport. Recommended, but make reservations well in advance.

Hincapie Guesthouse, Ave. Hincapie 18-77; $38, includes continental breakfast and transport to the nearby Guatemala City airport; 332-7771, fax 337-4469, arvedap@infovia.com.gt. Lots of hot water plus cable TV.

Hotel de las Américas, Avenida de las Américas 9-08; $150; 339-0666, fax 339-0690. Luxury quarters near the airport; 88 rooms.

Where to Eat in Guatemala City

Zone 1
Fast-food fanatics are amply supplied throughout Zone 1 by McDonald's, Burger King, Wendy's, Pizza Hut, and Pollo Campero.

A Guy from Italy, 12a. Calle 4-41 and elsewhere. Good pizza and pasta at reasonable prices.

Altuna, 5a. Avenida 12-31. Upscale prices combined with an Old World ambiance, specializing in shrimp dishes and Spanish cuisine (including paella). Try the seafood soup.

Canton, 6a. Avenida 14-20. Reliable, well-prepared Chinese food.

El Gran Emperador, 14a. Calle next to Chalet Suizo. A vegetarian restaurant, one of several in the neighborhood.

El Gallito, 9a. Calle between Avenidas 8 and 9. Long-time favorite, with a huge marimba band and giant dance floor.

El Mesón de Don Quijote, 11a. Calle 5-22. Popular nightclub run by a smiling Spanish expatriate who makes everyone feel welcome. The drinks are cheap, food mediocre, and live music so appallingly bad that it's great fun to listen to.

Los Cebollines, 6a. Avenida 9-75. Delicious local variants of popular Mexican dishes, served in an airy, festive atmosphere. Part of a chain.

Ranchón Antigüeño, 13a. Calle 3-50. Typical Guatemalan food.

Zone 4

The fancy multistory shopping centers along bustling 6a. and 7a. Avenidas, which are usually overlooked by foreigners, are surprising sources of good meals. Zone 4 has more than its share of fast-food outlets including the ubiquitous **McDonald's, Taco Bell, Burger King, Pizza Hut**, and **Pollo Campero**.

Alicante, 7a. Avenida 7-16. Typical dishes of Spain and Guatemala. Prices are low, and there is a pleasant upstairs balcony.

Franco's, 7a. Avenida 4-40. Decent Italian food and friendly service, near Alicante.

Las Espadas, in the upscale Conquistador Hotel's fancy atrium. The continental food served here is well prepared but pricey.

Zone 9

El Establo, Avenida de la Reforma 14-36. Book-lined soup and sandwich café.

El Tamal, 6a. Avenida 14-49. Part of a local chain offering low-cost, savory Guatemalan dishes.

La Miga de Yaacov, 7a. Avenida 14-46. New York–style take-out deli.

Martin's, 13a. Calle 7-65. Varied continental menu; expensive.

Ming Court, 6a. Avenida 14-24. Canton Chinese dishes served in a clean, modern atmosphere.

Palacio Royal, 7a. Avenida and 11a. Calle. Tasty and authentic Chinese fare.

Pea de los Charangos, 6a. Avenida 13-60. Famous for its large, well-prepared steaks.

Puerto Barrios, across the street from the Palacio on 7a. Avenida. Seafood specialist, housed in a fake sailing ship.

Zone 10
Firoella, 13a. Calle 4-44. A good bet for authentic Italian cuisine.

Hacienda de los Sánchez, 12a. Calle 2-10. Serves some of the best steaks in Guatemala.

Happy Days, 14a. Calle at 4a. Avenida. Homesick Americans and Canadians come here to indulge in classic burgers and Coke floats.

La Patisserie, 13a. Calle 4-44. You'll find the best bagels here as well as specialty cream cheeses and pastries.

Le Rendezvous, 13a. Calle 2-55. Recommended for French food.

Los Antojitos, Avenida de la Reforma 15-02. Delicious, moderately priced Guatemalan dishes. The name means "little snacks," which is what Guatemaltecos typically prefer to eat. Part of a local chain.

Samba, 1a. Avenida and 13a. Calle. Brazilian dishes.

William Shakespeare Pub, 13a. Calle 1-51. The favored pub-style expatriate bar.

Sushita, 2a. Avenida 14-63. Reasonably priced, popular Japanese restaurant.

DAY TRIPS FROM GUATEMALA CITY

LAKE AMATITLÁN
Lake Amatitlán is located about 20 miles (40 minutes) south of Guatemala City on the main highway to Escuintla and the Pacific, Route CA-9. Not to

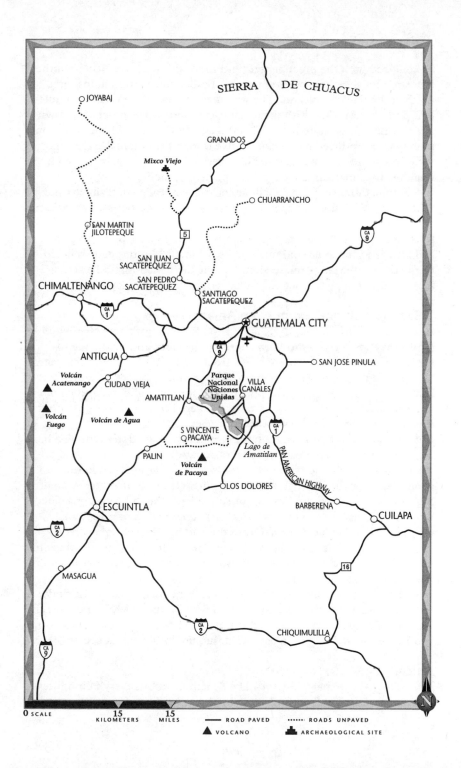

be confused with the much larger (and more scenic) Lake Atitlán in the western highlands, this body of water is nestled in the mountains directly north of the Pacaya volcano. The irregularly shaped lake is about 8 miles long and 3 miles wide, with the small sugar- and coffee-processing town of Amatitlán at its western tip. This is a largely Cakchiquel-speaking community that produced red cochineal dye during the colonial era. Lining the lake's shoreline are a number of vacation homes and cabins used by wealthy Guatemalan families who come here on holidays and weekends.

From a distance, Lake Amatitlán looks like a real gem. Sailboats and water-skiers skim along its sparkling surface, and the cottages along its banks are embraced by lush vegetation. A close look, however, reveals that the lake has become woefully polluted. A power plant chugs away on its shoreline, and litter is scattered around much of its perimeter. An unsightly railroad bridge crosses the lake's midsection. Despite these blemishes, the setting is lovely and an outing to Lake Amatitlán makes a pleasant day trip.

Things to See and Do in Lake Amatitlán

After a scenic drive around the lake, you can hike from **Las Ninfas National Park** on the southern shore up the steep mountainside to **United Nations Park**, where there are more trails and panoramic views. Horses and mules can be rented for rides through the countryside. The nearly vertical slope above the lake is ideal for hang-gliding, and competitions are held here from time to time. An aerial tramway line goes up the mountain but in recent years it has not operated.

The lake is not clean enough for swimming; instead, try renting a boat along the public beach near the town of Amatitlán. There are several privately owned pools and bathhouses (*balnearios*) at various geothermal hot springs in the area, although most are neither clean nor inviting. A small **Maya ruin** lies about 2 miles east of Amatitlán. The indígena considered this a sacred place, and pots and urns that contained their ceremonial offerings are still being retrieved from the bottom of the lake by divers.

The town's feast days are May 3 and June 29, when visitors flock to the 16th-century church housing Niño de Atocha, a sacred statue said to possess miraculous powers.

About 10 miles southwest of the lake, off the main road to Escuintla, is the **San Pedro Mártir cave complex**, noted for its underground river and waterfall. Because of the chamber's unusual twisted shape, the subterranean stream appears to be flowing backward. Inquire locally about access.

Getting There

Buses leave Guatemala City for Lake Amatitlán about every 30 minutes from the terminal at 20a. Calle and 3a. Avenida, Zone 1.

Where to Stay and Eat near Lake Amatitlán

There are a number of decent restaurants around Lake Amatitlán, but because of the polluted water, you are advised not to eat any fish caught here.

Blanquita Hotel, on the lakeshore east of downtown Amatitlán; $10. Basic clean rooms.

Hospedaje Kati, on the lakeshore east of downtown Amatitlán; $10. Basic clean rooms.

Other Options

Several campgrounds and trailer/RV parks are on the main road between Lake Amatitlán and Guatemala City, with others found along the highway to Escuintla and the access road to United Nations Park.

Turicentre Auto Mariscos (Km. 33) provides rooms and campsites, with free use of its outdoor pools included in the accommodation price. RVs are charged about $6 per night. About 200 yards away is **La Red** (Km. 33), a private campground (around $2 per night) with two warm pools.

PACAYA VOLCANO

On a clear day, steamy Pacaya volcano is clearly visible from Guatemala City, looming to the south above Lake Amatitlán. Rising to an altitude of 8,420 feet, this is one of five Guatemalan volcanoes currently considered active—the others are Fuego, Santiagüito, Santa María, and Tolimán. Pacaya has two cones, and the newer one occasionally spews ash, steam, and lava—an awesome spectacle, especially at night. The latest eruption period began in 1994, and there are occasional evacuations of nearby villages. In 1998, Guatemala City was showered with ash. For information (and warnings) about trekking to the top of Pacaya, see Chapter 4: Special Interests and Activities.

SAN PEDRO, SAN JUAN, AND SANTIAGO SACATEPÉQUEZ

These three small towns have the largest indígena populations in the department of Guatemala, the jurisdiction that includes the capital. The Sacatepéquez trio lies in a rich agricultural region interspersed with thick pine forests. When the Spanish arrived, this area was occupied by the Sacatepéquez Maya, hence the name. Most residents still speak the Cakchiquel language of their ancestors.

San Pedro, the smallest of the communities, is the first you will enter en route from Guatemala City. The huipiles and other textiles woven here are particularly well made and colorful. Friday's market is the best time to find them. The feast day is June 29. (Note: There is another town of the same name to the west, in San Marcos department.)

Surrounding **San Juan**, 4 miles past San Pedro, are terraced gardens of produce, sold in the capital, and greenhouses of flowers (mostly carnations), exported overseas by air. The purple and yellow huipiles of the community are very beautiful; some bear representations of two-headed eagles and horses. They can be purchased at the Friday and Sunday markets. June 24 is the annual feast day. A dirt road continues across the barren mountains north of San Juan Sacatepéquez to the ruins of **Mixco Viejo** (see following section).

About 6 miles southwest of San Pedro, north of the Pan American Highway and along the branch road to Antigua, is **Santiago Sacatepéquez**. This town is noted for its unique All Saints' Day celebration on November 1. Besides the traditional candles and gifts of food left in the community cemetery, the men of Santiago fly huge multicolored circular kites (*barriletes*) made of reed or bamboo sticks and painted paper. Each 9-foot kite is of intricate design and may take months to construct. If the kite begins falling apart after a few crashes, the paper is burned off so that the frame can be covered with a new sheet that will be decorated for the following year. The *barriletes* are flown as a way of sending messages of comfort, devotion, and affection to the spirits of the dead. It is a scene not to be missed!

Getting There
Each town can be reached by private car or via public buses that leave several times a day from the Zone 4 terminal in Guatemala City, and from 2a. Avenida at 2a. Calle in Zone 9.

MIXCO VIEJO RUINS
Location: About 40 miles northwest of Guatemala City near the Motagua River. The archaeological site is a 1-hour drive beyond San Juan Sacatepéquez at the bottom of the river valley.
Services: Camping is allowed at any of Mixco Viejo's thatched shelters, but you will need to bring your own food and water. There are no restaurants or hotels in the area, but drinks and snacks are sometimes sold here during the day.

Set in an arid, moonlike landscape, these dusty, excavated ruins date from about A.D. 1300 and have been badly damaged over the years by Spanish conquistadors, vandals, erosion, and earthquakes. Partial restoration has been carried out by France's Museum of Man and other academic institutions. Entering the ancient city by way of a single-file causeway, you can still see a number of temples, ball courts, altars, and observation platforms. One unusual aspect of the site is the absence of burial tombs, which suggests that bodies were cremated, an unheard-of practice among the highland Maya.

Mixco Viejo, with its 12 pyramid groupings, was the capital of the Pokomán, one of the many warring Maya tribes of pre-Columbian Guatemala. Surrounded by steep ravines, the city is believed to have been home to about 9,000 Maya when Pedro de Alvarado laid siege to Mixco Viejo for three months in 1525. The Spaniards used trickery, stealth, and starvation to finally storm the fortress, massacre its defenders, and relocate survivors to the new town of Mixco, now a suburb of the capital, where a few people still speak the Pokomán dialect.

There is very little traffic to these remote ruins, and you are likely to have them to yourself much, if not all, of the time.

Getting There

You can drive to the site from Guatemala City or Antigua in about 2 hours, or take a long bus ride to Pachalum on Route 2, which will pass by the entrance to the ruins. Ask the driver or ticket agent to make sure your bus passes the ruins, as some Pachalum buses do not. Several Guatemala City tour operators offer day trips to Mixco Viejo at reasonable rates.

SAN JOSÉ PINULA

This small village is only 30 minutes away from Guatemala City but has a distinctly rural feel, tucked as it is into the wooded folds of volcanic foothills. The main attraction is **Campo Ecologico de Pinula**, a family and nature-oriented resort (Km. 25.5, Ruta Nacional 18; 634-3047) offering horseback rides, bicycle rental, hiking, volleyball, picnicking, and even hay rides. Guatemaltecos come here for birthdays, family reunions, and similar celebrations.

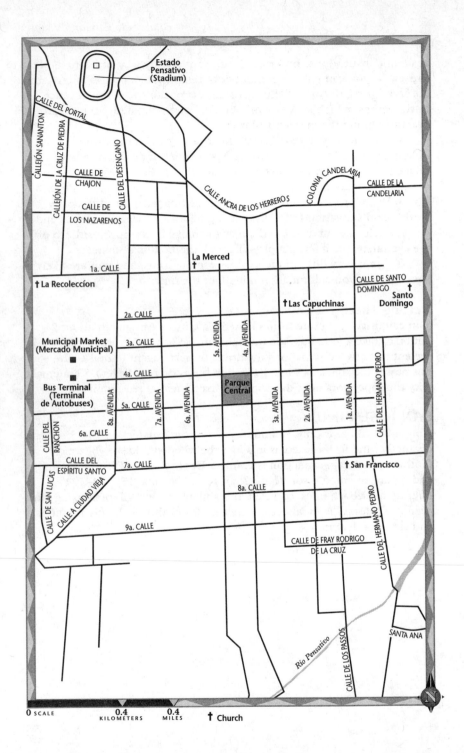

Estado
Pensativo
(Stadium)

CALLE DEL PORTAL

CALLEJÓN SANANTON

CALLEJÓN DE LA CRUZ DE PIEDRA

CALLE DE
CHAJON

CALLE DEL DESENGANO

CALLE DE
LOS NAZARENOS

CALLE ANCRA DE LOS HERREROS

COLONIA CANDELARIA

CALLE DE LA
CANDELARIA

1a. CALLE

La Merced
†

† La Recoleccíon

CALLE DE SANTO
DOMINGO

Santo
Domingo
†

2a. CALLE

† Las Capuchinas

Municipal Market
(Mercado Municipal)

3a. CALLE

5a. AVENIDA

4a. AVENIDA

CALLE DEL HERMANO PEDRO

4a. CALLE

Bus Terminal
(Terminal
de Autobuses)

8a. AVENIDA

5a. CALLE

7a. AVENIDA

6a. AVENIDA

Parque
Central

3a. AVENIDA

2a. AVENIDA

1a. AVENIDA

CALLE DEL
RANCHON

6a. CALLE

CALLE DEL
ESPÍRITU SANTO

7a. CALLE

† San Francisco

CALLE DE SAN LUCAS

CALLE A CIUDAD VIEJA

8a. CALLE

9a. CALLE

CALLE DE FRAY RODRIGO
DE LA CRUZ

CALLE DEL HERMANO PEDRO

Río Pensativo

CALLE DE LOS PASSOS

SANTA ANA

N

0 SCALE

0.4
KILOMETERS

0.4
MILES

† Church

6

ANTIGUA AND VICINITY

If you go to Guatemala, it's a safe bet that you will visit Antigua. Only 30 miles (and a world away) from Guatemala City, this mountain-hugged, coffee-scented community of 40,000 residents has become a tourist magnet of the highest order. Many travelers head for tranquil Antigua as soon as they exit airport customs, and a large number never seem to go anywhere else after that. All that may make this compact city feel a bit cozy and precious—one gets the impression that *gringos* outnumber *Guatemaltecos* at times—yet it doesn't seem to lessen Antigua's air of romance and mystery.

During the past century, the nation's *old* colonial capital of La Antigua Guatemala (this formal Spanish name is self-explanatory) has been fragrantly enclosed by lush plantations of macadamia nuts, oranges, roses, and, of course, coffee. Antigua is also a food and furniture manufacturing center and hosts hundreds of Spanish students each month in more than 50 language schools. Many of Guatemala's finest painters, writers, and craftspeople also make Antigua their home, resulting in a constant blooming of arts-related activity. In recent years, many wealthy Guatemalans have moved here as well, building luxury villas on hillsides and adding second-floor living quarters to older buildings downtown.

Antigua enchants visitors with its narrow cobblestone streets, tree-shaded parks, imposing religious monuments, and old colonial buildings. Many of the latter are protected from deliberate

115

destruction by the same strict architectural laws that forbid overhanging signs, garish advertising, and high-rise buildings. Even jostled cobblestones must be replaced exactly as they were. Many structures have been lovingly restored to their original beauty, while others have been taken over by shopkeepers and homesteaders. Some have been modified for use as public buildings or open-air markets. Earthquakes still rumble, and the nearby volcanoes sometimes spew steam, ash, and lava, but the *Antigüeños* have learned to take it all in stride.

A growing number of residents commute daily to jobs in Guatemala City, despite the narrow, twisty drive. Many North American and European retirees and expatriates have settled here, opening shops and restaurants that—along with hundreds of foreign-born Spanish students—giving the town a cosmopolitan feel.

Because of its small size and orderly layout, Antigua is best seen on foot or bicycle (beware the bumpy cobbles). Horses and motorcycles can also be rented at reasonable rates. Wandering among its colonial mansions, churches, and public buildings is like being transported in a time machine back to the days when this was the affluent cultural, religious, economic, and political capital of a powerful empire that stretched from Chiapas to Panama. In the early 18th century, an estimated 60,000 people lived here, making Antigua one of the biggest Spanish cities of the Western Hemisphere.

If nothing else, the presence of foreigners has succeeded in driving Antigua's rents and real estate prices up to U.S. standards. The irony is that so many people come to learn Spanish in a place where English will serve just as easily. Still, this is one of the best places in all of Central America to stroll, study, or shop, particularly for fine textiles, ceramics, furniture, and jewelry. And when you turn a corner and suddenly see a street vendor selling the most gorgeous orchids you've ever seen—well, how can you not marvel at a town like that?

HISTORY

Originally called Santiago de los Caballeros de Guatemala (Saint James of the Noblemen of Guatemala), Antigua was Guatemala's capital for more than two centuries after its founding in 1543. The first seat of government had been established by the Spanish conqueror Pedro de Alvarado in 1524 near the Cakchiquel capital of Iximché but was moved, after a Maya revolt in 1527, to the Almolonga Valley.

The site of the first Ciudad Vieja was the unstable lower slope of the Agua volcano, a few miles south of present-day Antigua, in what is now San Miguel Escobar. In 1541, only a few days after word arrived from Mexico of Pedro de Alvarado's death there, the *new* capital was wiped

Earthquake!

On July 29, 1773, Antigua was largely destroyed by the worst in a series of devastating earthquakes. The event was recounted in American writer Edna Fergusson's 1946 travel memoir, Guatemala: "Tremblings became shakes, shakes became quakes. Even the strongest buildings rocked. Men had to crawl through the streets...Tiles and stones leapt in the air . . . Prisoners were released. A monk saw the Virgen de la Luz dance in her niche and ran, crazed, until he fell dead . . . Priests prayed without ceasing. Day was dusk with dust; night a black horror lit by rivers of flame flowing down the volcano."

out by a giant mudslide after a volcanic eruption loosened a natural dam below Agua's summit. The tall façade of the second Ciudad Vieja's 18th-century Franciscan church, built by Diego de Porres, is the only structure remaining from the colonial period. Across the plaza stands a gnarled old tree beneath which the first Guatemalan mass reportedly was recited in about 1530.

The *third* capital was rebuilt in a flatter and presumably safer location in the center of the Almolonga Valley, still beneath the shadow of Agua and its taller volcanic neighbors, Acatenango and Fuego. Despite occasional droughts, epidemics, temblors, and eruptions, the new Antigua grew and prospered. By the mid-18th century the city was envied throughout the Americas for its gracious living, talented artisans, elegant estates, fine university, walled convents, stone monasteries, and ornate churches. The construction of the streets and avenues of Antigua began at the Plaza Real (now Parque Central) and moved out in the four cardinal directions. The symmetrical design of the city resembles a chessboard, and it is considered one of the better planned cities of Spanish America.

Excellent examples of centuries-old colonial architecture still exist in Antigua, typified by arabesques and stucco latticework, along with wrought-iron balconies and window framing. Many structures were reduced to hollow shells by a series of devastating earthquakes between

1558 and 1773 and, by decree and popular sentiment, were never rebuilt. The destruction wrought by the 1773 catastrophe was so complete that a decision was made to move the capital once again, to the tiny farming village that has become Guatemala City.

Ignoring many official orders, hundreds of families refused to abandon the ruins of Antigua, and the city was eventually revived and granted special status by the federal government as a national cultural monument, despite continuing damage inflicted by major earthquakes as recently as 1976. There are ruins of no fewer than 50 churches, convents, and monasteries. All are protected by law and preservation is regarded so seriously that it takes special permission to move so much as a brick.

GETTING AROUND

Orientation

Antigua is about a 1-hour drive or bus ride west-southwest of Guatemala City. Take the Pan American Highway west of the capital to the Antigua turnoff and then along a paved two-lane road that winds through steep canyons, thick forests, and shaded coffee plantations. (Coming from the opposite direction on the Pan American Highway, watch for the sign in Chimaltenango directing you southeast on a road that snakes through the Almolonga Valley to Antigua.)

At 5,050 feet, Antigua is slightly higher than Guatemala City and a bit cooler. It's good to have a sweater or light jacket available, particularly for evening and early morning use. You'll need a blanket on your bed at night. The average year-round temperature is 70 degrees.

After spending any length of time in the energetic capital, first-time visitors will find Antigua positively provincial and serene. It is a conservative town in both temperament and politics, and the commitment to tradition is much more than a ploy for tourist dollars.

Antigua was laid out by the Spanish in a classic grid pattern around the Parque Central, with *calles* running east-west and *avenidas* extending north-south. Newcomers often find it helps to get their bearings in relation to the Agua volcano, which looms south of the city. The urban zone system, ubiquitous throughout Guatemala, was never adopted here. The town is small enough that finding your way around is not much of a problem.

Streets here are identified by both their original colonial names and a modern numbering sequence. Some streets (and most maps) have signs with one designation or the other but seldom both. Unfortunately, a healthy percentage of intersections have no signs at all, and many buildings have no visible numbers. If they do, you'll quickly see that street numbers don't necessarily follow a logical order.

Transportation

Several bus companies schedule departures to and from Guatemala City as frequently as every 15 minutes between 5:00 a.m. and 7:00 p.m. Buses leave about every 30 minutes to and from Chimaltenango and Escuintla, more often to San Antonio Aguas Calientes and other nearby villages. Service to all destinations is less frequent (or non-existent) after 7:00 p.m, on Sundays, or on holidays. Fares are paid on board and never cost more than a few dollars. The bus terminal is at the foot of 4a. Calle Poniente (Calle del Ayuntamiento).

When you hear the shout, "Guate!" you'll know the bus is headed for Guatemala City. It will pick up passengers on street corners as it heads out of town along 7a. and 4a. Calles. The ride costs less than $1 and takes about an hour to Zone 1 (buses sometimes charge a small handling fee for large baggage, such as backpacks). When arriving on a public bus from Guatemala City, unless you're headed elsewhere, stay aboard until the very last stop: the terminal is opposite the public market near the center of Antigua.

Because of the slow, crowded conditions on Guatemala's public buses—often called "chicken" buses because live poultry often rides along—shuttle service between major tourist destinations has become a big business. Minibus services are offered by local travel agencies; expect to pay around $20 for the 2-hour trip to Panajachel, about $15 for the 1-hour ride to Guatemala City. Recommended is **Servicios Turísticos Atitlán** (832-0648, 6a. Avenida Sur 7).

Taxis wait for fares near the bus terminal and Parque Central. Ask at INGUAT about appropriate fares to Guatemala City and surrounding villages. In 1999 the taxi fare for destinations within Antigua was $3 or less. Drivers sometimes take advantage of new arrivals.

Autos can be rented at several agencies in Antigua, including **Avis** (832-2692; 5a. Avenida Norte 22), and **Tabarini** (832-3091; 2a. Calle Poniente 19A). Expect to pay about $55 a day (including insurance and unlimited mileage) for a small car. In mid-1999 unleaded gasoline sold for about $2.50 per gallon.

VISITOR INFORMATION

Tourism Offices

Walking-tour and country maps are available from the government-run **INGUAT** tourist information office (832-0763), located at the corner of 5a. Calle and 4a. Avenida in the Palacio. A stop at INGUAT at the start of your visit is recommended: The informed and (mostly) English-speaking staff will help you find a hotel or a private room with a family,

119

dispense restaurant and touring suggestions, offer information on language schools, and answer any other questions you might have. INGUAT is open daily from 8:00 a.m. to noon and 2:00 to 6:00 p.m

Comprehensive travel information is also available from the well-run **AmeriSpan Tourist Resource Center** (6a. Avenida Norte 40, 832-0164, fax 832-1896, amerispan@guate.net). The friendly staff directs visitors to hotels, schools, agencies, tour companies, homestays, and nonprofit agencies needing volunteers. Inexpensive tours, lectures, and transport services are available. An international fax and phone service is also provided at the AmeriSpan office, along with free maps and a discount card for local businesses.

Special uniformed Tourist Police patrol Antigua; most speak English and are well informed.

City Guidebooks

If you are going to be in Antigua for a while, it is helpful to have a detailed guide to the city. A good summary is found in the widely distributed brochure *Guide to Antigua* by Lynn Durán, but a more thorough treatment, with extensive maps and history, is found in the excellent *Antigua Guatemala*, by Elizabeth Bell and Trevor Long. Bell has also written a guide to Lent and Easter week events in Antigua.

Tours and Travel Agencies

The author's favorite local travel agency is **Viajes Tivoli** (832-4274 or 832-0892; 4a. Avenida 10), a computerized, full-service, multilingual facility, handling international and domestic excursions, including sailing charters and rental of bicycles, horses, motorcycles, and cars. The agency's owner, Cathy, speaks fluent English.

Centro de Viajes (832-3041, 5a. Avenida Norte 15A) and **Turansa** (inside the Radisson Hotel, 832-2928, and at 5a. Calle Poniente 11B, 832-3316) are other recommended agencies providing ticket reservations, organizing tours, and the like. Turansa can arrange volcano, coffee finca, and natural history outings as well as the usual excursions to Tikal, Chichicastenango, and Lake Atitlán.

These agencies are also recommended: **Sinfronteras** (832-2674, 3a. Calle Poniente 12), **Aventuras Vacacionales** (1a. Avenida Sur 11B, tel/fax 832-3532), **Rainbow Travel Center** (832-4202, 7a. Avenida Sur #8), **Adventure Travel** (832-0162, 5a. Avenida Norte 25B), and **Servicios Turísticos Atitlán** (832-0648, 6a. Avenida Sur 7).

The city's best walking tours are offered by author/historian Elizabeth Bell's **Antigua Tours** (tel/fax 832-0228, elizbell@guate.net), based in the Casa Santa Domingo Hotel, 3a. Calle Oriente 28. The long-time resident charges $15 (includes all admission fees) for a 2-hour outing, and meets participants Mondays and Thursdays at 2:00 p.m. in front of the fountain in the main plaza. Tuesday, Wednesday, Friday, and Saturday tours depart at 9:30 a.m. from the same location. Check out her Web site at www.tradepoint.org.gt/ redtp/ touroper/antitours.

Banks, Telephones, Shipping, and Post Office

Banking transactions are relatively fast and simple in Antigua, one apparent blessing from having so many foreign students and visitors. Most popular are **Lloyds Bank**, at the northeast corner of

The daughters of an Antigua handicrafts vendor relax in their backyard.

Richard Mahler

Parque Central (4a. Calle Oriente 2); **Granai & Townson Bank**, on the west side of the park (5a. Avenida); and **Banco del Agro**, on the north side of the park (Alameda Santa Lucía 63). **Banco Industrial** (5a. Avenida Sur 4) has a cash-dispensing Visa automatic teller machine. **Banco del Quetzal**, on 4a. Calle at Parque Central, has a Mastercard ATM and has among the best rates for exchanging U.S. dollars. Exchange rates vary slightly from bank to bank and you can save some money by shopping around. The same holds true for the cashing of traveler's checks, which usually have a more favorable rate than cash (note that many banks refuse to exchange American Express traveler's checks: Barclay's is more widely accepted).

The **post office** is at the corner of Alameda Santa Lucía and 4a. Calle Poniente. Packages heavier than 2 kilograms (4 pounds) must be sent from the main branch in Guatemala City or through a private shipping company.

A company called **Conexión** can arrange overseas courier shipments, and money transfers from its office at 4a. Calle Oriente 14. Several other firms also handle out-of-country shipping, including **Quick Shipping** (832-2545; 3a. Avenida Norte; Tlinda@guate.net), an air cargo and door-to-door parcel service that will ship your purchases to anywhere in the U.S. or Canada. English is spoken and credit cards are accepted. There's a Guatemala City office, too.

The **Telagua** (government telephone monopoly) office is on the southwest corner of Parque Central, at 5a. Avenida Sur and 5a. Calle Poniente (note that, like most every other business, they're closed during lunch). There are pay phones next to the San Carlos restaurant under the portal on the north side of the park, outside the police station, and at Doña Luisa's.

E-Mail and Internet

Conexión (832-3768, users@conexion.com.gt, www.cyberia.com.gt) is an Internet access provider, along with electronic mail, fax, and telex services. It's located in the La Fuente complex at 4a. Calle Oriente 14. **Tips & Chips Computación** (4a. Calle Oriente 28, tel/fax 832-3061, asbpower@guate.net) provides Internet access, computer repair, and computer rental, among other services. Also try **Cybernet**, 5a. Avenida Norte #25B, or **Café.net Mistral**, at 2a. Avenida Norte #6b. An increasing number of hotels offer e-mail and Internet access to their guests; inquire when booking your room.

Books, Magazines, and Newspapers

There are several good bookstores in Antigua, including **Casa Andinista** (4a. Calle Oriente 7A), opposite Doña Luisa's restaurant. Mike Shawcross, the expatriate British writer who owns the place, stocks a good selection in many languages, with an emphasis on English-language material on Guatemala's politics, indigenous cultures, and natural attractions. Detailed maps are sold here, and information on volcano treks and other outdoor adventures is posted.

Hundreds of books in English and Spanish are also found at **Un Poco de Todo** and **La Casa del Conde**, both open daily on 5a. Avenida, the west side of the Parque. The latter, which has a fantastic selection of art and photography books, is in the Casa del Conde shopping arcade. The owner of both stores, Jane Swezey, spearheaded a campaign to establish an excellent international library at **El Sitio** (5a. Calle Poniente 15). For used books, try the well-stocked **Rainbow Reading Room** (7a. Avenida Sur 8), which also offers good music and vegetarian meals.

The best local magazine by far is *The Revue*, published monthly in English by American expats. They are at 4a. Calle Oriente 23 (tel/fax 832-0767, Revue@conexion.com.gt), with reasonable rates for classified and display advertising. A Web edition is at www.revue.conexion.com.

Spanish and Art Schools

For a listing of reputable operators in Antigua (and the rest of Guatemala), see the Spanish-language schools section in Chapter 4:

Special Interests. Quality of instruction and prices vary widely, so be sure and check around. The best schools are happy to make arrangements long before you arrive, and if you're serious about learning Spanish you should definitely plan ahead.

Several groups offer backstrap weaving classes taught by indigenous Guatemalan weavers. **AmeriSpan** (532-0164) in Antigua is a good unbiased source of information about these opportunities, as well as Spanish schools in Antigua. They can arrange credit card payments to Spanish schools, which generally do not accept them. **Art Workshops** in Antigua (832-3584 or in the U.S. at 612/825-0747) offers excellent short-term classes in weaving, painting, photography, writing, and other art-related activities. Owner Liza Fourré can also arrange experienced Spanish tutors for those who want to include language study in their curriculum.

Other Services

Film stock and one-hour photo processing are available at **Foto Solis**, 5a. Avenida Norte 13 (832-0753). A limited selection of film is also sold at the larger grocery stores and pharmacies. Film and photo-processing are relatively expensive in Guatemala, so you may want to bring all the film you expect to shoot, then wait until you're back home to process it.

For comestibles, the biggest *supermercado* is **La Bodegóna** (4a. Calle Poniente 17), where English and French are spoken.

For visa extensions, auto papers, pet shipment, and other bureaucratic matters, try **José Caal** (7a. Calle Poniente 2A) or **Miguel Angel** (4a. Avenida Norte 4).

ENTERTAINMENT

Shopping

Shopping for handmade textiles, clothing, ceramic pottery, wood products, and jewelry in Antigua is a popular and recommended pastime. You will almost certainly find lower prices farther away from tourist areas like this one, but the selection and quality are likely to be much more limited; the public markets of Quetzaltenango and Guatemala City, however, are both very good.

Several shops in Antigua are set up to maximize profits and support for the indígena craftworkers whose work they sell. For example, **Ojalá** (4a. Calle Oriente 27) is a showroom for the nonprofit Proyecto Artesanal, which seeks to preserve, protect, and stimulate the ethnic heritage of more than 500 contributing artisans (mostly women) throughout the central and western highlands. Other stores selling high-quality Guatemalan arts and crafts include **Pues-Si** (4a. Calle Oriente 30-37 and 4a. Calle Poniente 30), **Al Pie del Volcán** (three locations), **Casa de los Gigantes** (7a. Calle Oriente 18), **La Casa Nuestra** (3a. Avenida Norte at 5a. Calle Oriente), **Casa de Artes** (4a. Avenida Sur 11), and **Nim Po't** (5a. Avenida Norte near La Merced). The latter shop, owned by Frank Mays, is a wonderful place to start your search for a well-made *huipil* to take home: Mays displays an extensive collection from over 100 villages and can provide expert commentary on their cultural history, fabrication, and design.

Antigua's INGUAT office can provide a complete list of local art studios specializing in ceramics, woodworking, weaving, candlemaking, and bronze sculpture, as well as information on cooperatives.

Fine jade jewelry is available from the factory and *típica* shop of **Jades S.A.** (4a. Calle Oriente 34, 832-0109, fax 832-0752), operated by former Indiana steelworker Jay Ridinger and his Mexico-raised archaeologist wife, Mary Lou. During the mid-1970s the couple helped discover and reopen an ancient Maya jade mine in the rugged Sierra de las Minas east of Guatemala City. Their company hauls out jade boulders by helicopter and mule, then cuts them to produce black, green, blue, and white jewelry at their factory in Antigua. A number of Guatemalans have subsequently started their own jade businesses, and the industry is now an important part of the local economy. Stop by **La Casa del Jade** (4a. Calle Oriente 3), **The Jade Kingdom** (4a. Avenida Norte 10), **Jades J.C.** (5a. Avenida Sur 6), or the studio of **Julio Hernández** (9a. Calle Poniente 2). Black jade is a particularly good buy in Antigua.

The area has several silver factories, including **Platería Típica Maya**, at 7a. Calle Oriente 9 (owner José Luis Barillas sells good-quality rings, chains, and other jewelry) and **Platería Típica La Antigüeña** (San Felipe de Jesús 46, 832-0411), founded in the village of San Felipe de Jesús by the Hector Portillo family.

High-quality custom furniture is built by **Francisco López** at his studio (832-2853) across from the Radisson Hotel. **Alfonso Velasco** has a woodcarving studio worth visiting at 1a. Calle Poniente 5.

Ceramic specialists include **La Familia Montiel**, **Marcelino C. Monroy**, and **Florencio Rodenas** (1a. Calle del Chajon 24). They make eave tiles and rain spouts in the traditional ornate manner.

Paintings by local artists are available at **Galería Estípite** (Avenida del Desengaño 22), **El Sitio Galería de Arte** (5 Calle Poniente 15), and **La Fuente** (4a. Calle Oriente 14).

Movies, Theater, and Art
A range of cultural activities, from live theater to video screenings, are held at **El Sitio** (5a. Calle Poniente 15), ensconced in a magnificently

restored old home near Parque Central. **Galería de la Fuente** (4a. Calle Oriente 14) and **Don Martín Asador** (4a. Avenida Norte 16) display contemporary Guatemalan art and host classical music performances. Also try **El Sereno** (4a.Avenida Sur 9) for art exhibitions.

Film buffs are well served by several entrepreneurs who offer evening video programs for an admission of about $1.50. You'll sit in a tiny "movie theater" and watch a tape played back on a big-screen TV. Check local bulletin boards and publications for the latest line-ups, and bring your own *palomitas* (popcorn).

There are occasional art openings, theater performances, and concerts in Antigua; the free monthly *Revue* is your best source of such information. Every two years (1999, 2001, etc.) the city plays host to **La Fiesta de las Artes**, a multimedia extravaganza sponsored by a Guatemalan grocery chain, Paiz. The events, held over a two-week period in February, include world-class opera, ballet, and classical music recitals.

Nightlife

Nightlife in Antigua centers around the restaurant and bar scene, with an occasional lecture, gallery opening, or concert thrown in. Some bars have discos and live music. Although there are a few tried and true favorites, these establishments come and go with such frequency that you are better off discovering them on your own. Most are clustered along 7a. Avenida and 5a. Calle Poniente near the center of town as well as 5a. Avenida Norte, near the arch.

Recommended bars include **Ricki's** (4a. Avenida Norte 4), known for its jazz, blues, and restaurant, and **La Fabrica** (next to Ricki's), which attracts lots of young people and student (both Guatemalans and foreigners). Good music options include the **Casbah**, for dance tunes (5 Avenida Norte, near the Arch); **Mistral**, a sports and coffee bar (2a. Avenida Norte 6B); and **La Gruta**, for jazz (Calzada Santa Lucía 17). Keep in mind that Guatemala's *ley seca* (dry law) forbids the sale of alcohol after midnight.

OUTDOOR RECREATION AND ADVENTURE TRAVEL

Adventure travel outfitters based here include the **Sinfronteras travel agency**, the Antigua representative for Maya Expeditions, a Gutemala City operator offering white-water raft trips and bungee jumping, among many other outdoor activities. Also recommended is Ken Johnson's **Guatemala Unlimited**, specializing in culture- and adventure-oriented travel itineraries, which can be contacted through **Maya Expeditions** (or, in the U.S., 800/733-3350). Nature and cultural tours are also offered by **Sensational Tours** (5a. Calle Oriente #2, 832-4297).

Horses are rented at the Radisson Hotel's **Adventure Travel Center** (5a. Avenida Norte 25B) or at the office of **R. Rolando Pérez** (832-2809, San Pedro El Panorama 28, Pérez offers reasonably priced guided horseback tours of nearby villages and mountains, including overnight trips. If you don't know how to ride, he will teach you. Expect to pay about $12 per hour for such excursions.

Inquire locally about bicycle tours and rentals. There has been much turnover in this segment of the business and AmeriSpan or the above-mentioned travel agencies are good resources for current information. **Maya Mountain Tours** (1a. Avenida Sur 15; 832-3383) has been recommended by travelers for bike tours, as has **Antigua Mountain-Bike Hire**, 5a. Avenida Sur Final 36 (832-2768, at El Rosario, #9).

Motorcycles are available for rent from **Jopa** (6a. Avenida Norte 3, 832-0794), **Rental** (6a. Avenida Sur 7), **Posada Refugio** (4a. Calle Poniente 30), and **Natura** (7a. Calle Oriente 11). Expect to pay about $22 a day for a 200cc bike, slightly more for a larger model. Rates are lower if you rent by the week or month. You'll need to leave a credit card or a large sum of dollars as a deposit.

Camping, trekking, and mountaineering gear may be rented at **Casa Andinista** (4a. Calle Oriente 7A) and **Club Andinista de Antigua Chicaq** (6a. Avenida Norte 34). Guides can be secured through the **INGUAT** office (832-0763) as well as most travel agencies or **Maya Mountain Tours** (832-3383 or 832-2768).

THINGS TO SEE AND DO IN ANTIGUA

As its Spanish founders intended, the **Parque Central** (Central Park) remains the heart of daily life in Antigua. Until the early 1900s this rectangle of land was an empty expanse of dirt—the site of a daily market as well as livestock grazing, public fairs, proclamations, hangings, floggings, and even bullfights. The **Fountain of the Mermaids** at the center of the park was built in 1739 by Diego de Porres. The market was eventually moved out, however, and trees were planted and permanent walkways laid down. Today the Parque Central is a lovely place to sit and read, get your shoes shined, practice Spanish with a friend, or simply watch street performers and the passing parade of humanity.

The layout of buildings around the park reflects strict conformity with colonial traditions: The various institutions of secular and religious power face off against each other on their own "turf" along each side of the Parque.

Looming over the eastern boundary of 4a. Avenida (Calle de Obispo Marroquín) are the ruins of Antigua's original **cathedral** (built in 1545) and the restored **Church of San José**, formed by merging the two

Tourist Police

For several years, the Guatemalan government has provided Tourist Police in areas that attract the largest concentrations of foreign visitors. Antigua has more than two dozen of these uniformed officers, whose primary purpose is to patrol the city's streets and prevent crimes before they happen. They also will accompany tourists, on request, to places such as peripheral ruins or parks where visitors might not feel safe on their own. Because one of the most common crimes against tourists is theft, the Tourist Police advise foreigners to carry only small quantities of money, stashed in different places around their bodies, and to wear little or no jewelry. Visitors are most vulnerable to pickpockets in crowded markets and on buses. The Tourist Police station is on 4a. Avenida just off 4a. Calle (832-0533 or 832-0577). Hours of patrol are 8 a.m. to 10 p.m., seven days a week.

chapels left standing after the 1773 earthquakes. Built between 1668 and 1680, the two chapels form the present structure of the cathedral. The impressive interior of San José (also called Metropolitan) features 17th-century ornaments and a magnificent carved figure of Christ by Quirio Cataño, the celebrated artist who also sculpted the renowned Black Christ of Esquipulas. Although the reference is not technically correct, this modified church is now popularly called "**La Catedral**." Beneath the adjacent ruins are the tombs of Spanish conqueror Pedro de Alvarado, the first bishop of Antigua, and other distinguished citizens. No one knows exactly where the Alvarados' actual remains are: Their burial box (now stored in Antigua's city hall) was opened some years ago and found to be empty. Since the early 1990s there has been extensive earthquake-proofing and restoration among these structures, although you are still allowed to browse among them. Ask to be shown the small underground chamber where local Maya still worship ancient effigies.

The entire south side of the plaza is taken up by the **Palace of the Captains-General**, seat of the colonial bureaucracy, first built in 1558 and restored to its present form (after a series of earthquakes) in 1764.

A stone plaque on the east site of the building commemorates its restoration.

The façade of the two-story *palacio* is a series of 27 consecutive archways running the length of the block. The building now houses the police department as well as offices for the department of Sacatepéquez, of which Antigua is the capital. Visitors are welcome to tour the interior courtyard and second-floor public rooms.

Facing the palace on the north end of the plaza is the solid-looking **Ayuntamiénto** (City Hall), built of thick *mampostería* (an earthquake-resistant mixture of brick, stone, and mortar that looks a lot like adobe) in 1740 to house the municipal government and prison. The city offices are still there—note the coat of arms hanging out front—but the jail has been turned into the **Museo de Santiago**, which displays paintings, pottery, costumes, cannons, and other artifacts from the colonial period (including leg irons and instruments of torture!). Operated since 1997 by the local Rotary Club, it is open weekdays (except Monday) from 9:30 a.m. to 4:00 p.m. for a nominal admission fee. Weekend hours are 9:30 a.m. to noon and 2:00 to 4:00 p.m. Next door is the **Museo del Libro Antiguo**, operating with the same hours. This "old book" museum contains examples of centuries-old printing and paper-making processes. It was in these rooms that the first Central American printing press began operating in the 1660s. A replica of Guatemala's first book is on display.

Finally, on the west side of the Parque Central, is a long *portal* (covered walkway) where vendors often sell fruit, candy, art objects, and souvenirs. The buildings behind them, representing the commercial face of secular society, are occupied by restaurants, bookstores, a pharmacy, and a travel agency.

West of the Parque

If you come to Antigua by bus, you will be let off at the terminal on the western edge of the city, at the foot of 4a. Calle Poniente (Calle del Ayuntaménto), three blocks west of Parque Central. Daily buses leave here for Guatemala City (about every 45 minutes during daylight hours), Chimaltenango (with connections to the western highlands), Escuintla (with Pacific coast connections), and nearby villages. Departing buses line up along 4a. Calle all the way to 8a. Avenida (Alameda Santa Lucía) and sometimes around the corner in front of the Pollo Campero restaurant, where you can also find taxis.

Across from the buses, along the north side of 4a. Calle, is the *mer-*

Richard Mahler

*The monument to Rafael Landivar, one of colonial Guatemala's
most beloved poets, near his Antigua home*

cado, or **public market**. Vendors here sell everything from fruits and
vegetables to handmade textiles and inexpensive jewelry. The market
operates every day, but there tend to be more vendors on Mondays,
Thursdays, and Saturdays. The selection is fairly extensive, and prices
(with hard bargaining) are reasonable.

Opposite the *mercado* and around the corner on 8a. Avenida is the
baroque **Monument to Rafael Landivar**, a colonial Jesuit poet who
died in 1793 in Italy, 26 years after all Jesuit priests were expelled from
the Americas on orders of the Spanish king, who felt they were becoming
too powerful. Landivar's beautiful home is behind the monument on 5a.
Calle Poniente.

Nearby, at Calle Recoletos 55 (near Alameda Santa Lucía), is **Casa
K'ojom**, a private music museum with an excellent collection of native
instruments and folkloric recordings. It offers a recommended slide-show
(accompanied by music) and occasional evening concerts. Guided tours of
the museum can be arranged for small groups. The Casa K'ojom museum
and gift shop are open Monday–Saturday from 9:30 a.m. to 4:30 p.m.
(832-3087), for a $1 admission. You can buy excellent tapes of the indige-
nous music of Guatemala—field-recorded during actual rituals, ceremonies, and fiestas—as well as replicas of some traditional instruments.

Antigua's annual Holy Week processions are the largest in the Western Hemisphere.

Richard Mahler

Following the street in the opposite direction, two blocks west of Parque Central at 7a. Avenida, you'll pass the restored **Convento de San Agustín**, destroyed by the massive 1773 quake and now the site of a hotel and several shops.

North of the market and bus terminal, at the corner of 8a. Avenida and Calle de la Recolección, are the ruins of the **Iglesia de San Jerónimo**, a small chapel and religious school built in 1739 and once used as a customhouse. Next to San Jerónimo are the impressive ruins of **San José de Recolección**, built in 1701, from which there are good views of all three nearby volcanoes.

Walking back to Parque Central on 4a. Calle Poniente, you pass the ruins of **La Compañia de Jesús** at the corner of 6a. Avenida. Completed in 1626, the crumbling brick walls of this Jesuit-run church and monastery housed Antigua's public market until the 1976 earthquake sent tons of debris crashing down. The ruin has been beautifully restored and now houses a conference center.

North of the Parque

Heading north from Parque Central on 5a. Avenida Norte (Calle de Santa Catalina), you will pass under the **Arch of Santa Catalina**, all that remains of a convent built here in 1609, and find many of Antigua's best restaurants and most fashionable shops. The arch was constructed in 1697 so that nuns could walk from one convent building to another without being seen by the public. This is a favorite spot for photographers, who can frame Agua volcano within the bow of the arch on a clear day. (Try coming in the morning, between the dawn and afternoon clouds that often shroud the summit.) In the evening, this district is a favorite hangout for foreign language students. There are many restaurants, coffeehouses, and nightclubs here, some with live music.

A half-block northward, 5a. Avenida dead-ends at 1a. Calle (Calle de la Real Aduana). Turn west (left) at this intersection, and you will run into **La Merced**, one of the most impressive religious buildings in

Guatemala. A huge church with an ornate Churrigueresque façade, La Merced has suffered little earthquake damage and has been in almost-continuous use since its construction in the late 1760s. The baroque cloisters, fountains, and gardens next to the church did not fare so well, however, and mostly lie in rubble. There is a fee for visiting the interior rooms and open ramparts, from which you can see a lovely panorama. The convent fountain is considered the most sumptuous in the city. La Merced houses an enormous wooden carving of the Virgin Mary and a splendid image of Jesus Nazareno carved by Alonzo de Paz in 1650. The latter is paraded through the streets of Antigua every Palm Sunday. In front of La Merced is a small, pretty park with several tall shade trees.

Walking back toward the Parque, at the corner of 1a. Calle Oriente (Calle de Platerías) and 4a. Avenida Norte (Calle del Obispo Marroquín), you will pass the **Convent of Santa Teresa**. Built several centuries ago by a Lima philanthropist to house Peruvian nuns, it now functions as the city jail. Two blocks farther south, on 3a. Calle Oriente (Calle de los Carros), are the ruins of **El Carmen**, a church built in 1638 that collapsed completely during the 1976 earthquake.

Two blocks to the east, at 2a. Avenida Norte (Calle de Capuchinas) and 2a. Calle Oriente (Calle de Santo Domingo), is the church and convent of **Las Capuchinas**, dating from 1736. Also called the Convent of Zaragoza, this is one of the largest and best preserved of Antigua's colonial

Antigua's Arch of Santa Catarina

INGUAT

buildings, with 18 nunnery cells extant and a curious two-story circular **Retreat Tower** (looming above a round courtyard). The convent originally housed Capuchin nuns from Madrid and was considered opulent in its day, boasting a sewage system, running water, and private toilets.

Up the mountainside is **Cerro de la Cruz** (The Hill of the Cross) with a lovely view. Don't go there after dark, however, and during the day only in groups with a member of the Tourist Police.

East of the Parque

The great colonial schools of Antigua were built immediately southeast of the plaza, facing the cathedral. Across 5a. Calle Oriente (Calle de la Universidad) from the church is the **Seminario Tridentino**, a seminary built in the early 1700s that is now used as a complex of private residences. It is one of the few buildings to survive Antigua's many earthquakes unscathed. Next door is the original **University of San Carlos**, founded in 1675 as Guatemala's first public college, the third-oldest in the Americas. The school was eventually moved to Guatemala City (where it continues to operate), and this building now houses the **Museum of Colonial Art**. The collection consists mostly of religious paintings, along with carved wooden saints (*santos*) and depictions of student life in early Antigua.

Continuing east of the Parque on 5a. Calle Oriente, between 2a. and 1a. Avenidas Sur, you will come upon a Jesuit church, the original location of the **Bernal Díaz del Castillo house**. Look for the commemorative plaque on the north side of the building. Castillo was a soldier who served under Alvarado during the conquests of Guatemala and Mexico. Dissatisfied with official whitewashed accounts of those campaigns, he wrote his own critically acclaimed versions after retiring here. Díaz del Castillo's descendants later sold the property to the Jesuits.

At the corner of 5a. Calle Oriente and 1a. Avenida Sur is **La Casa Popenoe,** an authentically restored colonial mansion full of antiques and artifacts collected by its expatriate owners. Wilson Popenoe, a North American botanist who died in 1972, left explicit orders that his home be kept open to the public part-time. As of 1999, it was open 2 to 4 p.m. Monday through Saturday, except holidays. Admission is about $2. Be sure to tour the interior courtyard gardens (which include one of the raised spice and herb gardens popular among many old-time Antigüeños) and low-ceiling attic (where you'll see the spacious coop for pigeons that carried messages tied to their legs). Lovingly restored by the Popenoe family, the mansion hearkens back to an era in which only four large homes were built on Antigua's city blocks, one occupying each corner.

The **Church and Monastery of San Francisco** is two blocks away on 1a. Avenida Sur (Calle de la Nobleza) at 7a. Calle Oriente (Calle de Chipilapa al Pensativo). Construction of a huge religious center was begun here in 1579 by Franciscan friars, but earthquakes wreaked havoc over the centuries, and it was not until 1960 that any significant restoration work was started. Not everyone in Antigua likes the idea of pressing ruined churches back into service, but that is exactly what has been done at San Francisco, and the visual results are splendid. The revered 17th-century humanitarian Fray Pedro de Bethancourt, founder of Antigua's colonial hospital and better known as "Padre Pedro,"

The ruins of the Convent of Santa Clara in Antigua

INGUAT

was once buried in San Francisco's Chapel of the Third Order. Although his remains were removed in 1990 to the transept of the same church, some of his many followers continue to pray before the shrine that marks his original grave. Some of Pedro's clothes and other artifacts are in a small museum adjacent to the main chapel. A fee is charged for self-guided tours.

Also on the east side of town, on 6a. Calle Oriente (Calle de los Peregrinos) near 2a. Avenida Sur (Calle de Santa Clara), is the **Church and Convent of Santa Clara**, founded by Mexican nuns in 1699 and rebuilt after a 1717 quake. The exterior walls are very ornate and there is a large courtyard in the building's interior. Daughters of the most affluent families of colonial Antigua often spent time here, apparently praying and meditating in considerable comfort.

The **Mesoamerican Regional Investigations Center** (Centro de Investigaciones Regionales de Mesoamérica) maintains an excellent Spanish/English library and photo collection at 5a. Calle Oriente 5 (832-0126). The facility, which focuses on Central American themes, is open to the public Monday through Friday from 9:00 a.m. to 5:00 p.m. and Saturday from 9:00 a.m. until 1:00 p.m. The carefully landscaped interior courtyard is magnificent.

South of the Parque

The southern quadrant of Antigua contains a number of colonial buildings—several in ruins but most still functional—and 12 small, crumbling chapels representing the Catholic Church's Stations of the Cross. They culminate at the far end of town at **El Calvario**, a formidable-looking church kept in daily use. There is a beautifully carved fountain outside El Calvario, next to a small tree-shaded plaza.

Walking directly south of Parque Central on 5a. Avenida Sur (Calle de la Sin Ventura) you pass the haunting ruins of the **Hermitage of San José el Viejo**, completed in 1761. This baroque church, in ruins for over 200 years, was built to house an image of Saint James, Antigua's patron, carved by sculptor Alonso de la Paz. It is situated between 9a. Calle Poniente and 7a. Calle Poniente.

One of the few reminders of "ordinary" life in colonial Antigua is the **Pila (or Tanque) de la Unión**, a series of public clothes-washing basins on 2a. Avenida Sur that has been used continuously, in one form or another, since 1853. It was named in 1920 in tribute to Central America's labor movement. Indígena women can be seen scrubbing clothes here by hand. Water bubbles up from a seemingly inexhaustible spring, which has served Antigua for centuries and is one reason the city was located here.

WHERE TO STAY IN ANTIGUA

Aurora Hotel, 4a. Calle Oriente 16; $46, includes breakfast; 832-0217. A family-run establishment in an old home, this 16-room posada is a good value, though not especially flashy. All rooms have private baths and hot water. Secure parking available.

Casa Santo Domingo, 3a. Calle Oriente 26; $90 and up; 832-0140, fax 832-0102. At the high end of the accommodations spectrum (and worth every quetzal), this unique and elegant hotel is situated in the carefully preserved and semi-restored ruin of an old Dominican monastery. It has 87 spacious rooms, a swimming pool, fine restaurant, and many other amenities, including antique furnishings and fresh flower arrangements daily. Many visitors regard it as Antigua's finest hotel. Recommended.

Convento Santa Catalina, 5 Avenida Norte 28; $30; 832-3086. Clean, basic rooms and a friendly atmosphere. Note that the nearby clock bell rings every hour through the night.

El Rosario Lodge, 5a. Avenida Sur 36, across from the Panza Verde restaurant; $20 and up; 832-0336. Basic, pleasant rooms at a serene location. Furnished apartments with kitchens can be leased long-term, and there is a decent Guatemalan-style eatery, **Café Ana**, adjacent at 5a. Avenida Sur 14.

Hotel Antigua, 5a. Avenida Sur and 8a. Calle Poniente; $105; 832-0288, fax 832-0807. Sort of a Spanish colonial country club with a fine restaurant, a bar, and a pool. Outsiders can eat and swim here (for a fee), although the ambiance is decidedly upper crust.

Hotel Casa Santiago de los Caballeros, 7a. Avenida Norte 67; $40; 832-0465, fax 832-5858. North of the center of town, with its own orange grove and well-appointed rooms. Recommended.

Hotel Van Gogh, 6a. Avenida Norte 14; $20; 832-0376. English-speaking personnel and the **Starry Night** café on the premises. Long-term stays can be arranged at reasonable rates.

Mesón Panza Verde, 5a. Avenida Sur 19; $50 and up; tel/fax 832-2925, mpv@infovia.com.gt. Located on a quiet street next to a convent and coffee finca, choose from six charming rooms (two with views and fireplaces) in a faithfully executed recreation of a colonial home. There's a very good—but overpriced—gourmet restaurant in the lower part of the building. (The term *panza verde*, or green stomach, is a local nickname for Antigüeños, who are said to have always eaten a lot of avocados and green vegetables.)

Posada Asjemenou, 5a. Avenida Norte 31; $20; 832-2670. A Dutch-run hotel consistently recommended by budget travelers, although the bell tower next door begins operation at 4 a.m.

Posada del Angel, 4a. Avenida Sur 24A; $115; 832-0260, in U.S. (800) 934-0065. Small luxury inn specializing in personal service (i.e., fresh flowers, bathrobes). Heated pool, cable TV, fireplace. Recommended.

Posada de Don Rodrigo, 5a. Avenida Norte; $68; tel/fax 832-0291. A lovely 34-room hotel in a restored colonial mansion near the center of town. An excellent restaurant looks out on a courtyard and rose garden.

Posada San Sebastian, 3a. Avenida Norte 4; $25; tel/fax 832-2621. Friendly, well-run establishment that's close to the action. The author's favorite low-cost lodging.

Quinta de las Flores, Calle del Hermano Pedro 6; $65; 832-3721, fax 832-3726. The author's favorite small luxury hotel is an old coffee finca

Religious Holidays in Antigua

The week before Easter, Semana Santa, is like no other in Antigua, or anywhere else in Latin America. For seven days, the streets are filled with religious processions and spiritual pageantry as hundreds of men, women, and children don multicolored robes and costumes to carry enormous Catholic icon platforms (andas) across carpets (alfombras) made of pine needles, hand-dyed sawdust, paper cut-outs, and flower petals. Some of the andas weigh several tons; all are carried on the shoulders of penitents (cucurochos). Behind the men of the procession are the penitent women of Antigua, carrying the andas of St. John, Mary Magdalene, and the Virgin Mary. They, in turn, are followed by orchestras and men burning containers of copal incense. Early in the week the churches of Antigua are filled with pilgrims attending solemn prayer vigils. Decorations within the churches include huertos, colorful and fragrant displays of flowers, fruits, and representations of birds. Events reach a climax on the morning of Good Friday with a reenactment of Pontius Pilate and his Roman soldiers (in uniform and on horseback!) arresting and condemning Christ, then leading him to his crucifixion, as a marching band plays funereal music behind them and clouds of incense fill the air. The procession always stops in front of the city jail, where one or two prisoners are chosen to join the spiritual quest and shoulder crosses heavy with chains. The custom dates back to the 16th century, when all the cell doors of the old prison are said to have miraculously opened as the procession passed by.

Antigua's population sometimes swells to 80,000 or more people during Holy Week, and wise visitors make room reservations as much as a year in advance. Most hotels (illegally) increase their rates, sometimes charging twice the standard fee. For those who have not made advance bookings, or would just as soon avoid the crowds, a practical option is to stay in Guatemala City and commute to Antigua for the various Semana Santa processions, which last 6 hours or more. Another idea is to rent a room in a private home, something that is also best arranged in advance. Antigua's INGUAT office and larger language schools can help in this regard.

If your visit to Guatemala coincides with Holy Week, you should plan to spend at least one full day observing the Antigua celebration, exceeded in size and scope only by the Semana Santa festivities of Seville, Spain. The days with the largest processions in Antigua are, in descending order of size, Good Friday, Palm Sunday, and Holy Thursday. For a more thorough description of Semana Santa, get a copy of Elizabeth Bell's helpful booklet, Lent and Easter Week in Antigua, *or timely issues of* The Revue, *a local English-language monthly that features a detailed rundown of events. Processions start at main churches throughout the city, including La Merced and San Francisco, but times and routes change slightly from year to year. There are similar religious processions involving andas every Sunday and a few Fridays during the Lenten season, as well as during the June festival of Corpus Cristi and the weeks leading up to Christmas.*

Other important festivals are held in Antigua on July 25 (the feast day of St. James), All Saints' Eve and Day, and All Souls' Day (October 31–November 2).

Richard Mahler

*Carpets of flower petals and colored sawdust adorn
the cobblestone streets of Antigua during Holy Week.*

on the quiet southern edge of town. Beautifully landscaped grounds shelter a swimming pool and patio restaurant. The 14 rooms are spacious and service is top-notch.

Radisson Villa Antigua, 9a. Calle Final Carretera a Ciudad Vieja; $70 and up; 832-0011, fax 832-0237. The biggest (182 rooms) and most modern-looking facility in the city. The architecture may be dull and the rooms like any other in the chain, but amenities include a pool, health club, restaurant, gift shop, horse stables, and travel agency. On the outskirts of town, about a 15-minute walk from Parque Central. Travelers in recreational or camper-type vehicles can park overnight at the Texaco gas station across from the Radisson for about $6 a night.

Other Options
Billing itself as "the only real spa in Central America," the **Antigua Spa Resort** (832-3960) is locally famous for its body and beauty treatments as well as therapeutic massage and other amenities. Prices are far lower than what you'd pay in the U.S., Canada, or Europe. A free shuttle brings visitors to its country location at San Pedro el Panorama (on the road to Ciu-

dad Vieja) or you can rent a luxury room on site. There's also a small café. Open daily from 9:00 a.m. to 6:00 p.m, with a shuttle service available.

Antigua has houses and apartments for rent on a short- or long-term basis and these can be less expensive than staying in a hotel. Check the bulletin boards around town (particularly at AmeriSpan, the Rainbow Reading Room, and Doña Luisa's Restaurant) and classified ads in *The Revue.*

WHERE TO EAT IN ANTIGUA

Asjemenou, 5a. Calle Poniente 4. Offers delicious pizza at lunch and dinner, and is a good value for breakfast as well (open at 8:00 a.m.).

The Bagel Barn, 5a. Calle Poniente near 7a. Avenida. Genuine bagels with cream cheese are served.

Beijing, 5a. Calle Poniente. Cantonese cuisine is on the menu here.

Café Condesa, 5a. Avenida Norte 4. The best Sunday morning brunch buffet, served from 10:00 a.m. to 2:00 p.m. Recommended for any meal.

Café Flor, 4a. Avenida Sur 1. Thai/Szechuan-oriented cuisine.

Caffé Mediterraneo, 6a. Calle Poniente 6A. Italian. Recommended.

Caffé Opera, 6a. Avenida Norte 17. Serves some of the best coffee drinks in Antigua or, for that matter, Guatemala. Two multilingual gentlewomen from Verona operate this friendly place, which offers good sandwiches and sinfully rich pastries (at painfully rich prices).

Deliciosa, 3a. Calle Ponienta 2. This is the finest gourmet deli in town, with sandwiches and snacks to go.

Doña Luisa's, 4a. Calle Oriente 12. This legend deserves at least one visit by everyone who comes to Antigua. Run by Dennis and Luise Wheeler, former Peace Corps workers who contribute generously to Guatemalan social welfare programs, Doña Luisa's offers a justifiably renowned bakery and restaurant—plus the best bulletin board in town, announcing everything from caving and snorkeling expeditions to yoga and shiatsu massage classes. The upstairs dining room offers tableside people-watching and fine views of the volcano.

El Asador de Don Martin (at the former location of **El Sereno,** which is now at 4a. Avenida Sur 9), 4a. Avenida Norte 16. A splurge, but perhaps the most romantic restaurant in the city. Across the street from Santa Teresa church in a perfectly restored colonial home that doubles as a fine art gallery.

La Cenicienta, 5a. Avenida Norte 7. Chocolate desserts to die for, plus delicious fruit-cheese combos. The downside: It closes at 8:00 p.m. and the coffee is watery.

La Fonda de la Calle Real, at 5a. Avenida Norte 5 and at 3a. Calle Poniente 7. For *caldo real*—soup that's a meal. Good Guatemalan fare.

La Fuente, 4a. Calle Oriente 14. One of Guatemala's best vegetarian restaurants, tucked into one of the many restored mansion courtyards that Antigüeños have divided into specialty shops. Coffee, tea, and pastries—served throughout the day—are excellent.

Las Antorchas, 2a. Avenida Sur 1. Steaks are a specialty here.

Masala, 6a. Avenida Sur 14A. The Japanese restaurant of choice.

Quesos y Vinos, 5a. Avenida Norte 31A, near the arch. A pizza/pasta menu and one of the best wine lists in town. Sandwiches, too.

Restaurante Ahumados Katok, 4a. Avenida Norte 7. A pleasant, moderately priced café with a diverse menu specializing in beef (the owner raises his own cattle).

Tostaduría Antigua, 6a. Avenida Sur 12A. Fresh-roasted gourmet coffee. Take a sack of roasted, locally grown beans back home!

Welten, 4a. Calle Oriente 21. High-quality German fare.

DAY TRIPS FROM ANTIGUA

Several villages close to Antigua are worth visiting, particularly for their handicrafts, hot springs, and religious sites. All are easily reached by car, taxi, or public bus and, in some cases, bicycle or horseback. The closest destinations are only a short walk from Antigua by paved road or footpath. Ask locally about scheduled tours; if you're enrolled in a Spanish school such excursions may be a planned part of your curriculum.

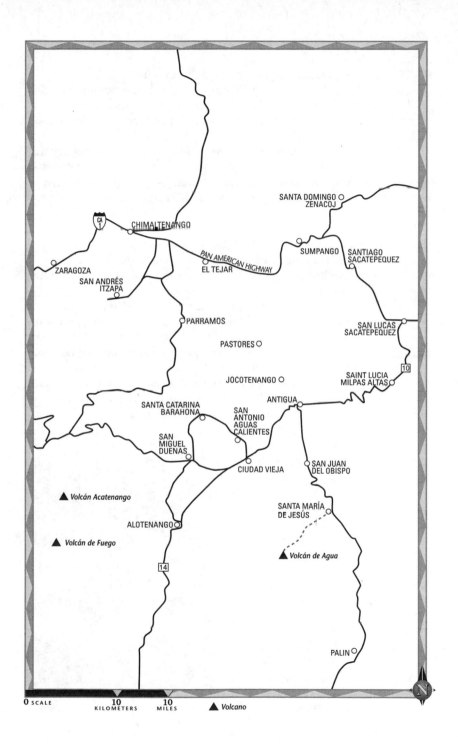

SANTA DOMINGO ZENACOJ

CHIMALTENANGO

CA 1

PAN AMERICAN HIGHWAY

SUMPANGO

SANTIAGO SACATEPEQUEZ

ZARAGOZA

SAN ANDRÉS ITZAPA

EL TEJAR

PARRAMOS

SAN LUCAS SACATEPEQUEZ

PASTORES

10

JOCOTENANGO

SAINT LUCIA MILPAS ALTAS

SANTA CATARINA BARAHONA

ANTIGUA

SAN ANTONIO AGUAS CALIENTES

SAN MIGUEL DUENAS

CIUDAD VIEJA

SAN JUAN DEL OBISPO

▲ Volcán Acatenango

SANTA MARÍA DE JESÚS

ALOTENANGO

▲ Volcán de Fuego

14

▲ Volcán de Agua

PALIN

0 SCALE

10 KILOMETERS

10 MILES

▲ Volcano

Specialized guided tours of local villages are offered by several Antigua residents. For visits to local coffee fincas and other plantations, try **Francisco "Pancho" Falla** (832-0409) or the **Turansa** travel agency (832-3316). Expect to pay $25 to $35 per person for these kinds of excursions.

Because of their proximity to Antigua, most villages and other day trip destinations in the area do not offer places for foreign visitors to stay or to eat. There are a few simple hospedajes and comedores, but travelers are better off returning to Antigua for meals and lodging.

JOCOTENANGO AND SAN LORENZO EL TEJAR

Practically adjoining Antigua, this coffee-processing center has an unusual **Seventh Day Adventist Herbal Institute** (Calle Real 30) where you can get low-cost steam baths, massages, and herb-based remedies (closed Saturday).

A wide variety of exotic butterflies can be seen at **Mariposaria Antigua**, a private butterfly reserve at Finca Las Gravileas de San Isidro, next to Fábrica Caoba in Jocotenango (363-2806). Guides will show you butterflies in various stages of growth and point out unique adaptations, such as wing patterns that look like tree bark.

In the nearby hamlet of **San Lorenzo el Tejar** you can pay a small admission fee and enjoy a small swimming pool fed by hot springs. Massage is also available at this rustic spa, open from 9:00 a.m. to 5:00 p.m. most days.

The nearest bus stop is at **San Luis las Carretas**, with hourly service from Antigua.

CIUDAD VIEJA

Literally wiped off the face of the earth more than 450 years ago, this old Guatemalan capital has little to interest the casual visitor aside from the massive white church (next to the small plaza), which was built during the colonial era and has been nicely restored. Only a few crumbling ruins, including that of the original city hall, date from before the catastrophic mudslide of 1541. A plaque in the plaza commemorates the first mass ever said in

Don Usner

Weavers of San Antonio Aguas Calientes

Traditional dance on El Día de la Concepción in Cuidad Vieja

Elizabeth Bell

Guatemala, beneath a tree that still stands. Most residents of this area are descendants of the Mexican Indians who were brought by the Spanish to help conquer Guatemala's highland tribes and given land around Ciudad Vieja as their reward. Buses leave Antigua many times a day for Ciudad Vieja, or you can walk the 3 miles in an hour or so.

SAN ANTONIO AGUAS CALIENTES

This village, about 4 miles southeast of Antigua, has an informal and highly regarded public market that sells a wide variety of fine handmade textiles. The traditionally woven huipiles and tapestries are particularly beautiful, and local artisans are known throughout Guatemala for the tightness of their weave and their colorful combinations of floral and geometric designs, usually on an orange background. If you are interested, some of the women work part-time giving expert weaving lessons. Among those who have been recommended are Rafaela Godinez and Felipa López Zamora, as well as Carmelo and Zoila Guarn. Rates are very reasonable, a dollar or two an hour. Another attraction is the fiesta held here every June 13.

As the name implies, there are several hot springs in the area, although recent volcanic eruptions have shifted things underground and lowered their temperatures into the lukewarm range.

You can get to San Antonio Aguas Calientes from Antigua by bus via Ciudad Vieja or walk from the latter village in about an hour.

SANTA CATARINA BAHARONA

This village, which adjoins San Antonio Aguas Calientes, is best known for the exquisite ruin of its Spanish Colonial church. There are many friendly artesanía vendors on the streets of this quiet community and prices are reasonable. If you're interested in nature hikes, some of the local children will guide you through a maze of lush gardens to the natural springs that supply Santa Catarina with a constant flow of clean, cool water (and fill a public swimming pool near the plaza). Buses run regularly from Antigua or you can easily walk from San Antonio.

SAN ANDRÉS IXTAPA

A fairly large, nondescript town a few miles from the main road, San Andrex Ixtapa has a Tuesday market that is worth visiting, particularly for those interested in its intricately woven huipiles. A major fiesta and parade stirs things up on the last Saturday in January. But the big local attraction is the dark and mysterious **Capilla de San Simón**, a venerated shrine to the Maya god of fortune, carnal love, and celebration (also worshiped under the name Maximón in Zunil, Santiago Atitlán, and a few other highland villages).

This particular version of San Simón is more Ladino than Maya: wearing a cowboy hat, moustache, and western clothing. The idol sits on a glass-enclosed altar, before which eager supplicants gesture, genuflect, and seek his divine intervention in their lives. Candles of various colors (each representing a different request) are lit on benches that fill Simón's chapel and the air is filled with the odors of cigars and rum (the lusty saint craves both). Inquire among townspeople for the exact location of this shrine, which is tucked away on a side street. Foreigners are welcome to visit as long as they're unobtrusive and respectful. You can buy cheap replicas of San Simón from nearby vendors. Discreet photography is allowed with a donation to the chapel. The best way to get to San Andrés is by bus or car from Antigua, which is 17 miles to the southeast.

SAN FELIPE DE JESÚS

The main attraction here is a restored, whitewashed Gothic church that contains an image of Christ (called Jesus Sepultado) that some Guatemalans believe can cure their diseases. Many pilgrims journey here on the first Friday of Lent, and a major procession begins at the church on the afternoon of Good Friday. There's a fiesta commemorating the arrival of the icon on August 30.

At a well-known silver jewelry factory (**Platería Típica la Antigüeña**) a couple of blocks off the main plaza, you can watch craftspeople at work and then buy their creations, made from silver mined in the mountains of Alta Verapaz. You can walk to San Felipe in about 30 minutes via 6a. Avenida Norte or take one of the many buses leaving the Antigua terminal.

SAN JUAN DEL OBISPO

The palace of the first bishop of Guatemala is in this village, a few miles south of Antigua. **Bishop Francisco Marroquín's mansion** is enormous, giving you some idea of the splendor enjoyed by members of Guatemala's colonial Catholic hierarchy. Knock on the door and one of the 25 resident nuns will show you around.

There are regular buses from the Antigua terminal, or you can walk here in about an hour, through shaded coffee plantations, via Calle de los Pasos. The buses to Santa María de Jesus will also drop you in San Juan del Obispo.

SANTA MARÍA DE JESÚS

Located a few miles up the slope of Agua volcano from San Juan del Obispo, this is a picturesque village with good views of all three volcanoes. The trail to the top of Agua starts here, just beyond the cemetery. Fine huipiles are made in Santa María, and they can be purchased directly from the women who weave them.

Buses run several times a day from Antigua, or you can take a taxi or join a tour group. You must leave Antigua at about midnight if you expect to see the sunrise from atop the volcano. There is a small pensión for overnight visitors.

PARRAMOS AND CHIMALTENANGO

These towns are nondescript, but local attractions worth mentioning include **La Posada de mi Abuelo** (839-1842; fax 476-2870), a country inn near Parramos that offers horseback riding, mountain biking, and hiking in the area's forested hills. All rooms have private baths, hot water, fireplaces, phones, and are about $30. The hotel's restaurant serves typical Guatemalan cuisine.

In Chimaltenango, **La Casa de la Leyendas** is a full-service restaurant at Km. 56 on the Pan American Highway. The country ambiance is augmented by fine art, music, and other entertainment.

ANTIGUA'S VOLCANOES

The three volcanoes closest to Antigua vary considerably in accessibility. **Agua** is the shortest and easiest to climb—a communications array near the summit is served by a dirt road—and **Acatenango** is the tallest and most arduous. **Fuego** is very active, regularly venting lava, ash, steam, and noxious gases. For details on volcano climbs see Chapter 4, Special Interests.

As on all Guatemalan mountains, security has become an important issue for prospective climbers. In recent years several foreigners have been assaulted in the vicinity of Agua; you should inquire locally about the best routes and guides before heading up this or any other volcano.

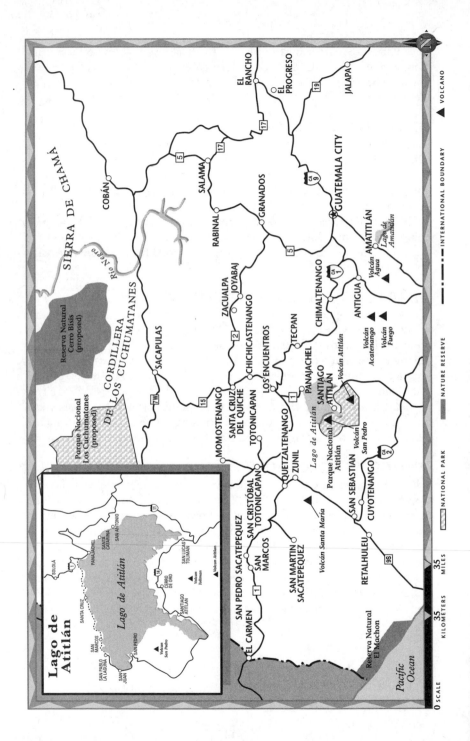

Lago de Atitlán

SIERRA DE CHAMÁ

Reserva Natural
Cerro Bisis
(proposed)

Parque Nacional
Los Cuchumatanes
(proposed)

CORDILLERA DE LOS CUCHUMATANES

Río Negro

COBÁN

SACAPULAS

7W

15

MOMOSTENANGO

SANTA CRUZ
DEL QUICHE

TOTONICAPAN

CHICHICASTENANGO

2

ZACUALPA

JOYABAJ

LOS ENCUENTROS

QUETZALTENANGO

ZUNIL

Volcán Santa María

SAN CRISTÓBAL
TOTONICAPAN

SAN PEDRO SACATEPEQUEZ

EL CARMEN

SAN
MARCOS

SAN MARTIN
SACATEPEQUEZ

RETALHULEU

9S

Reserva Natural
El Machón

Pacific
Ocean

PANAJACHEL

1

Lago de Atitlán

Parque Nacional
Atitlán

SANTIAGO
ATITLÁN

Volcán Atitlán

Volcán
San Pedro

SAN SEBASTIAN

CUYOTENANGO

CA
2

TECPAN

CHIMALTENANGO

CA
1

ANTIGUA

Volcán
Acatenango

Volcán
Fuego

Volcán
Agua

AMATITLÁN

Lago de
Amatitlán

GUATEMALA CITY

CA
9

GRANADOS

5

RABINAL

SALAMA

5

17

17T

EL
RANCHO

EL
PROGRESO

19

JALAPA

Lago de Atitlán (inset)

SOLOLÁ

17

SANTA CRUZ

SANTA
CATARINA

SAN ANTONIO

PANAJACHEL

SAN
MARCOS

SAN PABLO
LA LAGUNA

SAN
JUAN

SAN PEDRO

Volcán
San Pedro

Lago de Atitlán

CERRO DE ORO

14

1

SANTIAGO
ATITLÁN

SAN LUCAS
TOLIMÁN

Volcán
Tolimán

Volcán Atitlán

SCALE

0   35
KILOMETERS

0   35
MILES

▨ NATIONAL PARK

▨ NATURE RESERVE

INTERNATIONAL BOUNDARY

▲ VOLCANO

7

THE WESTERN HIGHLANDS

The western highlands, in the view of many travelers, are what a journey to Guatemala is all about. Indeed, it is hard to imagine any first-time visitor leaving the country without spending at least a few days among the "living Maya" in the towns and villages of these rolling hills and towering volcanic mountains, a land of eternal springtime.

The Spanish conquered this area in the early 1500s, a time when the long-feuding highland tribes were in disarray. But the conquistadors failed to find the gold and silver they were hoping for and, except in the form of readily exploited indígena labor and religious conversion, the area was largely ignored by European immigrants.

Besides the strong, vibrant indigenous cultures, regional attractions include Lake Atitlán—dubbed "the most beautiful lake in the world" by English novelist Aldous Huxley—and the colorful market town of Chichicastenango, a must-see on the itinerary of most visitors to Guatemala. If you have time, visits to the historic cities of Quetzaltenango and Huehuetenango, with side trips to Todos Santos, Chiantla, Aguacatán, and other villages in the Cuchumatanes range, are also highly recommended.

The most heavily populated parts of the western highlands range in altitude from about 5,000 to 8,000 feet above sea level, although some river valleys dip lower and a few volcanoes rise to over 13,000 feet. The temperature averages 60 degrees Fahrenheit all year long with a mild climate similar to coastal Southern California.

Buses are the main form of transportation in the western highlands, and here, as elsewhere, the aisles are no wider than a foreigner's hips and the vehicles are crowded with many more passengers than they were ever intended to carry. It is normal to cram four or five adults in a seat designed to hold two or three North American schoolchildren. There are no sanitary facilities and few, if any, rest stops.

If traveling for a distance of 60 miles or more, it is worth taking a first-class bus, or *pullman*, as they are known in Guatemala. The tickets are slightly more expensive, but for only a few extra dollars the comfort level is improved astronomically. A pullman offers assigned seats in Greyhound-style vehicles, usually with a bathroom (occasionally functional), air conditioning, and comfortable, reclining seats.

CHICHICASTENANGO

Location: In a high mountain valley about 90 miles (2 hours) west of Guatemala City and 24 miles north of Panajachel.
Population: 9,000 (1999 estimate).
Services: There is a Banco del Ejército on 6a. Calle, a block off the plaza, and, for a fee, the Mayan Inn will also change money for non-guests. The Telgua long-distance telephone station and post office are on 7a. Avenida near 8a. Calle, about ten blocks from the plaza. Besides the market vendors, several small stores sell food, drinks, and sundries. The town also has a couple of pharmacies.
For More Information: There is no tourist office in Chichi, but reliable registered guides hang around the market and plaza, ready to bargain over the price of a tour. The larger hotels are a good source of information about the specifics of what to see and do here.

Since the 1200s, Chichicastenango has been a trading center, mainly because historically it occupied a kind of geographically neutral zone between the domains of the frequently squabbling Quiché, Cakchiquel, and Tzutuhil Maya.

Things to See and Do

Chichicastenango is a Quiché Maya community famous for its dazzlingly **colorful markets**, held every Thursday and Sunday morning in the main plaza. This is one of the largest markets in all of Central America: Textiles, wooden masks, leather goods, hand-embroidered huipiles, jewelry, pottery, and other craftwork are found here, along with flowers, produce, hardware, and other domestic items. Even Spanish colonial coins and ancient pottery shards occasionally are sold.

Although heavily touristed, the "Chichi" market is a marvelous place to mingle with the full-blooded Maya of the 20th century, whose faces

Folk Catholicism

Indigenous and Roman Catholic customs are mixed freely and openly in Chichicastenango, and you will see the devout burning incense and lighting candles on the steps of both churches, then crossing themselves as they step inside to pray or to attend mass. During Semana Santa (Holy Week) the mingling of traditions is especially evident, as parish priests and Maya religious leaders from the ancient prayer brotherhoods known as cofradías join in the ritual parading of Christian icons from the cathedral through the streets of the village.

Because the expense of the community's many elaborate religious ceremonies is too great for a single individual or family to bear, the cofradías provide a means for villagers to work together to keep these important rituals alive. The brotherhood's members, called cofrades, are dedicated to the service of various Christian saints, whose images also symbolize sacred spirits or gods from the Maya religion. Throughout the western highlands, each god's distinctive dominion—the sun, moon, rain, clouds, and even corn—is inextricably woven with Christianity's Holy Trinity and the saints of Catholicism. Each year the most respected men of the village proudly take turns serving in the cofradías and carrying out the special spiritual and secular duties associated with them. In Chichi, the cofradía has 14 members, each with six to eight cofrades, who in turn look after the image of a particular saint.

Among the Maya the gods have always required a yearly round of sacrifice and prayer to perpetuate the miracle of life. Today the cofradía and shaman participate in the rites of baptism, fasting, supplication, and incense-burning that give their followers a sense of seamless infinity. Many of the Maya view Catholicism as something foretold in their ancient prophecies, which said that a day would come when bearded men would arrive from the ocean bringing new forms of religion.

could be models for the stone carvings at Tikal and whose clothing patterns are often the same designs found in paintings created a millennium ago. The marketplace itself is laid out according to a precise, age-old system: flowers sold on the steps of the Church of Santo Tomás, food sold around the plaza fountain, and so on. Sunday is always the bigger of the two weekly markets.

Market-day preparation begins the night before, and good bargains can be found at this uncrowded time, when poles and canvas are erected to shelter the individual stalls. Prices tend to go up with each passing hour on market day, especially after tourist buses begin discharging their more affluent passengers around 9:00 a.m.

The main attraction on the plaza is the massive, whitewashed **Church of Santo Tomás**, built around 1540 on the site of a Maya temple and still in daily use. Non-indígena should enter the church only through the side entrance, never through the front, since the Quiché believe that permission must be obtained from the guardian spirits of the massive front door—something you will see each indígena do as he or she approaches the doorway, while a holy man swings a coffee-can censer full of smoking *pom* (copal incense) or tends a perpetual fire in a concrete altar called a *quemada*. If you decide to sit in the pews of Santo Tomás, it is recommended that you also follow the custom of men on the left side, women on the right. Notice the blaze of candles throughout the church lighted in honor of the saints, ancestors, and Maya deities. Photography is not allowed inside Santo Tomás without permission. Here, as elsewhere, the modern Maya are tolerant of visitors as long as they are respectful.

Maya indígena in front of the Church of Santo Tomás

A few steps away from the church, on the south side of the plaza, is a **museum** housing the collection of hundreds of Mayan artifacts and jewelry pieces presented to Father Ildefonso Rossbach, a well-loved American-born priest at the church from 1894 until his death in 1944. There is a nominal admission fee to the museum, which is open from 8:00 a.m. to noon and from 2:00 p.m. to 5:00 p.m. every day except Tuesday.

Facing Santo Tomás on the

May I Take Your Picture?

A reminder: If you try to photograph indigenous people here, as elsewhere in Guatemala, many will turn or cover their faces. Photography is relatively new to rural Maya culture and some people feel it steals something from them. Many of those who agree to be photographed expect something from you in return. Most will be happy with a quetzal or two, but virtually all will be even more delighted if you send them a copy of the picture. Try to obtain a name and address and mail it to them after your return. Another option is to carry a Polaroid camera and hand them a print on the spot.

opposite side of the plaza is **El Calvario**, a smaller Catholic church used exclusively by the Maya for special prayers and services, particularly during Holy Week. Traditionally closed to outsiders, it should not be entered without permission or accompaniment by an indígena. The convent garden attached to it encloses the plaza on the west.

Next to Santo Tomás, enclosing a small courtyard, is a former **monastery** built in 1542 and now used as a church office. It was here that Spanish priest Francisco Ximénez became the first foreigner to see the **Popol Vuh**, the rarest and most sacred book of the Quiché (also spelled K'iche'). A kind of cross between the Bible and the Bhagavad Gita, this document revealed Quiché history and many details about traditional Maya spiritual beliefs and practices dating back to the Classic era. Unlike other Catholic officials, who destroyed such materials whenever they found them, Father Ximénez became fascinated by the Popol Vuh and in 1680 translated it into Spanish. His manuscript is preserved in Chicago's Newberry Library; the original text was lost over 200 years ago. It was Father Ximénez's respect for Quiché traditions that convinced indígena leaders in Chichicastenango to incorporate their own forms of worship into the Catholic faith.

Perched on a bluff northwest of the plaza, behind the Mayan Inn, is the *camposanto*, or **public graveyard**. At the front of the cemetery is a small chapel, surrounded by the large tombs of the prosperous. Toward

INGUAT

*Maya ritual in progress
at Pascual Abaj*

the rear are much simpler grave markers and a small yellow tomb that holds the remains of Father Rossbach. Like other Guatemalan cemeteries, the camposanto comes alive on November 1 and 2, All Saints' and All Souls' Days, when families come to clean the graves and honor their dead with flowers, candles, food, and drink.

Another occasion of great religious fervor is the Fiesta of Santo Tomás, held between December 14 and December 21. It is a week full of music, the selling of handicrafts, singing, dancing, processions, merrymaking, and fireworks. The crowning event is the Palo Volador, in which costumed men dangle by ropes from a 60-foot maypole. On the last day of this festival, all the babies born during the previous year are brought en masse to the church of Santo Tomás for a group christening.

As for the Thursday and Sunday markets, you are best off discovering them on your own. Merchandise and prices change slightly from week to week, but quality is uniformly high. Bargaining is considered mandatory and a fair price is often about one-half or two-thirds of the figure first quoted by the seller. If you don't want to bargain, simply ask the vendor for "a special discount" or for his or her "best price."

Don't overlook the small shops and stalls near the plaza selling carved masks and other artesanía: Some are particularly interesting and well worth a few minutes of your time. A few favorites are **La Fábrica de Máscaras** (The Mask Factory), about one block from the main plaza; **Típica Aj-Kmab** (5a. Avenida 6-34), specializing in leather goods; **Barroco Boutique** (4a. Avenida San Juan 2-12), offering clothing and accessories; and **Patojitos** (6a. Calle 5-30), selling 100-percent cotton clothes.

Getting There

Buses pass through the town at least once every hour during daylight hours, arriving from Santa Cruz del Quiché to the north and Los Encuentros (15 miles south, on the Pan American Highway) to the south. Unless you are on one of the few direct buses to Chichi from the capital or Pana-

The Shrine of Pascual Abaj

Some of the original Quiché shrines and rituals have been maintained by local people. The most accessible to foreigners is Pascual Abaj, a pre-Columbian monument located atop a small hill within walking distance of the Chichicastenango plaza. Ceremonies involving live chicken sacrifices and incantations are regularly held here in front of a carved stone Mayan face, next to which a Christian cross has been placed. Flower petals, candles, and incense can usually be found scattered amid the bones and ashes surrounding these altars. If a ceremony or sacrifice is in progress as you approach the shrine, it is best to stay back unless you are beckoned forward.

To get to Pascual Abaj, follow 5a. Avenida, the street that runs downhill (south) from Santo Tomás, and turn right at the first corner, 9a. Calle. The road eventually becomes a trail and is marked by signs and arrows pointing the way to Pascual Abaj. You will pass through a pine forest and patches of thorny bushes along the way. (Chichicastenango means "the place of the purple nettles.") There are other Maya shrines and sacred caves in the hills around this area, but they are all off-limits to non-indígena.

The path to Pascual Abaj traverses the yard of the man who repairs and stores the village's ceremonial costumes, which you are welcome to photograph and examine. Masks, souvenirs, and cold drinks are sold here.

jachel, you will need to change at Los Encuentros for one of the frequent local vehicles making the trip (the town is about 30 minutes away).

Buses leave Chichi from various points around the market and plaza, usually stopping to pick up passengers near the post office on 7a. Avenida if they are headed south to Los Encuentros.

Tourist shuttles from Antigua, Panajachel, and Quetzaltenango operate frequently on market days. Check with hotels or local travel agencies. Expect to pay between $15 and $20 for a minibus shuttle from Antigua; slightly less from Panajachel and a touch more from Guatemala City. These vans usually leave by 7:30 a.m. on market days.

Where to Stay in Chichicastenango

Hotels fill up quickly in Chichicastenango on evenings before market days, and the prudent course is to make a phone reservation well in advance.

Casa de Huespedes Girón, 6a. Calle 4-52; $10, $15 with bath; 756-1156. Motel-style rooms opposite the vegetable market.

Chalet, 3a. Calle "C" 7-44; $15; 756-1360, fax 756-1347. One of the better budget hotels.

Hotel Santo Tomás, 7a. Avenida 5-32; $70 and up; 756-1061, fax 756-1306. Expensive, modern hotel on the road from Guatemala City. Built in a colonial style around a central courtyard, it has a decent bar and restaurant. Many of its 43 rooms are furnished with antiques. Free overnight parking is available at the Shell gas station next to the Hotel Santo Tomás.

Hotel Villa Grande, on a hillside on the outskirts of town; $75; tel/fax 756-1053. The usual amenities in 67 upscale rooms.

The Maya Lodge, on the plaza, is a basic hospedaje and not to be confused with the Mayan Inn. It has received consistently mixed reviews from travelers and is not recommended. Terrible meals.

The Mayan Inn, 8a. Calle and 3a. Avenida; $80–$100; 756-1176, fax 756-1212. A 30-room hotel stuffed with colonial antiques and built around a shaded Spanish-style courtyard full of beautiful flowers. This inn is known for its excellent dinners, served by waiters dressed in traditional Quiché clothing and accompanied by a marimba orchestra. The Maya was built in 1932 by the American-Guatemalan family that owns Clark Tours. Each room has a fireplace, private bath, and hot water. The elegant bar and restaurant are pricey but worth a visit. Horseback and car tours can by arranged at the hotel desk. The best of the luxury hotels in Chichi.

Pensión Belén, 12a. Calle 5-55; $7, $10 with bath; 756-1244. The communal toilet is often dirty, but the rooms are clean enough.

Pensión Chugüila, 5a. Avenida 5-24; $35; 756-1134. Modest 35-room hotel about 2 blocks north of the plaza near the Arco Gucumatz, a distinctive arch across the roadway. Rooms, most with baths and some with fireplaces, overlook a courtyard and restaurant. Both the pensión and café are good values, highly recommended.

Where to Eat in Chichicastenango
Hotel restaurants serve the best food in town (at the highest prices), but there are also inexpensive eateries around the plaza. They include:

La Fonda Tzijclaj, above the produce market, is a good choice for both international and regional dishes. Excellent view of the plaza.

La Villa de los Cofrades, on the second floor of the Girón Building, above the interior courtyard (where produce is sold). Great people-watching and the best breakfast in town.

Tziguán Tinamit, at 5a. Avenida and 6a. Calle near Pensión Chugüila. Serves perfectly decent typical Guatemalan meals and even pizza. Big portions at reasonable prices. Recommended.

AROUND CHICHICASTENANGO

SANTA CRUZ DEL QUICHÉ
Location: About 30 minutes (14 miles) north of Chichicastenango.
Population: 12,000 (1999 estimate).
Services: There is a Banco de Guatemala on the concrete-paved central plaza where you can change money.
For More Information: There is no tourist office; your best bet is to inquire at local hotels for information about things to see and do here.

The capital of the department of Quiché lies north of Chichicastenango on a paved road that passes the Laguna Lemoa, a small lake said to have been formed by the tears wept by the wives of Quiché leaders after their husbands were killed by the Spanish.

Things to See and Do
Santa Cruz, called simply "Quiché" by the locals, is a good base for exploring the surrounding villages or for catching a bus into the Ixil Triangle and beyond. There are good markets here on Thursday and Sunday:

Palm-woven hats are a local specialty (often made by women while they amble down the street!), and high-quality textiles (especially the shoulder bags called *morrales*) are sold at excellent prices.

The plaza's large **colonial church** was built by Dominican friars, with stone blocks taken from the nearby Maya ruins of Utatlán, also known as K'umarcaaj. (Utatlán's ornamental stonework is also embedded in the walls of the nearby courthouse.) Inside the church is a poignant memorial to the many Catholic friars in the department who lost their lives during the unrest of the 1970s and 1980s. The violence became so severe that all priests were withdrawn from Quiché for a time.

There is a major fiesta on May 3 and another around the middle of August, plus eight other minor festivals each year.

Getting There
Buses arrive and depart at least once each hour for points to the south and north. The terminal is on the edge of town. Daily buses run to the Zone 4 terminal in Guatemala City (via Chichi), Joyabaj, Nebaj, Uspantán, Quetzaltenango, and San Marcos. Allow about 5 hours by bus from Guatemala City, 30 minutes from Chichicastenango. There is no first-class transportation and local buses are especially crowded on market days (Thursday and Sunday).

Where to Stay and to Eat in Santa Cruz del Quiché
The best meals are served in the more upscale hotels, or try the simple restaurants on or near the plaza, such as **Las Rosas**. Lodging choices are also limited, but you will find rooms at the following places.

Gumarkaah, 3a. Calle 8-05; $6; 755-1649; 17 rooms.

Posada Calle Real, 2a. Avenida 7-36; $7; 755-1438. With hot water, the best of a meager lot.

San Pascual, 7a. Calle 0-43; $6; 756-1107; 33 rooms.

UTATLÁN (K'UMARCAAJ) RUINS
Location: 2 miles west of Santa Cruz del Quiché.
Hours: Open (for a 25¢ fee) from 8:00 a.m. to 4:30 p.m. daily.
Services: Camping is permitted; pit toilet but no other services here.
For More Information: Inquire locally.

West of Santa Cruz del Quiché are the unrestored ruins of the ancient Quiché Maya capital, the most powerful city in the highlands before it was razed by the Spanish in 1524. Founded in the early 1400s as Gumarcaaj (sometimes spelled K'umarcaaj), the site was renamed Utatlán by Pedro de Alvarado after he proudly sacked the town.

Utatlán was never rebuilt after its destruction, and only a few temples, palaces, and stone monuments are still recognizable amid the mounds of pine-forested rubble and badly eroded foundations. Visitors may notice various trenches dug by archaeologists, treasure hunters, and local residents. Buried rubble lies beneath several square miles.

About 50 feet beneath the main plaza are several human-made tunnels (bring a candle or flashlight if you have one, although the latter are rented here for a few cents) that extend underground about 300 feet. About 100 yards from the site is a small ceremonial cave (look for the handwritten sign pointing "*a la cueva*"). These and other sacred monuments at the site are still used by local Maya shamans (or *K'ichee Aj Q'Ij*) and *brujos* (lay priests) for devotions to ancestors and the earth deity that include animal sacrifices and the burning of incense, candles, and sugarcane alcohol. One shaman, Manuel Pacheco, will sometimes perform blessing ceremonies for tourists in return for a donation to his fund for widows and orphans.

The chambers beneath Utatlán reportedly still serve as tombs for members of the Quiché elite. You will probably notice chicken feathers, ashes, and flower petals from recent ceremonies strewn about the tunnels and aboveground ruins. Be careful as you explore these catacombs— there are several very deep vertical pits.

A small museum near the entrance has a scale model of Utatlán as it originally appeared.

Getting There
You can easily reach Utatlán from Santa Cruz del Quiché by car or taxi, or on foot (in about an hour). Taxis will charge about $7 and wait while you visit the site. From the plaza, head south on 2a. Avenida to 10a. Calle; turn right and follow the road all the way to the ruins, set in a pleasant grove of pines.

NORTH AND EAST OF SANTA CRUZ DEL QUICHÉ
A winding road (Route 15) continues north through the hills from Quiché to the outskirts of Cunén, where one branch (Route 3) heads north to Nebaj (in the Ixil Triangle) and another branch goes east (Route 7-W) all the way to Cobán, via Uspantán and San Cristóbal Verapaz. The latter road is seldom traveled by foreigners, although it passes through beautiful mountain country and some very traditional Quiché villages.

Things to See and Do

On the way to Cunén, Route 15 passes through San Pedro Jocopilas, Rancho de Teja, and Sacapulas, where there is a turnoff (Route 7-W) for Huehuetenango. A hot, dusty town on the Río Chixoy, **Sacapulas** has a proud colonial church dating from 1554, and some geothermal hot springs are located nearby. There is a good market on the plaza (beneath the big ceiba trees) every Thursday and Sunday. You will see local women in lace huipiles who tie their hair with fancy pom-poms. If you get stranded in Sacapulas, there are a few basic *pensiónes* and *comedores*, but none to be recommended. Area Verde Expeditions of Antigua runs **white-water trips** down the Río Chixoy from here (see Chapter 4: Special Interests and Activities).

Near Cunén, 10 miles northeast of Sacapulas on Route 7-W, is a small cave that has been used by the local Maya since ancient times. It is often flooded by a swift-flowing river but may be accessible during the dry season.

A separate road (Route 2) heads directly east from Santa Cruz del Quiché through scenic hill country to the villages of Chiché, Chinique, Zacualpa, Joyabaj, and eventually, Guatemala City. Other than the Saturday market and church (a virtual replica of Santo Tomás in Chichicastenango) at Chiché, the most interesting destination is **Zacualpa**, where small shops sell exquisitely woven wool bags. The women also weave (and wear) unusually good-looking red and purple huipiles. Pretty huipiles are also made in otherwise drab Joyabaj, where the men of the village

How You Can Help

One of the most effective projects started on the displaced indígena's behalf is the nonprofit Shawcross Aid Programme for Highland Indígena (Apartado Postal 343, Antigua), which helps install potable water systems, build schools, buy vegetable seeds, and pay teachers. You can write to this worthy group if you would like to volunteer time, expertise, or money on behalf of the Ixil Maya. Weavings are sold at Shawcross headquarters in Nebaj.

are suspended from a 60-foot Palo Volador during fiesta (the second week of August).

THE IXIL TRIANGLE

Although not many tourists take the trouble to visit this remote part of Guatemala, it is one of the nation's richest areas in terms of indigenous culture and natural beauty. Inquire locally about hiking suggestions (some areas may be unsafe). These highland valleys of Quiché are the last stronghold of the Ixil Maya, who suffered tremendously during the social unrest of the 1970s and 1980s. Some of the indígena displaced by the civil unrest and government policies are gradually returning to their homeland.

The Ixil originally occupied a roughly triangle-shaped region bounded on the north by the Río Xaclbal basin, on the east by the Río Chixoy, and on the west and south by the rugged Cuchumatanes Mountains. The territory of this tight-knit ethnic group has shrunk to only three main villages. Many of the men still seasonally migrate to the coast to harvest coffee on the many large plantations there.

NEBAJ

Location: 55 miles north of Santa Cruz del Quiché.
Population: 6,000 (1999 estimate).
Services: Nebaj has the only bank in the area (Bancafé) and traveler's checks can be cashed here. Money cannot be drawn, however, from credit cards.
For More Information: The Ixil Hotel, Maya Inca, and Pensión de las Tres Hermanas (see below) are good sources of local travel tips.

The southern gateway to the Ixil-speaking area, Nebaj lies in the corner of a long, isolated valley. Almost all of the women still dress in the traditional manner, as do a few older men. The huipiles worn here are particularly stunning, with embroidered figures of dancing birds and animals. A twisted and braided strip of colored cloth is worn as a headdress, and a bright red skirt completes the outfit. Some of the men still wear short red jackets that imitate the design worn by Spanish officers stationed in Nebaj three to four centuries ago.

Things to See and Do

The quality of the weaving in Nebaj is excellent, and traje can be purchased at good prices during the Wednesday market or from craftspeople in their homes. Well-made crocheted cloth bags are also for sale. Some of the young girls and women sell huipiles to foreigners, and a few give weaving lessons.

There is a big annual fiesta here during the second week of August, ending—with processions and much drinking and dancing—on August 15.

There is not much to see in Nebaj itself beyond the daily routines of indígena life, although there is an interesting **colonial church** on the plaza. Some modest and unrestored **pre-Columbian ruins,** just outside the town, are still the site of sacred rituals. About 30 mounds and pyramid structures were excavated by the Carnegie Institution in 1947, yielding lovely ceramics, jade, and alabaster artifacts, some of which are now on display at the Museum of Archaeology in Guatemala City and the British Museum in London. Maya occupation took place between A.D. 600 and 800, and the site is noted for the explicit historical scenes found painted on polychrome burial pots.

The **mountain trails** around Nebaj are very lovely, especially one leading to the remote village of **Acul**. The morning crispness is well suited to trekking and in 2 hours you'll cross a mountain ridge through a cloud forest. Near Acul is the **Finca San Antonio**, owned by an Italian-descended family that is reputed to make the best cheese in the country. Stop by for a tour and low-cost samples. Don't forget that the locally grown apples are famous throughout Guatemala for their delicious flavor (and go well with cheese). You can walk back to Nebaj by the (much longer) road, passing a spectacular double-waterfall along the way.

Getting There

Several buses a day shuttle between Nebaj and Santa Cruz del Quiché via Sacapulas. It is a 2-hour bus ride from Santa Cruz del Quiché (departures between 7:00 a.m. and 11:00 a.m.) to Sacapulas and another hour to Nebaj. There is also direct service several times each week to Huehuetenango and Guatemala City.

Where to Stay and to Eat in Nebaj

Note: The community has no telephones but rooms are usually available. Other restaurants in Nebaj besides those listed below are very simple and are clustered on or near the plaza. **Irenés** and **Delicias** are acceptable. A woman named Juana Marcos Solís offers meals in her home that can be combined with a traditional Maya "sweat lodge" behind her house (she also gives weaving lessons).

Hospedaje Esperanza, at the corner of 6a. Avenida and 3a. Calle; $4, shared bath with hot water. The upstairs rooms are nicest.

Ixil Hotel, 5a. Avenida at 10a. Calle; $4. Near the town's entrance, this hotel offers seven basic rooms.

Los Viejitos, Batxbaca 6-92. Splendid soups and Italian dishes. Look for the green door.

Maya Inca, 5a. Calle near the plaza. Delicious Peruvian and Guatemalan food, cooked by Lima-born Alberto Heredia and his Ixil wife, Elena Gómez. Tasty pastries and good coffee, too.

Pensión de las Tres Hermanas, a block off the plaza; $2, shared bath. Damp, basic sleeping rooms clustered around an interior courtyard. The straw mattresses are notoriously uncomfortable and blankets are in short supply. Hearty meals ($1.50, order in advance) are prepared by the friendly, 70ish sisters who run the place.

SAN JUAN COTZAL
Location: 11 miles northeast of Nebaj.
Population: 3,000 (1999 estimate).
For More Information: Inquire locally.

The town of San Juan Cotzal lies east of Nebaj over a scenic mountain road. This road is often very muddy and therefore the town is time-consuming to reach by the infrequent bus. Cotzal is even more traditional in its dress and customs than Nebaj, although less interesting as a place to visit. Cotzal's old mission church, for example, was bombed during the recent civil war and never rebuilt. (A carved image of cigar-smoking, rum-drinking San Judas—known elsewhere as Maximón or San Simón—holds court on the steps of the ruin during Holy Week.) The residents grow maguey cactus and weave ropes and bags from the plant's stringy fibers. The women wear elaborate green huipiles. Market day is Thursday.

Getting There
There are infrequent buses from Nebaj or you can try hitching a ride on a supply truck. You can also hike from Nebaj in a few hours.

Where to Stay and to Eat in Cotzal
Other than what may be offered in private homes, there are no accommo-dations or services, except for a pharmacy that is said to rent rooms and serve meals to Cotzal's infrequent visitors.

CHAJUL
Location: 13 miles northeast of Nebaj.
Population: 4,500 (1999 estimate).
For More Information: Inquire locally.

Along with Nebaj and San Juan Cotzal, Chajul is the only sizable community in Guatemala where the Ixil language is still widely spoken. Chajul was established during colonial times through the forced merger of 11 separate villages. As in Nebaj, the women wear gorgeous hand-woven huipiles, decorated with fanciful animal figures, and brilliant red skirts. They also wear unusual earrings made from strands of cloth to which colonial era coins have been affixed. The men's red coats are a stylistic adaptation of those worn by the Spanish conquistadors. Some of the men and boys still hunt with blow-guns, a practice that dates back to pre-Columbian times. Among the more interesting weavings here are a napkin (*servilleta*), headcloth (*caragador*), scarf (*bufanda*), and cape (*perraje*). Market day is Tuesday.

An intriguing Christ of Golgotha figure in the massive **Chajul Colonial Church** is flanked by two carved figurines dressed like vigilant soldiers and is the object of pilgrimages on the second Friday of Lent, when there is a community-wide fiesta.

Several other traditional Ixil villages north of Chajul—including **Bisich, Visiquichum,** and **Batzchocola**—can be reached only by long hikes through the mountains.

About 6 miles north of Chajul is 9,000-foot **Cerro Bisís,** a forested wilderness that is under consideration as a government-decreed nature reserve. Although this is one of the last remnants of relatively pristine mountain habitat in the region, funding to protect the slopes of Cerro Bisís was still lacking as this book went to press. See it while you can.

Getting There
There is irregular bus service (about twice a week) from Nebaj. Unless you drive or hitch a ride, you will have to walk 2 hours from Cotzal to Chajul.

Where to Stay and to Eat in Chajul
Like San Juan Cotzal, Chajul receives few visitors, and you will have to ask around to find a sleeping room and meals. Inquire at the post office regarding a small pensión on the south side of town.

LAKE ATITLÁN
Location: Next to the town of Panajachel, about 70 miles west of Antigua and 100 miles west of Guatemala City.
For More Information: Panajachel Tourist Services (762-2337, fax 762-2112) on Calle Santander near Calle Principal, in Edificio Rincon, in Panajachel, can arrange local tours and shuttle transportation. Also recommended are Servicios Turisticos Ixchel (on Calle Santander) and Servicios Turisticos Atitlán (762-2246), both in Panajachel.

The World's Most Picturesque Lake

Traveling through the highlands by mule in the 1850s, American visitor William Brigham was stopped in his tracks by Lake Atitlán, which fellow writer Aldous Huxley later described as "too much of a good thing." Brigham wrote: "We lingered to photograph the view of Atitlán and its volcanoes. The sun was in our face, and shone over the silvery waters with the effect of moonlight. The three black giants — once so terrible, now so solemnly grand — kept back the surging sea cloud from the Pacific."

The famous 50-square-mile Lake Atitlán, dominated by the three towering volcanic peaks and the sheer cliffs that surround it, changes colors and moods by the minute. A few glimpses of Lake Atitlán can be seen along the Pan American Highway, but it must be seen close up to be fully appreciated.

Atitlán means "abundance of waters," and the lake more than lives up to its name. It is over 11 miles long, nearly 8 miles wide, and more than 1,000 feet deep in some places. Unfortunately, it is also becoming increasingly polluted: Swim here at your own risk. Note that a dangerous southern wind (called the *xomil*) often picks up in the afternoon.

Santiago Atitlán, wedged at the base of the volcanoes, is the most accessible traditional village on the shoreline, but most of the hotels, restaurants, and services are across the lake in the city of **Panajachel**, which can easily be reached by public bus, private car, or shuttle van. There is no airport. Hiking trails link some of the villages.

Getting There

A two-lane paved road winds for over an hour (some 25 miles) through the mountains from Chichicastenango to the town of Panajachel, on the northeast shore of Lake Atitlán. The zigzag route heads first to the four-way intersection of Los Encuentros, then along the Pan American Highway for a short distance before the El Cuchillo turnoff to Sololá and Panajachel.

Richard Mahler

The Panajachel ferry on Lake Atitlán

Where to Stay at Lake Atitlán

If you are planning to spend more than a few days at Lake Atitlán, you may prefer staying at one of the handful of small hotels located away from Panajachel. The most comfortable of these are around the villages of Santa Catarina and San Antonio Palopo, on the northeastern shore, as well as the west and south sides of the lake in Santiago, San Pedro, San Marcos, and Santa Cruz (see entries later in this chapter). All are much more isolated communities than Panajachel, which means you will have a chance to see a more traditional indigenous community close up. These locations are also considerably quieter and less touristy than Panajachel, but with fewer amenities.

PANAJACHEL

Location: About 100 miles west of Guatemala City.
Population: 6,000 (1999 estimate).
For More Information: INGUAT maintains an office on Calle Santander near its intersection with Calle Principal. This office is open from 8:00 a.m. to 6:00 p.m. except for the noon to 2 p.m. lunch break. It is also closed Monday afternoons and all day Tuesday. Transportation schedules are posted and the well-informed staffers speak English. Next door is a message center where you can send letters, faxes, and packages overseas. Tourist information is also

available at El Toro Pinto, opposite the Texaco station. A second INGUAT office has operated from time to time on the main public beach.

Nicknamed "Gringotenango" on account of its touristic image and substantial expatriate community, Panajachel ("Pana" to the locals) is home to many foreign-born exporters and entrepreneurs. Many Guatemaltecos also maintain vacation homes here, and the streets are full of *turistas* and urban Guatemalans alike on weekends and holidays. This surreal, almost carnival atmosphere is a turn-off to many visitors, yet this city is a good base for forays into the "real" Guatemala of the rural highlands. And where else in this blessed country can you attend a dream workshop, meet with a past-life regression counselor, or get your body adorned at a shop called BMW Tattoo?

Things to See and Do
There are few specific attractions in Pana itself, beyond the well-stocked daily market, creature comforts (a French bakery and Italian restaurants, for example), broad assortment of artesanía shops, and nicely restored colonial church. (The latter contains a statue of St. Francis of Assisi, patron saint of the city, in who's honor a festival is held October 1 through 7.) Panajachel is an ideal place to relax, however, particularly for those who have been shuttling around Guatemala in overcrowded buses on kidney-busting roads. The laid-back ambiance, pleasant beach, stunning sunsets, comfortable accommodations, and wide variety of bars and restaurants may be a welcome indulgence.

The main **shopping area** for artesanía is along Calle Santander above the public beach, although street vendors seem to be everywhere. Be prepared to bargain aggressively if you want to avoid paying tourist-targeted prices. You'll immediately be descended upon by children, who will pester you for the duration of your visit in their attempts to sell you hair ribbons, "friendship" bracelets, wood carvings, and other inexpensive items.

Panajachel is a good place for participating in the many forms of **outdoor recreation** available on and around Lake Atitlán, which maintains a year-round average water temperature of 65 degrees. The lake is well suited for fishing, sailing, canoeing, windsurfing, kayaking, and even snorkeling or diving. Conditions for each of these sports are excellent. The cliffs above Atitlán are also considered ideal for hang-gliding: Several national and international championship competitions are held here. On the placid waters below, regattas and sailboat races are regularly scheduled. And, of course, there is always volcano climbing. There are hiking trails that encircle the lake, but some sections are extremely steep and you should check locally about safety.

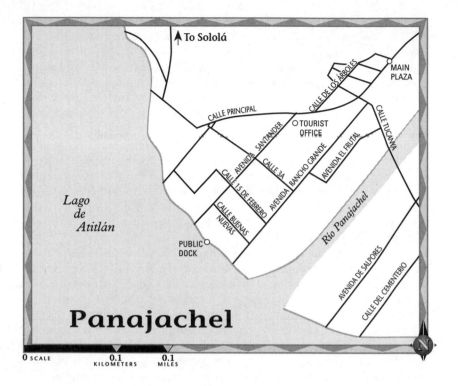

↑ To Sololá

MAIN PLAZA

CALLE DE LOS ÁRBOLES

CALLE PRINCIPAL

CALLE TUCANA

TOURIST OFFICE

AVENIDA SANTANDER

AVENIDA EL FRUTAL

AVENIDA RANCHO GRANDE

CALLE 3A

CALLE 15 DE FEBRERO

Lago de Atitlán

CALLE BUENAS NUEVAS

PUBLIC DOCK

Río Panajachel

AVENIDA DE SALPORES

CALLE DEL CEMENTERIO

Panajachel

0 SCALE   0.1 KILOMETERS   0.1 MILES

N

If you stay for more than a day, a visit to one or more of the 11 **traditional villages** around the lake is in order. Some can be reached on foot or by private car, motorcycle, or bicycle, others by public boat, bus, or horseback.

Orientation

Getting around in Panajachel itself is easy on foot or bicycle. Street names are somewhat confusing, however. The main street (part of the highway that continues on to Santa Catarina) is variously referred to as Calle Principal and Calle Real, with the latter predominating. Calle Rancho Grande is also known as Calle del Balneario. The Guatemalan government once renamed all the streets, giving them number and zone designations, so you will sometimes see two signs posted: One is the designated "government" name and the other is the name everybody uses.

Note that most businesses (except restaurants and *típica* shops or stalls) close from noon to 1:00 or 2:00 p.m.; most don't open at all on Sunday.

Transportation

The bus ride from Panajachel to Santiago Atitlán takes almost 2 hours; you're better off taking the public boat (1 hour) to this or any other community on the lake (except for those immediately adjacent to Pana). Each day between 8:30 a.m. and 10:30 a.m., several public passenger boats leave for Santiago Atitlán from docks along the beach. Check in front of the Hotel Tzanjuyu and Brisas del Lago restaurant. Some of the boats continue on to San Pedro la Laguna and other lakeside villages, making a complete circuit of the lake several times a day; alternately, you can be taken directly to these smaller communities by smaller craft. The bigger boats return from Santiago between 12:30 p.m. and 1:30 p.m. Passenger fares (the boats don't carry vehicles) are inexpensive, averaging around $3 for the 1-hour trip across the lake to Santiago (bigger boats sometimes take longer). You can buy tickets on board.

Because schedules, watercraft, and prices change fairly often, it is best to ask around to get current information about boat trips. Individual private boats can be chartered to specific destinations, but the price may be steep unless spread among several passengers. Try not to schedule any boat trip across the middle of the lake after 3:00 p.m., because the breeze from the coast inevitably kicks in and can make the surface very choppy.

BIGSA Moto Rent (762-1253 on Calle de los Arboles) is about the only place to rent an insured car (about $45 per day) or motorcycle. You can also try **Hotel Dos Mundos** (762-2251) or **Hotel Atitlán** (762-1429), which sometimes rent vehicles.

Taxis park in front of the Banco Inmobliario and charge about $2 for most Pana destinations. Some can be hired for day trips around the lake (price negotiable).

Visitor Information

One of the best all-round travel agencies is **Panajachel Tourist Services** (762-2337, fax 762-2112) on Calle Santander near Principal, in Edificio Rincón, across from INGUAT. They can arrange local tours, shuttle transportation, and airline ticketing. Also recommended are **Servicios Turisticos Ixchel** (Calle Santander) and **Servicios Turisticos Atitlán** (762-2246) on Santander in front of the Hotel Regis. The latter arranges good local sightseeing tours as well as reliable shuttle transportation to Guatemala's main cities.

Tour companies run direct minivan shuttles daily and these are a good value. They'll even pick you up at your hotel. Other private shuttles to and from Antigua, Chichicastenango, Guatemala City, Copán, Belize, and the Mexican border can easily be booked from travel agents and large hotels.

Colonial-era church on the main plaza of Panajachel

Richard Mahler

You'll pay a lot more than for a chicken-bus ticket, but you'll get there much faster and with some degree of comfort. Rates in 1999 were about $10 for a minibus to Chichicastenango, $15–20 to Antigua, and $25–30 for a ride to Guatemala City.

Services

The biggest bank in town is **Banco Agrícola Mercantil**, in the center of Panajachel next to the Mayan Palace Hotel. Changing foreign currency here is faster than in most Guatemalan cities and there is an ATM (*cajero automatico*) at **Banco Industrial** on Calle Santander. There is a third bank (**Inmobliaro**) in Panajachel on Principal and another in Sololá. Hours for all are 9 a.m. to 3 p.m.

Packages can be shipped to the U.S. and Europe from **Get Guated Out** (762-2015), a well-run parcel service on the second floor of the building next door to Café Al Chisme, on Calle de los Arboles. The same office handles overseas mail, faxes, and telegrams. **Américos Exports**, on Santander (762-2064), also provides parcel and air cargo service.

Panajachel Tourist Services at 1-30 Calle Santander (opposite INGUAT) offers e-mail services and Internet access (ungringo@ guate.net or panamail@guate.net).

The post office and a taxi stand are opposite the downtown cathedral, and a **Telgua** phone office is located on Calle Santander.

There are several bookstores in town, but current foreign newspapers and magazines are virtually impossible to find.

Spanish schools seem to come and go regularly in Panajachel (see Chapter 4), but they are not highly rated and there are much better places to study.

There are multiple laundry services in Pana: Look for signs reading *servicio lavado* or *lavandería*. Expect to pay $2 a load for an automatic washer (manual washing is much less expensive, but harder on your clothes).

The public market is past the city hall at the far end of Calle Principal. The main market day is Sunday, but you can buy fruits, vegetables, and incidentals here throughout the week. The police station is next to the town plaza, opposite the cathedral.

Shopping

For artesanía, try any of the shops and stalls along Calle Santander or Calle de los Arboles. Besides every item of clothing and textile imaginable, several will sell you the bolts of cloth, ribbon, yarn, and thread you need to make your own garments. High-quality antique masks and furniture are sold at **Ojalá**, located next to Café Cinema on Arboles. Original lithographs and other art objects are the specialties of **La Galería**, in a rambling, architecturally unique house on Calle del Balnearo (near the Hotel Rancho Grande).

Nightlife

There are several sports and disco bars in Pana. Among the more popular are **Nuan's**, **Circus Bar**, and **Ubu's Cosmic Café** (on Calle de los Arboles), and **Atlantis Mixer**, on Calle Rancho Grande. Nightlife here is pretty much limited to drinking, hanging out, watching videos (there are several "video bars," charging about $2 per movie), and more drinking. Recreational drugs are available, but why risk spending time in a Guatemalan jail?

Outdoor Recreation and Adventure Travel

A number of outfits rent bicycles and motorcycles for reasonable hourly rates (about $2 for bikes and $6 for motorcycles): Try **Moto Servicio Quiché** (762-2089) on Calle Principal and either **Taller Bicicletas Tono** or **Bicicletas Gaby** on Santander. Make sure you check the machine out and inquire about road conditions before going anywhere.

Entrepreneurs at the beach and larger hotels rent sailboats, rowboats, canoes, kayaks, motorboats, and other water recreation equipment. Touts will accost you constantly along the beach, trying to sell "tours" and to rent boats. Check around for the best prices, equipment, and guides. The **Atitlán** and several other large hotels can arrange horse and boat rentals. **Diversions Balam** (762-2242) rents water skis, windsurfers, sailboats, kayaks, canoes, and power boats. Rates start at about $2 for the use of such items. You can arrange a guided catamaran sailing excursion with **Veleros de Lago** for about $15 per person (about 5 hours). Sailing tours are also offered by **Ecotourism & Adventure Specialists** (361-3104).

Americans **Jim** and **Nancy Matison** offer guided horseback tours, starting at about $15 per hour or $40 per person for a day trip (meals included, inquire at 721-7167 or 201-5527), along Lake Atitlán and to its

The Butterfly Farm

About a mile northwest of Panajachel, tucked in a broad, lush valley (with the Hotel Atitlán), is El Mariposario San Buenaventura de Atitlán, a commercial butterfly breeding facility on a private nature reserve. Visitors are welcome to tour the farm and see some of the 35 native species it manages in screened, open-air cages. A few of these butterflies, like the magnificent Blue Morpho, are exported to butterfly parks around the world. There's a 25-minute loop nature trail with identification of shrubs, trees, and flowers native to the Lake Atitlán basin, as well as an old wagon road used by early residents.

For those who would like to spend the night along this peaceful, verdant stretch of beach, full-furnished vacation homes and hotel suites are available for rent. For information about the butterfly farm or to make lodging reservations, call 762-2059. Admission to the park (8:00 a.m. to 5:00 p.m.) is about $3.50 for adults, $2 for children. The butterfly farm is open from 10:00 a.m. to 3:00 p.m.

shoreline villages, with longer excursions to El Mirador (a viewpoint and nature reserve above Santiago Atitlán) and nearby volcanoes. Use the same numbers to inquire about recommended nature hikes and boat trips led by American expatriate **Lee Valenti**, a knowledgeable long-time resident.

Skydiving *(parapente)* is offered by **Ecotourism & Adventure Specialists** (361-3104), which also guides volcano trekkers.

Getting There
Hourly buses shuttle daily between Panajachel and Guatemala City from 5:00 a.m. to 2:00 p.m. The trip takes a minimum of 3½ hours on

a second-class bus (an hour less to Antigua) and costs less than $2. A more comfortable option is to take a first-class Quetzaltenango bus as far as the Pan American Highway turnoff at Los Encuentros, where there is frequent local service to Panajachel (some buses go only as far as Sololá). There are only a few direct public buses between Antigua and Panajachel; you will usually transfer at Chimaltenango en route, and possibly again at Los Encuentros. Buses leave from Calle Principal across from the Banco Inmobliario.

From Panajachel, there are several direct buses each day to Quetzaltenango, Chichicastenango, and around the lake to San Lucas Tolimán and Cocales, and from there on to the Pacific Coast. Avoid traveling on the "old road" through Patzún that approaches the lake from the southeast: many robberies have been reported along this route, and the roadbed is in poor repair. If you are going to Panajachel by rental or private car from anywhere, avoid driving at night.

Where to Stay in Panajachel

Cacique Inn, Calle Real; $60; 762-1205, fax 762-2053. Bar, restaurant. Pleasant lodge on the quiet western edge of town, popular among upscale tour operators. Each of 34 rooms is large; all have fireplaces for the surprisingly chilly nights. Non-guests can use the swimming pool for a small fee.

El Rosario, above the public beach; $20; 762-1491. Clean, well-maintained, with eight bungalows surrounded by lawns and gardens. A friendly indígena family runs the place.

Hotel Atitlán, Finca Buenaventura; $115; 360-8405, fax 334-0640, hotinsa@infovia.com.gt. Luxury resort isolated from the main part of Panajachel by a ridge along the Sololá road. Has 66 well-appointed rooms, a restaurant, bar, private beach, and gift shop. Nearby is a private nature reserve. If you don't mind being a long walk from town and cocooned in a rarefied upper-class atmosphere, this may be the place for you. Recommended.

Hotel Barceló del Lago, 2A. Avenida 6-17; $90–$135; 762-1555, fax 761-1233. $90-$135; Luxury hotel near the lake with premier views, good restaurant, large pool, and small health club. Popular with tour groups.

Hotel Dos Mundos, Calle Santander 4-72; $45; tel/fax 762-2078. Satellite TV, phones. Owned by an Italian and set in a shady, walled courtyard. Good *Italiano* restaurant on the premises.

Hotel Rancho Grande, Calle Rancho Grande; $40 and up, includes large breakfast; 762-1554, fax 762-2247. On one of Panajachel's more pleasant (and quiet) side streets. There are 12 rooms, several with fireplaces. German-Guatemalan owner Marlita Hannstein and her staff are well informed and helpful. Recommended as an excellent value.

Hotel Maya Kanek, Calle Principal; $15; 762-1104. Decent rooms, private showers, shaded courtyard. Recommended.

Hotel Regis, Calle Santander; $40; 762-1149, fax 762-1152. A long-time favorite, with a restaurant, satellite TV, and the heavenly hot showers that derive their water from an underground thermal spring. Recommended.

Las Casitas, on Calle Principal near the cathedral; $12; 762-1224. Clean bungalow-style rooms, lots of hot water, and the option of three home-cooked meals a day.

Mario's Rooms, Calle Santander; $12; 762-1313. Small, basic rooms, and a tiny restaurant where you can eat delicious crepes for breakfast.

Monterrey, Calle Monterrey, near the beach; $40; 762-1126. On a secluded street near a coffee finca. Good value.

Müller's Guest House, Calle Rancho Grande; $30; 776-0409, fax 334-4294. Quiet, well-kept; stellar reputation. Secure parking.

Paradise Inn, Calle del Río; $18; 762-1021. Near the Río Panajachel and the lake; it has a bar and small café.

Zulema's Rooms, Calle de Balneario; $7. At the bottom end of the price scale are basic accommodations such as Zulema's marked by simple hand-painted signs in the back alleys of town. Expect little more than a room with a mattress, and a bathroom down the hall. Zulema's is the author's favorite.

Other Options

A public campground is near the beach, across the Río Panajachel from the city itself, next to the cemetery and a residential area called Jucanyá. This area has a reputation for theft, however, so campers may want to try the private campground (762-2479) next to the cemetery, which rents tents, camp stoves, and hammocks ($1 or $2 each).

Yet another option is the more expensive private campground at

Hotel Visión Azul, on the opposite side of Panajachel. It has electrical hook-ups and water for recreational vehicles.

Small houses or rooms with kitchens can also be rented by the day, week, or month in Panajachel. Monthly rates begin around $130. Look for posted signs or simply ask around. Rates vary considerably depending on what is being offered and whether it is high season. During Semana Santa rooms of any kind may be difficult to find.

Where to Eat in Panajachel

There are plenty of inexpensive fast-food restaurants and comedores along Calle Santander. Some of Pana's cafés hire itinerant musicians who provide excellent dinner accompaniment, from flamenco to folk.

Al Chisme, Calle de los Arboles. A festive and fun expatriate hangout that serves food of consistently high quality (if a bit overpriced).

Cafetería las Palmeras, Calle Santander near the Regis. Sit outside and watch the world walk by while you sip your beverage of choice.

Casablanca, corner of Calle Principal and Calle Santander. For those ready to splurge: high-quality meals (especially fish) in elegant surroundings.

The Deli Restaurant, on Calle Principal next to Hotel Galindo. Arguably the best breakfast in town: homemade waffles, oatmeal, fruit *licuados*, fresh eggs, and more. Excellent value.

El Bistro, at the beach end of Calle Santander. Excellent Italian food and salads; the portions are large, but unfortunately so are the prices.

El Cisne, Avenida Rancho Grande. Inexpensive and satisfying. A typical Guatemalan menu that includes fresh lake fish (usually *lobina*, which is non-native black bass).

El Tocoyal, at the foot of Avenida Rancho Grande, above the beach. Fine food and drink, plus views of spectacular sunsets. Watching the sun's orange disk slip behind the San Pedro volcano is a sight not soon forgotten.

Hsieh and **Selvananda's**, both on Calle los Arboles, serve reliably delicious vegetarian cuisine.

La Laguna, Calle Principal. Serves *pepián*, the wonderfully-spiced chicken stew that is Guatemala's national dish. Outdoor dining, too.

La Posada del Pintor, on Calle los Arboles. Pizza and mixed drinks.

Mama Luna, on Calle Principa. Features everything from burritos to bagels.

Manchón Típica Atitlán, Calle Santander. A simple eatery that does a fine job with local fish.

Pana Pan, Calle Principal. Breakfast is good but the coffee is terrible.

Restaurante El Dragon, Calle Santander. German-run specialist in vegetarian dishes and curries. The cuisine is creative and delicious (all veggies and salad ingredients are carefully disinfected).

LAKE ATITLÁN VILLAGES
A road (not completely paved) goes around the eastern and southern sides of the lake but does not reach all Atitlán villages. Some are accessible only on motorbike, bicycle, or foot via narrow trails. The villages on the northwest shoreline are the most difficult to get to because the trails becomes steep and arduous: not passable for motorcycles or bicycles. Each community can be reached by boat, however, and you might consider walking for part of your journey, then returning by water.

INGUAT publishes a detailed map of the Lake Atitlán area that is distributed free in Panajachel at hotels, shops, and restaurants as well as the local INGUAT office (on Calle Santander near Calle Principal).

Public buses shuttle daily between Panajachel and all villages served by roads. The first bus to San Lucas Tolimán leaves about 6:30 a.m. and takes about an hour. Passenger boats run daily to all the villages between Panajachel and Santiago Atitlán, on the north and west sides of the lake.

SANTA CATARINA PALOPÓ
This shoreline village, 5 miles east of Panajachel, has gradually shifted from an economy based on fishing and fresh-water crab collection to one geared to textile production, mostly for the tourist market. The local women's costume is made up of three panels, its waistline displaying geometric figures handwoven in a brocade of bright colors, with violet dominating. The men's clothing repeats the pattern in a tighter brocade. Fiesta day is November 25. Buses run frequently from Pana, or you can easily walk or take a taxi.

Where to Stay and Eat in Santa Catarina Palopó
Villa Santa Catarina, $50; 762-1291. With 31 rooms and a restaurant, at a spectacular location overlooking the lake.

SAN ANTONIO PALOPÓ

San Antonio, 2 miles east of Santa Catarina, is a larger and more traditional village than Santa Catarina. The indígena dress is traditional costumes of red shirts and wool skirts, sometimes accompanied by turban-style hats. Residents tend terraced hillside gardens of onions, anise, beans, and corn, also working maguey and reed fibers into ropes and mats. The village fiesta is held June 13. Buses run frequently from Panajachel, or you can walk or take a taxi.

Where to Stay and Eat in San Antonio Palopó

An unmarked pensión, run by a Peruvian woman, is a budget alternative: Ask locally for directions. No phone, $7.

Hotel Terrazas del Lago, $26; 232-8741. Run by a Polish expatriate, beautifully located near the lake, with 15 rooms. Serves fine meals.

SAN LUCAS TOLIMÁN AND CERRO DE ORO

A largely Ladino village in a heavily cultivated area (mostly coffee) on the southeast arm of the lake, San Lucas has little to recommend it except a stunning colonial church, Friday market, and the trailhead to the top of the Atitlán and Tolimán volcanoes. About 20 miles south of Panajachel, the paved road from the Pan American Highway branches at San Lucas, with one fork heading to Santiago and the other to Cocales and the Pacific Coast. A small dirt road continues 2 miles northwest to the tiny village of Cerro de Oro, whose old, recently restored church has an unusual mural showing Christ dressed in the purple and white costume of the local Maya. Some artifacts from this church have been moved to a modern structure nearby. Buses run frequently from Pana and the Pacific Coast.

Where to Stay and Eat in San Lucas Tolimán

Brisas del Lago, $10; no phone. The only hotel/restaurant in town.

SANTIAGO ATITLÁN

Location: About 16 miles southwest of Panajachel, across the lake.
Population: 17,000 (1999 estimate).
Services: There's a post office near the mercado and a Telgua phone station a block past the Hotel Tzutujil.
For More Information: For suggestions on where to go and what to do, stop by the tourist information kiosk (on the right as you walk up the steps from the dock). INGUAT maintains modern showers and restrooms next to the kiosk. The American-owned Posada de Santiago (see below) is also a good information resource.

Santiago's Maximón

As in many highland villages, Santiago's religious customs mix indigenous beliefs with Catholic ideology. For instance, residents still pay their respects to the puppet-like image of Maximón (also called San Judas or San Simón), a figure dressed in indígena clothing and a fedora, that is paraded during Holy Week alongside solemn statues of Jesus and the Virgin Mary. This is one of the few places remaining in Guatemala (Zunil, near Quetzaltenango, is another) where this curious, cigar-smoking, rum-drinking native deity is openly worshiped. Maximón's exact origins are shrouded in Maya antiquity, but today he is an embodiment of the god of carnal love, celebration, and good fortune. On his own feast day, just before Easter, members of the village cofradía remove the wooden figure from his chapel, located in front of the town's Catholic church, stuff a cigar in his mouth, set a drink in his hand, and march Maximón in procession through the streets of Santiago. At the end of Holy Week he is returned to the house of a specially chosen cofrade, who is responsible for his well-being for the following year. (The Maximón cult is expanding throughout Guatemala and is no longer a rural phenomenon—even the capital now has its adherents.). Ask around and you will be guided (for a fee) to Maximóm.

The largest of the lakeside towns after Panajachel, Santiago is famous for its Friday market and beautiful textiles. Other popular souvenirs are wood carvings of St. James (*Santiago* in Spanish), the town's patron saint. The traditional dress here includes white-and-purple-striped short pants for the men and intricately embroidered huipiles for the women, some of whom still wear tightly wound halos of red cloth on their heads. (It is tempting to photograph the older people in full regalia, but many of them resent picture-taking and either cover their faces or ask to be paid a small amount of money. Please respect their wishes.)

Santiago is the traditional capital of the Tzutuhil Maya (also spelled Tzutujil or Zutuhil), a fiercely independent tribe. From 1979 into the early 1990s, the Tzutuhiles had a series of violent conflicts with the Guatemalan military, commemorated by a shrine in Santiago's colonial church to the village's many dead, "disappeared," and wounded. The roster includes Stanley Francis Rother, a popular American-born Catholic priest who became a local martyr after his 1981 assassination in the church by unknown assailants, probably members of a right-wing death squad. Santiago was occupied for 11 years by the Guatemalan Army, which was forcibly driven from the town after a 1990 massacre.

Things to See and Do

Walking from the *muelle* (boat dock) up the main street you will immediately be accosted by some of the most rude and aggressive souvenir sellers in Guatemala, many of them children. Unlike most communities, Santiageños have difficulty taking "no" for an answer. Fortunately, there are shopping bargains to be found: The embroidered and needlepoint textiles (many with animal images) are particularly good values. Wall-hangings and *mantels* (tablecloths) may catch your eye, along with the woodcarvings for which this area is known. Several art galleries (Chávez, Sisay, Nim Pot) are open along the main street, display-ing a naturalistic tempura and oil painting style practiced by a growing number of local artists. The market is semi-permanent here and you can always find handicraft vendors.

The thick, cool interior walls of the enormous **Franciscan church**, built on the main plaza in 1568, are lined with wooden stat-ues of Catholic saints clothed in indígena scarves and traje embroi-dered by the women of Santiago. Carvings on the wooden pulpit include the image of a quetzal reading a book and Yum-Kax, the Maya god of corn. (According to the Maya, human beings were cre-ated from sacred corn.) Although

Richard Mahler

Santiago Atitlán is one of the few highland villages where men continue to wear at least some of their traditional clothing.

the Catholic Church in Santiago has come under heavy competition in recent years from Protestant evangelists, sit in the pews of this ancient building for a few minutes and you'll see one devout resident after another coming to light candles and ask favors from the icons, who are viewed as the embodiment of Mayan gods by many locals.

The best way to get a feel for Santiago Atitlán's culture and history is by taking a highly recommended walking tour ($15) offered by Dolores Ratzan, a Tzuithuil guide who speaks excellent English (she lived in the U.S. for 12 years) and has worked as a healer, weaver, lecturer, and interpreter. If you want her to take you to a *cofradía* house, add $2 or a small gift of food. (Ratzan was formerly married to Martín Prechtel, an American who was trained here as a Maya shaman. For a fascinating account of Prechtel's spiritual journey, read his 1998 memoir, *Secrets of the Talking Jaguar.*)

Excellent backstrap weaving lessons are available from Dolores' daughter, Concepción Ratzan Mendoza, who also speaks English. The rate is about $2 an hour and you can learn the basics in 4 to 6 hours. Materials for such instruction cost about $6.

Visitors can also take a walk east of Santiago along the southern shoreline to San Lucas, and there is a circuitous trail behind San Pedro volcano to the town jof the same name.

Local canoes can be hired (for $2 to $3 an hour) to visit what remains of the nearby **Atitlán Grebe Nature Reserve**, designed to protect the flightless Atitlán giant grebe, locally called *poc*, which became extinct here in the mid-1980s. The disappearance of the poc is a tragic tale in which overdevelopment, earthquakes, politics, greed, and human stupidity each play a role. A boat ride to the reserve is a pleasant excursion, however, and you may also see some of the lake's migrants, including the American widgeon and the ruddy duck. You can camp here if you like, but keep a close eye on your belongings.

Horseback tours of the area can be arranged through Panajachel Tourist Services (762-2333) or Jim and Nancy Matison (721-7167). Guided tours range between $30 and $60 per hour. For a guided hike to forests and volcano summits, expect to pay between $20 and $30. A guided trek to **El Mirador**, a lookout point above Santiago, costs about $5. Bring water, a hat, sunscreen, and insect repellent. Ask at local hotels for suggestions on experienced guides for any of these activities. A Spanish school (703-2562) operated by Jim and Cecilia Conroy opened in 1998.

Santiago's annual feast day to its patron, Saint James, is July 25.

Nature Treks Around Santiago Atitlán

It's a fairly easy hike of 1 to 2 hours from Santiago Atitlán to the top of the volcanic ridge that separates the lake from Guatemala's fertile Pacific slope. At **El Mirador** (The Lookout), the highest point on the dirt trail that winds through coffee plantations from Santiago, you'll be rewarded with a sweeping view that takes in hundreds of square miles and includes, on a clear day, the Pacific Ocean. A cloud forest preserve near El Mirador is one of the area's last habitat remnants for such increasingly endangered birds as the horned guan, crested curassow, bushy-crested jay, and boat-tailed grackle. Sharp-eyed birders can also see chachalacas, emerald toucanets, green parakeets, hummingbirds, doves, and wrens. Guides (Spanish-speaking) can be hired in Santiago for the trip. Wear hiking shoes and expect to pay about $5.

More ambitious trips, each requiring about 7 hours of trekking, will bring you to the virgin tropical forest called **Xebula** (home of spider monkeys, quetzals, armadillos, wild pigs, and pavóns) or a pine forest on the back slope of San Pedro volcano called **Lidio** (where a few quetzals and other rare birds still survive). These guided adventures will cost about $14 each.

The true thrill-seeker may want to try an overnight (or one very long day) trip to Cerro Cabeza del Burro, a mountain that looms above the arm of Lake Atitlán wedged between San Pedro and Santiago. The peak is not very high (6,200 feet, or a thousand feet above the lake), but its virgin tropic forests are home to many colorful orchids and exotic wild animals, including the elusive quetzal. The fee for this guided trip (which includes a boat ride up the narrow arm of the lake) starts at about $24; it costs more if you camp out.

It's possible to take a guided full-day hike up the Santiago side of the San Pedro volcano and come down the other, finishing the trek in the village of San Pedro. You'll need to arrange boat transportation from Santiago to the western slope and a guide to show you the way. Expect to pay $16 or more. The most fit climbers will make the summit in 2 hours, couch potatoes will need 4 or 5 hours. Getting down is easy: 1 to 2 hours for everybody. For details, see Chapter 4, Special Interests.

Getting There

Large passenger ferries leave daily at 8:35 a.m., 9:30 a.m., and 10:30 a.m., and at 1:00 p.m., 3:00 p.m., and 4:30 p.m. for Santiago from Panajachel's public beach and the Hotel del Lago dock, returning at 6:00 a.m., 7:00 a.m., 11:30 a.m., 11:45 a.m., 12:30 p.m., 2:00 p.m., 3:00 p.m., and 4:30 p.m. The trips take about an hour in either direction and you'll pay your $1.75 fare on board. Some vessels continue to San Pedro (30 minutes) and around the lake back to Pana (at 7:00 a.m., 10:30 a.m., 12:00 p.m., 1:00 p.m., 3:30 p.m., and 5:00 p.m.) and also cost about $1.75. The author recommends coming to Santiago on the direct boat, then take a leisurely, village-hopping "local" for the return trip. Chartered boats cost about $25 (one-way).

During Holy Week the ferries are sometimes woefully overcrowded, and at least one boat has sunk, resulting in numerous drownings. If a ferry looks too full, don't board it.

There are several direct buses a day to Santiago from Cocales, but none from Panajachel (you must connect in San Lucas Tolimán). From Guatemala City, second-class buses to Santiago (via Escuintla) leave daily from the Zone 4 terminal at 6:00 a.m. and 7:00 a.m., and again at noon and 2:00 p.m. Buses (about $2) leave the south end of Santiago's market for Guatemala City at 2:30 a.m., 3:00 a.m., 4:00 a.m., 5:00 a.m., 7:30 a.m., and 11:30 a.m., and 12:45 p.m. and 2:00 p.m. Minivan shuttles to and from Santiago can be arranged from Panajachel's major travel agencies. The road to San Lucas was paved in 1998.

Where to Stay and to Eat in Santiago Atitlán

In addition to the hotels listed below, some homeowners also rent rooms by the day, week, or month; ask around.

Hospedaje Chi-Nim-Ya, on the lake near the main dock; $5. Best in-town accommodations, 12 rooms (one with private bath). Across the street is **Restaurant El Gran Sol**, with a nice view and good food.

Hotel Bambú, on the lake; $30; 201-8913 or 832-3038. Bungalows and rooms, with restaurant on the premises.

Hotel Tzutuhil Atitlán, center of town; $12; 762-7174. Four floors and 19 simple rooms.

Posada de Santiago, southwest of the village on the road toward San Pedro; $40and up; tel/fax 721-7167, e-mail: posdesantiago@ mail2guate.net., www.myphonebook.com. One of the loveliest hotels on the lake and highly recommended. Set amid lush gardens with six elegantly appointed casitas made of local stone, plus two larger suites. A couple of budget rooms are available. Americans David and Susie Grenville also operate the best restaurant in town, open to non-guests and serving three meals a day. Dinners ($10) may include such gourmet delights as Thai coconut shrimp soup and chocolate macadamia-nut brownies. There is a small gift shop on the premises, and the owners can suggest things to do in the area such as mountain biking, cultural touring, swimming, canoeing, hiking, snorkeling, and horseback riding.

SAN PEDRO LA LAGUNA

Location: About 20 miles southwest of Panajachel, across the lake.
Population: 7,000 (1999 estimate).
For More Information: Inquire locally at hotels and restaurants; there is no tourist office.

Quiet San Pedro la Laguna, a Cakchiquel Maya village on the opposite side of the San Pedro volcano from Santiago, receives relatively few visitors, although budget backpackers often take advantage of its low prices (like the *old* days in Panajachel). San Pedro is mainly oriented toward the cultivation of coffee, corn, avocados, and other produce, as well as the manufacture of shirts, rugs, and Maya-style curios for the tourist market. Some of the men still carve *cayucos* (canoes) out of the trunks of large cedar trees growing on the slopes of the nearby volcano, which can be climbed from here in roughly 2 to 5 hours, depending on one's physical condition (see Chapter 4: Special Interests for details). With widespread adoption of evangelical Protestantism, many residents have discarded their traditional ways, although a modified form of indígena dress is still worn by some.

Things to See and Do

You can visit rug-making workshops in San Pedro, and some of the women teach foreigners how to weave on their backstrap looms; Rosa Cruz has been recommended. Horses and guides can be hired for excursions to coffee plantations or up the nearby volcano; expect to pay about $2 an hour for horse or guide, about half that to rent a kayak. Market day is Sunday and fiesta in San Pedro is June 29.

One of the village's most unusual attractions is **Thermal Waters,** an outdoor hot-tub complex operated by an entrepreneur named Antonio. For a reasonable price ($5) you can take a 2-hour soak in these soothing tubs and emerge to munch on healthful snacks—a soothing indulgence after climbing the nearby volcano. Daily sunset saunas in the sweat lodge are about $3 each; for more money you can undergo a 2-day "body cleansing" regimen. Look for the signs between the first and second boat docks.

There are some nice beaches east of the village (toward Santiago) and you might want to rent a small boat to do some exploring. All in all, San Pedro is much more tranquil than Santiago, with many fewer touts, beggars, and artesanía vendors. Swarms of tourists never disembark here, although there are some worthwhile art galleries and típica shops on the main street.

Getting There

Several boats each day head directly for San Pedro from Panajachel and many more indirectly via Santiago. Note that there are two boat docks here, one on each side of the small peninsula upon which the village is sprawled. Some boats for Pana leave from both docks, but the last one each afternoon leaves only from the smaller of the two, in front of Restaurante Johana.

Where to Stay in San Pedro la Laguna

Hotel San Pedro, conveniently located near the main (second) boat dock; $8; no phone. Budget rooms.

Punta d'Oro Hotel, near the lake, next door to the Villa Sol, between the two docks; $8; 762-2487. Bungalows, campsites, volleyball, horseback riding, a Jacuzzi, and a beach. Also a bar and restaurant. Recommended.

Villa Mar, set back from the smaller dock, on the main street; $6; no phone. A good value for budget travelers.

Where to Eat in San Pedro la Laguna

Caia Rosario Guest House. Offers Spanish classes and weaving lessons, as well as basic rooms. No phone; write c/o Sololá, Guatemala.

Comedor Ranchón, in the Chuasinahi Hotel, on the beach northeast of the village. Typical Guatemalan fare and the usual "traveler meals."

Hospedaje Chuazanahi, near the first boat dock, toward Santiago; $5; 331-0997. Serves drinks and simple meals; 32 basic rooms.

Nick's Place, overlooking the main dock. Basic Guatemalan food.

Restaurant Chez Michel, on the eastern outskirts of the village, next to a coffee plantation, is your best bet for meals, with some truly delicious and imaginative offerings.

Restaurante Ti Kaaj, near the center of town, down a winding dirt road that veers off from the main dock. Nightlife (that is, drinking and swapping travel stories) in San Pedro happens here.

SAN JUAN LA LAGUNA AND BEYOND

Location: The west and northwest of Lake Atitlán, between 5 and 20 miles from Panajachel.

The Coffee Connection

Did you know that consumers in the U.S. drink more than one-third of the world's coffee? This helps explain why coffee remains the biggest single income producer in Guatemala, a grower and exporter of fine beans for more than a century. Unfortunately, only a tiny percentage of the industry's revenues trickle down to the people who do the actual planting, cultivating, and harvesting of Guatemalan coffee.

In 1989, Rhode Island coffee roaster Bill Fishbein founded a nonprofit organization that tries to give something back to the people growing coffee. Coffee Kids does this by supporting self-directed, grassroots projects that address a wide range of community needs, from clean water to immunization, from renewable energy to public schools. The organization helps create partnerships between local micro-lending groups and local development activities as a means of providing long-term solutions to quality-of-life problems. Working with the citizens of San Pedro la Laguna, for example, Coffee Kids has helped fund health education programs and shot clinics.

For information or to make a tax-deductible donation, contact Coffee Kids at 1305 Luisa Street, Santa Fe, New Mexico 87505, (800) 334-9099, or www.coffeekids.org/kids.

Population: *From 400 to 4,000 in each village (1999 estimate).*
Services: *This area is considered relatively free of banditry, although accommodations, clean water, and services are very limited. Camping is permitted along the lakeside, but finding even a small patch of unused level ground can prove difficult.*
For More Information: *There is no tourist office; inquire at the INGUAT offices in Panajachel or locally among hotel and restaurant operators.*

The small fishing and farming village of San Juan, less than a mile (20-

minute walk) beyond San Pedro, specializes in the weaving of lake-reed mats called *petates*. At the Tuesday and Saturday markets, these and other locally produced crafts are sold at good prices. Follow the signs from the boat landing to **Las Artesanías de San Juan**, a store that sells textile, hammocks, and bags, locally manufactured since 1988 as part of a village self-help project. The quality is excellent and buying items here supports a worthy cause.

Continuing on foot for several miles along rough, steep trails, you can reach, in order, the tiny settlements of Santa Clara, San Pablo, San Marcos, Tzununa, Jaibalito, and Santa Cruz la Laguna. Allow at least 3 hours for the hike from San Marcos to Santa Cruz, and another 3 from there to Sololá by a steep but well-marked trail.

The industrious and clever people of **Santa Clara** and **San Pablo** produce and sell cane baskets, hammocks, ropes, bags, and clothing from local materials. **San Marcos** is well known for its weavers of fine reed mats and maguey ropes, as well as a natural steam bath called **Temascal** (used by local Maya for centuries; ask for directions). Kayaks and mountain bikes are available for hire in San Marcos and the hiking hereabouts is superb.

After passing through a couple of miniscule coffee-growing hamlets (with no lodging or restaurants), travelers come to the basket-weaving village of **Santa Cruz**, which is accessible only by a steep trail from the lake and has the feel of a whitewashed Greek island community. Its impressive 16th-century church is surrounded by very old homes (and a post office). A well-marked trail continues from here up a steep hillside to Sololá.

Getting There

There are about eight daily boats between San Pedro, Santa Cruz, and Panajachel; allow about 20 minutes for the ride from Santa Cruz to Panajachel. A mail boat makes the run about 9:30 a.m. Don't attempt to walk the direct trail between Pana and Santa Cruz. The terrain is dangerously rugged, and even locals don't attempt the hike. If you want to make the trip by foot, it's best to stay on the longer trail from Sololá to Santa Cruz.

Where to Stay and Eat in San Juan la Laguna and Beyond

Arca de Noé (Noah's Ark), Santa Cruz; $25, includes dinner; write Apartado Postal 22, Panajachel, or fax 762-1196. Recommended bungalow-style hotel and home-style restaurant. The expat managers can suggest nearby places to hike and swim. With only eight rooms, you'd best book ahead. Lunch and breakfast are open to the public; dinner meals are served only to guests (family style). The food at Arca de Noé is excellent and the setting fabulous, with a nice stretch of beach near the hotel and a pier (this is one of the few places on Lake Atitlán where the water is both deep and clean, though not very warm).

Hospedaje García, near the dock, Santa Cruz; $7; no phone. Very basic rooms that will serve in a pinch. Owned by a friendly local family.

Hotel San Marcos, San Marcos. Offers hammocks spaces for a few dollars. This and other lodges in San Marcos can be reached via the community telephone, 998-0481.

La Paz Bungalows, San Marcos; $25 per person for four-person casitas with sleeping lofts; no phone. Eco-friendly and architecturally unique. Very good health food restaurant and a sauna. Neighboring **Mañuela's** sells Italian-style bread loaves baked in clay ovens.

Posada Abaj, Santa Cruz; $8; 762-1196, fax 762-1196. Offers Spanish lessons and a veggie café.

Posada de Iguana, Santa Cruz; $4; fax 762-1196. Rustic cabaña accommodations, a sauna, a small restaurant, and that rarity at Atitlán: a dive shop and scuba school! PADI certification courses are $150 and tank dives are $40 each.

Posada Schumann, San Marcos; $8; 873-1326 or 360-4049 in Guatemala City. Inviting stone-straw-and-wood bungalows (with kitchens and showers). The owners of Posada Schumann also operate **La Ché** restaurant. Nearby is a meditation center, **Las Pirámides,** with "overnight pyramids," a bakery, a medicinal plant garden, and a vegetarian café.

SOLOLÁ
Location: About 6 miles northwest of Panajachel, on a mountain slope above Lake Atitlán.
Population: 7,500 (1999 estimate).
Services: There is a Banco Granai on 7a. Avenida where you can change money as well as a post office, pharmacy, and market.
For More Information: Inquire at the INGUAT office in Panajachel, or locally at hotels and restaurants.

One of the major market centers of the western highlands is Sololá, perched on a ridge high above Lake Atitlán. The plaza market (and adjacent streets) fill up every Tuesday and Friday morning with sellers from throughout the area. The traditional costume, still very much in evidence, is unusually

J.W. Smith

The public street-markets of highland Guatemala are a highlight of any trip to the region.

colorful. Men are dressed in red-striped pants with blanket aprons and waist-length woolen coats modeled after those of Spanish colonial officers. Women wear long, multi-hued skirts and red pin-striped huipiles.

Founded in 1547, after the Spanish destroyed a nearby indígena settlement, Sololá is the capital of the department of the same name and a stronghold of Cakchiquel Maya traditions, as indicated by the distinctive bat-shaped emblem on the back of the men's jackets, the symbol of the last ruling clan of the Cakchiquel nation. The ancient cofradía brotherhood is still strong here, and on Sunday mornings shortly before 10:00 you can see its members walking to the colonial cathedral in their elaborate costumes. Outsiders have tried for many years to fathom the rituals and traditions played out in Sololá, but the local residents are jealous of their secrets and share little information with non-indígena.

A colorful fiesta is held here every August 15 on Mim Ajij Sololá, which translates as "the great day of Sololá."

Getting There

The town is served by frequent daily buses from Panajachel and Los Encuentros, both about 6 miles away, where connections can easily be made to Chichicastenango, Quetzaltenango, and other cities.

Where to Stay and Eat in Sololá
El Pasaje, 9a. Calle 5-41; $3; no phone. Basic rooms and meals.
You're better off eating and sleeping in Panajachel or another community on the lake.

SANTA LUCÍA UTATLÁN
Santa Lucía is a good-sized, Quiché-speaking town, 9 miles beyond
Sololá, surrounded by pine and oak forests. Seldom visited by outsiders,
it can be reached by a branch road off the Pan American Highway. There
is a good market each Sunday. A few miles farther down the road is the
community of **Santa María Visitación**. There are no hotels or restaurants of note in Santa Lucía or Santa María.

NAHUALÁ AND SANTA CATARINA IXTAHUACÁN
*Location: Nahualá is at Km. 155 on the Pan American Highway, between
Los Encuentros and Quetzaltenango. Santa Catarina is about 3 miles to the
southwest of Nahualá.*
*Services: No accommodations or tourist services, so consider these towns a
day trip.*

These twin towns, about 3 miles apart along the Pan American Highway
and known collectively as **Los Pueblos Chancatales**, are noteworthy in
that they have deliberately and successfully resisted the influence of the
non-indígena world. At one point during the last century the entire able-
bodied male population walked the 100 miles to Guatemala City and con-
fronted the president face-to-face about government land confiscation.
Today only a handful of Ladinos live here, although casual visitors of any
nationality are welcome.

Set in cool, high mountains, Nahualá and Santa Catarina Ixtahuacán
are good places to buy wood carvings and weavings. For the former, try
Carpentería Emmanuel on Nahualá's main street. Fine textiles can be
purchased in either town directly from those who produce them (ask
around or come to the weekly markets). Folk Catholicism is especially
strong in this mountainous region, and ancient ceremonies are often carried
out on the steps of the huge Spanish colonial churches. The towns' jointly
held fiesta is November 25. Highly recommended markets take place every
Sunday in Nahualá.

Getting There
You can take a bus to Puente Nahualá on the Pan American Highway,
then walk to either village in 30 minutes or so. A taxi or private car would
be more convenient.

THE IXIMCHÉ RUINS

Location: *About 30 miles east of Los Encuentros and about 30 miles west of Antigua on the Pan American Highway is a well-marked turnoff to the town of Tecpán and nearby ancient Maya ruins of Iximché. Tecpán is only a few hundred yards beyond the highway, and the archaeological site is about 3 miles farther south.*

Hours and Fees: *The ruins are open to visitors daily from 7:30 a.m. to 4:00 p.m. for about 25¢.*

Services: *No lodging or restaurants in the area; make this a day trip from Antigua, Chichicastenango, or Panajachel.*

For More Information: *There are no services or tourist offices in either Tecpán or Iximché. Use caution in the area: Some violent robberies involving tourists have been reported.*

About halfway between Lake Atitlán and Antigua is an old Maya capital, which also served as the first seat of government for Spanish-ruled Guatemala. Founded in about 1470 by the Cakchiquel Maya as a defense measure against the aggressive Quiché Maya to the north, Iximché is on a strategically located promontory bordered on three sides by steep pine-covered ravines.

This site was the capital of the Cakchiquel when the first conquistadors arrived in the early 16th century. The Spanish and Cakchiquel formed an alliance against the Quiché and other rival indígena tribes in the area, and a provisional Spanish colonial capital was established at Iximché in 1524. After a few months the Cakchiquel revolted against the European invaders, forcing them to retreat first to the nearby village of Tecpán and then to the Almolonga Valley, where they founded Ciudad Vieja and, 16 years later, Antigua.

The Cakchiquel were defeated by the Spanish about 1530, and their capital was ransacked and burned. The destruction was not absolute, however, and some of the original plaster and paint remain on a few buildings. Still extant are several temple pyramids, a main plaza complex, a couple of ball courts, and some uncovered mounds, plus the foundation of the royal palace. Unfortunately, many of the original building materials have been hauled away for use in construction projects.

The setting is lush and very peaceful (it was purposely chosen as a ceremonial center to be used for sacrifices and other religious rituals), and today Iximché is a good place for quiet contemplation: There are no guides. In fact, you are likely to be the only visitor present.

As you enter Iximché, there is a small museum on your right where you can obtain a Spanish-language pamphlet describing the results of research done here from 1959 to 1961.

Getting There

You can walk to Iximché in about 45 minutes from Tecpán or drive from Tecpán to Iximché in a few minutes by car. Another option is a Tecpán taxi: about $10 round-trip.

QUETZALTENANGO (XELA) AND VICINITY

The primary tourist sights of Quetzaltenango can be taken in over a couple of days. Beyond that, the city is a good springboard for day trips to nearby villages and hot springs. Most can be reached easily by public bus, private car, or taxi. In some cases, the destinations are even close enough to reach on foot. During the annual fairs and fiestas mentioned below, colorful indígena dances are often performed in village plazas. The dances may include performances of the popular La Conquista Española (the Spanish Conquest), El Mono (the Monkey), and El Venado (the Deer). Very few of these villages have accommodations or restaurants catering to foreign visitors, and the recommended strategy is to return to Quetzaltenango each evening for meals and lodging.

QUETZALTENANGO (XELA)

Location: About 130 miles northwest of Guatemala City and 10 miles southwest of the Pan American Highway on Route 9-S.

Population: 100,000 (1999 estimate).

Services: Telgua is just across the street from INGUAT, on Parque Centro América in Zone 1. The post office is at the corner of 4a. Calle and 15a. Avenida, also in Zone 1. Banks are near Parque Centro América and the main public market. Shipping and communications services are offered by Alfa (763-2104, 15a. Avenida 3-51, Zone 1).

For More Information: For local tours and rentals of autos and bicycles, try SAB (761-2042; 1a. Calle 12-35) or Guatemala Unlimited (761-6043; 12a. Avenida C-35), both in Zone 1. There is a well-staffed INGUAT (761-4931, 9a. Calle and 12a. Avenida) in the foyer of the Casa de Cultura building on the south side of the Parque. Hours are 8 a.m. to noon and 2 p.m. to 5 p.m. weekdays. Inquire at INGUAT about local volcano guides and Spanish schools.

Guatemala's second-largest city is more commonly referred to locally as **Xela** (SHAY-lah), an abbreviated version of its original indígena name, Xelajuj, a Quiché word referring to the ten principal gods members of this Maya ethnic group worshiped.

Xela is located in a cool part of the country, and temperatures can

189

Quetzaltenango

0 SCALE   0.15   0.15
         KILOMETERS   MILES

drop into the low 30s during the dry season, although daytime highs usually reach a balmy 70 or 80 degrees.

Quetzaltenango, incidentally, means "place of the Quetzals,"
although these birds became locally extinct many years ago.

Things to See and Do

Mountains and volcanoes surround Xela, located in a large flat plain at
about 7,700 feet. For an excellent view of the city, climb to the top of the
hill called **El Baúl**, where there is a monument in tribute to Tecún Umán,
the Quiché leader who defended this area against its Spanish conquerors.

Xela is famous for its many 19th- and early 20th-century structures
built in classical, neoclassical, and Italian Renaissance architectural styles,
most constructed using local volcanic stone with detailing by expert indígena stonecutters. Among the best examples of Xela's fine architecture are
the deteriorating façade of the **Espiritu Santo Cathedral**, built in 1535,
facing the tree-shaded main plaza—**Parque Centro América**—and the
adjacent **Church of the Los Altos Diocese**, completed in 1899. Fronting

the same plaza (also called Parque Municipal), are the Corinthian-style **Palacio Municipal** (City Hall) and the Greek-revival **Casa de Cultura del Occidente**, where INGUAT, a recital hall, a library, and the **Museo de Historia Natural** (Museum of Natural History) are located. The museum is recommended for its eclectic assembly of artifacts, ranging from pickled Guatemalan animals (including dogs!) to dramatic photographs of the severe damage sustained by Xela during volcanic eruptions in the early 1900s. Exhibits are poorly marked, in Spanish only.

The downtown **Parque Centro América** is a great place for people-watching, especially on balmy summer evenings. Unlike most Guatemalan cities, in Xela many of the townspeople proudly wear traditional indígena dress as everyday clothing and love to promenade each evening beneath the shade trees and monuments.

The **Municipal Theater** (1895), at the corner of 1a. Calle and 14a. Avenida, is another good example of solid neoclassical style. The inside of the building is very fancy: Theater-goers can rent private boxes equipped with individual vanities for women. Other attractions near the city center include the **Guatemalan Art Museum**, at 12a. Avenida and 7a. Calle, and **Iglesia de San Nicolás** (4a. Calle and 15a. Avenida), a neo-Gothic structure with concrete flying buttresses and other eccentricities, now used as an evangelical church.

On the west side of town, near the bus terminal and adjacent municipal market in Zone 3, is **Parque Minerva**, where the neoclassical Templo de Minerva (now falling apart) was erected to inspire Guatemalan youth to study hard. Minerva was the Roman goddess of wisdom and has always been revered in Xela, home to many of Guatemala's foremost artists and intellectuals. There is also a small zoo in the park.

The large **La Democracia market**, located between 16a. and 15a. Avenidas near Calle Rodolfo Robles in Zone 3, sells craftwork from throughout the highlands and offers high-quality goods, especially textiles, at reasonable prices. It is open every day. Do not confuse this with the "new" municipal market, a much smaller collection of shops and stalls at the southeast corner of Parque Centro América, where there is also a three-story shopping mall catering mainly to tourists. A good handicraft market is held on the main plaza the first Sunday of each month.

One of Guatemala's biggest federations of weaving and textile cooperatives is based in Quetzaltenango and sells handmade products through its **Tejidos Guadalupanos** store. Another recommended shop called **Artexco** (7a. Avenida at 16a. Calle) represents more than 2,000 artisans whose work is of exceptionally high quality. Profits from Artexco's sales support a weaving and dyeing school that is open to foreigners. Another good source of artesanía is **Alternativas** (16a. Avenida 3-35, Zone 3),

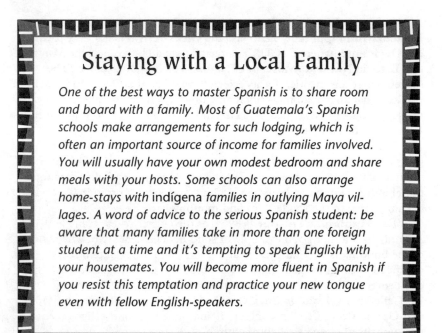

Staying with a Local Family

One of the best ways to master Spanish is to share room and board with a family. Most of Guatemala's Spanish schools make arrangements for such lodging, which is often an important source of income for families involved. You will usually have your own modest bedroom and share meals with your hosts. Some schools can also arrange home-stays with indígena *families in outlying Maya villages. A word of advice to the serious Spanish student: be aware that many families take in more than one foreign student at a time and it's tempting to speak English with your housemates. You will become more fluent in Spanish if you resist this temptation and practice your new tongue even with fellow English-speakers.*

which specializes in hand-crafted gifts. A recommended shipping specialist for such goods is **Cropa Panalpina**.

After you have seen the markets, museums, shops, and dignified public buildings of Xela, there is not much for a casual visitor to do unless you want to use the city as a base for further excursions to highland villages that have minimal or no accommodations (or restaurants). If you have the time and inclination, you may also wish to enroll in one of the city's several language schools (see Chapter 4.)

The colorful **Quetzaltenango Fair** takes place September 12 through 18. As in most other Guatemalan towns, Holy Week and Christmas are also occasions rich in tradition, with high-spirited ceremonial processions through the city's streets.

E-mail and Internet access is available at **Salon Tecún** (on the Plaza Central in Zone 1, 761-2832). Many hotels and language schools also offer such services.

A goldmine for travelers is **VRISA**, which operates an excellent English-language bookshop at 15a. Avenida 3-64 and a bicycle rental service at 15. Avenida 0-67, both in Zone 1. Expect to pay about $3 a day

The southern skyline of Quetzaltenango, with the Santa María volcano at left

for mountain bikes, $2 for town bikes (maps available). The bookstore boasts over 4000 titles and an espresso/tea counter.

Getting There

If driving, turn southwest at the Pan-American Highway crossroads called Cuatro Caminos. In terms of miles, it is actually a slightly shorter distance from Guatemala City to Quetzaltenango via the Coastal Highway, turning north at Mazatenango, but that route is much less scenic.

Xela is easily reached by bus from Guatemala City, Antigua, Panajachel, Huehuetenango, and other major towns. From Chichicastenango and Panajachel there are few direct buses, so you will have to change at Los Encuentros or Cuatro Caminos. Passengers from Antigua change in Chimaltenango. The main bus terminal is in Zone 3 near Parque Minerva, a 10-minute taxi ride from the main plaza, where there are always cabs. Several companies run first-class buses every day between Xela and Guatemala City, with arrivals and departures from their own private terminals near Parque Centro América. This option is highly recommended for long-distance travelers. The trip takes 5 hours.

Where to Stay in Quetzaltenango

Casa Kaehler, 13a. Avenida 3-33, Zone 1; $7 and up; 761-2091. Cozy, somewhat rundown old house. Accommodations are clean and inexpensive, although noise can be a problem. Some of the seven rooms have private baths; others share.

Casa Suiza,14a. Avenida A 2-36, Zone 1; $8; 763-0242, fax 763-1378. Popular among budget travelers.

Hotel Casa del Viajero, 8a. Avenida 9-17, Zone 1; $12; 761-4594. Good, low-priced hotel in the downtown area.

Hotel Modelo, 14a. Avenida A 2-31, Zone 1; $30; 761-2529, fax 763-1376. Old-fashioned, centrally-located establishment (with new annex) popular among Guatemalan travelers. The rooms and meals are an unusually good value: Both are recommended.

Pensión Altense, 9a. Calle 8-48; $8; 761-2811. Clean and centrally located, although in an unappealing neighborhood.

Pensión Bonifaz, 4a. Calle 10-50, Zone 1; $50 and up; 761-2279, fax 761-2850. Although built in the early 1930s, this hotel radiates colonial elegance. Each of its large, suites has a sitting room, TV, and private bath. Good restaurant and comfortable bar off the lobby. Recommended.

Parque Centro América, the main plaza of Quetzaltenango

Río Azul, 2a. Calle 12-15; $14; 763-0654, fax 763-0554. Excellent value in this price range. Convenient, non-stylish establishment run by a retired university professor and his family, all eager to make you feel at home. Travel tips cheerfully dispensed. Security is tight, rooms are clean, and each has a private bath with plenty of hot water. Next door is the nonprofit handicrafts shop, **Mujeres al Año 2000** (2a. Calle 12-13).

Where to Eat in Quetzaltenango

Among the hotels, **Modelo** serves excellent fixed-price meals in a pleasant colonial-style dining room. **Bonifaz** has the most elegant dining rooms in town, and its prices are not excessive. High tea is served late afternoons, with blonde German-Guatemalan ladies chatting each other up. At breakfast, try the *huevos monteleños*, a tasty egg dish.

Bazar del Café, 15a. Calle 2-23, Zone 10. One of Xela's great coffee bars, Bazar del Café roasts and grinds export-quality beans on the premises.

Café Baviera, 5a. Calle 12-50, Zone 1. Excellent bakery, coffeehouse, and restaurant, serving perhaps the best coffee drinks in the country. Sit back and relax while reading the morning paper and sipping a café latte and listening to George Winston. There's also a worthwhile used-paperback exchange (and plenty of Spanish school students).

Cafetería El Kopetin,14a. Avenida 3-31, Zone 1. Salt-of-the-earth Guatemalan fare and Spanish-style tapas.

Giuseppe Tutto Italiano, at 4a. Calle and 15a. Avenida, Zone 1. One of two excellent Italian restaurants to choose from in Xela.

Il Padrino, on Calle de Calvario, opposite the post office, Zone 1. The other excellent Italian restaurant.

La Taquería, two locations on 13a. Avenida. Head here for Mexican food, particularly chile-spiced tacos.

Pizza Ricca, 14a. Avenida 2-42, Zone 1. Tasty pizza served in a family-oriented atmosphere at low prices.

Pollo Frito Albumar, 4a. Calle 14-16, Zone 1. The place to go for good fried chicken and grilled beef.

Rincón de los Antojitos, 4a. Calle at 15a. Avenida, serves typical, well-prepared Guatemalan food.

Shanghai, 4a. Calle 12-22. The best Chinese food in town, with large, inexpensive combination plates.

Taberna Don Rodrigo, 14a. Avenida 47, Zone 1; across from the Municipal Theater. Recommended convivial night spot, with draft beer, hamburgers, and sandwiches.

Utz'Hua, 3a. Calle and 12a. Avenida, offers good Guatemalan fare.

ALMOLONGA
Location: 2 miles southeast of Quetzaltenango.
For More Information: Contact the INGUAT office in Quetzaltenango or consult with local hotels and travel agencies.

This Quiché Maya town is known for its delicious fruits and vegetables as well as the nearby **Aguas Amargas** (Bitter Waters) and **El Rosario hot springs**. The latter have been developed as a family-oriented attraction. High-quality textile and leather goods are also made and sold in Almolonga. Market days are Wednesdays and Saturdays, with a fiesta June 27 through 29. The easiest way to get here is on foot, or by either public bus or taxi.

ZUNIL AND FUENTES GEORGINAS
Location: Zunil is about 6 miles southeast of Quetzaltenango and Fuentes Georginas is another 7 miles into the surrounding mountains.
For More Information: Contact the INGUAT office in Quetzaltenango or consult with local hotels and travel agencies.

The village of Zunil is a short distance southeast of Almolonga and 6 miles from Xela, on the banks of the Río Salamá. Its indigenous people wear traditional clothing made using pre-Columbian weaving techniques, with designs representing objects from their environment. The women wear unusually long purple shawls. Textiles are sold at the artisans' cooperative in town and at the colorful Monday markets.

There is a local fair in Zunil on November 25. A stunning colonial church dominates the village, which is one of the places the image of Maximón is still openly revered with pomp and ceremony, especially during Holy Week. Also known as San Simón or Alvarado (after Spanish conqueror Pedro de Alvarado), Zunil's Maximón is a comical-looking, plastic tailor's dummy dressed in ski wear, gloves, and sunglasses.

About 7 miles away by a rough but scenic road are the idyllic Fuentes Georginas mineral hot springs, which emanate from the dormant **Cerro Quemado** volcano and are said to have curative properties. Guatemala's largest geyser is located nearby. Outdoor pools ($1 admission) are surrounded by lush cedar and pine forests adorned with ferns, lichens, and orchids. These waters are said to have curative powers.

After fluctuating during the early 1990s, water levels in the hot pools returned to normal in 1995. Gates to Fuentes Georginas close at 6 p.m., although you can lie in the pools until long after sunset.

Getting There
There are regular buses from Xela to Zunil, but you will have to walk, drive, or take a taxi to Fuentes Georginas. Another option is to walk between Zunil and Almolonga; it takes about 1 hour. Allow about 45 minutes for the bus ride to Zunil from Xela. You can take a taxi to and from the springs from Zunil for about $12. Another option is to hop one of the trucks ($4, if there are four or more passengers) that lines up in front of the church to take visitors there, then walk back (it's downhill and takes about 2 hours).

Where to Stay and to Eat in Fuentes Georginas
Fuentes Georginas Hotel, in the complex next to the hot springs; $6; no phone. A modest seven-cabin complex; simple meals are available. Each cabin is equipped with a spring-fed bathtub and a fireplace (wood provided). You can camp on the grounds for a nominal fee.

LOS VAHOS
These hot sulfur and mineral springs, 12 miles south of Quetzaltenango by car, have been used by locals since the days of the ancient Maya. Today several bathhouses (with steam rooms and showers) and bungalows are available at Los Vahos for day ($3) and overnight visits ($7). Like nearby Georginas, Aguas Amargas, and El Rosario, the Vahos spring is in a scenic mountain setting. Unlike the others, however, it is neither particularly clean nor private. You can take a public bus from Almolonga to the Los Vahos junction, then walk the remaining mile to the geothermal baths. Taxis from Xela are another option.

Above the springs are the Cerro Quernado volcano and lava field, which make an interesting day hike from Los Vahos.

OLINTEPÉQUE
About 6 miles northeast of Quetzaltenango on the old road to Huehuetenango, Olintepéque is near the place where the proud Quiché emperor Tecún Umán is said to have been killed in 1524 during a fierce battle

against the forces of Pedro de Alvarado. The story claims that the nearby Río Xequijel was tinted bright red by the blood of the indígena warriors, hence its name, which means "blood." Markets are held here on Tuesdays, and the local fair is June 24. Handweaving of silk and cotton textiles is the main occupation. There are frequent public buses to Olintepéque from Xela or you can take a taxi.

SALCAJÁ
Location: A few miles east of Olintepéque on the road to the Pan American Highway.
For More Information: Contact the INGUAT office in Quetzaltenango.

This old and mostly Ladino village is famous for its *jaspe* cloth, hand-woven from tie-dyed yarn for subsequent use by weavers throughout the highlands. This knot-based technique is also known as ikat. Salcajá is also renowned for its delicious alcoholic beverages: *Caldo de frutas* is a powerful fruit punch, and *rompopo* is a bit like eggnog. Worth seeing is the stately **Church of San Jacinto**, said to be the first colonial building erected in Guatemala. Market day in Salcajá is Tuesday. A local fiesta takes place on August 25. Many buses from Quetzaltenango pass through here each hour.

Where to Stay in Salcajá
La Mansión Don Hilario, on 3a. Avenida; $6; 763-9594. A basic hotel, with private baths and hot water.

Salcajá, on 3a. Avenida; $7; 761-6101. Another basic hotel.

SAN JUAN OSTUNCALCO
Location: 9 miles northwest of the provincial capital, Totonicapán.
For More Information: Contact the INGUAT office in Quetzaltenango.

This Mam-speaking trading center is a good place to buy wicker furniture, musical instruments, and regional weavings, especially during the Thursday and Sunday markets. San Juan is located in an enchanting mountain valley and holds an annual fair from January 29 to February 3. Buses run here often from Quetzaltenango, or take a taxi.

CANTEL
Location: About 15 minutes by car from Xela on the paved road heading southeast toward the Pacific Coast.
For More Information: Contact the INGUAT office in Quetzaltenango.

Cantel is justifiably famous for the quality of both its delicious fruit and its lovely textiles. In fact, Guatemala's largest textile company is head-quartered here. Market day is Sunday, and the annual fiesta is August 15. Bus service is frequent from Xela.

SAN MARTÍN CHILI VERDE
Location: *About 30 minutes by car or bus from Xela.*
For More Information: *Contact the INGUAT office in Quetzaltenango.*

One of the most traditional villages in the region, San Martín is near **Lago de Chicabal,** a volcanic lake considered sacred by local indígena. Much of the land is devoted to cultivation of green chili peppers, and many residents are skilled basket-weavers. The five-day village fair begins November 7.

SAN CRISTÓBAL TOTONICAPÁN
Location: *About 14 miles northeast of Xela on the Pan American Highway, easily accessed by car or bus.*
For More Information: *Contact the INGUAT office in Quetzaltenango.*

An important center for the weaving of silk, wool, and cotton textiles, San Cristóbal has an outstanding Franciscan church with an unusual altar made of chiseled silver and crystal. Sundays are market days, and a week-long fair begins July 20.

TOTONICAPÁN
Location: *About 17 miles northeast of Quetzaltenango.*
For More Information: *INGUAT has prepared a guide to Totonicapán artisans and studios that is available at any of its offices, as well as at many travel agencies in Guatemala.*

The departmental capital of Totonicapán is well worth a visit, especially for those interested in native and colonial Guatemalan craftwork. Nestled in high mountains and surrounded by tall pine and oak forests, it is famous for its pottery, wooden toys, leather goods, ceremonial masks, and weavings. The principal markets are on Tuesday and Saturday, and there is a fair the last week of September. Smaller handicraft markets are open each Sunday and Thursday.

Getting There
Totonicapán is about 8 miles off the Pan American Highway on Route 1 via San Cristóbal. The nearby village of Andres Xecul has an unusual church

dominated by a façade that reproduces the design in the huipile worn by local women. Both communities can be reached easily by car or bus.

SAN FRANCISCO EL ALTO
Location:12 miles northwest of Totonicapán, 30 minutes from Xela.
Services: There are a couple of basic hospedajes here, should you wish to get to the market early (it starts at 4:00 a.m!).
For More Information: Contact the INGUAT office in Quetzaltenango.

Friday is market day in this stunning highland village located on a steep mountainside and surrounded by tall volcanoes and pine forests. The view to the valley far below is spectacular.

The buying and selling of farm and hunting animals at the big San Francisco el Alto **livestock market** held every Friday morning on the outskirts of town is not to be missed. For tourists, the in-town Friday market is also special. Besides consumer goods, fruit, and coffee, there are good buys on handmade woolen blankets bearing intricate geometric designs.

A large fiesta is held October 5 and includes some especially big and exotic markets. An old colonial church dominates the main plaza.

Getting There
Frequent buses come from Quetzaltenango; a few continue from San Francisco to Momostenango (see below). Some travel agencies and Spanish schools in Quetzaltenango arrange shuttle transport for the Friday market.

MOMOSTENANGO
Location: About 20 miles north of San Francisco.
Services: There are a couple of very basic hotels and restaurants.

This village is known throughout the world for its superbly made woolen blankets, scarves, and rugs, woven on large foot-looms. Market day is Sunday, and a regional fiesta called Octava de Santiago is held from July 28 to August 2. Traditional Maya rituals are also held throughout the year in Momostenango, one of the most traditional and spiritual communities in the western highlands. The ancient 260-day Tzolkin calendar is still in use here, and there are said to be as many as 300 indígena shamans living in the area, each specializing in a different kind of practice. About 2 miles from the village is a hot spring called **Palo Chiquito**, used for bathing (by locals only) and for the shrinking of newly made blankets.

The **Momostenango Riscos**, located in a rural area about .5 miles north of the town, are an unusual set of eroded pillars and caves composed of consolidated volcanic ash derived from eruptions that took place centuries ago. Ask locally for exact directions to the site (an easy walk or short taxi ride). It takes about an hour by car or bus from San Francisco on Route 2.

SAN MARCOS AND SAN PEDRO SACATEPÉQUEZ
Location: About 50 minutes by car northwest of Quetzaltenango.
Services: Several basic hotels and restaurants, most of them in San Pedro.

These twin cities (less than .5 miles apart) are located in a Mam-speaking region of the western highlands. The San Marcos department's largest market, famous for its colorful textiles, takes place in San Pedro every Tuesday, Thursday, and Sunday. (*Note:* There is another town of the same name near Antigua.) A local fair is also held in San Pedro the week of June 24. Tuesdays and Fridays are market days in the town of San Marcos, noted for its natural hot spring bathing center, called **Agua Tibia**.
Another local attraction is the **Maya Palace**, a strange-looking building situated between the two towns that is government headquarters for the department. The structure is elaborately decorated with imitation Maya friezes, and a sculpted pair of roaring jaguars guard the entrance.
A fiesta takes place in San Marcos April 22 through 27. Buses run each hour to Quetzaltenango, and several first-class pullmans leave for and from Guatemala City every day.

SANTA MARÍA, SANTIAGÜITO, TAJUMULCO, AND TACANÁ VOLCANOES
One of these four peaks—**Santiagüito**—is still active, and current conditions should be checked among outfitters before climbing it. The crater of Santiagüito is a 2- or 3-hour hike from the Llanos de Pinal, about 10 miles directly south of Quetzaltenango. **Santa María**, the higher peak of the same mountain (at 12,376 feet), is a fairly arduous climb. **Tajumulco** and **Tacaná**, north of San Marcos near the Mexican border, are not especially difficult climbs, but the altitude takes some adjustment. At 13,846 feet, Tajumulco is the highest mountain in all of Central America. Tacaná checks in at 13,429 feet. (See Chapter 4 for more on volcano climbing.)

HUEHUETENANGO AND VICINITY

HUEHUETENANGO
Location: About 90 minutes by car (about 55 miles) northwest of Quetzaltenango. If heading to or from Mexico, the border is an easy 52 miles to the west. Guatemala City is 160 miles southeast.

Population: 20,000 (1999 estimate).
Services: The post office is at 2a. Calle 3-54, Telgua is next door, and the Mexican Consulate is inside the Farmacia del Cid on the plaza at 5a. Avenida and 4a. Calle; all are in Zone 1. Banco de Guatemala, at 5a. Avenida and 4a. Calle, Zone 1, is the only bank that will exchange Mexican pesos.
For More Information: Tourism office on 2a. Calle opposite Hospedaje el Viajero.

Affectionately known as "Huehue," this small Ladino town is a good encampment for day trips to the many surrounding indígena villages, each with its own distinctive Maya markets and fiestas. Bus connections can be made here to scores of tiny settlements in the Cuchumatanes Mountains, the highest range in Guatemala, where life has changed very little in the last few hundred years.

Huehue is 4 miles off the Pan American Highway, at the base of the Cuchumatanes. It is an important trading center, with one of the best public markets in the highlands (indoors, at 3a. Avenida and 4a. Calle, open daily), and has an interesting neoclassical church overlooking the plaza. The best artesanía shop is **Ixquil**, at 5a. Avenida 1-56. Several Spanish schools operate here (see Chapter 4) and Huehue is not a bad place to study thanks to its lack of touristy distractions and low prices.

Getting There
Huehue is most easily reached from Guatemala City by first-class bus, and several depart each day from the capital. Allow about 6 hours. The best service is Los Halcones (7a. Avenida 15-27). If arriving by car, turn north from the Pan American Highway on Route 9-N for the short drive north into Huehue.

Where to Stay in Huehuetenango
Hotel Centro, 6a. Avenida 4-29; $8; no phone. A great place to meet fellow backpackers, though it is noisy and not very clean.

Hotel Mary, 2a. Calle 3-52, Zone 1; $7, or $20 for a room with TV; 764-1618. Not flashy, but a good value. Basic restaurant.

Hotel Zaculeu, 5a. Avenida 1-14, Zone 1; $38; 764-1086. The best place in town, with some rooms better than others. Those facing the older, inner courtyard are recommended. Acceptable restaurant.

Where to Eat in Huehuetenango
The best meals in Huehue are served in the hotels, but other recommendations are listed below.

Eboni, at 3a. Calle 5-11, Zone 1. Guatemalan and "international" cuisine in a youth-oriented atmosphere. Unusual "tiki bar" decor.

Pizza Hogareña, on 6a. Avenida between 4a. and 5a. Calles, Zone 1. Giant pizzas at rock-bottom prices. Terrific people-watching.

Restaurante Jardín, at 4a. Calle and 6a. Avenida in Zone 1. Inexpensive and tasty Guatemalan or American-style lunches and dinners.

Ven al Callejón, 6a. Avenida 4-40, Zone 1. One of the few night spots; live music, Spanish tapas.

Two women of Zunil

Richard Mahler

ZACULEU

Location: About 3 miles northwest of Huehuetenango.
Hours and Fees: Admission is about 25¢, and a small museum is open from 8:00 a.m. to noon and 1:00 p.m. to 6:00 p.m.

These restored ruins date from the pre-conquest period and are all that remain of the former capital of the Mam, one of the main highland Maya tribes. The archaeological park includes a few large temples, plazas, and a ball court, laid out in a strategic defense pattern. The walls of the constructions contain no hieroglyphic writing, and there are no stelae or figurative objects, possibly because of clumsy restoration work carried out by the United Fruit Company in the late 1940s. There is a picnic area, and the surroundings are pleasant, with a good view of the Cuchumatanes Mountains.

Getting There

Several buses and minivans head this direction (on 2a. Calle) each day from Huehuetenango (there is a stop in front of the Hotel Maya), or you can take a taxi. Walking to Zaculeu from Huehue takes about an hour. The route can be confusing, so be prepared to ask locals for directions.

TODOS SANTOS CUCHUMATÁN

Location: 30 miles northwest of Huehuetenango via the Paquix junction.
Population: About 2,000.

For More Information: There is no tourist office; inquire locally at hotels and restaurants that cater to foreigners.

Todos Santos is an isolated valley town ringed by tall, forested mountains. Its friendly Mam-speaking residents have maintained their traditional way of life. Men wear red-and-white-striped pants, black woolen breeches, straw hats, and elaborately embroidered collars; women wear dark blue skirts and brilliant red blouses. Even the saints in the old Catholic church are dressed up in local *traje*.

The elevation of Todos Santos is 8,154 feet, so temperatures are always fairly cool and it's often foggy in the morning and evening.

Things to See and Do

A good time to visit Todos Santos Cuchumatán is during the local All Saints' Day fiesta, October 31 to November 5, when an unusual kind of all-day horse relay race and other traditional celebrations can be observed, all with the accompaniment of marimba orchestras. Year-round attractions include the high-quality traje sold at the Saturday market, along with locally made pottery and woolen goods. There's a small Spanish- and Mam-language school, **Proyecto Lingüístico de Español**, as well as superb mountain hiking.

The 260-day Maya calendar is still used in Todos Santos, and shamans continue their ceremonies and rituals at nearby ruins. Nights can get very cold in the upland pastures where men tend their sheep. You will sometimes see the shepherds wearing a traditional overdress of long-haired black monkey skin.

Ask around and you may be invited to a traditional Mam sauna: Rocks are heated in a small enclosure, water is poured over them, and participants stay inside as long as they can stand it, sweating profusely.

A pathway next to Comedor Katy leads to the small Mayan site of **Tojcunanchén** above the village. A small museum ($1 admission) is located just off the plaza.

Getting There

Only a couple of buses run each day between Todos Santos and Huehuetenango (leaving Huehue at 4:00 a.m. and 11:00 a.m.); they continue up the valley to smaller communities where there are no services or accommodations. Because of difficult connections (the return buses leave Todos Santos at 4:30 a.m., 11:30 a.m., and 1:00 p.m.), it's best to plan on spending the night in Todos Santos if you're coming from Huehue, otherwise you'll leave soon after arriving. Allow about 4 hours each direction, with more crowded buses on Monday and Friday.

Where to Stay and to Eat in Todos Santos

A few simple comedores and taco stands are on or near the plaza, or try **Tres Olguitas,** known for its "starch extravaganza" meals. Avoid Comedor Katy: The food is expensive and not very good, but it's a popular hangout.

Basic lodging is available at **Pensión Lucía, Pensión Tres Olguitas,** and **Hospedaje La Paz,** all near the bus stop and all about $2 a night. Bring your own padlock if you wish to lock your room.

Casa Familiar, just up the street from the museum, may be your best choice. It's a step above the usual rice-and-beans with a balcony-type terrace on which to dine. They also sell new and used traje, including scrap cloth. Basic, clean rooms rent for $4.

Other Options

Hikers may be interested in the 5-hour trek through mountain passes and cloud forests from Todos Santos to **San Juan Atitán** (no lodging). Here the people still wear their traje and maintain a traditional Maya way of life. You can time your hike so that you can catch the infrequent bus back to Huehuetenango from San Juan. Shorter hikes can be arranged through Proyecto Lingüistico de Español.

Reached by a separate bus route from Huehue, **Jacaltenango** sits on a high limestone plateau near the Mexican border. Inquire locally about visiting **Cooperativa Río Azul, a** coffee finca where a brilliant blue stream flows along a bed of terraced travertine deposits emanating from the area's many caves, a sight that recalls the famous Agua Azul in Chiapas.

A local group called **Proyecto los Aislados** is helping provide environmental education for villagers in these isolated mountains; for information (in the U.S.) call (909) 659-0199.

SAN MATEO IXTATÁN AND AGUACATÁN

Location: San Mateo is about 8 hours by bus northeast of Huehuetenango. Aguacatán is about a 1-hour (17-mile) bus ride east of Huehuetenango, from which there are several daily buses along 1a. Calle, some continuing along Route 7W to Sacapulas.

Services: Aguacatán has a few basic hotels and restaurants but not much else. San Mateo's services are equally minimal.

Markets are held each Thursday and Sunday in the village of San Mateo Ixtatán, with a good selection of well-made textiles and other típica, including the warm woolen cape called a *capixay*. San Mateo is at a high altitude (above 8,000 feet) where wheat is grown and sheep are grazed. A scenic road continues to Nentún, near the Mexico border.

Thursday and Sunday are also market days in Aguacatán, the garlic and avocado center of the highlands. Aguateca is spoken here and in the surrounding countryside, but nowhere else on earth. The Spanish colonials tried to integrate the Aguateca Maya with the nearby Quiché but had little success. There are ruins of an early colonial church here, and nearby is the historic site of **Pueblo Viejo**, a pre-Columbian village with several unexcavated burial mounds.

Aguacatán's large Sunday market (which actually begins Saturday afternoon) is an excellent place to shop and people-watch. The women of Aguacatán are distinguished by their unusual headdress, a fanciful embroidered ribbon of bright reds, yellows, greens, and blues. Outside Aguacatán is the source of the **Río San Juan**, which bubbles from a nearly hidden limestone cave.

CHIANTLA

The village church in Chiantla is famous for its solid silver image of the Virgin Mary, which is said to have special restorative powers. Pilgrims come from throughout the country every February 2 to pay homage to the **Virgen del Rosario**. This is a spectacle worth seeing, although there are no hotels and few restaurants in the community itself. The silver for the icon was mined locally during the colonial era. Chiantla, located 3 miles north of Huehuetenango, has a market every Sunday near the plaza. Buses shuttle frequently between the village and Huehue (about a 15-minute trip).

THE HIGH ROAD TO NEBAJ AND COBÁN

From Huehuetenango, Route 7W twists and turns through the Cuchumatanes to Aguacatán, Sacapulas, and, after it intersects Route 3, the Ixil-speaking town of **Nebaj**. It is a scenic (usually two-day) bus ride along this road through eastern Quiché department and into the lush Sierra de Chuacús and Chamá of **Alta Verapaz**. Route 7W eventually meets the Cobán Highway north of Tactic. It is about 10 more miles from that intersection to the city of **Cobán**. This road is seldom taken by travelers, but there are a few very basic hospedajes and comedores along the way in **Cunén, Uspantán, Chicamán**, and **San Cristóbal Verapaz**. The adventurous would do well to inquire about local transportation, criminal activity, and services before heading east of Cunén along Route 7W. Several bicyclists have recommended this route as a scenic alternative to the busy Guatemala City-to-Cobán highway.

THE HIGH ROAD TO BARILLAS AND BEYOND

Route 9-N continues north from Huehuetenango into the Cuchumatanes and through mountain villages that are among the most traditional and undisturbed in Guatemala. It takes at least a full day (preferably two) to travel the 90-odd miles to **Barillas,** where the road runs out in a lowland forest that stretches deep into Mexico. There is talk about extending the one-lane road all the way to **Playa Grande,** on the Río Chixoy in Alta Verapaz, but further construction is unlikely while the Guatemalan government remains strapped for funds. The best restaurant in the area is El Comedor Central, serving up tasty roast-chicken dinners at their Barillas plaza location.

THE MEXICAN BORDER AND BEYOND

LA MESILLA
There are buses every 90 minutes or so between Huehuetenango and La Mesilla, on the Mexican border, a journey of about 2 hours. The border crossing is open from 6:00 a.m. to 9:00 p.m., sometimes later. Mexican tourist cards are always issued here; if you are coming from the other direction, however, Guatemalan visas are sometimes not available at this frontier. If needed, get those documents in advance (i.e., from the Guatemalan consulate in Comitán, Mexico).

Buses for San Cristóbal de las Casas and other Mexican cities start arriving in Ciudad Cuauhtémoc, Mexico, across from La Mesilla, at about noon each day. Heading south, you can catch a direct bus to Quetzaltenango and/or Guatemala City from La Mesilla starting at 6:00 a.m.

Be advised that this border crossing has been closed occasionally in recent years, during periods of civil unrest in Chiapas, the Mexican state immediately across the frontier. Check locally about political conditions before traveling in this part of Mexico.

There are a few basic hotels and restaurants in La Mesilla, but none are recommended and you are better off continuing your journey in either direction rather than staying here.

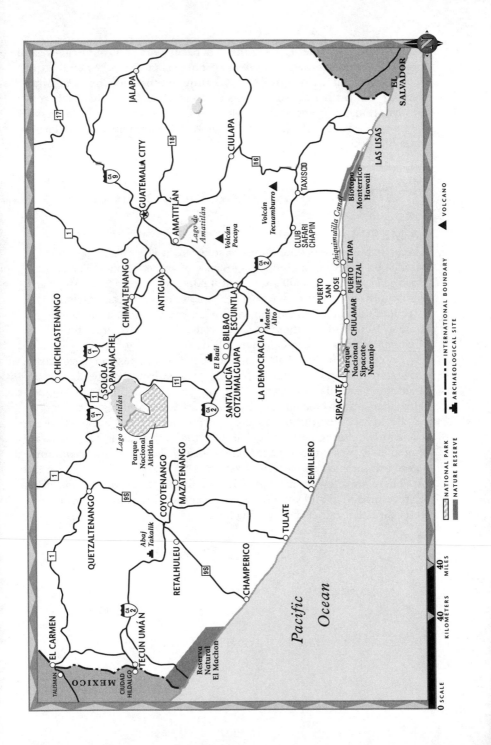

MEXICO

TALISMAN
CIUDAD HILDALGO

EL CARMEN

TECÚN UMÁN

Reserva Natural El Machon

Pacific Ocean

CHAMPERICO

RETALHULEU

Abaj Takalik

QUETZALTENANGO

COYOTENANGO

MAZATENANGO

TULATE

SEMILLERO

CHICHICASTENANGO

SOLOLÁ
PANAJACHEL

Lago de Atitlán

Parque Nacional Atitlán

CHIMALTENANGO

ANTIGUA

El Baúl
SANTA LUCÍA
COTZUMALGUAPA

BILBAO
ESCUINTLA

Monte Alto

LA DEMOCRACIA

SIPACATE

Parque Nacional Sipacate-Naranjo

CHULAMAR

PUERTO SAN JOSE

PUERTO IZTAPA
QUETZAL

Chiquimulilla Canal

Biotopo Monterrico-Hawaii

CLUB SAFARI CHAPIN

Volcán Pacaya

Lago de Amatitlán

AMATITLÁN

GUATEMALA CITY

JALAPA

CIULAPA

Volcán Tecuamburro

TAXISCO

LAS LISAS

EL SALVADOR

N

SCALE
0   40   KILOMETERS
0   40   MILES

NATIONAL PARK

NATURE RESERVE

ARCHAEOLOGICAL SITE

INTERNATIONAL BOUNDARY

VOLCANO

8

THE PACIFIC COAST

Guatemala's hot, humid Pacific coast is understandably low on the destination list for most visitors, although it does have some secluded beaches, ancient ruins, and nature reserves to recommend it. And in the winter, the balmy, dry weather is almost perfect.

The South Coast (known locally as La Costa Sur) is heavily cultivated, with a largely Ladino resident population and a sizable number of migrant indígena workers who come from the highlands to the area's labor camps during harvest times. There are many sugarcane fields, cattle pastures, tropical fruit plantations, and food-processing plants.

Many destinations along the Pacific coast are within an easy day's drive or bus trip of the capital, Antigua, Quetzaltenango, or Lake Atitlán. In addition, most of Guatemala's major tour operators have regular and reasonably priced trips to Pacific coast attractions by car or minivan.

Things to See and Do

The Pacific coast's beaches are scenic and relatively empty, but the afternoon sun can make them uncomfortably hot (due to their black volcanic sand) and offshore currents create treacherous swimming conditions. With one important exception—**Monterrico**—the resorts of the region cater primarily to Guatemalan families, most of whom visit on weekends and holidays.

Best bets for foreign travelers include the several archaeological sites and wetland nature reserves. There is also excellent deep-sea

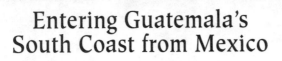

Entering Guatemala's South Coast from Mexico

There are several border posts for those approaching Guatemala's Pacific Coast from Mexico. El Carmen is the 24-hour Guatemalan crossing of CA-2 over the Río Suchiate into Talismán, Mexico. Because only a small number of services are available, it's best to plan your trip so that you'll be able to stay overnight or change buses in a larger town, such as Malacatán or Huehuetenango in Guatemala or Comitán in Mexico. There are better first-class bus connections here than farther south in Tecún Umán, a traffic-clogged village opposite the town of Ciudad Hidalgo, Mexico, with railroad and highway connections north as far as the United States. There is a 24-hour customs and immigration office, plus several small restaurants and basic hotels. Buses head from here in a steady stream into the interiors of Mexico and Guatemala.

fishing offshore, and ample opportunities for birding, volcano climbing, white-water rafting, and kayaking.

Getting There

By bus: Buses serve most coastal towns with frequent, reliable schedules. As in the rest of the country, these vehicles (except for first-class coaches) are usually uncomfortably crowded old school buses. From the Zone 4 terminal (4a. Avenida near 1a. Calle) in Guatemala City buses depart each day for such communities as Puerto San José, Las Lisas, and Escuintla (which is also served from the Zone 1 terminal at 18a. Calle and 9a. Avenida). Connections serving smaller communities can be made via Escuintla, Retalhuleu, and other big towns.

By car: The main road through the region is the Pacific Coast Highway, marked on signs and maps as CA-2. It runs roughly parallel to the Pacific (east/west) from the Mexican frontier to El Salvador. The highway is actually some distance from the ocean, but feeder roads connect it to virtually every Costa Sur community and to the western highlands. From Guatemala City, take CA-9 southwest past Lake Amatitlán to intersect the Coastal Highway at Escuintla. From Lake Atitlán, head south on CA-11 and meet CA-2 near Patulul. From Quetzaltenango, the coast route is reached by heading south on 9-S, which continues to the seaport town of Champerico.

ESCUINTLA
Location: 40 miles southwest of Guatemala City.
Population: 45,000 (1999 estimate).
For More Information: Consult the Guatemala City office of INGUAT.

The largest of the coastal towns, located at the junction of the Pacific Coast Highway and the main road between Guatemala City and Puerto San José, Escuintla is a dull but bustling commercial center that has little to recommend it beyond a busy daily market near the plaza (terrific watermelons and coconuts), convenient bus connections, and easy access to the archaeological sites around Santa Lucía Cotzumalguapa, 12 miles west on the Coast Highway.

Getting There
Buses operate frequently from the Zone 4 and Zone 9 terminals in Guatemala City. Connections are easily made in Escuintla to other towns up and down the Pacific Coast.

Where to Stay and Eat in Escuintla
There are many budget hotels ($10 or less) near the market on 3a. and 4a. Avenida. Along 4a. Avenida, Escuintla's main street, you can find plenty of inexpensive eateries serving everything from Chinese fried rice to fresh seafood. None are noteworthy.

Hotel Texas, Avenida Centro América 15-04, Zone 3; $20; 888-0183. Centrally located, with 26 rooms. Also serves meals.

Sarita, Avenida Centro América 15-32, Zone 3; $30; 888-0482, fax 888-1959. The best among undistinguished lodging choices, with restaurant and other amenities.

PUERTO SAN JOSÉ
Location: 25 miles south of Escuintla, on the Pacifica coast.
Population: 12,000 (1999 estimate).
Main Activities: Shipping, tourism.

Located about a 2-hour drive south of Guatemala City, this city is a
major cargo port, although somewhat overshadowed by the new Puerto
Quetzal a few miles to the east. Nearby also are the beach resorts of
Chulamar and Likin, which tend to be crowded and noisy on weekends
and during school vacations.

Things to See and Do
San José and adjacent holiday retreats are separated from the beach by
the **Chiquimulilla Canal**, a human-made inland waterway that runs
from Sipacate, 15 miles west of San José, all the way to the Salvadoran
border. There are plenty of small ferries transporting beach-goers across
the canal throughout the day and evening. You can also hire a boatman
to transport you along the canal in either direction, dropping you at the
secluded beach, campground, or resort of your choice. This is one way
to get to **Monterrico** (via ferry and bus from Itzapa), but you're better
off going by way of Taxisco and La Avellana further east.

Getting There
Buses run here frequently from Escuintla, or you can make the drive in
about 40 minutes via CA-9.

Where to Stay and Eat in and Around San José
The larger hotels have reliable restaurants, and a number of inexpensive
comedores serve good shrimp dishes and other seafood.
   Note: Be advised that prices at all of the better hotels in the San José
area vary dramatically, depending on whether it is a weekend or a holiday
(expensive), weekday or slow season (moderate). It's recommended that
you bargain for your room rate if you visit during an off time, especially if
you wish to stay more than a day or two.

Agua Azul, Km. 106.5; $45; tel/fax 881-1667. Thirty-two rooms.

Posada del Quetzal, Avenida 30 de Junio; $40; tel/fax 881-1601.
Eighteen rooms, with a more expensive annex in Barrio Miramar.

CHULAMAR, PUERTO QUETZAL, AND LIKIN
Chulamar, a self-contained, moderately priced resort about 3 miles
west of San José, has several restaurants, swimming pools, and decent
beaches. Heading east, past the container cargo and cruise ship terminal of Puerto Quetzal, is the fully planned (and security-conscious)
community of Balneario Likin. Boats can shuttle you to the broad
beach, but otherwise there is not much to do here.

Ripe coffee beans are Guatemala's most important commodity.

Where to Stay and Eat in Chulamar, Likin, and Puerto Quetzal

As an alternative to renting a room at one of the lodgings below, you can camp on the beach at Iztapa, but the environs are rather dirty and polluted. Watch your stuff! You will have better luck near El Cenacaste and Madre Vieja, beach villages farther along as you head toward Monterrico.

Hotel Santa María del Mar, in Chulamar; $38; 881-1293. Rooms and cabañas are usually filled on weekends and holidays, when the rates triple.

Turicentro Likin Hotel, in Likin; 756-1061. Bungalows and a small restaurant.

IZTAPA AND THE CHIQUIMULILLA CANAL

The main road east of San José along the beachfront ends at the town of Iztapa, a quiet and crumbling old port used by the early Spanish as the main Guatemalan naval station.

There are hourly buses from Guatemala City. You can take the car ferry across the Río Naranjo to Pueblo Viejo and a bus from there to the pleasant beachside village of Monterrico, or hire a boat and follow the Chiquimulilla Canal, which winds its way for another 25 miles to Las Lisas on a course roughly parallel to the ocean. Unfortunately,

213

what could be a peaceful journey with plenty of birding is often interrupted by noisy speedboats.

Where to Stay in Iztapa

Iztapa has several lodging choices, all of reasonable quality and some with modest cafés. None, however, are exceptional.

Sol y Playa Tropical, on the riverfront; $15; no phone. Basic rooms for budget travelers.

MONTERRICO–HAWAII NATURE RESERVE

Location: About 50 miles south of Guatemala City, on the Pacific Ocean.
Population: 800 (1999 estimate).
For More Information: There's no tourist office, but the Hotel Baule Beach is an excellent source of travel tips, as is Michael's Pig Pen Bar (both on the beach; see below).

This isolated area and the **Río Samalá** wetlands near Champerico are the only parts of Guatemala's Pacific lowlands that enjoy specific environmental protection.

Things to See and Do

Located near the tiny village of Monterrico, the 7,000-acre **Monterrico–Hawaii Biotope** includes several miles of pristine coastline, a stretch of inland mangrove swamp, and some lowland forest. This is an extremely important habitat for many species of waterfowl, such as herons and egrets, plus the many small fish, crabs, insects, worms, and other creatures on which they feed. Quite a few migratory birds also make this their winter home. The maze of mangrove roots provide a kind of underwater nursery, where hatchlings can grow to adulthood with plenty of nutrients and some measure of protection from predators. Raccoons, opossums, anteaters, weasels, iguanas, and other water-loving animals are found here. You can hire a guide to take you through the wetlands in a boat (expect to pay at least $3 an hour) or rent a canoe or pole-powered *cayuco* of your own.

The reserve's management has been embroiled in controversy in recent years, and the headquarters and sanctuary have been virtually deserted. There are few interpretive signs and visitation appears minimal. Things are most active on Sundays, when tours are offered for a nominal fee. The main facility is on the beach immediately east of the El Baule Hotel, which posts some information about the turtles that come here.

Sea turtles are raised and released at the sanctuary in the hope of increasing their numbers, which have been devastated by human hunters (who continue to gather, eat, and sell their eggs despite the animals' endangered status). Sea turtles nest and lay their eggs along the beach from June to February before returning to the ocean. Farther inland, the reserve protects the habitat of freshwater turtles. If your visit corresponds with the hatching period, you can help the newborn turtles make their successful escape to the Pacific. Iguanas and caiman are also bred here in cages at the reserve in an effort to produce young reptiles for release in the wild. All in all there's not much to see and one feels like a witness to a great idea that's slowly fallen apart. (For more information, see Chapter 3, Flora and Fauna.)

The Monterrico reserve, with its overgrown, self-guided nature trail and neglected-looking breeding facility, is bisected by the meandering **Chiquimulilla Canal**, which offers good birding opportunities. The reserve extends south to the fishing village of **Hawaii**, accessible by boat or on foot, the site of a few vacation homes and one simple hospedaje (you can also rent rooms in a private home). **Las Lisas** is the next village along the beach, with very basic lodging, but foot access is blocked by the Chiquimulilla Canal.

The reserve incorporates the village of **Monterrico**, which has simple accommodations and restaurants, plus a few meager gift shops and groceries. A Spanish school (not recommended) has operated here intermittently. You can arrange deep-sea fishing trips by inquiring locally: Marlin, tarpon, sailfish, and tuna are in ample supply offshore, along with the occasional dolphin and whale.

A word of warning about the beach: Undertows and surf are dangerously strong; a number of people have drowned here. Swimming and surfing are not recommended, although you can wade in far enough to cool off without much risk. Bring your own beach towels— and sandals to walk on the warm black sand. The sand is very littered and you are likely to encounter both beggars and fast-moving vehicles at regular intervals. Mosquitoes come out in force at dusk, so bring insect repellent.

Nightlife is pretty much limited to a handful of bars including the Canadian-owned **Pig Pen**, 50 feet west off the main street on the beach, which also rents surfboards and whose colorful owner, Michael, cheerfully dispenses tourist information. There's often a party scene here on weekend nights: This may be the only bar in Guatemala where you can get waited on in a hammock.

Despite its sundry negatives, Monterrico is a pleasant place to hang out and relax for a while, especially if you've had your fill of bone-rattling chicken buses and nerve-racking verb conjugations. This is the only budget-priced, foreigner-friendly beach community on the country's Pacific Coast.

Getting There

Monterrico can be reached by public boat (20 minutes, 50¢) from La Avellana, a small town at the end of a road that intersects with the Pacific Coast Highway at Taxisco. You can even transport a car or RV through the swamp on simple, one-vehicle barges.

If arriving by public bus from the north; you'll need to transfer to the La Avellana bus in Taxisco, about 30 minutes north. (Make sure you find the right bus stop: The Escuintla-bound bus doesn't take the road to La Avellana.) From Guatemala City's Zone 4 or Zone 13 terminals, the trip to Monterrico takes 3 to 4 hours and costs about $3. (Although it's less convenient, you can also take a public bus and ferry from Puerto San José to Pueblo Viejo, then hop one of the three or four local buses that run each day to Monterrico.)

From the public boat dock in Monterrico it's about a 10-minute walk (or faster taxi ride) straight south on the village's main street to the beach. Turn left (east) for most of the beachside accommodations and restaurants as well as the reserve headquarters and turtle sanctuary.

Where to Stay and Eat in Monterrico

The most expensive hotel in the area is also the least recommended. The **Monterico Paradise**, 238-4690, west of the village, is noted for its bad food, unfriendly staff, and inconvenient location. Meals are available at various local hotels, cafés, and comedores, but your best bets are the dining rooms at the **Hotel Baule** and **Pez de Oro**, both east of the main street along the beach. Food is somewhat cheaper in the village itself (try **Divino Maestro**), but the ambiance is different (there are no sunset views).

Hotel Baule Beach, on the beach; $12, rates lower for stays longer than three days; 473-6196 or fax 471-3990 in Guatemala City, ask for Lorena. Run by former Peace Corps worker Nancy Garver. Although the rooms at this hotel are basic and not particularly clean, amenities include a decent restaurant and fabulous swimming pool. Tours of the reserve by *cayuco*, foot, or horseback can be arranged here. Recommended.

Johnny's Place, on the beach; 336-4193 in Guatemala City. For about $8 you can rent a four-bed bungalow.

Kaiman Inn, on the beach; $15; no phone. The Kaimann Inn is an overpriced Italian-run hotel/restaurant with a pool and nice landscaping. You can do better.

Las Marías Sea Cottages, on the beach; $12; no phone. Rustic cabañas, away from the crowds.

Pez de Oro, on the beach, past the sanctuary; $14; 331-3768 in Guatemala City. The best value among the seaside bungalow lodges, with a small swimming pool, attractive restaurant, and friendly Italian-managed staff. The best food in Monterrico.

Other Options

Some of Monterrico's lodges will let you camp on their grounds, but theft is a big problem in this area, especially on weekends. The area can sometimes become crowded with Guatemalans who escape from the city to hang out at their *ranchos* (beach houses), which dot the coast for miles in either directon. Inquire locally and you may find a rancho for rent. During the rainy season (June through November), the area can be unpleasantly humid and buggy, with very rough surf.

The margay is one of five cats native to the forests of both Belize and Guatemala.

Belize Tourist Board

CLUB SAFARI AFRICA CHAPIN
Location: A few miles west of Taxisco, at Km. 87.5 on the coast highway.
Hours and Fees: The park is open Tuesday through Sunday from 9:30 a.m. to 5:00 p.m. An all-day ticket costs about $2.

Guatemala's one and only "wild animal park" is seldom visited by foreigners. The facility is on the grounds of a large ranch, whose owners were once big-game hunters. The family's younger generation is more conservation-minded and has used part of the property to protect and breed lions, hippos, giraffes, black rhinos, cats, and other large mammals, along with many kinds of snakes and birds.

You can ride through the park on a minibus and stroll through a small zoo, mostly devoted to native species of Guatemala. Your entry ticket entitles you to use the swimming pools and picnic grounds, plus the tour. There is also a restaurant on the premises, which gets crowded on weekends and holidays, when Guatemalan families like to visit.

ARCHAEOLOGICAL SITES

Unlike other parts of Guatemala, the archaeological sites of the Pacific piedmont are spread out and in some cases difficult to access. A few are on private land, surrounded by cultivated fields of sugarcane and other crops. Many of the remarkable carved stone monuments for which the region is famous have eroded considerably over the years or have been carelessly disassembled. A good number have also been carted off to museums and private collections. Because of these circumstances, visitors may be better off taking an organized tour from Guatemala City, hiring a local guide, or securing a well-informed taxi driver, rather than trying to find some of these obscure archaeological sites on their own. Violence against tourists has been a problem here in recent years.

MONTE ALTO ARCHAEOLOGICAL PARK
Location: In the town of La Democracia on Route 2, about 6 miles south of the Pacific Coast Highway and just east of Santa Lucía.
For More Information: Contact the INGUAT office in Guatemala City (331-1333, fax 331-4416) or Antigua (331-2060).

Little is known about the origins of the Olmec-style carved stones and fig-ures that are strewn about the fields of the Monte Alto Archaeological Park, in the La Democracia town plaza. Many archaeologists believe that Mexico's ancient Olmec, in addition to the Maya, occupied this part of Guatemala for some time. These experts point out that some of the carved figures wear Mexican-style clothing and headdresses or have faces that resemble Olmec gods, such as those represented at the Monte Alban site near Oaxaca, Mexico. Other historians disagree, preferring to connect these ruins more closely with the highland and Petén Maya of Guatemala, although no Maya glyphs have yet been found here. Still others feel that these sculptures may be the work of neither group. Whatever their origin, some of the carvings may be well over 4,000 years old, which would put their creation during the most formative years of the Maya civilization.

Things to See and Do
The park features colossal carved stone heads from the Late Pre-Classic era (300 B.C. to A.D. 300), which are believed to have been created by the Olmec. The collection also includes enigmatic pot-bellied stone figures that were hauled in by Europeans from their original location 4 miles away at Monte Alto, where there are no longer any ruins. Smaller speci-mens are found in the city's archaeological museum (open 9:00 a.m. to

noon and 2:00 p.m. to 5:00 p.m., Tuesday through Sunday, except holidays). Also on display are obsidian blades and carvings of mushrooms, which lead some observers to speculate that hallucinogenic fungi may have been used in ceremonial rituals by these early residents.

Other fat-jowled, Buddha-like heads and eroding zoomorphs (carved, animal-like figures) are scattered throughout the rolling hills of this area. Some are still used by local indígena in rituals that involve the anointing of the rocks with sugarcane liquor (which is then burned) along with incense, flower petals, and sacrificial blood.

Getting There
Buses pass through frequently en route from Escuintla, or you can arrange transport through a tour operator in Guatemala City or Antigua. Yet another option is to rent a car and drive yourself.

Where to Stay and Eat near Monte Alto Archaeological Park
Caminotel Santiagüito, Km. 90.5, Santa Lucía Cotzumalguapa; $40; 882-5435, fax 882-5438. One of the few upscale options hereabouts, there is a large swimming pool and the restaurant usually has fresh seafood or paella available, along with cold drinks and sandwiches.

Hotel El Camino; $10; 882-5316. Across the highway from the Caminotel Santiagüito: less flashy but perfectly acceptable, with 19 rooms.

EL BAÚL, EL BILBAO, AND LAS ILUSIONES
Location: Near Santa Lucía.
Services: There are no accommodations or restaurants in the area worth mentioning, beyond those detailed in the Monte Alto Archaeological Park section.
For More Information: Inquire among taxi drivers in Santa Lucía, or at INGUAT offices in Antigua, Quetzaltenango, or Guatemala City.

Each of these sites contains monumental stone sculptures of the little-known Cotzumalguapa-Pipil culture, which flourished here during the Classic era and was apparently linked to both the highland Maya and the Mexican Olmec.

The **El Baúl** site is about 3 miles north of Santa Lucía on a sugar plantation and is the most accessible to visitors. There are several stones at the top of a hill, both still used in animal sacrifices, flower offerings, and the burning of incense. The tallest of these is a fertility symbol, used in supplications for pregnancy and safe births. Another carved stone resembles an enormous head, blackened now by countless burning rituals. Yet another stele shows a presumed ruler in ritual paraphernalia holding a

El Manchón Nature Reserve

The truly adventurous nature lover or fisher may want to arrange an excursion into the mosquito-infested wetlands northwest of the scruffy seaport town of Champerico. This is a government-protected area intended to preserve the habitat of native crocodiles, armadillos, coatimundi, and the occasional jaguar, along with scores of species of water birds. You will need an experienced guide to show you around, which should be possible to arrange in the coastal village of Manchón or Champerico, about 10 miles to the southeast. This remote area is seldom visited, yet remains rich in the flora and fauna that has otherwise all but disappeared from Guatemala's Pacific coast. Bring plenty of insect repellent and sunscreen!

wavy-bladed flint knife. As at other ceremonial centers, you should stay away when the shrine is in obvious use unless specifically beckoned forward by participants. A number of sculptures, some with non-Maya glyphs, have been stacked haphazardly next to a sugar refinery.

The **El Bilbao** site is immediately north of Santa Lucía and consists of four sets of stelae, all that remains of a much larger ceremonial site that was shipped off to Germany—nearly in its entirety—in the 1880s. The stones were carved by artisans of the Pipil culture between A.D. 400 and 900. The glyphs bear some resemblance to others found in southern Mexico from the same era. The monuments are well hidden by sugarcane, and the services of a local guide are strongly advised.

Las Ilusiones is a mile or so east of Santa Lucía, also surrounded by sugarcane fields. The attraction here is a jumbled but impressive collection of stone carvings and artifacts, some with Olmec characteristics, others that look like Maya creations. You will have to ask at the main house of the finca for someone to unlock the building that houses this eclectic private museum. Particularly interesting are the finely carved stelae and zoomorphs. The site can be visited for a small fee between 8:00 a.m. and 5:00 p.m. Again, a guide is recommended.

Three other small Pipil sites are within a few miles of Santa Lucía: **Pantaleon, El Castillo**, and **Santa Rita**. Ask locally for directions to these stone monuments.

ABAJ TAKALIK
Location: Located between Coatepeque and Retalhuleu, on CR-6W. Retalhuleu is about 25 miles south of Quetzaltenango, inland from the coast; the Abaj Takalik monuments are roughly 6 miles northwest of Retalhuleu. *For More Information:* INGUAT office in Quetzaltenango (761-4931) or Guatemala City (331-1333, fax 331-4416).

Researchers believe this is one of the first places along the coast where carved stone stelae became a public and religious art form, at about 100 B.C. Monumental structures at the Abaj Takalik site, also known as El Asintal (the name of the town where it is located), include some carved stones with Olmec and others with Pre-Classic Maya characteristics. Apparently both groups lived here at different times. Some stelae found here bear hieroglyphic dates in the Long Count notation corresponding to A.D. 200. Others, which have been damaged, may be older. Altogether there are about 50 stone monuments at Abaj Takalik, the 12 largest averaging nearly 15 tons each.

Getting There
There are frequent buses to Retalhuleu from Quetzaltenango and Escuintla. You can then arrange private transport to the archaeological site. Tours depart regularly from Antigua, Quetzaltenango, and Guatemala City.

Where to Stay and to Eat near Abaj Takalik
Hotel Astor, 5a. Calle 4-60, Zone 1; $24; 771-0475. Good alternative for bed and board if the Don José is full. The city plaza, two blocks away, has marimba bands at night.
Posada de Don José, 5a. Calle 3-67, Zone 1; $32; 771-1080, fax 771-1179. TV, a/c, good restaurant, bar, and a large pool. Recommended.

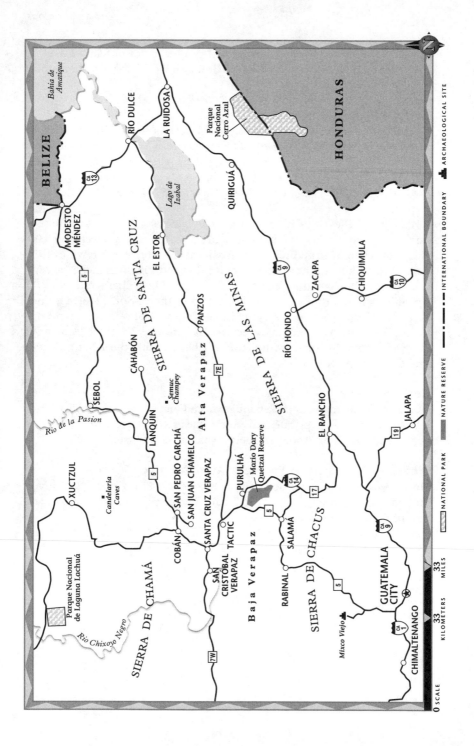

THE VERAPACES

This mountainous area immediately northeast of the central highlands was one of the last to be brought under Spanish domination, in the late 16th century.

The departments of **Baja** (Lower) and **Alta** (Upper) **Verapaz** cling tightly to their indigenous traditions and bloodlines. The Ladino presence is largely confined to larger towns and the most recently settled farmlands. Coffee is the number one cash crop, although there is also much cultivation of cardamom, corn, cacao, allspice, and maguey.

There is a paved highway to the area's largest city, Cobán, which is of most interest to the traveler as a base for touring local Maya villages, caving, hiking, white-water rafting, and visiting nearby nature reserves. En route you will pass a cloud forest remnant dedicated to the preservation of Guatemala's endangered national bird, the quetzal.

HISTORY

Known as the Land of War in the early years of the conquest, this region was defended by fierce indigenous Maya who thwarted successive waves of conquistadors.

Finally, the king of Spain granted liberation theologist and pacifist priest Bartolomé de las Casas five years in which to peacefully convert the Quiché, Pokomán, and Kekchí Maya who inhabited the area. Las Casas distinguished himself among the tribes by allowing them to worship Christ in their own languages, something that was then unheard of. His respectful outreach worked, and the area was renamed La Tierra de la Verapaz (Land of the True Peace). Las Casas continued to fight for justice throughout the country and returned to Spain to argue against the enslavement of Guatemalan indígena, inspired by his belief that all humans share the same basic civil rights.

Even after its conversion to Christianity, isolated Verapaz existed for centuries almost as if it were a separate country. Until the mid-1970s there were no paved roads, and all trade was via pack animals, forest trails, and river boats. A rail link to the Caribbean coast was abandoned earlier this century and air traffic was infrequent.

Cobán, the capital of the department of Alta Verapaz, was founded by Bartolomé de las Casas in 1538. By 1900 it had become like no other city in Central America. Many German coffee growers moved to the area, beginning in the 1880s, enticed by the promise of virtually free land and labor. They created a cosmopolitan, cultured society of their own in Cobán that dominated the coffee industry for more than half a century. Under pressure from the U.S., the Guatemalan government expelled most of the Germans during World War II and took over many of their coffee plantations.

BAJA VERAPAZ

Guatemala's department of Baja Verapaz is a land of steep mountains and rolling hills, some of these bare and studded with cacti, others thick with pines or hardwoods.

Most visitors enter the region by turning north off the Atlantic Highway at El Rancho, a hot and dusty town at the bottom of the Río Motagua gorge. The road immediately begins winding its way into the westernmost foothills of the Sierra de las Minas through a hot desert landscape. Within minutes, however, the cacti become fewer as the air becomes cooler and more humid at the higher altitudes. Trees, mostly pines and other softwoods, become the rule rather than the exception. In less than an hour, the terrain has become lush and pastoral.

Things to See and Do
The view toward the provincial capital of **Salamá**, reached by a side road that heads from the main highway into the San Jeronimo Valley, recalls the wine country of Northern California. The large colonial church at Salamá contains 14 finely carved and gilded altars as well as a figure of Christ made by the celebrated Guatemalan artist Evaristo Zuñiga.

The Pokomchí village of **San Miguel Chicaj**, 6 miles west of Salamá, is famous for the beauty and quality of its textiles, which you can buy in local public markets. A gorgeous and historic church, damaged in the 1976 earthquake, was carefully restored and reopened in 1997. The community's annual fiesta is September 27–28.

A short distance farther west is **Rabinal**, known for the production of its pre-Columbian-style *nij* ceramics, unique musical instruments, and painted gourds. Nij is an unusual dye extracted from insects found in the area. On January 25 each year, the town puts on its dramatic **Rabinal Achí Ballet**, which dates back to before the Spanish conquest. Rabinal was the first village "peacefully" converted in 1537 by the Dominicans under Fray Bartolomé de las Casas. Also nearby are **Los Chorros Springs**, an outdoor bathing complex.

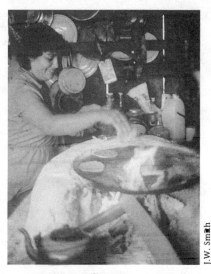

Making tortillas from scratch, the Guatemalan way

On a hill above Rabinal is the **Cahrup** (also called Xecoc) archaeological site, the original Pokomchí capital, with its sweeping vista of the Urrán Valley. A few miles to the northwest are the ruins of another pre-Columbian city, the quarries from which the Quiché hauled stones to build their far-off capital at Utatlán. Route 5 now follows this path to Guatemala City.

About 25 miles west of Rabinal is the isolated town of **Cubulco**, in a valley surrounded by lush, forested peaks. The annual fiesta that peaks on January 23 features the rarely seen pre-conquest ritual of the **Palo Volador**, in which men fling themselves from the top of a 90-foot pole with coiled ropes tied to their legs, then spin to the ground while the rope unravels (hoping to land on their feet). The spectacle, which finds its Western equivalent in Bungee-jumping, is as amazing (and dangerous) as it sounds. If you decide to spend the night, a room in the downtown *farmacia* is one of the very few options. Simple meals are available at stands in the public market.

SIERRA DE LAS MINAS BIOSPHERE RESERVE

Location: *About 50 miles east of Guatemala City, encompassing portions of the Baja Verapaz and Izabal departments.*

Size: 143,000 acres.
Hours and Fees: *There were no posted hours or entrance fees as of 1999.*
Services: *Accommodations and services are very limited and very basic.*
For More Information: *Contact the park's management, Defensores de la Naturaleza at its Guatemala City office (Avenida las Americas 20-21, Zone 14; 337-3897, defensores@pronet.net.gt), or through one of the group's local offices in Chilasco or Salamá.*

One of the last truly wild places in Guatemala is a tall, 30-mile-wide, east-west mountain range that runs for roughly 100 miles, from near Salamá in Baja Verpaz to the ridges above Mariscos, in the department of Izabal. Saving the ecologically dynamic wilderness of the rugged Sierra de las Minas is the main focus of the Guatemalan conservation group Defenders of Nature (Defensores de la Naturaleza). With assistance from Conservation International, World Wildlife Fund, Swedish Children's Rain Forest, and several other nonprofit organizations, Defenders of Nature and the Guatemalan government have been able to give much of these mountain lands protective status.

A great deal of the range's habitat has been largely protected from agriculture by its natural features: steep hillsides, shallow soils, and fickle weather. Because the heart of the mountains is made of jade and marble, however, mining has been carried out here for centuries (thus the name).

Created in 1990, the reserve offered only limited access to casual visitors as this book went to press in 1999, pending approval of a long-term management plan. Roads are so rough as to be virtually impassable in bad weather; trails are equally strenuous.

Protection of the Sierra de las Minas range is especially important because it contains an estimated 60 percent of Guatemala's remaining cloud forest habitat, home of the elusive quetzal. Because of its geographic isolation, forbidding terrain, and wide range of elevation (from 15 feet to 10,050 feet above sea level), the Sierra is home to at least 885 species of birds, mammals, amphibians, and reptiles—fully 70 percent of all the species from these groups known to exist in Guatemala and neighboring Belize.

Forest experts refer to these mountains as "an important tropical gene bank of conifer endoplasm," noting that 17 distinct species of evergreens are found here and nowhere else on earth. The area is thus considered an irreplaceable seed resource for reforestation and agroforestry throughout the tropics.

Besides its robust population of diverse flora and fauna, the Sierra de las Minas plays an important role in providing fresh, clean water to the many farms and villages in valleys below. More than 63 permanent rivers drain from the reserve, making it the country's biggest water resource. This is particularly important because the area southeast of the Sierra is a rain-shadow desert heavily dependent on irrigation. The dense forests in the northern part of the reserve and on mountain summits naturally filter rainwater, prevent topsoil erosion, and inhibit river siltation.

The reserve's managers are engaged in an environmental education program designed to convince community leaders of the project's value and teach soil conservation techniques to local farmers, many of them Kekchí Maya. The goal is to discourage their ongoing migration into the forest and to establish "sustainable" agricultural activities—those that do no long-term damage to the environment—in the buffer zone surrounding the reserve. Tourism is an important alternative to such destruction; therefore, your visit may help encourage locals to protect their forests.

Hiking the Sierra de Las Minas

In 1994 a rugged, 20-mile wilderness trail was completed through the western end of the Sierra de las Minas Biosphere Reserve between the villages of San Agustín Acasaguastlán, east of El Rancho, and Chilascó, past the northern boundary of the protected area. The trek requires overnight camping and two long days of strenuous hiking (the first day is mostly uphill, the second mostly down). The trail winds through some of the wildest territory remaining in Guatemala (with greater biodiversity than even the Petén), and the first trekkers who used the trail reported many animal sightings and fantastic bird life. Large cloud forests dominate the peaks, interspersed with stands of bamboo and moss-covered hardwoods. Recommended times to visit are the months of January through March, which have lowest rainfall. In any season, this hike is recommended for only well-equipped, fit, and adventurous individuals.

Getting There

Visitors dependent on public transportation are best off starting in Chilascó (take a bus to the CA-14 turn-off, then hitch a ride or hike to the village) and ending their trip at San Agustín Acasaguastlán (which is close enough to CA-9 to catch a bus to Guatemala City or Puerto Barrios). Guides, who can be hired in Chilascó, will take visitors to several sightseeing points within the reserve. Roads to these villages are passable by private car during the dry weather.

Where to Stay and Eat near Sierra de las Minas

Lodging closest to the Sierra de Las Minas consists of the two hotels next to the Mario Dary Quetzal Reserve (see below). Chialascó and San

Agustín Acasaguastlán, at either end of the Sierra de las Minas trailhead, have few tourist services except for a few guides. See Proyecto Ecológico Quetzal later in this chapter for nearby eco-travel services at Chicacnab.

Hotel Tezuluylán, Ruta 4 in Salamá; $8; no phone. Basic rooms and meals.

MARIO DARY QUETZAL RESERVE

Location: About 35 miles southeast of Cobán, on the main road to Guatemala City. It is about a mile south of the small village of Purulhá at Km. 162.
Size: 2,849 acres, of which 62 are open to the public.
Hours and Fees: The reserve is open from 6:00 a.m. to 4:00 p.m. and has no telephone or hotel. Donations are gladly accepted.
Services: There is ample parking at the visitors center, which encompasses a small museum, store, and picnic area. Adjacent to the center are restrooms, hammock shelters, and campsites.
For More Information: Contact the conservation organization CECON in Guatemala City (Avenida Reforma 0-63, Zone 10). Local guides, who can be hired for a small fee at the visitors center, are excellent sources of information about the plants and animals of the region.

You can experience firsthand one of Guatemala's rarest ecosystems, the tropical cloud forest, along the main Baja Verapaz highway. With luck, you may even glimpse Guatemala's elusive national bird.

Only a small portion of the Mario Dary Quetzal Reserve, also called Biotopo del Quetzal, is open to the public, to assure future generations the chance to see this almost mythic bird. Revered by the ancient Maya and long a symbol of freedom for all Guatemalans, the male quetzal (the female is a dull brown) bears a crown of brilliant green feathers and a chest of crimson, followed by an umistakable train of golden-green tail feathers. He almost never survives in captivity. The quetzal is a notoriously shy creature, and this protected habitat may be one of its last hopes for survival in this country, although substantial cloud forests yet remain in the Sierra de las Minas, southeast of the reserve, and in the mountains east of San Juan Chamelco. (See Chapter 3, Flora and Fauna, for more information about the quetzal.)

An environmentally friendly sewage system processes human wastes in the reserve, and biodegradable materials such as tree-fern trunks are used in building trails. Several interpretive nature trails of varying lengths and steepness begin near the visitors center. Guides can take you deep into the forest to such destinations as **Xio Ua Li Che** (Grandfather Tree), a living shrine said to be nearly five centuries old.

The Mario Dary Legacy

A bust of Mario Dary near the entrance to the park commemorates the tireless campaign this University of San Carlos environmentalist waged to establish a cloud forest sanctuary for the quetzal. Dary was assassinated in Guatemala City in 1981, not long after the preserve was created by the government in cooperation with the environmental studies department Dary founded at the university. Some speculate that lumber interests, unhappy about his efforts to protect the highland forests, may have had a hand in Dary's still-unsolved murder.

Things to See and Do

Nature Trails

The reserve's shady pathways are well maintained and regularly patrolled, turning and twisting into the steep embankments and canyons of the nearby hills. An easy 30-minute hike on **Musgos (Mosses) Trail** passes beneath tall, orchid-covered trees and giant ferns, ending at a small but spectacular waterfall. Longer treks of up to 3 hours follow the Río Colorado toward its source on a lush ridge of the **Chuacús Mountains**, where spider monkeys, toucans, and parrots can sometimes be observed in the high canopy.

The vegetation in the reserve is lush and thick, with a profusion of vines, epiphytes (air plants), liverworts, mosses, lichens, palms, and ferns that thrive on the nightly mists cascading down from the surrounding peaks. Trees include varieties of oak, cypress, walnut, and pepper. Remember to wear good (preferably water-repellent) walking or hiking shoes, and bring along a bathing suit if you wish to dip into any of the reserve's several swimming holes.

Birding

Most visitors leave the park without having seen a quetzal, although many other birds are in evidence. Quetzals are most active in the evening and early morning, immediately after dawn, when they stir from their perches and move to higher or lower altitudes. Even then, the birds spend most of their time in the highest tree branches. Your chances are slightly better during the April–May breeding season, when the rites of courtship make the quetzal a bit bolder. You may also be able to see quetzals around the beginning of the rainy season, in late May and June, when the young are being raised in nests that their parents have built in dead trees. There are many other bird species in the park, however, and even some monkeys, so keep your binoculars handy.

Getting There

The quetzal reserve can be reached easily by car, taxi, or bus, although it is almost too far for a comfortable day trip from Guatemala City. Public buses pass the reserve's entrance every hour or so throughout the day, continuing to or from Cobán, El Rancho, and terminals as far away as Guatemala City and Flores. Allow about 3 hours from the capital, at least 16 from Flores. Make sure you tell the driver you want to be left off at the *biotopo*, as the turnoff is not posted very far in advance. When you wish to leave the park, simply flag down a bus passing on the highway in either direction. Taxis can be hired in Cobán, about 35 miles away. Many tour companies arrange day trips to the quetzal sanctuary from Guatemala City, leaving the capital early in the morning. If you're on a white-water rafting trip down the Cahabón River, you will most likely stop here for a visit.

Where to Stay and Eat Around Mario Dary Quetzal Reserve

Food of variable quality is served at the Posada Montaña del Quetzal, Pensión El Ranchito, and Comedor San Antonio in Purulhá. Cold drinks and snacks are sometimes available at the visitors center. There are a couple of small *tiendas* and street vendors in Purulhá from which you can buy fruit, crackers, and other basic supplies.

Pensión El Ranchito de Quetzal (also known as Hospedaje los Ranchos), Km. 157.5 Ruta a Cobán; $9; no phone. Only a few hundred yards north of the reserve's entrance, in the direction of Purulhá. Simple wooden huts, plus some fancier rooms with private baths. Quetzals are often seen on the grounds around dawn and dusk.

Posada Montaña del Quetzal, Km. 156 Ruta a Cobán; $40; 331-4181 in Guatemala City. Modest 18-room hotel in pleasant surroundings 2 miles south of the park. Bar, restaurant, pool, laundry service, and fireplaces. Credit cards are accepted and reservations are advised (especially on weekends). Views are wonderful and the area holds considerable wildlife. Despite its considerable physical attractions and amenities, several visitors have complained about overbooking, overcharging, and poor sanitation.

Other Options

If Pensión El Ranchito is closed or full, try the *farmacia* in Purulhá, which has basic rooms to let. The friendly biotopo personnel will allow vehicles to park overnight there, in return for a small donation to the park.

Camping and hammock-hanging in the biotopo is free; it's best to make advance arrangements for campsites through CECON (see above). A waterproof, bugproof tent is recommended. You can bathe in the cool Río Colorado, which flows down from the mountains through the reserve.

ALTA VERAPAZ

Several miles beyond the quetzal sanctuary, heading north through spectacular mountain landscapes, travelers cross into the department of Alta Verapaz. Soon the road descends into a narrow, cultivated valley bracketed by steep, forest-covered hillsides. At one point, near the town of Tactic, a large waterfall can be seen shimmering in the distance, surrounded by dense vegetation. Called **Cascada Patal** by locals, these are the headwaters of the Río Cahabón, one of Guatemala's longest and most scenic rivers. Rain that falls here will be carried to Lago Izabal, then down the Río Dulce to the Caribbean Sea. A trail leads through cattle pastures and cornfields, up a streambed to the waterfall.

TACTIC AND SAN CRISTÓBAL VERAPAZ
Location: 10 to 20 miles south of Cobán.
Population: 4,500 (Tactic) and 9,000 (San Cristóbal), 1999
estimates.
For More Information: Información Turística (1a, Calle 1-11, 952-
1305) in Cobán, open daily except Sunday.

Tactic is a mostly Pokomchí-speaking center for the production of beef, cheese, and other dairy products, plus some silver jewelry, textiles, and other craftwork. The old part of the town is dominated by a colonial-era baroque church built by the Spanish. Inside are paintings showing Byzantine influence, in addition to some interesting altars. The Maya of Tactic have traditionally kept small clay animals in their homes, ancient protective symbols for humankind. The strikingly picturesque **Chi-ixim**

Chapel is on the side of a hill overlooking the settlement.

Just beyond Tactic a road branches west at Santa Cruz toward San Cristóbal Verapaz, situated on the banks of **Lago Cristóbal**. This small lake is said to have been created in 1590 when heated disputes between local Pokomán and a Spanish priest caused the earth to shift, entombing the indígena and flooding the area with water. Lago Cristóbal is now used for fishing, boating, and swimming, mostly by locals. In the past, San Cristóbal was the home of Guatemala's largest shoe factory, which has polluted its waters.

Kekchí Maya fishermen display their catch along an Alta Verapaz river.

Richard Mahler

The San Cristóbal road, Route 7-W, continues for about 60 miles beyond this coffee- and sugarcane-producing village to Cunén. From there travelers can continue to Nebaj and, by a separate highway, to Huehuetenango. Transportation and accommodations are rough, however, and not for the faint-hearted.

On the main road, about 14 miles beyond Tactic, the terrain becomes more gentle and rolling, with large coffee fincas on either side of the highway. It gradually descends into Cobán, set on the edge of a small valley ringed by tree-covered ridges. These towns are accessed by frequent bus or private vehicle from Cobán, via the main highway to Guatemala City.

Where to Stay and Eat in Tactic and San Cristóbal Verapaz

There are a handful of very simple hospedajes and comedores in Tactic, none of them recommended.

Hotel del Parque, Km. 196, near Lago Cristóbal in the community of Santa Cruz Verapaz; $20; tel/fax 950-4539. With 48 rooms, the best place to stay, offering basic rooms and meals.

COBÁN

Location: About 100 miles northeast of Guatemala City.
Population: 17,000 (1999 estimate).

Main Activities: *Coffee, cattle, spices, tourism.*
Services: *There are a few taxis on the plaza next to the bus stop and some of the drivers will guide you to local attractions for a reasonable fee (remember to bargain). The local Telgua office is on 1a. Calle between 1a. and 3a. Avenidas. Telephone calls may be made from 7:00 a.m. to midnight, seven days a week. Banco de Guatemala is on the plaza and a post office is at the intersection of 2a. Calle and 2a. Avenida, Zone 2.*
For More Information: *U and I Tours (952-1547 in Cobán), operated by Marcio Acuña, specializes in caving and nature treks. Información Turística (1a, Calle 1-11, 952-1305) is open daily except Sunday, 9:00 a.m. to 2:30 p.m., 2:00 p.m. to 6:30 p.m.*

The largest town in either of the Verapaces, Cobán has a laid-back atmosphere that confirms its status as capital of one of Guatemala's more isolated departments. Navigating the almost-empty streets, you have the sense that busier times have come and gone here, and that no one really cares.

At the invitation of then-president Barrios, hundreds of German immigrants came to this area in the 1880s and 1890s, creating huge plantations of tea, jute, cardamom, vanilla, sarsaparilla, and (especially) coffee. They also cut down thousands of acres of tropical hardwoods, shipping lumber down the Río Polochic to Lake Izabal, and from there down the Río Dulce and across the Atlantic to Germany. It is said that until an airport and road were built here in the 1930s, the self-sufficient residents of Cobán had stronger ties to "the old country" than to the rest of Guatemala.

Today the main evidence of German influence in Cobán are the blonde-haired, blue-eyed, Spanish-speaking Ladinos you encounter and the occasional Teutonic surname. The owners of the nearby fincas, some still foreign-born, are now mostly based in Guatemala City, and many of the local men leave for months at a time to work in parts of the country where jobs are more plentiful.

The colonial-era **El Calvario Church**, located on a hill on the edge of town, is interesting for the carved tiger cubs guarding its entrance, placed there in tribute to a local Maya legend.

A Spanish school operates here, offering full room and board as well as instruction (see Chapter 4).

Getting There
Buses (some first-class) leave for Cobán from Guatemala City about once each hour between 5:00 a.m. and 5:00 p.m. Travel time is about 4 hours. There are also daily buses to Cobán from El Estor (via the Polochic Valley), Huehuetenango, Nebaj (the latter two towns requiring connections in Sacapulas), and Flores, via Sayaxché and Sebol. Only the route from

Guatemala City is paved, and the others may be subject to suspension during the rainy season or periods of reconstruction. Driving time to Cobán from Guatemala City by private vehicle is 3 to 4 hours. Several tour companies offer excursions to Cobán and the surrounding area.

Where to Stay in Cobán

Central, 1a. Calle 1-79, Zone 4; $7; 952-1442. Basic pensión near the cathedral, with 14 rooms.

Hostal de Acuña, 4a. Calle 3-17, Zone 2; $10; 952-1547. Travelers interested in nature and the outdoors will want to stay at this clean and friendly place, run by one of the region's leading environmentalists, Macio Acuña, who also operates a reasonably priced adventure travel agency, U and I Tours. Both the bunk-style hotel and eco-friendly excursions are recommended. The food is fabulous, too; the kitchen works miracles with Italian dishes and fruit pies. You can stock up on local artensanía in Acuña's "green store."

Hotel La Paz, 6a. Avenida 2-19, Zone 1; $6; 952-1358. A dozen worn rooms and a small restaurant. A nearby building also houses Proyecto Quetzal, which operates a guest house on a private reserve in the Polochic Valley (discussed later in this chapter).

La Posada, 1a. Calle 4-12, Zone 2; $29; 952-1495. Wonderful colonial-style inn, consisting of 14 rooms clustered around a beautifully landscaped courtyard. The authentic Guatemalan food is excellent, and the staff helpful. Staffers can arrange sightseeing trips to plantations, rivers, caves, parks, and other points of interest. Highly recommended.

Where to Eat in Cobán

In addition to the eateries listed below, cheap meals are also available around the main market, about a block north of the plaza, and from numerous sidewalk vendors who do business in the evening. A local specialty is macadamia nut pie.

Café Triol, 1a. Calle 3-13, Zone 1. The best coffee shop in Cobán.

La Cafetería Santa Rita, on the main plaza, Zone 2. Good basic meals.

Pizzeria El Molino, in the Hotel Rabin Ajau. Serves reliable fare.

Tico's Pancakes, la. Calle 4-40, Zone 3. Inexpensive tasty meals.

LAS VICTORIAS NATIONAL PARK
Location: Just south of Cobán.
Hours and Fees: Open from 8:00 a.m. to 4:30 p.m. daily. No entrance fee.
Services: No services are provided so consider this a day trip.

A short walk south of Cobán takes visitors to Las Victorias National Park, a formerly German-owned coffee plantation that was confiscated by the government in World War II and since then has been allowed to revert to its natural state. About 8 miles of trails wind through this second-growth forest, now home to many birds and small animals, as well as myriad flowering plants. Follow Avenida 7a. west of Cobán past El Calvario church and follow the signs northwest to the park's entrance.

VIVERO VERAPAZ
Location: About 2 miles outside Cobán on the Old Guatemala City Highway (now Diagonal 4a.).
Fees: There is a nominal admission fee to enter Vivero Verapaz and you'll be taken on a brief tour of the facility.

One of the country's more unusual natural destinations is the Vivero Verapaz "orchid rescue station." On display are more than 80,000 orchids representing more than 800 species. The project was launched in 1989 on this former coffee *finca* by a Guatemalan-German family as a means of saving the many varieties of orchids that would otherwise be destroyed by the ongoing logging throughout the country. Whenever possible, representatives of the farm go to where trees are being felled and rescue any orchids they find. (Because they are tree-dwelling epiphytes, the orchids will die if not salvaged.) The owners then propagate rescued plants and sell them to domestic visitors. (Guatemalan law forbids orchid export, thus they are not sold to foreign travelers.) It's estimated that about 2 or 3 percent of the country's orchid species have been rescued here so far, with many others lost forever. The best time to see the orchids blooming is at the end of the wet season (November and December). Almost none bloom during the relatively dry months of April and May.

Getting There
The best way to get to Vivero Verapaz is by drving your car or hiring a taxi from Cobán. You can walk here in about an hour (turn left at the bottom of the hill, past Pensión Familiar, as you exit Cobán on 3a. Calle and Diagonal 4a.). You can spend the night among the orchids at **Ecocabañas Verapaz** (361-3104, in Guatemala City), which has four cabañas, each with a private bath and kitchenette. Birding is excellent.

SAN PEDRO CARCHÁ
Location: 4 miles east of Cobán on the road to Lanquín.
Population: 6,500 (1999 estimate).
For More Information: Información Turística (1a, Calle 1-11, Cobán;
952-1305), open daily except Sunday, 9:00 a.m. to 12:30 p.m., 2:00 p.m. to
6:30 p.m.

Several miles beyond Cobán on the main highway is San Pedro Carchá, a good-sized town referred to locally as "Carchá." This is one of the few communities in Guatemala with a long history of indígena self-government. The Kekchí-speaking majority has been pretty much in control of its own affairs since Carchá was founded in the mid-1500s by Dominican friars from nearby Cobán.

The small museum, **Museo Regional de la Verapaz** (across the street from Radio Imperial), is open weekends from 9:00 a.m. to noon and 3:00 p.m. to 5:00 p.m. Knock during the week and you may be allowed to enter. The museum contains Maya artifacts and samples of local craftwork.

Also worth visiting nearby is a large **colonial church**. It houses a wide variety of locally carved masks and silver filigree jewelry, such as chains, bracelets, and Kekchí "elder wands," which are available from some of the shops in Carchá as well as at the daily market. The annual fiesta is June 29.

Getting There
Many buses make the short commute to Cobán during the day. You can also walk from one town to the other in about 45 minutes.

Where to Stay and to Eat in San Pedro Carchá
Carchá has only a couple of basic hotels and restaurants: None can be recommended. Travelers are advised to stay in Cobán or at an outlying lodge.

SAN JUAN CHAMELCO
Location: 6 miles south of Cobán.
Population: About 2,000 (1999 estimate).
For More Information: Contact Don Jeronimo's (see below) or Hostal de
Acuña in Cobán (951-4547).

The **Balneario Las Islas** bathing resort is a developed mineral hot spring on the road heading southeast of Carchá, one of several such springs in the area. All are within a 30-minute walk of the city and cost about 25¢ admission. (Recommended are **La Colonia** and **Los Hermanas de León**.)

Ask local tour guides about day-trip nature walks to the nearby
Finca El Arenal waterfall and the scenic **Río Pasamulhá canyon**.
Cavers can explore the underground **Río Uqueba** (part of the
extensive San Juan Chamelco Cave system). These caves, located near
the village, are part of a complex aquifer system that seems to appear and
disappear in a haphazard manner. Some of the galleries are quite large,
but do be careful when entering the passageways during times of heavy
rainfall—water levels can change suddenly. A flashlight and a sturdy pair
of shoes are advised.

On a separate road that heads south from Cobán is the village of **San
Juan Chamelco**. The market here is a perfect place to buy the renowned
braided or twisted Tzy'bil textiles, which display images of ducks, pineapples, and butterflies. They also utilize an unusual braiding technique.

A nearby waterfall, **La Presa**, is also worth a visit, and there are several developed bathing "resorts" along the Río Chío. Along the
Chamelco road you'll pass **Té Chilipee**, an agricultural cooperative that
is one of the only tea plantations in North America offering guided tours.

Beyond Carchá the paved road toward the northeast narrows and
turns to dirt, with slow going from here to **Sebol** and (in the dry season)
all the way to the Petén. The countryside is beautiful, however, as you
wind through the lush **Sierra de Chamá**. In the distance are sweeping
views of pristine forest, still too remote for farming. On either side of the
road, much of the land has been turned over to coffee, cardamom, corn,
beans, squash, wheat, and maguey. Happily, some reforestation has also
begun and the results are visible along roads in the area.

Getting There
Buses run frequently from the main terminal in Cobán, or arrange private transportation. The Monja Blanca/Escobar line is most frequent.

Where to Stay and to Eat in San Juan Chamelco
Don Jeronimo's, about 3 miles outside of San Juan Chamelco at Aldea
Chajaneb; $35; no phone, write c/o San Juan Chamelco, Alta Verapaz
16010, or contact Hostal D'Acuña in Cobán. Rustic, forest-enclosed
bungalow-style lodge; three vegetarian meals a day (from a biodynamic
garden that also raises blueberries!). Activities include swimming, hiking,
and inner-tubing on nearby waterways. American expatriate Jerry
Makransky has lived off the land here for about 20 years. His place is
reached via local pickup truck "bus" (it stops at the Tienda Maranatba
in Chamelco) or foot (take the Chamil Road from Chamelco to Barrio
San Luis). Recommended. Ask Makransky about day trips from here to
cloud forests, caves, and hot springs.

THE CANDELARIA CAVES

Location: About 40 rough-road miles north of Cobán in the verdant Sierra de Chamá. The main entrance is on private land near the hamlet of Mucbilhá, between Raxujá and Chisec.

For More Information: Mucbilha Lodge arranges guided tours ($8) for guests of the lodge only. Guests and non-guests can make tour arrangements through Monkey Ecotours (361-3104 in Guatemala City or 204-8826 in Flores), Maya Expeditions (363-4965, fax 337-4666 in Guatemala City), or Hostal D'Acuña (951-4547 in Cobán). A portion of the tour fees goes to local residents, who act as cave guides. If traveling from Guatemala City, allow at least two or three days for a round-trip visit to the caves. A public "pick-up" bus from Chisec, an hour south, passes by here daily about 6:00 a.m.

A French-Guatemalan team undertook a systematic exploration here in 1968 and counted more than 200 separate small caves totaling at least 20 miles in length. A documentary film on their effort, *Cuevas y Siguanes de Guatemala*, was released in 1972. Many of the passages are "technical caves," which should be explored only by experienced personnel with the proper equipment. A further complication is that the Candelaria network is often flooded and much of it must be explored on specially equipped, inflatable rafts. Best months to visit are March through May.

The Río Candelaria emerges from the main cave, within which are rooms as large as 240 feet in height and 360 feet in diameter—big enough to hold a football field! These galleries were sacred to the Maya, who left pottery, paintings, and murals in some of them. In fact, it's believed that an ancient indígena tribe actually lived in the caves. A complete archaeological study of the complex has yet to be undertaken.

Where to Stay near the Candelaria Caves

Mucbilha Lodge, near the mouth of the main cave; $40; no phone. French expatriate Daniel Dreux, who helped explore the caves in the 1970s, runs this lodge. Two meals included. There is also a campground on site; $5. Neither have been visited by the author. Dreux can be reached through Monkey Eco Tours at the number above.

LAGUNA DE LACHUÁ NATIONAL PARK

Location: Between Cantabal and Cruce Rubelsanto, in the far north of Alta Verapaz.

Fees: Admission is about 25¢ and you can rent a canoe, campsite, or hammock space for not much more.

Encompassing a lush subtropical jungle and a picturesque lake, Laguna de Lachuá National Park is only accessible to the most adventurous travelers, preferably those who bring their own camping equipment. Scientists now believe that this deep, limestone-rimmed lagoon was formed by a large meteor that crashed to earth millions of years ago. The impact left a crater that is filled with water draining in from one stream, out from two.

This is a magnificent setting for those who want to experience Guatemala's subtropical forest with minimal human presence. Except for the caretakers—who keep the park's amenities in great shape—you may well be the only person for miles around. Hiking trails here tend to be overgrown.

There are no hotels, restaurants, or outfitters in this area. The park provides basic cooking facilities, but you'll need to bring your own food and water (or a water filtration system for the local well-water).

Getting There
Public transportation is by the daily bus from Cruce Rubelsanto (90 minutes away) or one of the several "pick-up" buses that drive by the entrance to the park in the early morning. It's about a 1-mile hike from the road to the lagoon itself, a little farther to the rustic campground.

LANQUÍN CAVE
About 30 miles northeast of Cobán is Las Grutas de Lanquín, a cave complex from which flows the Río Lanquín. These subterranean passageways are a national park and worth at least a brief inspection. The main entrance to the Lanquín Cave is a short walk from a shaded picnic and camping area on the banks of the river, where you can take a refreshing swim. On first glance, the Río Lanquín seems to burst forth from the side of a mountain. A closer look reveals an underground channel bubbling up beneath a rock face at the right side of the cave. On the opposite side is an attendant's hut, where a small fee will be collected if you wish to have the cave's lights turned on (this covers the expense of firing up a diesel generator). If you bring your own candles or flashlights, admission is free and you are allowed to proceed beyond the short section illuminated by overhead bulbs. Be sure to bring extra batteries. (Lit candles in caves are dangerous and not advised.)

Although Lanquín is relatively small, it has a long, rich history. Stone altars located about 100 yards inside the cave have been used by local Maya for centuries in sacred ceremonial rites. At least one such altar is still regularly used in rituals, which are still practiced in the traditional manner and include blood sacrifices of chickens and the burning of copal incense.

Unfortunately, insensitive visitors have scrawled graffiti on some of the sacred stones and broken precious stalactites from grotto ceilings. Others have left empty bottles and litter. Nevertheless, a profound sense of majesty pervades these dank rooms. Even during the driest months of the year, Lanquín's well-marked trails and stairways are very slippery. Be sure to wear shoes with plenty of traction.

Getting There

Two hours (about 30 miles) past Cobán, a narrow and twisting road branches off from the main highway at Pajal and heads east toward the village of Lanquín. (The other branch continues north to the villages of Sebol and Fray Bartolomé de las Casas.) A few hundred yards before the settlement, a sign points the way to Las Grutas de Lanquín.

Where to Stay and to Eat near Lanquín Cave

There are a few modest accommodations in the village of Lanquín, plus a couple of small restaurants.

Hotel El Recreo Lanquín Champey, situated near the cave entrance; $20, price higher on weekends; 952-2160. A 25-room lodge and restaurant. Also serves meals and arranges local tours.

SEMUC CHAMPEY

Six miles south of the village of Lanquín, across a ridge and in the canyon of the Río Cahabón, is a remarkable natural bridge and series of limpid freshwater pools called Semuc Champey. This amazing natural limestone structure stretches nearly a thousand feet across a narrow mountain gorge. The river runs underneath the overhanging rock through a cave, reemerging a few hundred yards downstream.

An ongoing campaign to preserve this natural attraction has secured funding from the United Nations, and in 1995 a nonprofit group called Project Champey received a 30-year lease on the land, enabling Director Eric Barrientos and others to build trails and a primitive campground. You can camp for free but there are theft problems in the area; don't leave your belongings unattended.

An unusual interplay of minerals (mostly calcium carbonate, a product of dissolved limestone) and light gives these pools a magical blue-green color. The setting is idyllic, and the warm, turquoise water is a soothing antidote to the strenuous hike to the top of Semuc Champey. Stretching out in one of these outdoor bathtubs and gazing into the jungle, you'll feel like you've found paradise.

Inherently beautiful, Semuc Champey is a wonderful place to camp, picnic, relax, and swim. Be careful of the sharp edges around the sides of the water-eroded travertine basins. Also keep in mind that at least three tourists have toppled to their deaths from the top of this high archway.

Getting There

The traditional means of getting to Semuc Champey involves hiking from the Finca Arenal bridge over the Río Cahabón. This is also a put-in point and campground for white-water expeditions. Some outfitters include a trek to Semuc Champey in their itinerary.

Public transportation in the area consists of about three buses a day passing along the road between the Pajal junction and Cahabón, a small village 14 miles east of Lanquín. About the same number of buses continue north toward Sebol-Fray Bartolomé de las Casas and the Petén province, depending on road conditions. Pick-up trucks will also take you from Lanquín to Semuc Champey for about $1.

In the past it has been possible to arrange "eco-tours" to Semuc Champey from Hostal D'Acuña, near Cobán (951-4547). Another option is the 8:00 a.m. daily shuttle (about $4) from Hotel Recreo, which returns in the early afternoon. You can walk from Lanquín to Semuc Champey in about 2½ hours, but this is a hot and strenuous way to go.

RÍO CAHABÓN TO CAHABONCITO

Location: Put-in point above the village of Lanquín.

For More Information: Highly recommended for white-water adventures are Maya Expeditions in Guatemala City (15a. Calle 1-91, Zone 10; 337-4666) and Ecotourism & Adventure Specialists in Guatemala City (Avenida de la Reforma 8-60, Zone 9; 361-3104, ecoadventure@mail2.guate.net) The 1999 cost of such a four-day Río Cahabón trip was about $600, including all equipment, food, and domestic transportation (for details, see Chapter 4: Special Interests).

Richard Mahler

A stream of hot mineral water makes a refreshing diving spot on the Río Cahabón.

The Cahabón is Guatemala's most popular white-water river, offering about 30 miles of navigable stream and a drop of about 1,600 feet.

The waterway offers many Class II and III rapids, and a few Class IV. At the Chulac dam-site is

Richard Mahler

Rafting on the Río Cahabón

an unrunnable rapid that must be portaged. Floating the Río Cahabón usually takes about four days from the put-in point above Lanquín, but you can cut a day or more from the trip by putting in farther east at the village of Cahabón, at the end of a dirt road.

RÍO POLOCHIC VALLEY TO LAGO IZABAL
Travelers heading from Alta Verapaz to such east-coast destinations as Lago Izabal, Río Dulce, Puerto Barrios, or Lívingston may want to consider the Tactic–El Estor-El Relleno road as an alternative to backtracking on the return trip via the Atlantic Highway.

The unpaved road follows the Río Polochic as it winds its way between the Sierra de Santa Cruz to the north and rugged Sierra de las Minas to the south. Although the valley floor has been cultivated, the steep hillsides are still heavily forested. The Pokomán Maya are dominant in the area, however only a few now wear their traditional clothing. The Pokomán here are known for their beautiful ceramics and hand-painted calabash gourds.

Buses pass several times a day between Cobán and El Estor, stopping at farming villages en route and continuing on to the Río Dulce at El Relleno.

From El Estor, about 20 miles from Cahaboncito, travelers can either hire a boat to continue their journeys or take the daily 6:00 a.m. passenger ferry ($1, no autos) across Izabal to Mariscos, where a paved road passes through rubber plantations to connect with the Atlantic Highway near the Maya ruins of Quiriguá. Heading the other direction, from Mariscos to El Estor, the ferry leaves at 5:00 a.m. and returns at 1:00 p.m. daily. Buses wait for the ferry and continue on to communities along the Atlantic Highway as well as Guatemala City.

Things to See and Do

One of the main attractions of touristic interest in the **Polochic Valley** is **Proyecto Ecológico Quetzal**, a non-governmental initiative whereby visitors may take guided hikes into the cloud forest near the village of **Chicacnab**. Guide fees of about $10 per day also include food and lodging with Kekchí Maya families in their nearby homes. **Hikes** are 2 to 3 hours long and fairly strenuous, therefore you should be in good physical shape before starting out. Though decidedly rustic, the experience is extremely rich in cultural exchange and natural beauty. You'll have a good chance of seeing a quetzal, howler monkey, and other indigenous wildlife. Orchids, bromiliads, and tree ferns abound, as well as caves, lagoons, and lookout points. All fees go directly to the host family, providing them with a rare bit of non-farm income in an otherwise subsistence-based economy.

Contact Proyecto Ecológico Quetzal in Cobán at 2a. Calle 14-36, Zone 1; phone/fax 952-1047, Bidaspeq@guate.net. Chicacnab is reached on foot from **Chamil**, which in turn is served by a daily bus from **San Juan Chamelco** (accessible by the Monja Blanca/Escobar bus from Cobán). Note that these rural buses begin their runs very early in the morning. From Chamil you can make a number of side-trips to several lovely mountain-side communities, including the coffee-growing village of Senahú, north of **Tucurú**.

There is a swimming beach at Mariscos, and boats can be hired there for trips around the lake or along the Río Dulce as far as Livingston. Inquire locally near the ferry dock. Hiking and birding in nearby mountains is excellent, and day trips can be arranged to the scenic Río Polochic wetlands. Expect to pay about $30 for all-day rental of a guided cayuco.

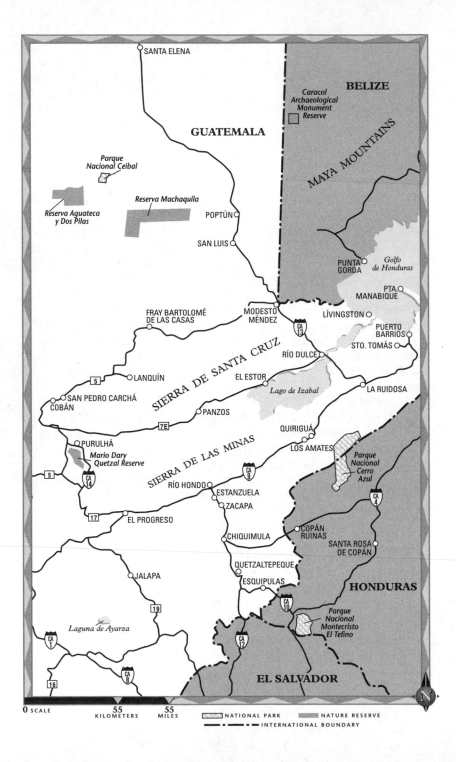

10

EAST TO THE CARIBBEAN

As you head south and east from Guatemala City, the character of the land and its people changes dramatically. The mountainous terrain becomes dry and dusty, the climate desert-like. The Maya faces disappear and cattle pastures are instead patrolled by Ladino cowboys wearing T-shirts, blue jeans, and broad-brimmed straw hats.

Natural and historical forces—deforestation, colonization, and fickle weather patterns—have conspired to create a region that is generally lacking in scenic beauty and cultural appeal. Powerful landowners and faceless companies have molded the departments of El Progreso, Jalapa, and Chiquimula into agricultural machines whose lands are to be exploited as much as possible. Exceptions to this rule are the highest and most inaccessible mountain slopes. Traversing this region is the Atlantic Highway, also known as CA-9 or La Ruta al Atlántica. From the southeastern suburbs of Guatemala City, the two-lane road winds through cactus-studded hills. The road is often crowded with trucks and buses, shuttling between the capital and heavily populated areas near Zacapa and Morales.

At El Rancho, next to an idle pulp mill, the highway intersects with the road to Cobán, capital of Alta Verapaz. The highway parallels the Río Motagua for most of the next 140 miles, through a series of farm towns that have little to recommend them to visitors. At Km. 126 is a turnoff to Zacapa and Chiquimula, 8 and 21 miles away, respectively. From Chiquimula, separate routes continue onward to the Copán ruins in Honduras and the shrine of the Black Christ in Esquipulas.

ZACAPA, ESTANZUELA, AND CHIQUIMULA

Heading south from the Atlantic Highway, paved Route 3 passes through a heavily cultivated area before entering Zacapa, seat of the department of the same name. This city is best known for its beautiful parish church, **San Pedro Zacapa**, and the nearby **Santa María hot springs**.

Estanzuela, a village 6 miles north of the regional capital, is home to the **Bryan Patterson Museum of Paleontology, Archaeology, and Geology**, which contains a large collection of Pleistocene Age animal fossils, ceramics, and archaeological items. Admission to the facility is free, open from 9:00 a.m. to 5:00 p.m. daily. The same community is famous for the fine embroidery produced by its resident artisans, available at the public market.

Chiquimula, 18 miles south of Zacapa, has one of the busiest and most colorful daily markets in the country, offering plenty of bargains. This commercial center is a changing point for hourly buses to Copán and Honduras, as well as Puerto Barrios, Guatemala City, and Esquipulas. It has several basic, inexpensive hotels and restaurants, if you choose to spend some time here. About 25 miles southwest of Jalapa, on CA-1, is **Laguna Ayarza**, a large volcanic lake with boating, hiking, and ancient Maya rock art. Unfortunately, the slopes around the lake have become overgrazed and there is little shade.

ESQUIPULAS

Location: 6 miles northwest of the Honduras border.
Population: 10,000 (1999 estimate).
Main Activities: Commerce, agriculture, spiritual tourism.
For More Information: There is no tourist office. Try INGUAT in Guatemala City or a local travel agency.

Esquipulas, about 30 miles south of Chiquimula on CA-10, is known throughout much of Central America as the home of the **Black Christ**, a venerated carved image housed in an impressive twin-domed basilica. Pilgrims converge on the shrine throughout the year, but especially on January 15 and (to a lesser extent) March 9, when the *Cristo Negro* is said to embody its greatest powers. According to legend, those who visit may have their ills cured by praying and burning incense or candles within the aura of the carving, which takes its dark color from the balsam wood of which it is made. Miraculous powers have been ascribed to the icon since its installation in 1595, but it has been particularly popular since a Guatemalan bishop claimed to have been cured in Esquipulas in 1737. Some nearby caves and hot springs are also said to have soothing and curative powers.

There is a Honduran border crossing close to Esquipulas at Agua

Caliente on Route CA-10. If you are going to Copán, however, it is much easier to take a bus from Chiquimula to the frontier at El Florido, on Route CA-11. The route may be longer, but it is also more scenic and the road is in better condition.

Getting There
Buses run frequently via CA-10 from Guatemala City and Puerto Barrios, or you can arrange private transport.

Where to Stay and Eat in Esquipulas
The restaurants of Esquipulas are unexceptional, and you would do well to stick to those in hotels. The better kitchens are at the Payaqui and El Gran Chorti.

Hotel El Gran Chorti, Km. 222 on the Pan American Highway; $45; 943-1448, fax 943-1551. The most charming (and expensive) of the lot. On a hill overlooking the city. Offers meals.

Payaqui, 2a. Avenida 11-56, Zone 1; $20; 943-1143, fax 943-1371. Two dozen rooms, bar, restaurant, pool, and other amenities. If full, try the cheaper **Los Angeles Hotel** next door.

Posada del Cristo Negro, at Km. 224 on the outskirts of town; $18; tel/fax 943-1482. A good value; 32 rooms.

THE COPÁN RUINS
Location: *About 8 miles south of the Guatemala border crossing at El Florido.*
Hours and Fees: *Admission to the Copán ruins costs about $5; guides charge around $12 for an English-language tour. The site is open from 8:00 a.m. to 4:00 p.m. daily.*
Crossing the Border: *Special travel permits are issued at the border that enable travelers to enter Honduras, visit the ruins, and return to Guatemala without having to obtain a new Guatemalan passport stamp or visa. The Copán travel permits cost about $5. Be aware that the last public transportation from the ruins to the Guatemala border leaves Copán at 1:00 p.m. and that bribes may be demanded by officials on both sides of the border. Money-changers at the frontier offer better rates than you'll get in Copán Ruinas, where there are banks and ATMs.*
For More Information: *The Honduras government's tourism bureau is at 299 Alhambra Circle, #510; Coral Gables, FL 33134 (305-461-0600). The Tunkul Bar and Los Gemelos Hotel are good informal sources of tips and information. On the internet, www.honduras.net/copan.*

Things to See and Do

In northwestern Honduras, about 7 miles south of the Guatemalan border and about 30 miles northeast of the El Salvador frontier, lies the magnificent Maya ruin of Copán. A tour of this ancient city is highly recommended.

The area was last occupied around A.D. 830, although a few Maya continued to use it for religious purposes as farmers tilled their fields nearby. Here the Classic Maya reached the height of their artistry, and fortunately a good deal of this work has been preserved due to the area's relatively benign climate. Even some of the original paint remains on a few monuments and temples.

Knowledgeable local guides are available for hire at the site and the nearby town of Copán Ruinas, home to about 25,000 people. Young (and surprisingly well-informed) boys with flashlights will help you navigate your way through the maze of dark tunnels, corridors, stairways, and tombs. During the dry season there are usually archaeologists working here who may be willing to answer questions you may have about their discoveries.

The best times to visit are during the dry months of December through April. Also, try to see the ruins during early morning or late afternoon hours, since the heat of the midday sun can be intense. Two outlying ruins are within hiking distance of the main site.

A modern new museum (modest admission) was opened near the ruins in 1996 and displays many of the artifacts found there, including some stelae that have been moved indoors to protect them from theelements.

There are a growing number of Spanish schools in Copán Ruinas and their prices are reasonable. A developed hot spring is about 30 minutes from the village, and there are other natural attractions worth visiting if you want to spend a day or two here.

Getting There

A secondary road to Copán begins 5 miles south of Chiquimula and it's about 35 more miles to the frontier. A long journey by car or van from Guatemala City (150 miles and 5 or 6 hours each way), it is nevertheless possible to make it from the capital to Copán and back in one exhausting day. The trip can be made by private car, but you will have to present appropriate documents at the El Florido border crossing.

Planes can be chartered to the ruins from Guatemala City or Flores–Santa Elena. The best charter operator is **Jungle Flying Tours** (360-4920, fax 331-4995, jungleflying@guate.net) in Guatemala City. Expect to pay at least $200 per person.

Buses are also available from Chiquimula to the frontier (**Trans-**

The Magic of Copán

An old watchman at the ruins recognized Copán's potential to serve as a spiritual connection with humanity. "This is imposing," he told one of the first archaeologists to work here, early in the 20th century. "Here the people excelled, particularly in art. You can see it at other Maya ruins, but not the way you see it here. The skill that they had for carving the stone is magnificent. Even today, with our special tools, we couldn't make one of their stelae. A memory has remained here through unknown hands . . . Every day the love of mine for these ruins has grown more and more. I value these ruins as I would my own house."

portes Vilma is recommended), where you must transfer to a Honduran bus for the onward journey to the Copán ruins. Total fare is about $1.

If you are coming from San Pedro Sula, the second-largest city in Honduras, Copán is about a 3-hour trip by a winding paved road. Flights from San Pedro Sula connect that city with Belize City, Guatemala City, the Bay Islands, and Tegucigalpa (the Honduran capital). Tegucigalpa can also be reached overland in about 4 hours from San Pedro Sula. En route from San Pedro Sula you will pass several small Maya sites, including a recently excavated ruin near **La Entrada**.

Where to Stay and Eat near the Copán Ruins

There are no hotels in El Florido, on the Guatemala side of the border, although you may find places to camp there and the very basic

Hospedaje Las Rosas ($5) will do in an emergency. Besides the generally unexceptional hotel restaurants and the eateries listed below, there are plenty of comedores and tiendas in Copán Ruínas.

El Jarral, near the ruins; $15; no phone. A tranquil place, offering horseback riding, bicycling, swimming, and even rafting down the Río Chamelecon in season.

Hotel Brisas de Copán, near plaza; $10; no phone. Friendly and clean, but no hot water.

Hotel Casa de Café, Guatemala City; $42, includes breakfast; 361-3104. Four blocks west of the main plaza. Owners cheerfully dispense travel tips. Recommended.

Hotel Marina, just off the plaza; $70; 98-3070. Hacienda-style pensión with nice rooms, hot water, restaurant, bar, intermittent electricity, pool, and a new annex with private baths as well as a/c. The best place to stay or eat in Copán (huge breakfasts and $10 buffet lunch).

La Llama del Bosque, across from the Tunkul Bar and Restaurant, two blocks west of the plaza. Hearty Honduran fare and money exchange.

La Madrugada, two blocks west of the plaza; $40; 898-0330. Beautifully appointed accommodations in an old adobe house formerly used to house archaeologists, with 18 rooms, hot water, and ceiling fans. The popular, adjacent Tunkul Restaurant & Bar has a happy hour from 6:00 p.m. to 7:00 p.m. nightly. Mediocre food but convival atmosphere.

Los Gemelos, one block east of the plaza, $6; 898-3077. Basic rooms with shared baths (no hot water). Nice courtyard. Recommended, excellent value.

Vamos a Ver, near the southwest corner of the main plaza. Serves delicious meals, prepared by a Dutch couple.

THE QUIRIGUÁ RUINS
Location: Quiriguá is about 1.5 miles south of the Atlantic Highway. About 100 miles northeast of Guatemala City and 65 miles southwest of Puerto Barrios.
Hours and Fees: Open from 7:00 a.m. to 5:00 p.m. daily. There is a nominal admission fee. Overnight parking is free at the ruins.
For More Information: INGUAT in Guatemala City, or local tour operators.

Located on a 75-acre, high-canopy forest preserve that once belonged to the United Fruit Company (and which helped pay for its preservation),

Río Hondo to Puerto Barrios

The Pan American Highway rejoins the Atlantic Highway at Río Hondo. Heading east, it is about 100 miles to the latter road's terminus at Puerto Barrios.

The vegetation becomes lusher near the coast, as the total average annual rainfall rises to more than 120 inches. Dense groves of bananas, citrus, and other fruits crowd the highway, interrupted from time to time by cattle pastures and cornfields. About 10 miles east of Quiriguá, at La Trinchera, an intersecting road winds through rubber plantations to Mariscos, on the south shore of Lago Izabal. Daily passenger ferries (no autos) leave here at 5:00 a.m. and 1:00 p.m. for the 1-hour trip across Izabal to El Estor, from which there is a rough road to Cobán via Tactic, and bus connections from there to Guatemala City, Huehuete-nango, Flores, and El Relleno. Buses also now run directly between Río Hondo and El Estor.

At La Ruidosa the Atlantic Highway intersects the road to the vast department of the Petén. Route CA-13 is mostly paved all the way to Flores. All Petén buses stop at the village of Río Dulce (called El Relleno or La Frontera on some maps), where it is easy to catch a boat to Lívingston or a bus to El Estor.

From this point on the Atlantic Highway it is a 33-mile drive through the tree-covered Montañas del Mico (a federally protected rain forest ecosystem) to the broad coastal plain where Puerto Barrios sprawls in the tropic sun. The road divides on the outskirts of town, the left fork heading into Santo Tomás, the port facility that has largely replaced Puerto Barrios as the main harbor for commercial vessels on Guatemala's east coast.

Quiriguá stands out as a green oasis amid miles of orderly Del Monte–owned banana plantations. Much of this ancient Maya site remains sheltered by lush tropical foliage, and its huge, inscrutable carvings—the tallest ever found in the Maya lowlands—are well worth a visit of at least an hour or two. The ruins are often very hot; it is advisable to carry water, apply insect repellent, and wear a hat.

Things to See and Do

Because its deep-relief, intricately carved stelae and altars are quite similar to those found in nearby Copán, Quiriguá is believed to have been a colony or outlier of that much larger city. Only here and in Copán have there been found large boulders carved into bizarre, fearsome monsters. All of these zoomorphs were created between A.D. 780 and 795.

Translations of the hieroglyphics at Quiriguá suggest that this was a trading center and perhaps an important source of cacao, the rich chocolate bean the Maya used as currency. In A.D. 737, the leaders of Quiriguá are believed to have taken the priest-king of Copán prisoner and sacrificed him. The former dependency then appears to have gone on a building boom and remained autonomous for many years. Until further archaeological work is done, the true origins, demise, and purposes of Quiriguá are likely to remain a mystery.

The brown and red sandstone stelae found here are massive, standing up to 35 feet tall and weighing as much as 65 tons, and their artistry is finely detailed. The Maya apparently moved them on wooden skids or rollers from a river quarry several miles away, then stood them on end like silent sentinels. They can now be viewed under thatched shelters that protect them from the torrential rain. There is also an acropolis and central plaza at Quiriguá, plus a ball court. The western platform of the acropolis once supported an elaborate mosaic wall, part of which remains. The site was excavated

Ancient Maya stone monument at the ruin of Quiriguá

INGUAT

bit by bit in the 19th century and partially restored by the University of Pennsylvania in the 1930s.

Birding is a satisfying activity among the ruins. Parrots, toucans, kiskadees, blue-crowned motmots, Aztec parakeets, hawks, and woodpeckers thrive in the lush foliage here, having been driven out of the surrounding countryside by deforestation and human activity.

Traffic on the Quiriguá access road is sometimes stopped for a few minutes to let conveyor belts full of bananas go by. Wrapped in plastic to promote uniform ripening and discourage insects, they look more like dry-cleaned garments than America's favorite tropical fruit. Several tour companies offer one-day trips to Quiriguá, which may be combined with overnight excursions to (or from) Copán, the Río Dulce, or Lívingston.

Getting There

Many buses travel this route in both directions; during daylight they pass about every 30 minutes. When arriving, ask the driver to be let out at the Quiriguá access road (Km. 205) rather than the regular stop in Los Amates, about 2 miles away. Taxis, buses, and motorbikes to the site are available; you can also walk in less than an hour.

Where to Stay and to Eat in Quiriguá

There isn't much to choose from here and Quiriguá is best regarded as a day trip from Guatemala City/Antigua or Lívingston/Puerto Barrios. You will find several produce stands and a supermarket/gas station at the Quiriguá turnoff from the Atlantic Highway, where you can hail a passing bus. Vendors usually sell cold drinks and snacks near the entrance to the ruins, along with maps and souvenirs.

Hotel Royal, in Quiriguá village; $7–$12; no phone. Clean but very basic rooms with or without bath. The only lodging near the ruins.

PUERTO BARRIOS

Location: About 170 miles northeast of Guatemala City, on the Caribbean coast.

Population: 40,000 (1999 estimate).

Services: There are several banks on 7a. Calle between 6a. and 7a. Avenidas, and another at the corner of 7a. Calle and 2a. Avenida. The Banco del Café will change money for those traveling to or from Belize.

The money-changers on the docks in Puerto Barrios and Punta Gorda offer a fair rate, and it's often more convenient to deal with them than to find a store or bank to exchange currency. The post office is at 6a. Calle and 6a. Avenida, Telgua at 10a. Calle and 8a. Avenida.

For More Information: There is no tourist office; inquire locally at hotels and restaurants, or try the INGUAT office in Livingston.

The capital of the department of Izabal, Puerto Barrios was founded in the 1880s by President Rufino Barrios as an eastern railroad terminus. This now-shabby city was Guatemala's chief port for much of the 20th century. The United Fruit Company used it to ship bananas from its nearby plantations, and the country's coffee growers have sent tons of their product from these docks. Puerto Santo Tomás, just a mile across the bay, now handles about 75 percent of Guatemala's exports and half its imports (plus a good portion of El Salvador's foreign trade).

Streets are poorly marked in Puerto Barrios, and the town is spread out. Ask locals for directions if you get lost; most are friendly and eager to help. This can be a rough place at night, however, and you're advised to stay indoors.

If you're heading to Belize, consider packing the companion volume in this guidebook series, *Belize: Adventures in Nature* (John Muir Publications), written by the author.

Things to See and Do
As you would expect in a down-on-its-luck port city, there are lots of bars, brothels, strip joints, cheap hotels, and grubby restaurants here. Other than checking out the lively market, marveling at a few stately Caribbean-style mansions, and watching bananas being loaded onto container ships, there is not much for the foreign traveler to see or do in Puerto Barrios. The beaches north of town are one recommended diversion while waiting for transportation somewhere else. Near the entrance to Barrios is the town cemetery, which reflects the town's multicultural background. You'll see Hindu mausoleums with elephant sculptures next to the tombstones of French-surnamed Haitians next to the colorful, flower-adorned graves of highland Maya.

Getting There
About two dozen buses each day shuttle between Guatemala City and Puerto Barrios. Most are slow, crowded, second-class buses, and it is advisable to spend a couple of extra dollars for a first-class coach (*pullman*), with an assigned seat and sometimes even a working bathroom and air conditioning. These *primera clase* buses also shave 4 or 5 hours off what might otherwise be an all-day trip. Recommended is the **Litegua** line, which runs about 8 buses daily, departing from 15a. Calle 10-30 in Zone 1 (in the bank building). Allow about 4½ hours for the Guatemala City–Puerto Barrios trip by pullman, including a refreshment stop at Tres Marías. Buses also leave the

Puerto Barrios market hourly for the Esquipulas-Chiquimula area, and there is at least one bus each day from Puerto Barrios for the frontiers of El Salvador and Honduras, with connections to Copán and to Mariscos on Lago Izabal. (You can easily walk to the bus terminal from the ferry dock in about 10 minutes.)

The long-running, twice-daily **passenger ferry** (no vehicles allowed) between Puerto Barrios and Lívingston continues to chug along, although its days may be numbered. The boat leaves the municipal dock in Puerto Barrios at 10:30 a.m. (10:00 a.m. Sundays) and again at 5:00 p.m. The same ferry departs Lívingston for Barrios at 5:30 a.m. and 2:30 p.m. daily, taking about 90 minutes to make the trip. The boat fills up quickly; try to arrive 45 minutes before departure. Tickets ($3) are sold on board or at the ALM shipping office on 1a. Avenida between 11a. and 12a. Calles.

A faster trip to Lívingston is via one of the **15-passenger powerboats** known locally as *lanchas*. You'll pay double the price of the ferry ticket but arrive at least twice as quickly. *Lanchas* leave the municipal dock about once an hour, or whenever they have enough passengers to make the trip worthwhile.

There is no ground transportation to Lívingston, which is inaccessible by road, and the small airport has no commercial flights.

The municipal dock is also a good place to hire private powerboats (about $50 round-trip) to make the 45-minute trip to **Punta Manabique,** the peninsula east of Barrios that is a popular recreational destination (see listing that follows this section).

If your destination is **Punta Gorda, Belize,** *lanchas* leave around noon each day from the municipal dock for the 90-minute ride, although private operators will often make the trip whenever they can gather 10 or 12 passengers. The cost is $15, with an occasional stop in Lívingston en route. Boats depart Punta Gorda for Barrios at about 9:30 a.m. Requena Tours is the recommended operator.

When heading for Belize, remember to stop at Guatemalan **customs and immigration** at the foot of 9a. Calle in order to have your passport stamped. There is no exit fee for either country; the tax to enter Belize is $2.50. Banks in Punta Gorda will not change Guatemalan currency so be sure to avail yourself of the money-changers at the docks, who generally offer fair exchange rates.

As this book went to press, Maya Island Air was offering twice-weekly (Monday and Friday, 9:30 a.m.) airplane departures from Punta Gorda to Puerto Barrios, returning from Guatemala at 10:20 a.m. the same days. Fares are about $35 one-way, $65 roundtrip. This schedule has been subject to change in the past, so it would be prudent to call Maya Island Air in Punta Gorda (7-22856) for confirmation of flights.

Where to Stay and Eat in Puerto Barrios

Caribeña, 4a. Avenida between 10a. and 11a. Calles; $10, with private bath; 948-0860. Recommended for budget travelers. Restaurant on premises offers inexpensive daily specials.

Del Norte, 7a. Calle Final y 1a. Avenida; $30; 948-0087. A genteel relic of a bygone age, not to be missed. Serves some of the best meals in town. Bar, restaurant, 36 rooms: a wonderfully ramshackle, clapboard British Caribbean–style edifice that has been wedded to an uninspired modern stucco monstrosity. The mood is something out of a Somerset Maugham novel and the view of the harbor is exactly the right backdrop. Recommended.

Hotel Canadá, 6a. Calle between 6a. and 7a. Avenidas; $20; 948-0025. Private baths, ceiling fans, and low prices at a central location, not far from both the bus station and ferry terminal.

Hotel Europa, 8a. Avenida between 8a. and 9a. Calles; $20 and up; 948-0127. Clean, comfortable, friendly. Some private showers.

Hotel Patty, 6a. Avenida between 6a. and 7a. Calle; $33; 948-0394. Garden patio and American-style bar. Arranges fishing and nature tours by yacht or *lancha*.

Puerto Libre, Km. 292, at the turnoff for Santo Tomás; $50; 948-3065, fax 948-3513. Most luxurious hotel in town, with 43 rooms, a/c, TV, a restaurant, and pool. Credit cards accepted.

PUNTA MANABIQUE
Location: About 20 miles north of Puerto Barrios.
For More Information: Contact Ecotourism and Adventure Specialists (361-3104) or Pirate's Point Lodge (594-6950, see below).

Geographically isolated from the rest of Guatemala, the 12-mile-long peninsula known as Punta Manabique reaches like an arm into the Caribbean northeast of Punta Barrios, forming the Bay of Amatique. The peninsula's handful of residents—most of whom subsist on fishing, hunting, and small garden plots—do without roads, electricity, health clinics, or treated drinking water.

Several luxury hotel groups have expressed interest in developing fancy resorts on the unspoiled beaches of Punta Manabique (also called Cabo de Tres Puntas). Although the threat of large-scale construction contradicts the stated government policy of preserving this pristine area, things may have moved forward by the time you read this.

For more information about the Mario Dary Foundation and its efforts to improve Manabique's standard of living while at the same time preserving its environment, contact its Guatemala City office (331-094) or the Massachusetts-based EcoLogic Development Fund (617/491-3608, spaul@ecologic.org).

Things to See and Do

Pirate's Point is an excellent place for swimming (off a nice sandy beach), beachcombing, sunbathing, snorkeling, and fishing. Divers can explore a shipwreck offshore. Boat trips can be arranged to the **Canal de los Ingleses** (an artificial waterway dug across the peninsula decades ago by English sailors) and **Río Estero Lagarto** (a small village on the Bay of Amatique shoreline), as well as **Punta de Cocolí, Cayo Zapotillo,** and **Punta de Palma** (on the mainland). Nature-lovers can be assured of seeing many species of marshland animals and waterbirds, possibly including pink flamingos, which have a rookery on the peninsula. The snorkeling and diving is only fair, however, and you'll see much more in Belize. Another favored destination and possible day trip from Puerto Barrios is to **El Paraiso Beach,** near the fishing hamlet of Matías de Gálvez.

Getting There

No regularly scheduled transportation serves Punta Manabique. You must hire a power boat from Puerto Barrios or Lívingston, a distance of an hour or so. Expect to pay at least $50 for a round-trip. The best tours are offered by Guatemala City's Ecotourism and Adventure Specialists (361-3104), which arranges a Garifuna-guided day trip that includes Estero Lagarto, the Canal de Ingleses mangrove tunnel, and a visit to a turtle/crocodile reserve on a Caribbean beach near San Francisco del Mar. Be sure to bring plenty of fresh water, something in very short supply on the peninsula. Trips leave the 17th of each month, except for September and October.

Where to Stay and Eat on Punta Manabique

Food is available from local fishermen and villagers, or your outfitter or hotel will provide it.

Pirate's Point Lodge, near the village of San Francisco del Mar; $20, includes all meals; call 594-6950 in Guatemala City for bookings and directions. Offers simple huts and hammock hooks near the tip of the peninsula. The expatriate German manager describes his modest establishment as "primitive but comfortable."

CERRO SAN GIL

The tall, green mountain that (3,900 feet) separates the Bay of Amatique from the Río Dulce holds the only true rain forest in Guatemala (by ecologists' standards) and has one of the highest annual rainfall averages in the country (200 inches or more). As such, Cerro San Gil (part of the protected rain forest range called Montañas del Mico) is home to a vast array of wildlife and exuberant vegetation. More than 350 bird species have been counted here.

Parts of the mountain are now off-limits to development, thanks to the tireless work of environmentalists and the local water company, which realizes that clean runoff from San Gil provides safe drinking water for the area. The **Río las Escobas**, reachable by road, is a limestone-bedded stream that cascades through scenic lowland jungle. The most verdant protected areas of the mountain are difficult to reach, but you can inquire about access through FUNDAECO, th conservation group managing the protected area (7a. Calle A-20-53, Zone 11, Guatemala City).

Where to Stay near Cerro San Gil

Punta de Palma, at the end of the four-wheel-drive road. An unimproved beach camping area southeast of Lívingston.

Playa Real (known locally as Ramoncito), midway between Lívingston and Santo Tomás; $4. This private beach and campsite has showers and restrooms. No phone.

LÍVINGSTON

Location: About 16 miles—and a 90-minute ferry ride—northwest of Puerto Barrios, on the Caribbean coast.
Population: 10,000 (1999 estimate).
For More Information: There is an INGUAT office (irregular hours) off the main street, next to the Garifuna Museum. Exotic Travel, to the left of the main dock, is one of several agencies that dispenses reliable information.

Lívingston is one of Central America's true cultural oddities. With its coconut palms and brightly colored wooden homes, the place looks more like Belize or Jamaica than Guatemala, yet it is really a world unto itself. The ancestors of most of the town's residents include African slaves and Carib Indians. (Lívingston's name commemorates the contributions of a 19th-century U.S. judge to refinement of the Guatemalan judicial system.)

In Livingston one is as likely to hear the Garifuna language as Spanish. The melodic native tongue is a unique mixture of African, English, Dutch, French, and Carib words and grammar. Also called Black Carib or *gariganu*, the Garifuna culture began in the mid-1700s, when shipwrecked West African slaves escaped to the British-controlled islands of Dominica and St. Vincent in the West Indies. The freed Africans intermarried with Red and Yellow Carib Indians, and the two groups later mixed their customs and rituals.

The Garifuna remained staunchly independent, refusing to bargain with the Europeans who repeatedly tried to subdue them and take their lands. For many years they successfully resisted colonization, but in 1795 their chief was killed by an English soldier's bullet. The Garifuna were subsequently rounded up and deported to the Bay Islands of Honduras, then a British colony. Today there are an estimated 120,000 Garifuna, most of them in Honduras. About 15,000 live in the greater Livingston area, most descended from migrants originally from Puerto Barrios and southern Belize.

Things to See and Do
Perhaps the best times to visit are during the Christmas season or May 13–15, when Garifuna dance festivals are underway and the Black Caribs reenact their arrival in Guatemala with much joy and celebration. The three days of hand-clapping, singing, dancing, and music-making culminate on the morning of May 15 with Yuriman, a simulation of the first farm plantings by the newly arrived Garifuna.

Other festivities occur during Holy Week (with a live performance of the passion of Christ, including a reenactment of Jesus' crucifixion), November 26 (feast of San Isidro Labrador), December 12 (the feast of the Virgin of Guadalupe, when local Kekchí Maya dance the sacred *pororo*), and December 24 through 31 (the Virgin of the Rosary festival, with December 28 the principal feast day).

During these religious celebrations call-and-response singing and energetic costumed dancing is accompanied by musicians pounding out a rhythmic Afro-Caribbean beat on turtle-shell drums. Visitors can sometimes witness the lively punta and Yacunú dances performed, the latter by men only.

Although more and more Ladinos and Kekchí have moved to Livingston in recent years, along with some East Indians and Asians, the Garifuna culture still dominates. On side streets you can see families living in traditional windowless, single-door, palm-roofed houses with mud and cane reed walls. In their backyards you may also see women pounding and straining cassava root, a starchy potato-like vegetable that is a

Garifuna drummer at a traditional dance in Lívingston

INGUAT

staple of the Garifuna diet. Its flour is used to prepare many kinds of breads and pastries. The cultural significance of cassava cannot be overestimated: In fact, the word Garifuna translates as "the cassava-eating people." The **Museo de la Cultura Garifuna** (just off Calle Principal) provides an introduction to this culture for visitors.

Garifuna cuisine is excellent and you won't go hungry here. Typical dishes include *tapado* (a stew of shrimp, lobster, clams, fish, coconut, sweet potato, and coriander), enchiladas (baked stuffed tortillas), *pan de coco* (sweet coconut muffin), cassava bread, and drinks such as *horchata* and *rosa de Jamaica*. Other local specialties are boiled fish in coconut sauce (*sere*) and *caldo de mariscos* (fish soup).

Lívingston is a popular hangout for young backpackers, who take full advantage of the community's tolerant and relaxed atmosphere, lilting reggae soundtrack, and low-cost restaurants. Although there isn't much of a beach in Lívingston proper (and it's filthy), several are within easy walking distance north of town, such as Río Blanco. Other pastimes include birding in the jungle and hiking about 3 miles north of town to **Paraje de los Siete Altares** (Resting Place of the Seven Altars) waterfalls, where you can swim in several fresh-water pools or picnic by the bay. The hike to Los Siete takes about 90 minutes. During the dry season the pools are sometimes virtually empty and hardly worth the effort. Litter and crime are recurring problems. Inquire locally about conditions and the best route. Nearby, in the village of Cocolí, is La Chimiguilla, a small bungalow lodge and restaurant, not visited by the author. For more pristine swimming, try **Cayo Sapodillo**, a beach where you can camp and buy fish or shrimp from local fishers (bring your own water and tent). Inquire at the Lívingston dock about arranging boat transport to this and other isolated coastal destinations, including **La Buga**, a sacred site of the Garifuna people.

There is no traditional market day in Lívingston; informal stands are set up along the main streets of town each morning. Prices, because of the isolation, tend to be notably higher than in the rest of Guatemala.

Day trips are a favorite activity and many locals make a living using their *cayucos* to transport visitors to remote beaches, islands, or rivers. Excursions can also be arranged to each of the three Garifuna villages north of Lívingston: **Cocolí, San Juan,** and **Sarstún.**

Orientation and Services

Lívingston is easy to get around in and most businesses are within two or three blocks of each other on the three paved streets. The **Telgua** and post office are to the right as you walk up the main road (Calle Principal) from the main wharf, across the street from the *migración* office (for some reason, the customs department is a few blocks away, opposite Comedor los Cocos). The one and only bank, **Banco de Comercio**, is on the first street to your left as you leave the wharf. It's open weekdays from 8:30 a.m. to 5:00 p.m. and Saturdays from 9:00 a.m. to 1:00 p.m. There are several gift shops; try McTropic on Calle Principal for one of the better selections.

There are a number of travel agencies and tour guides, but because they seem to come and go with great frequency it's best to check around before making a commitment to any one of them. One of the more reliable in recent years has been **Happy Fish Travel,** housed in the Restaurante Happy Fish on Lívingston's main street. The friendly staff can arrange jungle river tours, beach and waterfall trips, and excursions to Belize or Punta Manabique. Also recommended is **Bahía Azul,** in the restaurant of the same name.

The town has one Spanish school (see Chapter 4: Special Interests), although it occasionally suspends operations. Between June and November the area receives its heaviest rainfall, and traveling is discouraged. May is the hottest month, often exceeding 95 degrees at midday.

Getting There

Lívingston can only be reached by boat or private airplane: There is no road connecting it to the rest of Guatemala. As of 1999 there was still no scheduled air transportation to Lívingston, although this could change in the future. Those who haven't been to the town for a while will be pleased to learn that boat transfers have become much more efficient and reliable. There still are very few phone circuits to the town, however, which is why almost no one has a telephone.

The daily ferry ($3.00) from Lívingston to Puerto Barrios leaves at 5:30 a.m. and 2:30 p.m. daily, arriving 90 minutes later. Power boats ($6) depart from the same dock whenever a boat is full for the 45-minute ride to Lívingston.

Passenger boats (locally called *colectivos* or *lanchas*) leave at

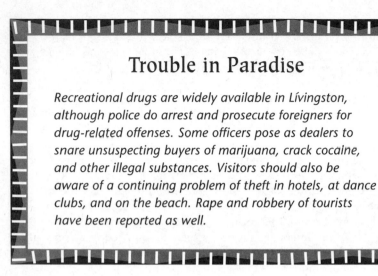

Trouble in Paradise

Recreational drugs are widely available in Lívingston, although police do arrest and prosecute foreigners for drug-related offenses. Some officers pose as dealers to snare unsuspecting buyers of marijuana, crack cocaine, and other illegal substances. Visitors should also be aware of a continuing problem of theft in hotels, at dance clubs, and on the beach. Rape and robbery of tourists have been reported as well.

7:00 a.m. Tuesdays and Fridays for Punta Gorda, Belize, and for Puerto Omoa, Honduras. A boat returns from Belize the same day at 8:30 a.m. and from Honduras at 1:00 p.m. Expect to pay about $15 one-way for Belize and $35 for Honduras (3 hours). For information, contact the Happy Fish Travel Agency on Calle Principal. Be sure to have your passport stamped before you leave.

Private boats up the Río Dulce leave the dock every morning beginning at dawn. Be sure to bargain for your fare, which will largely depend on how far you are going and how many passengers will be on board. Be prepared to pay at least $8 for a one-way trip ($14 round-trip) to the village of El Relleno (also referred to as Río Dulce or La Frontera) that may include a half-hour visit to the Manatee Reserve en route. With a stop there and at Río Dulce hot springs, the journey takes about 3 hours. It is usually slightly more expensive to hire a boat in the opposite direction, from El Relleno back to Lívingston. The only public transport is an inexpensive mail boat that shuttles between Lívingston and El Relleno daily ($2) at 8:30 a.m.

Sightseeing day trips are provided by many local operators; expect to pay about $15 (includes lunch). Departures are usually between 8:30 a.m. and 9:30 a.m., returning about 6 hours later.

Where to Stay in Lívingston

The African Place, on an unmarked side street, past the Catholic Church; $6 and up; no phone. This odd Spanish-Moroccan-looking establishment attracts many young travelers, particularly Europeans, and may be too noisy for some. Some rooms share baths. Good food, English paperback exchange, lively atmosphere, and bizarre decor.

Hospedaje Doña Alida, east of the main dock, overlooking the water; $10; 948-1567. A six-room lodge with its own private beach.

Hotel Caribe, 150 feet to the left of the main dock; $5 without bath, $8 with; no phone. Some vistors have complained about insects and lack of cleanliness, but it'll do in a pinch.

Hotel Garifuna, on a quiet, nameless side street in a residential part of Lívingston (follow the signs); $9; no phone. Secure, two-story structure owned and operated by a local Garifuna family. Private baths, big rooms, and ceiling fans. Recommended, though a bit away from the action.

Hotel Tucán Dugú looms over Lívingston harbor, to the right of the main street; $65; 448-1512 or 331-5213 in Guatemala City. Upscale 42-room complex, originally designed, owned, and managed by a Swiss hotelier. Exotic, steeply-pitched thatch roofs, mahogany interiors, and terraced balconies (kind of Maya Modern). Offers fishing, river trips, bird and animal watching, sailing, and diving trips to Belize's barrier reef. Excellent (but relatively expensive) bar and restaurant offer the best views in Lívingston.

La Casa Rosada, upriver from the main pier (on the same street as the bank); $15; 947-0303 or (510) 525-4470 or fax (510) 525-5427. Ten tiny seaside cottages; shared bath, non-smoking. Good (but overpriced) meals served in the hotel's restaurant. The American owners are helpful in arranging tours, and Cathey Lopez also runs the reasonably priced, recommended Spanish school, Escuela Idiomas Tropical, up the street. Recommended.

Rigoletto Guest House, a short distance past the bank; $9; no phone. Clean and friendly. Run by a Mexican-Guatemalan couple who operate a pretty good pizza parlor on the premises. Recommended.

Where to Eat in Lívingston
In addition to the listings below, several comedores on the main street serve tasty breakfasts and snacks. If you have a means to cook them, you can buy fresh fish on the beach for about 50¢ a fistfull. There's a Saturday

morning produce market (in front of the police station), stocked with tropical fruits and vegies.

The African Place, on an unmarked side street, past the Catholic Church. Particularly recommended for its tasty Garifuna dishes that will only set you back about $4. Amenities include a sunny patio and extensive wine list featuring many Spanish and Chilean vintages.

Bahía Azul, across from Banco de Comercio. Serves fresh yogurt, exotic tropical fruit, and yummy juices.

Dante's, one block off the main street; turn left at the Happy Corner Store. An upscale option (and popular travelers' watering hole) that serves excellent seafood and pasta.

El Tiburón Gato, on the main street. Open-air restaurant with good food.

Hotel Tucán Dugú, on Lívingston harbor, to the right of the main street. This hotel's dining room—offering the best views in Lívingston—is the place to go if you want to splurge.

Margoth, one block off the main street; turn left at the Happy Corner Store; across the street from Dante's. Recommended for its good, inexpensive Garifuna fare.

Restaurant Raymundo, on the main street just up from the dock. Serves good, low-priced regional specialties such as seafood soup and garlic shrimp.

UP THE RÍO DULCE

Location: This broad waterway is between Lago Izabal and the Caribbean, between the communities of Río Dulce (the largest town on the river) and Lívingston.

For More Information: Inquire locally among hotels and travel agencies. La Casa Rosada in Lívingston (902-7014) provides reliable tips.

A boat trip inland from the Caribbean first takes the visitor across the broad mouth of the Río Dulce, under a sky full of swooping fish-loving birds of all descriptions: gulls, pelicans, cormorants, frigate birds, ospreys, herons, kingfishers, and egrets. Here, where the nutrient-rich fresh water of the mainland jungle meets the salty Caribbean, is an unusually high concentration of marine life. Despite the proximity of

Where's Nito?

During three centuries of Spanish rule, the Río Dulce and Lake Izabal drainage served as one of the main trade routes between Central America and the Caribbean. In 1990, archaeologists began a four-year survey of Spanish colonial and pre-Columbian activities in the area. Over 100 new sites were found, including more than a dozen with 50 or more structural mounds. This suggests a large population of little-known residents who interacted closely with their Maya neighbors. However, researchers were unable to pinpoint the exact location of Nito, the place near present-day Lívingston where Spanish explorer Hernán Cortéz described contact with indígena in 1524.

Lívingston, the ecosystem is fairly healthy, and as a result there is plenty to occupy the birder or sportfisher.

If you're visiting Guatemala on a yacht, note that there are occasionally break-ins on unlocked, unguarded boats. A word to the wise should be sufficient.

Things to See and Do

Only a few hundred yards from the mouth of the Río Dulce, the river abruptly funnels into a 50-yard-wide gorge enclosed on either side by sheer cliffs up to 300 feet high. It is an incredible sight, especially in the early morning hours when large water birds congregate in the huge trees that loom over this slow-moving stream. The rain forest is unusually thick along this stretch and virtually impenetrable, draped with vines and clogged with shrubs.

Eventually the Río Dulce widens slightly and a few thatch huts are visible along the embankments, home to the **Kekchí Maya** seen spearfishing or hauling produce in their dugout cayucos. Bank-to-bank gill-nets are sometimes used to trap virtually all the fish in the river. A rapidly growing number of riverside houses have powerboat moorings, used by Guatemalans on holiday outings.

At one point the Río Dulce is warmed on its north bank by an underwater hot spring, where you can take a soothing swim—while holding your nose against the hydrogen sulfide fumes. Then, several miles from the sea, the river opens into a broad lagoon called **El Golfete**, the banks of which constitute **Río Dulce National Park**.

This 4-mile-wide body of water and much of the land bordering it is a nature reserve protecting the Caribbean manatee. Enormous walrus-like mammals that nurse their young and use lungs to breathe, manatees are said to have given rise to the mermaid myth. According to legend, sailors who saw the vaguely human face of the creatures peering out of the water speculated that what they were seeing was half woman, half fish. Local people have never suffered such delusions, however, and the manatee are still hunted (illegally) throughout their range in Guatemala. A full-grown adult can weigh a ton or more, and its meat is considered a mouth-watering delicacy by some.

The **Manatee Reserve** (officially called Biotopo Chocón Machacas) is jointly overseen by the Center for Conservation Studies of the University of San Carlos and INGUAT, with financial support from the World Wildlife Fund. The biosphere encompasses all of the water area of El Golfete and a tract of nearly 18,000 acres on its northern bank. There is a $5 admission fee.

Manatees are notoriously shy, and the best way to catch a glimpse of these endangered mammals is to approach their grassy shoreline domain very slowly in a non-motorized boat. The manatees surface regularly to breathe and seem to favor certain "blowholes" and feeding grounds known to local guides. Try the Escondida, Negra, Calix, or Salvador lagoons west of the visitors center (where maps are available). Early morning hours seem to be the best time to observe these magnificent creatures, but do not be surprised if you come away without seeing one.

The Manatee Reserve is about 10 miles by water southwest of Livingston and 16 miles northeast of the Río Dulce Bridge (a link in Route CA-13). There are aquatic trails that non-motorized, shallow-draft boats can navigate through various rivers and lagoons. The reserve also has several land trails leading into dense tropical rain forest frequented by monkeys, boa constrictors, tapirs, jaguars, and many other animals. Birders will be rewarded by the many local and migratory species in evidence. In fact, this area is believed to have the greatest variety of plants and animals anywhere in Guatemala.

Before setting out on foot, remember that this lowland jungle is also relentlessly hot (averaging 80 degrees Fahrenheit) and rainy (more than

INGUAT

A Garifuna boy proudly displays his catch.

180 inches in a typical year). Bring plenty of insect repellent, and keep an eye out for snakes.

Boats can tie up at a dock at the headquarters (the park has no roads). This is also a good spot for snorkeling or a refreshing swim, although the water is rather shallow and full of grasses. Camping and hiking are permitted in the compound just beyond the pier. The main trail takes about 20 or 30 minutes and features mahogany, cohune palm, orchids, and bromeliads, as well as tropical birds and other wildlife. There are no vendors or services, only a small open-air museum and rudimentary restrooms, so bring your own food and drink. Guides can usually be hired at this location.

At the western end of El Golfete, the Río Dulce narrows again and passes through a picturesque area that has long been a favorite for vacationing Guatemalans. There are a few hotels along the way, catering primarily to boating enthusiasts heading up the Río Dulce from the Caribbean.

Water-recreation gear can also be rented at many of the lodges along the river. Local guides and boatmen can be hired at the docks near the Río Dulce Bridge for fishing and nature trips or onward journeys to El Estor, El Paraíso, or Livingston. They are good sources of information about docking facilities, river tours, and boat rentals. As always, be prepared to bargain on excursion prices.

For chartering sailboats for use on Lake Izabal, the Río Dulce, or offshore waters, contact **Aventuras Vacacionales** (832-3352 in Antigua, fax 702/255-3641 in Las Vegas, Nev.), which runs three- and six-day excursions on a 46-foot catamaran. Also try **Adventure Travel Center** in Antigua (832-3228) or **Ecotourism & Adventure Specialists** in Guatemala City (361-3104).

Getting There

A modern bridge crosses the Río Dulce about 10 miles west of the Manatee Reserve. This road is the main artery in and out of the Petén, and you can catch buses at the village of Río Dulce (on the north side of the bridge—note that the community is also called El Relleno and La Frontera) to Flores, El Estor, Puerto Barrios, Guatemala City, and other destinations. Bungee jumping from the 150-foot bridge is offered by Guatemala City–based Maya Expeditions.

It is about 170 miles (4 to 5 hours) to Guatemala City from here, and a comparable distance (but 7 to 8 hours) to Flores. The buses are usually full by the time they reach the Río Dulce junction, and you will probably have to stand up inside or sit on the roof for the rest of the journey if you board here. There are about 10 buses a day passing through en route to Flores. One option is to overnight in Poptún, about halfway to Flores. Heading south, you will reach the Puerto Barrios–Guatemala City highway at La Ruidosa, about 24 miles away. There are two banks in Río Dulce that will change money.

Where to Stay and Eat Around the Río Dulce

There are many cheap hotels and restaurants in the village of Río Dulce, but it is a dirty and noisy community. You're better off heading up or down the river, where better lodging and food are available.

Catamaran Island Hotel, on tiny Punto del Chorizo; $50; 947-8361, fax 331-8450 in Guatemala City, in U.S. (813) 685-9545. Popular among sailors from Texas and Florida. Owned and operated by a retired American pilot and his Guatemalan wife, who built it in the 1970s. Good upscale base for trips along the Río Dulce or around Lake Izabal.

Hotel Marilu, in Río Dulce; $7; no phone. Stay here if you get stranded in Río Dulce.

Los Palafitos, accessible by water; $16; no phone. Recommended nature-oriented, family-owned bungalow-style hotel. Restaurant on the premises. Canoes available for water exploration.

*The 17th-century fort of San Felipe defended Lake Izabal
against incursions by British pirates.*

Pensión Don Humberto, within walking distance of the fort; $15; no phone. One of the few modestly priced lodging options along the river, this 11-room hotel has a boat dock and an open-air restaurant.

Hacienda Tijax, on the river, east of the bridge; $16 per cabana, $25 per bungalow; 902-0858, rio@guate.net. Horses can be hired (for about $6) here for rides into the nearby jungle and rubber plantations. Also offers sailing, hiking, birding, and plantation tours. Owner Eugenio Gobbato is a goldmine of useful information and speaks English, French, Italian, and Spanish. Recommended.

Turicentro Marimonte, Km. 275 on the Petén highway; $65; 947-8585. A 26-room hotel, campground ($6), and boat ramp east of the bridge on the south side of the river. Amenities include a swimming pool and small zoo.

EL CASTILLO DE SAN FELIPE

A short distance past the Río Dulce bridge is the old Spanish fort of San Felipe de Lara, overlooking the entrance to **Lago Izabal**, Guatemala's largest lake. This medieval-looking structure, more commonly called El

Castillo de San Felipe, was built in 1652 to discourage the many British and Scottish pirates who plundered this area throughout the 17th century, raiding mule trains and stealing provisions. The raids persisted even after the fort's construction, however, and San Felipe was burned by buccaneers in 1686.

After El Castillo was rebuilt, the Spanish went so far as to stretch an iron chain across the river to discourage unauthorized ships from entering the lake, but even this imaginative ploy was unsuccessful. A series of treaties between Spain and England ultimately put an end to the piracy problem, so San Felipe was converted into a prison, then abandoned.

Now a national historic monument cared for by INGUAT, San Felipe has been fully restored and is worth a tour. The fort is the only one of its kind in Guatemala and can be reached either by boat (about 2 miles and 10 minutes from the Río Dulce Bridge) or via a short unpaved access road off the main highway. The scenic area around the fort, maintained as a park, is an excellent spot for swimming, kayaking, waterskiing, windsurfing, boating, and fishing.

EL PARAÍSO AND BOQUERÓN

One of the area's most unusual attractions (and a recommended day-trip destination) is El Paraíso, a private coffee finca on the north shore of Lago Izabal where a waterfall of hot water cascades into a cool river from an underground thermal spring 30 minutes downstream from the entrance to an extensive cave network. The cave itself is partially flooded (with cold water) and you'll need an experienced guide if you want to explore (French cavers reportedly surveyed 8 miles of passages without coming to an end). Travel agencies in Lívingston can arrange transportation and permission for a visit, which requires some moderate hiking and a small admission fee. Arrangements can also be made through Hugo's Restaurant, at 5a. Avenida and 3a. Calle in El Estor.

El Paraíso is about a half-hour east of El Estor by bus on the recently built road to Río Dulce. Buses run from El Estor to Río Dulce hourly from 6 a.m. to 11 a.m., returning from Río Dulce between 1 p.m. and 6 p.m. The thermal waterfall is a terrific place for a picnic, or you can walk down to the lake, where there is a restaurant.

Equally impressive—and closer to El Estor—is Boquerón, where the Río Sauce cuts through a deep gorge covered in mosses, trees, and epiphytes. You can swim or take a cayuco ($1) up the river and explore the cliffs and caves en route. Monkeys and exotic birds can sometimes be seen in the treetops. The easiest access is by renting a bicycle in El Estor and cycling the six miles to Boquerón (30 minutes), or by taking a Río Dulce bus (about 10 minutes).

Ecofriendly Biology

During 1997-98, Defensores de la Naturaleza built a large biological station/eco-lodge (about $3 per night) in the village of Selmepin at the foot of the Sierra de las Minas, adjacent to the Bocas del Polochic Wildlife Reserve. The lodge is equipped with bunk-beds for up to 30 guests. Amenities include showers, composting toilets, solar electricity, and a nearby biological research station. Local residents provide cooking and guiding services on forest trails. The lodge is about one and one-half hours from El Estor via lancha or cayuco. Arrangements can be made at the wharf in El Estor, or at the Defensores office there (942-7237; defensores@pronet.net.gt). A 1997 Peace Corps survey found 321 bird species (plus 74 migrant species) in and near the Río Polochic wetlands, nearly half of the 664 species thought to exist in all of Guatemala. Other wildlife in the region includes howler monkeys, iguanas, bats, snakes, ocelots, and turtles. Contact Defensores de la Naturaleza about other regional ecotourism projects, including in the villages of Chilascó and Los Albores.

EL ESTOR AND LAGO IZABAL

Location: *On the north shore of Lake Izabal, about 23 miles west of the Río Dulce Bridge.*

Population: *About 3,000 (1999 estimate).*

Services: *You can take a one-day **rafting trip** on the Cahabón from El Estor through arrangements with Guatemala City's **Maya Expeditions** (337-4666). **Mountain bikes** can be rented for exploration of nearby wilderness areas (50¢ per hour; 6a. Avenida 4-26).*

For More Information: *There is no tourist office; try Hugo's Restaurant (see below).*

Guatemala's largest lake covers 228 square miles and reaches a maximum depth of 60 feet. Most of it is fairly shallow and muddy: ill-suited for swimming but terrific for most water sports.

Unfortunately, overhunting and overfishing have taken their toll on marine life here. An April–June moratorium on fishing is virtually ignored. Most of the indigenous crocodiles and caimans have been killed for their hides, manatees and turtles for their meat, and iguanas for their eggs and skins. Parrots, toucans, and other exotic birds are captured for illegal export to stores and collectors. There are still perch, tarpon, snook, catfish, and large-mouth bass in Lake Izabal, however, and an experienced fishing guide can advise you of the best times and places to catch them. The wetland estuary of the Río Polochic at the west end of the lake is a protected area with a tremendous amount of bird life, plus some monkeys, caimans, and manatees.

El Estor, on the northwest shore of Lake Izabal, was once a source of provisions for British ships, thus the name: a Spanish corruption of "The Store." It is now a hot, sleepy backwater, a good base for adventures in the nearby mountains. Birders sometimes use this as a connecting point for boat trips up the Río Polochic, which for many years was the principal transportation link between Alta Verapaz and the outside world. Today there is little river traffic in the area, and what exists mostly consists of white-water rafters and kayakers who float down the smaller Río Cahabón, overnighting at El Estor.

Another worthy attraction is the a weaving co-op and training center (AFQ), which has a retail outlet on the central plaza. You can buy fine handicrafts at this store and get directions to the weaving center (5 blocks away) for a tour.

Getting There

Valenciana runs buses every 2 hours (starting at 5 a.m.) to Cobán (about 6 or 7 hours away); Fuentes de Polochic has morning and afternoon buses to Guatemala City via Tactic. A side trip north from Telemán takes you to Senahú, famous for its lovely cave (on the outskirts of the village). In 1998 a new road was opened between **El Estor** and **Río Dulce**, which can be reached in one to two hours by bus for about $1. Departures via the *Fuentes del Norte* bus are at 1 a.m. and 5 a.m., continuing on to Guatemala City (another 5 hours from Río Dulce). Other buses to El Estor pass through Río Dulce between about 3 p.m. and 7 p.m. daily, returning from El Estor between 6 a.m. and 11 a.m. daily.

A passengers-only ferry leaves El Estor every day at 6 a.m. for Mariscos, on the southern lakeshore, where buses connect to the rest of the country. The crossing takes about 2 hours and costs $1.50.

Where to Stay and to Eat in El Estor

Hospedaje Santa Clara, 5a. Avenida 2-11; $6 with private bath, $5 without; 948-7244. Delightful upstairs balcony/lounge overlooking the lake.

Hotel Marisabela, on the lake, three blocks east of the municipal pier; $15; no phone. Quiet, plenty of hot water. Very good Italian restaurant.

Hotel Villela, near the lake, 6a. Avenida 2-06; $10; no phone. Basic, clean rooms, private baths, courtyard. Doña Flora is friendly and can help arrange boat transport and tours. Recommended.

Hotel Vista al Lago, on the lake; $27; 949-7205. A colonial-style structure on the lake; upstairs rooms have nice views (all have private baths). Owner Oscar Paz speaks some English and seems to know everything about the area. Paz can arrange boats and guides for fishing, hiking, and touring.

Hugo's Restaurant, on the plaza, at 5a. Avenida and 3a. Calle; no phone. The best restaurant in town. Its friendly owner is a native of southern Guatemala who learned fluent English while taking pre-med courses in Canada some years ago. Hugo is a wonderful source of information about Lake Izabal's attractions and the surrounding mountains. He occasionally takes travelers on boat trips up the nearby Río Boquerón canyon, known for its spectacular scenery and caves (about $10 per person).

Turicentro El Paraíso, on the lake; $25; no phone. The most upscale accommodations, with cabañas and a nice café.

SIERRA DE SANTA CRUZ NATURE RESERVE

The newest area set aside to protect the elusive quetzal (and associated flora and fauna) is part of the relatively low (3,500-foot) mountain range immediately north of El Estor and Lago Izabal. The Sierra de Santa Cruz Nature Reserve achieved its protected status in the mid-1990s thanks to a coalition of international nonprofit organizations (including the Lions Club) working with the Guatemalan government. Said to contain one of the country's largest concentrations of quetzals, the mountain range has limited access and there were no developed trails or services as this book went to press. A four-wheel-drive dirt road winds through the foothills of the Sierra de Santa Cruz, providing access to remote villages and the lower reaches of the reserve, eventually entering the southern Petén wilderness. Inquire locally about guided treks into the reserve. A good information resource is Hugo's Restaurant in El Estor (see above).

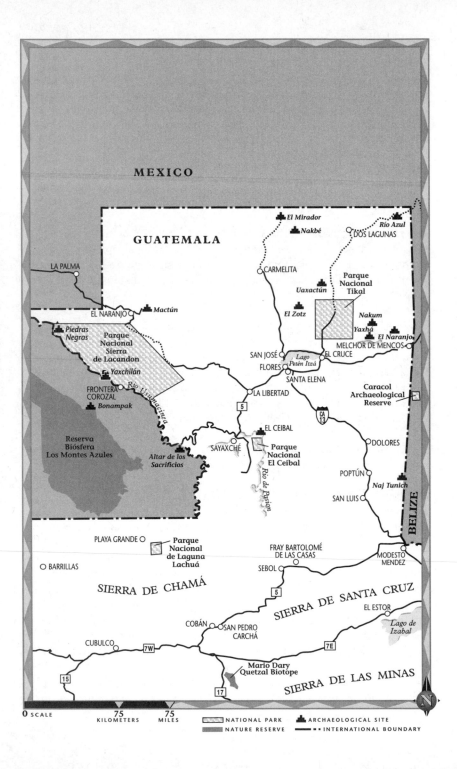

11

THE PETÉN AND TIKAL

Guatemala's department of El Petén, consisting of roughly 14,000 square miles and located about 150 miles north and east of Guatemala City, is the setting for one of the world's largest remaining subtropical moist broadleaf forests, teeming with wildlife and lush with vegetation. Although not a true rain forest—annual rainfall is not high enough for that designation and there is a sustained dry period—the Petén nevertheless has very impressive flora and fauna. Scientists have inventoried more than 4,000 plant species in the Petén (including more than 800 tree species and 500 orchid species), plus more than 350 different resident birds and nearly 100 migrants, along with 57 snake species and five cat species.

Occupying fully one-third of Guatemala and home to a population of approximately 360,000, the Petén is one of the fastest-growing regions in Central America. Immigrants, arriving at the rate of 300 or more a week, are mostly farmers, loggers, and cattle ranchers, who have been cutting down the forest at a cumulative rate of up to 100,000 acres a year. The Guatemalan government has finally—albeit belatedly—taken meaures to ease this rate of destruction, recognizing that if strong action is not taken, the Petén could look like a subtropical Kansas within the next 20 years. Go now!

History
Experts now believe that a million or more Maya lived in the Petén during the height of that civilization's influence here, some 1,200 years

ago. Sprinkled throughout the region are thousands of archaeological sites, many unexcavated and 80 of them considered "major," plus vast sacred cave systems and navigable waterways, used by the Maya as trade routes.

This area was so cut off from the rest of Guatemala during the Spanish conquest that the colonizers did not get around to subduing local inhabitants until 1697, more than 150 years after the Europeans settled into the western highlands. Even after Spain staked its claim to the Petén, its hostile climate, limited transportation, and lack of easily exploitable resources discouraged Europeans from developing the area. Forest products such as chicle, rubber, balsam, and mahogany have been commercially exploited here only during the last century. Bear in mind that until 1970, the Petén was virtually inaccessible by road. As recently as 1940, the population density averaged less than one person per square mile. It was 25 times that figure in 1999.

When to Go

Consider visiting the Petén early in your trip to Guatemala, unless you are exiting the country through this department en route to Belize or Mexico. Many travelers put off their excursion to Tikal and other Petén attractions until the end of their journey, which often results in a hasty visit that may necessarily take place during bad weather or involve poor accommodations. Remember that planes to and from Flores–Santa Elena, the area's only commercial airport, fill up quickly, and reservations should be made as far in advance as possible.

Because of the Petén's perpetually hot, humid climate, the best times of day to see and enjoy its attractions are early morning and evening, when the air is cool and the birds and other animals are most active. Therefore, it is worthwhile to plan on spending at least one night and two full days in the area.

The high season for Petén visitors is mid-November through mid-April. Mornings from December through February can be cold enough to warrant a light sweater or jacket. March and April are the driest months, with cool nights and warm days. Heavy rains begin in May and continue intermittently at least through December. In August there is often a dry spell that lasts up to 3 or 4 weeks. Months with the fewest visitors are May and September.

INGUAT (926-0533) maintains an office inside the terminal at the Santa Elena airport, open daily except Monday from 8:00 a.m. to 5:00 p.m. The INGUAT representative is happy to suggest the best resources for local tours, transportation, and guide services. Most local travel agencies also have plenty of information about the Petén.

Getting There

By plane: Flying is unquestionably the fastest and easiest way to get to this remote region. A trip that requires at least a dozen hours by car takes just 35 minutes by jet. As of 1999, six airlines were flying daily between the Flores–Santa Elena airport and Guatemala City. Aerovías, Tapsa, Mayan World Airlines, Aeroquetzal, and Tikal Jet flights leave Aurora at about 7:00 a.m. and depart Santa Elena around 4:00 p.m. Aviateca makes the round-trip twice a day, with morning and afternoon arrivals and departures. The planes are almost always full departing Guatemala City, but because many passengers continue from Tikal to Belize or Mexico, there are usually empty seats on return flights. Round-trip airfare in 1999 was about $160; one-way, $90. From Santa Elena, it is another 37 miles over a smooth paved road to Tikal National Park. The trip by shuttle van takes about 45 minutes, a little longer by public bus. There is an airstrip at the ruins, but it is no longer in use. Air connections can also be made from Flores–Santa Elena to Belize City, Chetumal, Cancún, and Mérida. Charter flights are also possible to Copán, in Honduras, and other destinations.

By bus: A number of Fuente del Norte, La Peteñera, Rosita, and Maya Express buses leave Guatemala City each day for Santa Elena, most departing between 6:00 p.m. and 8:00 p.m., although a few leave in the early morning and late afternoon. The trip is scheduled for 12 hours but often takes much longer, due to flat tires, bridge closures, military blockades, and occasional holdups by *bandidos*. (Thankfully, the route was upgraded in 1998.) Try to buy your ticket a day ahead or you may be forced to stand up all the way or ride on the roof amid piles of luggage. Tickets are about $10 each way and can be purchased on board, but those who have already paid their fare are given first crack at seats. Buses advertised as "express" or pullman are slightly faster (and more comfortable), give you an assigned seat, and cost about $22 each way. Most departures are from 19a. Calle between 8a. and 9a. Avenida in Zone 1. Contact: La Petenera bus line (16a. Calle and 10a. Avenida, Zone 1, Guatemala City), Fuente del Norte (7a. Calle 8-46, Zone 1), or Maya Express (17a. Calle 9-36, Zone 1, Guatemala City). Maya's first-class return buses leave Santa Elena at 4:00 a.m., 7:00 a.m., and 8:00 a.m.

From Flores–Santa Elena it is about an hour by local public bus to the Tikal ruins, or 45 minutes by private vehicle or tourist van.

By car: It is about 300 miles from Guatemala City to Flores, and under ideal conditions the route can be driven in about 9 or 10 hours. Unfortunately, the second half of the trip is over narrow, potholed, winding roads that may take twice the "normal" amount of time or be completely impassable during wet weather. If you do decide to drive, be sure to bring at least one spare tire, tools, a stout tow rope, and extra water. Be advised that most Guatemala City rental agencies will not allow their vehicles to be driven in the Petén. Avoid driving at night if at all possible; other vehicles sometimes drive without lights, animals congregate on the roadway, and criminals sometimes accost travelers. Locally, cars can be rented at the Santa Elena airport.

By tour: Packaged tours to Tikal can be arranged for as short a visit as 2 hours, but it is better to spend at least one full day at the site if at all possible, preferably overnighting in the park itself. Some of the more reputable operators shuttling visitors to and from Tikal by air are **Clark Tours, Ney's Viajes y Turismo, Expedición Panamundo, Ecotourism & Adventure Specialists**, and **Servicios Turísticos del Petén** (see Chapter 4: Special Interests and Appendix B). Some of these companies offer regularly scheduled excursions to Ceibal National Park, the Yaxhá ruins, Lake Petén Itzá, Santa Elena caverns, Lake Petexbatún, and other worthwhile destinations in the region.

Local Transportation

Public buses, invariably slow, unsafe, and crowded but dirt cheap, maintain regular schedules on the few main roads of the Petén. The most popular routes, each costing a few dollars, are between Flores–Santa Elena and the Belize border (note that the U.S. State Department has issued warnings about the presence of bandits on this isolated stretch of road); Flores–El Naranjo (with boat connections to Mexico via the Río San Pedro); Flores–Sayaxché (with connections to Cobán via Sebol and to Frontera Corozal via Betél); and Flores–Guatemala City (via Poptún and Río Dulce–El Relleno). Express buses leave at 5:00 a.m. daily from the San Juan Hotel terminal in Santa Elena for Belize City, Belize, and Chetumal, Mexico. (Belize-based bus companies do not allow their vehicles to cross into Guatemala.) Rosita offers direct, round-trip buses from Guatemala City to Belize City.

Other alternatives to bus travel include renting a private vehicle or airplane charter (both expensive) and traveling with a tour group. The latter often makes the most pragmatic sense, especially when going to remote archaeological sites, rivers, or caves that are not served by public transportation. Some destinations, however, can be reached only on horseback, by boat, or on foot.

As of 1999, regular flights were scheduled between the Petén's Santa Elena international airport and Belize City (Tropic Air, Aerovías), Chetumal (Aerovías, AeroCaribe), Mérida (AeroCaribe), and Cancún (Aviateca, Aeroquetzal, Mayan World, AeroCaribe). Connections can be made to other Belizean and Mexican destinations from these cities.

INGUAT

The ancient city of Flores is reached by a causeway across Lake Petén Itzá.

FLORES AND SANTA ELENA

Location: *Flores is about 2 miles north of the Santa Elena airport, on an island in Lake Petén Itzá. Santa Elena is a larger town, facing Flores across a human-made causeway.*

Population: *Flores 2,000; Santa Elena 7,000 (1999 estimates).*

For More Information: *There is an INGUAT office at the airport in Santa Elena. A tourist information and ecology center (CINCAP) now occupies the old Flores city jail. It is a good source of tips on where to go and what to see throughout the Petén.*

Flores is the capital of the department of El Petén. It is linked by a causeway to the neighboring "mainland" towns of Santa Elena and San Benito. San Andrés and San José, twin Itzá Maya villages immediately north of Flores across a narrow neck of the lake, are reached by boat or car.

With its pastel-colored buildings, cobblestone streets, dense housing, and flooded shoreline, Flores more closely resembles a village of the Aegean than Central America. Its main street circumscribes the island in ever smaller spirals as it winds toward the top of the hill on which the town is built, crowned by a whitewashed church with a few weathered Maya stelae in the plaza nearby.

Learning Eco-Friendly Spanish in the Petén

At least one Spanish school operates in Flores, under the auspices of G.A.P. Adventures and Conservation International, a nonprofit environmental organization based in Washington, D.C., and very active in the promotion of Guatemalan conservation through its ProPetén program. Eco-Escuela de Español, based in the nearby village of San Andrés, offers high-quality Spanish instruction along with companion programs in tropical ecology and conservation. Costs are low, and students have the option of staying with local families (meals included). The San Andreños are noted for their warmth and friendliness. Profits from the school are turned over to community development and conservation projects. For information, contact Conservation International at c/o G.A.P. Adventures at (800) 465-5600 or adventure@ gap.org.

History

The attractive island city of Flores, called Tayasal by its Itzá Maya founders, was one of the first indígena cities visited by the Spanish but the last to be conquered. Hernán Cortés marched through here in 1524 on his way to Honduras and reported that the local people were friendly and welcoming.

When Spanish priests arrived in 1618, they found the Maya worshiping the stone image of a wounded horse left by Cortés almost a century earlier. (The horse had died after the Maya fed it flowers and meat.) The appalled Franciscans ordered the stone sculpture destroyed, but several residents of Tayasal tried to carry it away on a small boat. The sculpture was lost in a sudden storm, and some local people insist that they can still see the blurry image of the carved horse beneath the waters of Lake Petén Itzá.

In 1697, soldiers from Spain returned to conquer Tayasal, well aware that according to a 257-year "cleansing cycle" of the Maya calendar, a major disaster was expected to occur during that year. The Maya, who had fled generations earlier from Campeche and the Yucatán, appeared almost fatalistic about the outcome of the brief but decisive battle in which this last outpost of the Maya empire fell to European hands. (Exactly 257 years later, the Maya were again rocked by the successful coup against reform-minded President Jacobo Arbenz.) On the same day as their attack, the conquerors destroyed the ancient temple at the crown of the hill on the island and celebrated mass there that night. The occupiers subsequently built a large Catholic church on that same spot, which still stands. In 1700, the island of Tayasal, renamed Flores, was fortified and turned into a penal colony. On a peninsula immediately north of present-day Flores are some low mounds, the last remnants of the Maya city.

Services

Money-changing can be carried out at the **Banco de Guatemala** branch office in Flores. Both Flores and Santa Elena have post offices, and the latter town also has a **Telgua** office. You can buy plane tickets at airport airline counters; the **Hotel San Juan** and **Hotel El Petén** also change money and sell tickets, but you can expect to pay extra when not buying directly from the airline. The latter two hotels also have reliable minivans running back and forth to Tikal, as do several other operators. Cars can be rented at the airport or Hotel Tziquinaha, on the outskirts of Santa Elena. Buses leave from Santa Elena's public market and, for some routes, from the Hotel San Juan in Santa Elena.

In addition to local travel agencies, a few adventure-oriented tour operators, such as **Expedición Panamundo, Ecotourism & Adventure Specialists**, and **Servicios Turísticos del Petén**, maintain representatives in Flores and arrange trips to remote archaeological sites, caves, and rivers. We also recommend San Andrés-based **Monkey Eco Tours** for nature treks and excursions to the more exotic Maya ruins and national parks. See Chapter 4: Special Interests and Appendix B for additional information.

Things to See and Do

Boats can be hired at reasonable rates ($10 or less) for trips to any of the several small islands in the lake (one, **Petencito**, has a small zoo and amusement park with a popular water-slide) or around the lake, which has been gradually rising over the years, putting many buildings underwater. Destinations include an old Maya observation tower (affording a good view of the lake) and forested areas with much bird life and an occasional Morelet's crocodile or turtle.

Fishing for peacock bass is good throughout the lake, particularly away from inhabited areas. There are 24 identified fish species in Petén Itzá, although this may change due to continued pollution of the lake by untreated sewage, uncontrolled development, and unregulated infilling. On the north side of the lake, near the village of San José, is the **Bio-Itzá Ecological Reserve**, a tract of tropical forest established by the local Itzá Maya and funded by the Austrian government in a bid to preserve a last vestige of their natural heritage. Sadly, this group of local indígena is rapidly becoming outnumbered: In 1999 it was estimated that only 100 speakers of Itzá Maya remained. Inquire locally about access to the reserve; a Canadian-run hotel in the area has arranged tours in the past. You can also make arrangements through Ni'tun Ecolodge in San Andrés and its co-owned Monkey Eco Tours.

Maya Handicrafts
ProPetén has conducted Maya artisan training projects since 1992, with the goal of creating a cottage industry that will reduce pressure on forest resources by reducing reliance on subsistence farming. As a result of these efforts, tourists can now buy carved alabaster and limestone plaques, painted and carved gourds, musical instruments made from gourds, and carved bones (similar to the ancient Maya canoe incised on a bone displayed at the Tikal museum). Ancient Maya quarries are now being used to obtain the alabaster and limestone for these products, which are now sold throughout the Petén.

The Scarlet Macaw Trail
In 1996, ProPetén-Conservation International and local residents completed work on the Guacamayo (Scarlet Macaw) Trail, a route that extends by road, waterway, and footpath for many miles through the Maya Biosphere, from Lake Petén Itzá to the headwaters of the Río San Pedro. Inquire locally about guided treks on this trail. Recommended local outfitters include Monkey Eco Tours (San Andrés).

In 1999 the trail was divided into three segments of various lengths: Scarlet Macaw, El Zotz-Tikal, and El Mirador.

Getting There
A short, inexpensive ride from the airport by taxi or minibus takes you to Santa Elena. Some of the hotels provide free shuttle service. If arriving by public bus, you will be let off at the terminal in Santa Elena, a dusty 10-minute walk across the Lake Petén Itzá causeway from Flores.

Where to Stay in Flores, Santa Elena, and Vicinity
In addition to the accommodations below, there are a few basic places to stay across the lake in San Andrés and San José, or you can sometimes arrange to stay in a private home in any of the area towns.

Smiling police officers relax during their patrol through Flores.

Don Quixote, in Flores; $10; no phone. Clean and friendly: perfect for budget travelers. Has a good café. Recommended.

Hotel del Patio Tikal, near the lakeshore in Santa Elena; $59; 926-1229, in U.S. (800) 327-3573. Each of the 21 rooms has private bath and satellite TV. Bar and restaurant.

Hotel Petén, in Flores; $35; 926-1692, fax 926-0662. Courtyard and roof-terrace gardens, 14 well-kept rooms, and hot water. Breakfast is available; an on-site travel agency will change traveler's checks.

Hotel San Juan, 2a. Calle, Santa Elena; $26; 926-0726. Travel agency and (noisy) bus terminal on ground level, where vans depart regularly for Tikal ($10) and Belize City (about $30). Sometimes helpful at making connections, but travelers complain about dirty and unsafe hotel conditions as well as unfriendly staff.

Hotel Tayasal, Calle Union, Flores; $25; tel/fax 926-0333. Relatively clean rooms, roof-top terrace, and private showers. Arranges Tikal tours. Recommended.

Hotel Tziquin-Ha, on the road to the Santa Elena airport; $50; 926-0175. This 36-room, modern-looking accommodation has a swimming pool, tennis court, restaurant, gift shop, and car rental agency.

Hotel Yum-Yax, at the foot of the causeway, Santa Elena; $25; 926-0686. The largest hotel on the island, with 43 basic, undistinguished rooms. Fairly noisy for Flores.

Jaguar Inn, Calzado Rodríguez Macal 879, Santa Elena; $28; 926-0002. Operated by the family that owns a hotel/restaurant of the same name in Tikal National Park. English spoken, good food served, personnel at either accommodation can make reservations for the other. Recommended.

Maya International, on the lake in Santa Elena; $54; 926-1276, fax 926-0032. Good restaurant, 20 bungalow-style rooms. Tours arranged here, as at the Villa Maya and other large hotels.

Ni'tún Ecolodge, 1 mile west of the village center, on the lake, San Andrés; $55, includes transportation from Flores; 204-8826 or 361-3104, ecoadventure@mail2.guate.net. Thatched, stone cabañas and an excellent restaurant. The author's favorite area accommodation specializes in organizing adventure trips to remote Maya ruins and natural destinations. Boats can be hired here for transportation on Lake Petén Itzá. Co-owned with Monkey Eco Tours; also recommended for tours, camping, trekking, and birding.

Sabana, in Flores; $25; tel/fax 926-1248. Large rooms, fine service. Lakeside terrace bar.

Villa Maya, several miles outside of town on Laguna Peténchel, an arm of Lake Petén Itzá; $85; 926-0086. Full-service, 36-room resort. The grounds are a rehab zone for wounded wild animals.

Where to Eat in Flores, Santa Elena, and Vicinity

Restaurants in the Petén are generally poor, although those located in hotels are somewhat better than the others (**Jaguar Inn** is especially recommended). Some Petén restaurants may have wild game on the menu, including deer, tepizcuintle, armadillo, and wild birds. Because these animals are already in decline locally, area biologists and environmentalists discourage tourists from eating them.

Café Maya, on the west side of the island, near Hotel Petén, Santa

Elena. Visitor-recommended. There is also a restaurant with a similar name, La Mesa de los Mayas, serving equally delicious food on Calle Centro America in Santa Elena.

Chaltunhá, next to the Hotel Petén, in Flores. Try the *chile rellenos* and *pescado blanco* here.

El Tucán, on the lakefront, just east of the causeway in Flores. Best view among Santa Elena eateries. Visitor-recommended. Try the fish.

Las Puertas, on the east side of the island, near the waterfront, Santa Elena. Healthy food, jazz at night, classical music during the day. Visitor-recommended. Good coffee, ice cream, and pasta.

Restaurante Jacal, on the main street, in Flores. Try the garlic lake fish.

THE ACTUN KAN AND JOBITZINAJ CAVES

Location: An hour's walk or a short taxi ride from Flores.
Fees: There is a nominal entrance fee and a guard will turn on the lights at the Actun Kan cave and answer your questions. Young boys will also serve as guides for a dollar or less. There are no electric lights at the Jobitzinaj Cave, so you will need to bring your own flashlight.

An easy half-day trip from Flores, the Actun Kan cave system is the legendary home of a huge serpent and is sometimes called La Cueva de la Serpiente. There is not a lot to see in the cave, however, except for some unusual rock formations shaped like animals, a marimba, and a waterfall. The usual bats, stalactites, and stalagmites are in evidence.

The eastern outlet of the underground network is called the Actun Kan; the western outlet, Jobitzinaj Cave. The galleries of both caves are often very narrow, and you can expect to get muddy, if not completely soaked.

Getting There

The Actun Kan cave can be reached by car or on foot by following the causeway into Santa Elena, turning left when the road forks in front of a small hill, and then taking the first right to the well-marked cave entrance. The walk from Flores takes an hour or so. The Jobitzinaj Cave can be reached by turning right instead of left at the fork in the road at Santa Elena. Proceed left around the low hill until you reach the marked entrance. You'll pay about $3 for a taxi ride to either cave.

Naj Tunich

Filled with ancient painted images and hieroglyphic texts, this cave has been closed to casual visitors for many years in an attempt to reduce vandalism. No one can get into Naj Tunich without specific permission from the Guatemalan government. As this book went to press, the only scheduled tour was offered by Albuquerque-based Far Horizons. This trip is guided by archaeologist James Brady, who has been conducting fieldwork at this remarkable site.

The first modern discovery of Naj Tunich was by American innkeeper Mike DeVine and his companions in 1980. The cave holds a trove of ancient Maya art, the largest underground collection yet found. The walls of Naj Tunich (also called La Cueva de las Inscripciónes) are adorned with extensive charcoal drawings and texts, some relating to characters found in the Popol Vuh, the sacred history book of the Quiché Maya, who now live in Guatemala's western highlands. Pottery and other artifacts have also been found in this cave, one of many sacred spaces believed by the Maya to be the portals to the underworld called Xibalba. Some archaeologists now believe that Naj Tunich may have been the most sacred Maya cave of all. Experts date the objects found here from A.D. 733 to A.D. 762, although a massive construction at the entrance is from the first century A.D. and some areas have not been fully studied.

Recent work at the cave involves excavation and mapping of an unexplored tunnel as well as videotaping of inscriptions and paintings using a high-tech camera developed by the U.S. Defense Department for use during the 1991 war with Iraq. The technology has been used successfully in recording the Bonampak murals of southern Mexico.

THE POPTÚN HIGHLANDS

Location: *65 miles and 3 hours southeast of Flores, about the same distance and 4 hours riding time from Río Dulce.*
Population: *10,000 (1999 estimate).*
Services: *In addition to several simple hotels and restaurants, Poptún has a gas station, a produce market, a bank, a Telgua office, and several groceries.*
For More Information: *There is no tourist office; try Finca Ixobel or Villa de los Castellanos (see below).*

Whether you're traveling by private vehicle or public bus, the unpaved road linking Flores and Guatemala City via Río Dulce is long and arduous, although it is gradually improving. Many visitors wisely break the journey at or near the town of Poptún.

The elevation here is not very high—about 2,000 feet—but enough to demonstrably change the climate and vegetation from the lowland forest that lies along much of this route. For example, you'll notice pines and other evergreens here that can't survive at the hotter, wetter elevations.

Worth a visit is **Finca Ixobel** (see below), a working farm started in 1971 by U.S. citizens Mike and Carole DeVine and Dennis and Luise Wheeler. Mike was brutally murdered in June 1990, and several members of the Guatemalan military were later arrested for and convicted of his killing. Carole and several friends now run the finca. (The U.S. government had long been pressuring Guatemala for resolution of the Mike DeVine case, linked in 1995 to a paid CIA informant who was an officer in the Guatemalan army.)

If you decide to spend some time in Poptún, a trip into the nearby countryside is highly recommended: Ask locally about hiking, horseback riding, and inner-tubing options. Several caves (including a river cave with an underground waterfall) are easy day trips. At Finca Ixobel you can also arrange a camping trek of up to four days into dense forest.

Getting There

Buses run frequently on this route between Flores and Río Dulce, or drive yourself. The tiny airstrip is served only by charters.

Where to Stay and to Eat in Poptún and Machaquilá

Finca Ixobel, 2 miles south of the town; $10 or less; tel/fax 927-7363. Pitch a tent, hang a hammock, or sleep in one of several rustic bungalows or treehouses. Places to swim and hike; most of the food is organic and home-grown. Travelers from all over the world swap stories over the delicious family-style meals, paid for on an honor system at checkout time. Solar panels heat water and make electricity. You can go swimming, or hire horses and guides for forest excursions. The farm is an easy walk from the road, but do *not* attempt to walk here from Poptún after dark: The highway is not safe.

Finca Ixobel II, downtown Poptún across from the gas station, budget-priced hotel. Operated by the same owner, its **La Fonda Ixobel Restaurant**, is also recommended.

Less than two miles north of Poptún is the village of Machaquilá, where you can find budget lodging along a river at **Cocay Camping** (no phone; run by former Finca Ixobel employees and similar to that operation) or pricier accommodations at **Villa de los Castellanos** (927-7541, fax 927-7307, peten@inforia.com.gt), a cabaña-style lodge run by the friendly Castellanos family, who also offer camping and horseback tours to the local caves, local forest reserves, and various ancient Maya ruins, as well as El Tapir Wildlife Sanctuary. Recommended for adventurous travelers.

THE ROAD TO BELIZE
Location: Melchor de Mencos is on the Belize border, about 70 miles east of Flores.
Population: 4,500 (1999 estimate).
For More Information: Aventuras sin Límites, in Hotel Frontera (see below), runs trips of up to six days' duration to the Maya ruins of Naranjo, Tikal, Yaxhá, Río Azul, El Mirador, and Ceibal.

Flores is about 70 miles west of the Belize border, via a dirt road that has severe problems with armed banditry: Inquire locally before proceeding. (Tourist vans are held up much more often than are public buses, but you should avoid taking chances: Consider flying from Santa Elena to Belize City.)

Melchor de Mencos is a nondescript town on the Guatemalan side of the frontier that has a few hotels, restaurants, and swimming holes (along the Mopán River), and a small public market. Across the international boundary is **Benque Viejo**, Belize, which has little more to offer.

Crossing the Border
Immigration and customs formalities are fairly straightforward, although bribery requests (implicit and explicit) can be expected and you may be charged for a passport stamp, which is technically illegal. Tourist cards are no longer required on the Guatemala side of the border, although some nationalities still need visas (not always available at Guatemala's land borders).

Guatemalan border officials are notorious for assessing illegal transit "taxes" at the Melchor border crossing,. There are no longer any entrance or exit "fees" at Guatemalan land borders. A polite refusal or a request for a detailed receipt will sometimes lead officials to drop this demand, but paying such bribes is sometimes unavoidable. You can fill out a complaint form at the INGUAT (Guatemala Tourist Commission) office at the Santa Elena airport. If you are part of an organized tour group, make your complaint known to the tour operator and request that your comments be forwarded to INGUAT. Such filings have, on at least one occasion, resulted in the firing of unscrupulous border personnel. Officials on the Belize side of the frontier always have tourist cards but will not necessarily issue visas. If you are traveling with a tour group, these formalities are usually taken care of in advance. (For more details about traveling in Belize, see *Belize: Adventures in Nature*, by Richard Mahler, also published by John Muir Publications.)

If you are driving a car, be sure to have your registration and insurance papers in order. Vehicles entering Guatemala are fumigated to kill agricultural pests, a 5-minute procedure for which there is a fee. Try to get rid of your quetzales before crossing into Belize, where they can usually be exchanged only at banks or among money-changers. There is a bank at the border (closed on weekends).

Getting There

Many buses head east from Benque Viejo to Belize City. The most reliable companies are Batty Bus Service and Novelo's Bus Service. Depending on which Guatemalan bus has transported you, you may have to walk or take a taxi the short distance across the border to the bus station. The trip from Benque Viejo to Belize City takes about 3 hours and costs only a few dollars. You can also take a 5:00 a.m. express bus from Flores–Santa Elena directly to Chetumal, Mexico, a 12-hour trip that will bypass Belize City entirely. Inquire at the Hotel San Juan. If you take the 8:00 a.m. public bus from Santa Elena, you should reach Melchor in time to catch a noon bus to Belize City.

Heading in the opposite direction, there are usually several minivans each day that head for Tikal from the cottage-style hotels of Belize's western Cayo district (although most will not pick up non-guests). Public buses originate here about five times a day for the trip to Flores–Santa Elena, which ordinarily takes about 3 to 4 hours.

Where to Stay and to Eat in Melchor de Mencos

Hotel Frontera, on the Mopán River; $10; 926-5196. The hotel— which has private baths, a restaurant, a car rental agency, and a minibus service—is operated by Marco Gross, a local entrepreneur affiliated with Aventuras sin Límites travel agency. For reservations call 092-2823 or stop at Arts & Crafts of Central America in San Ignacio.

Hotel Melchor Palace, near the border and on the river; $16; 926-5196. The best place to stay, with restaurant, travel agency, and auto rentals. The friendly, English-speaking staff can arrange trips to Yaxhá, Naranjo, and other Maya ruins in the Petén and Belize.

Mayab, on the main street; $8; no phone. Basic rooms, a coffee shop, and secure parking. Recommended for budget travelers.

THE ROAD AND RIVER TO MEXICO
Travelers can take one of two daily buses (about $5) from Flores to El Naranjo, a village on the Río San Pedro, and continue from there into Mexico by motorized river launch. The Pinita line bus ride takes 5 or 6 hours over a rough unpaved road, with departures at 5:00 a.m. and 12:30 p.m. The onward (twice daily) boat trip to the Mexican border outpost of La Palma is another 5 hours ($25); the bus ride from there to Tenosique takes about one hour ($4). From Tenosique there is a passenger train to Palenque and Mérida, or you can make bus connections to those destinations or just about anywhere in Mexico. Be sure to have your passport stamped as you enter the country.

El Naranjo
El Naranjo has only the most basic services, including a few comedores and two hotels, the better of which is Lodge El Naranjo ($5, no phone), which also serves meals and changes currency. The boats to La Palma are privately owned and will not depart with fewer than four passengers, usually early in the morning. A small customs and immigration office handles formalities, and, again, you may be asked (illegally) to hand over a few extra dollars to speed "processing."

The trip down the Río San Pedro goes through an extensive wetland habitat, and the channel narrows and widens dramatically en route. A few stilt houses are perched on the riverbanks, and there is a fair amount of boat traffic, as there has been here since the days of the ancient Maya. The swimming, birding, and fishing are good along the way.

An alternate route from Mexico into the Petén involves taking a boat up the Río Usumacinta from Frontera Corozal to Sayaxché via the Río de la Pasión, an Usumacinta tributary. A road connects Sayaxché with Flores and the rest of Guatemala. The journey can be made by private motor launch in a day or two. You will need to bargain over the fare and have your passport checked by Mexican officials in Frontera Corozal and by Guatemalan authorities in Sayaxché or Betél.

Mosquito-borne malaria is endemic throughout the Petén but especially along such waterways as the San Pedro, Usumacinta, and Pasión. You're advised to take preventive medication when traveling in these areas. Also, widespread banditry has been reported in this area, and the Usumacinta is widely regarded as unsafe downstream from Yaxchilán.

THE ROAD TO SAYAXCHÉ AND COBÁN

Sayaxché is a jungle town located on a bend in the Río de la Pasión, which is crossed by an auto ferry. It is an important supply, storage, and shipping center for local farmers, cattle ranchers, and timber cutters. In recent years it has also become the center for excursions to several nearby Maya ruins as well as river trips down the Pasión to Lake Petexbatún and, eventually, the mighty Usumacinta, which can be navigated all the way to the Gulf of Mexico.

SAYAXCHÉ

Location: About 40 miles southwest of Flores.
Population: 2,500 (1999 estimate).
For More Information: Try the INGUAT office at the airport in Santa Elena, or inquire among local hotels and outfitters.

There is not much to do in Sayaxché besides making onward travel arrangements and resting up for your next adventure. If you have not done so prior to your arrival, you can inquire at local hotels and among boat operators on the Pasión about trips to the area's various attractions. As you would expect, it is often much cheaper to join a larger group than to head out on your own. **Servicios de Lancha Don Pedro** (928-6109) rents boats and provides guides for trips up or down the river to Maya sites and natural destinations.

South of Sayaxché road conditions deteriorate rapidly, although it is usually possible in the dry season to take a public bus or drive a four-wheel-drive vehicle all the way to Cobán (where the pavement resumes). Under ideal conditions, it is a 4- or 5-hour journey from Sayaxché to Raxrujá, a village on the upper Río de la Pasión in the department of Alta Verapaz. Raxrujá offers some basic rooms and a few simple comedores. A poorly maintained road branches off at Raxrujá for Playa Grande, about 60 miles west. Bus service from Sebol to Playa Grande is sometimes available.

About 15 miles west of Raxrujá is the village of Xuctzul, where a second road heads 50 miles south to Cobán. Although transportation in this area is poor, you may wish to take this route if you are keen on seeing the **Candelaria Caves,** about 8 miles south of Xuctzul on a poorly maintained access road. (See Chapter 9, the Verapaces, for details).

There are plans eventually to extend an overland highway from Playa Grande all the way to Barillas, making it possible to continue to Huehuetenango and the Mexican border. Such an extension will greatly improve what is now an arduous and perilous journey across largely uninhabited wilderness.

It is also possible to travel between Sebol and Sayaxché by boat on the **Río de la Pasión** and its tributaries, via the hamlet of El Pastor, but arrangements must be made locally.

Getting There

At least two buses a day leave Santa Elena for Sayaxché, a journey of 2 to 3 hours. An airstrip at Sayaxché is open only to charter aircraft. Direct flights from Flores and Guatemala City are available from **Aviones Comerciales** (331-4955). At least one company (**La Pinita**) regularly operates buses on the rough road that runs southwest of Flores to Cobán via Sayaxché. The trip to Guatemala City takes about 20 hours, longer when the ground is muddy. It is recommended that travelers break the journey into two or three segments, overnighting in Sayaxché, Lanquín, or Cobán.

Where to Stay and Eat in Sayaxché

Guayacán Hotel, on the river next to the ferry terminal; $6; 926-6111. Eight basic rooms (some with bath), a small restaurant, and parking. The Guayacán's friendly owner is a former hunting guide and very knowledgeable about the area. Recommended.

Mayapán Hotel, down the street from the Guayacán ($4, no phone) and equally hospitable.

Posada de San Mateo, on Lake Petexbatún ($100, including meals), 232-4483 in Guatemala City. Owner John Schmidt is definitely the one to handle all logistics to such nearby ruins of Dos Pilas and Aguateca. The lodge is some distance from Sayaxché, but it's fabulous.

La Montaña, on the riverfront. Among the town's very basic restaurants, whose owner, Julián Mariona, arranges trips and transportation for travelers.

Yaxkin, in the village center. Another acceptable restaurant. You can stow luggage here (for a modest fee) while making day trips.

Bob Mahler

Ancient stairways and living quarters dot the ruins of Tikal.

THE ROAD TO TIKAL

Heading east from Flores, the paved and well-maintained road to Tikal passes through savannas and cultivated farmland until the turnoff to Belize at El Cruce, after which it follows the edge of Lake Petén Itzá. The village of El Remate clings to the shoreline, a number of its low-lying houses inundated by the rising waters of the lake.

The coastal road continues along the north side of the lake but does not make a complete circuit. At the village of San Andrés, opposite Flores, the road heads north for about 40 miles to the tiny outpost of Carmelita, where horses, mules, and guides can be hired for trips to El Mirador, Nakbé, and other remote Maya sites. Check road conditions, as flooding is a problem beyond the Hotel Camino Real, and a four-wheel-drive vehicle is usually required.

Where to Stay and Eat on the Road to Tikal

El Gringo Perdido, near the intersection of the paved road to Tikal and the dirt road to El Remate and Cerro Cahuí Biotope; $30, includes breakfast and dinner; 926-0605, in Guatemala City 337-0674 or 334-2305. Recommended restaurant, campground, and 40-bed lodge. Rustic bungalows, hammocks, swimming beach, and a campsite. Its name, "the lost Gringo," refers to American David Kuhn, who built a campground here after

293

becoming confused about which of the routes led to Tikal. (The compound is now run by a Guatemalan named Manuel who is married to a German.) The restaurant serves basic but good food. The 12 camp-space platforms are on packed sand and clay, near a thatch-covered dining hall and hammock-hanging space. The toilet is an outhouse, the bathing facilities are the lake. Natural history tours are offered by Manuel's son, Mauricio, who is very knowledgeable and can take you to see turtles, caimans, and a bat cave. If El Gringo is full, try nearby **Casa Roja**, (no phone), a nearby rustic eco-lodge with vegetarian meals, thatch bungalows, and mountain bikes.

Westin Camino Real Tikal, in a 72-room jungle compound about 15 miles from Tikal adjacent to Cerro Cahuí Biotope; $132; 926-0206 or (800) 373-3573, fax 926-0222. First-class service and amenities include cable TV, radio, a/c, telephone, and mini-bar. Three restaurants, lounge, gift shop, beauty parlor, room service. Car rentals and tours, as well as canoeing, windsurfing, diving, fishing, and birding excursions, can be arranged from here to archaeological sites. Credit cards accepted.

La Mansión del Pajaro Serpiente, in El Remate; $90, no phone. A moderately priced alternative to Hotel Camino Real Tikal that also arranges nature-oriented trips and Tikal tours. Recommended.

TIKAL NATIONAL PARK AND RUINS
Location: About 25 miles northeast of Flores.
Size: 222 square miles.
Hours and Fees: In 1999 an admission ticket cost about $6.00 and was good for the date of purchase only. If you wish to visit the ruins at sunrise or sunset, be sure that "special hours" are indicated on your ticket. Normal visiting hours are 6:00 a.m. to 6:00 p.m. and the park's guards are aggressive in their enforcement. If you stay overnight at Tikal, you will have to buy a new, full-price ticket each day to reenter the ruins.
For More Information: All INGUAT offices have information about Tikal, but the one at the airport in Santa Elena is a particularly useful resource. There are also several helpful guidebooks that describe Tikal's attractions; they can be purchased at stores and hotels throughout Guatemala, including those at the park. The best of these guidebooks is Tikal: A Handbook of the Ancient Maya Ruins, *by the University of Pennsylvania's William R. Coe, director of archaeology from 1962 to 1969. For birders, Frank B. Smythe's* The Birds of Tikal *is an indispensable guide to the hundreds of species observed within the park's boundaries. The same volume is useful throughout the rest of Petén and, for that matter, in the rest of lowland Guatemala. Good background on Maya history and culture is found in* The Rulers of Tikal, *by Genevieve Michel; The*

Maya, *by Michael D. Coe; and* The Ancient Maya, *by Sylvanus Morely (fifth edition, updated by Robert Shaves). Spanish-speakers may wish to call the Tikal Visitor's Center at 926-0102.*

Artifacts of the mysterious Maya civilization are found throughout almost all of Guatemala, but nowhere is the documented concentration of ancient buildings greater than in the Petén. Of these, the most impressive excavated site is Tikal.

The massive ruins of Tikal are among the largest in the Maya world, covering some 10 square miles and encompassing thousands of individual constructions, including temples, plazas, ball courts, ceremonial platforms, residences, shrines, palaces, causeways, and reservoirs. On display are over 200 stone monuments, such as altars and plain or sculptured stelae. The latter served an important role in the Maya's religion-based political system, documenting important historical events and deifying autocratic rulers.

Excavation and restoration activities are almost continuously underway at the site, and it is believed that thousands of structures, monuments, and artifacts still lie below the shallow topsoil.

The ruins are on a low ridge at approximately the center of Tikal National Park and are surrounded by forest that has been neither cut nor significantly tampered with since the lowland Maya empire collapsed around A.D. 850 (except for the main plaza, which is planted with grass). Because of the special character of this primary broadleaf forest, Tikal attracts many scientific researchers as well as birders and other lovers of exotic flora and fauna.

The variety and abundance of life found here are truly mind-boggling. As they have enjoyed protection from hunters since the early 1930s, many of the resident creatures show little fear of people and thus can be easily approached and photographed, much like wildlife on Ecuador's Galápagos Islands. (Some of Tikal's animals, including its scarlet macaws, have been confiscated elsewhere from poachers and released here after becoming locally extinct.)

Nearly 300 bird species have been identified in Tikal National Park, including unusually large concentrations of crested guans, ocellated turkeys, king vultures, and great curassows. Among the diverse mammal species found here are jaguar, puma, ocelot, margay, jaguarundi, white-lipped peccary, brocket deer, agouti, paca, and kinkajou. Spider monkeys and black howlers swing through the treetops. Sixteen species of bats have been recorded in Tikal and over 350 kinds of butterflies. Few of these creatures pose any serious threat to visitors. Notable exceptions include several snake species, such as the fer-de-lance and coral.

Besides the famous ruins, the park has several nature trails extending for some distance into the thick jungle. One of the best of these begins on the grounds of the Tikal Inn and takes visitors past a tall treehouse platform built by scientists to study insect populations at various levels of the forest habitat. If you climb to the uppermost point, you will penetrate the canopy and have an unusual panoramic view of the *selva* (undisturbed forest). Do not continue on this trail beyond the observation platform without a knowledgeable companion. Several tourists have become lost here.

Orientation

At the park boundary several miles west of the ruins themselves, all vehicles must stop so that each visitor can register and pay the entrance fee. The author's recommendation is to spend at least one night at the ruins if at all possible. While conditions are far from luxurious, you'll be rewarded with a close-up view of Tikal's wildlife (many animals are active at sunset and sunrise) and a chance to see the ruins at your leisure (an abundance of tour groups and hot temperatures can make the ruins feel oppressive from 11 a.m. to 3 p.m.).

As you approach the compound south of the ruins, where Tikal's hotels and services are located, you will first notice a string of simple cafés along the right side of the road. These open-air restaurants provide simple and relatively inexpensive meals, though far from gourmet. They also sell cigarettes, matches, postcards, and souvenirs.

On the left as you continue driving into the main compound is a small telegraph and post office (there are no telephones in Tikal), next to which is a modern building that serves as the park's visitors center. It is worth stopping here first to see the impressive scale-model replica of the ruins in the lobby and a large collection of stelae and other sculpture housed in the central part of the building. At the opposite end of the center are restrooms, a gift shop, and Tikal's most expensive restaurant (although not necessarily its best).

The entrance road dead-ends beyond the visitor center in a parking lot that is actually part of the airstrip that was used for many years to ferry archaeologists and tourists in and out of Tikal. A decision was made in the late 1970s to discontinue flights because of vibrational damage to the Maya structures and disturbance of wildlife, as well as the danger of plane crashes.

Along one side of the old airstrip are the park's three bungalow-style hotels and their respective restaurants. On the northern end of the compound is the small but worthwhile **Sylvanus G. Morley Museum of Archaeology, History, and Nature** (open daily 9:00 a.m. to 5:00 p.m., for a small admission fee) and a gift shop selling Guatemalan *típica*. On the

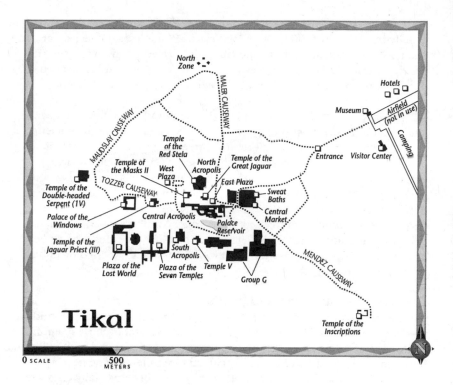

Tikal

opposite (east) side of the airstrip is a grassy area that serves as a public campground, with hammock hooks, restrooms, water tap, and showers.

If you enter Tikal by tour bus, your driver will probably head up the short access road that passes between the Jungle Lodge and the Inspector's Checkpoint, where you must show your ticket. Passengers are discharged at the gated entrance to the archaeological site, then walk several hundred yards to the ruins.

If you come by private car or are on foot, simply walk the short distance from the parking lot up the access road to the entrance gate to the ruins. On the right side of this road, through the trees, you may glimpse the encampment that houses several hundred employees of the park, most of whom return to their home villages for eight days each month. They also have Sundays off.

No matter what time of year you visit, it is likely to be hot during the afternoon. During the dry months of March and April, daytime temperatures at Tikal can often exceed 90 degrees Fahrenheit. For this reason, you are strongly advised to visit the ruins during morning hours if at all possible. In the early morning it may be very damp and misty, but this usually burns off by 9:00 a.m. or 10:00 a.m. Remember to wear a hat and apply sunscreen. Carry a map (the ruins are vast and maps are widely available) and bring water (only a few soft-drink and snack vendors operate in the park). Touring the ruins is fairly strenuous: The ground is uneven and there are stairs to climb.

Plenty of shade trees grow among the ruins and it is helpful to have a guide point out the most important species: ceiba (sacred to the ancient Maya and modern Guatemala's national tree, also called the kapok or silk cotton), mahogany, Spanish cedar, chicozapote (from which chicle is tapped and ironwood is cut), ramón (whose breadnuts are a favorite food of spider monkeys), and xate palm (its ornamental leaf is an important Petén export). You will also see flowering orchids and bromeliads clinging to the highest branches of many of these trees. Monkeys, coatimundi, deer, cats, and other mammals freely roam through the ruins, and scores of parrots, red-crested woodpeckers, oropendolas, and other colorful birds fly overhead.

Overview of the Archaeological Site

Tikal is dominated by five enormous temples—tall stone-block pyramids that rise as much as 212 feet above the ground. Several of these magnificent structures are clustered around a Great Plaza, decorated with tall limestone stelae and other delicately carved monuments. The nearby North and Central Acropolis complexes have also been partially excavated and restored. Other structures, scattered for many acres among the tall trees that have taken over the site, include ancient mansions, storehouses, ball courts, and sacrificial platforms. All told, more than 4,000 structures have been mapped in Tikal, about half of them in the excavated core area. A complex network of causeways, aqueducts, and reservoirs—remnants of which are still visible—provided this ancient city with water for drinking, construction, and irrigation during the long dry season.

Guide Services

Because of Tikal's immense size and the confusing maze of trails linking clusters of buildings, you are strongly urged to hire a guide or join an on-site tour group, at least for your first foray into the ruins. Expect to pay $25 to $35 for a general tour of 2 to 4 hours' duration, more for a personal guide.

There are usually plenty of English-speaking guides looking for customers near the parking lot. If not, inquire at the inspector's hut or any of the hotels. The author also recommends Raul Calvillo, who speaks fluent English and operates through a company called Jades R.C. Señor Calvillo

also arranges horseback tours of the
El Mirador ruins west of Tikal.

History

Tikal first became known to the
non-Maya world in 1848, after two
officials of the Petén's regional government, Modesto Méndez and
Ambrosio Tut, toured the vast
overgrown site. Their findings were
published in a European archaeological magazine and created new
interest in the area. Sadly, they also
inspired a Swiss adventurer to
visit—and cart a load of beautifully
carved temple doorway lintels off to
Switzerland.

*One of the many carved stone
monuments at Tikal*

Richard Mahler

British archaeologist Alfred
Maudslay began scientific exploration here in 1881, clearing
mounds from the jungle and taking the first photographs of Tikal. The
published pictures stirred worldwide interest and brought the head of the
Carnegie Institution's archaeology program to the site to lead a large
research team. This respected investigator, Sylvanus G. Morley, is cred-
ited with deciphering many of the hieroglyphic inscriptions on the stelae
found here. His group remained in Tikal through most of the 1920s and
1930s, followed in the 1950s and 1960s by experts from the University of
Pennsylvania who worked under contract with the Guatemalan government's Institute of Anthropology and History, which continues to oversee
excavated ruins that cover about 6 square miles.

Tikal National Park was created in 1955 and occupies a square measur-
ing about 16 miles on each of its four sides. It was the first fully protected
archaeological preserve in Central America.

Based on archaeological evidence uncovered here, scientists believe
Tikal was founded around 700 B.C., although habitation in the area may
have begun as much as 1,800 years earlier. Because there is no consistent
source of water in the area, the Maya were forced to develop an intricate
system for storing and distributing rainwater before Tikal could develop
into a sizable city. This technology, developed about 500 years before
Christ, probably saved much of the nearby forest from destruction at
least through the Classic era, since Tikal's farmlands were able to produce enough food to feed the local population.

*This doorway arch has been exposed to the elements
for more than a thousand years.*

Richard Mahler

During this early period thousands of workers were used to build
and flatten the stone platforms on which large structures were constructed out of cut limestone blocks. The architectural achievements of
the Maya are particularly impressive considering that they had no pack
animals, wheels, metal tools, or pulleys. Their builders never mastered
the formal arch, however; therefore it was impossible for them to create
rooms wider than 8 feet.

By approximately A.D. 1250, the beginning of the Early Classic
period, the Maya were ready to build the largest of their temples and
other monuments. Many of these commemorate the lives and deaths of
individual rulers, who were often buried in a chamber beneath their pyramids. Curiously, no cemeteries have been found at Tikal, and it is
believed that peasants were buried under their modest houses on the
fringe of the city.

Commissioned artists were kept busy carving stone stelae with
inscriptions telling the history of the Maya and the accomplishments of
their specific leaders. Friezes were carved as building ornaments in the
shapes of animals real and imagined. Particular care was given to the
sculpting of wooden lintels made from the ziracote tree (also called ironwood). Many of these have been stolen or unrecognizably eroded,

though a few are still visible after more than a dozen centuries of exposure to the elements.

During the mid-Classic period, around A.D. 550 to 650, Tikal became the wealthy center of a vast trade network that extended throughout Central America and Mexico, perhaps even as far as South America and the southwestern U.S. The discovery of large amounts of jade, obsidian, copper, coral, and other non-native materials suggests the Maya had developed a sophisticated system for exchanging precious goods.

The population of Tikal probably peaked at roughly 70,000 residents during the Late Classic era, which began around A.D. 650. With the city's infrastructure and largest ceremonial structures virtually complete, more attention could be paid to metaphysical pursuits, such as religion, mathematics, and astronomy.

Because the Maya had a habit of constructing new edifices on top of old buildings—and smashing the carved images of rulers after their deaths—most of what we now see at Tikal is believed to date from A.D. 700 to 750. What we do not know is why the city suddenly became depopulated around the end of the eighth century, after perhaps 1,500 years of continuous occupation. Some buildings were even abandoned in the middle of construction. Theorists have sought to explain this abrupt decline, citing drought, land exhaustion, disease, social disorder, and internecine warfare as possibilities. There is evidence that, late in Tikal's history, Belize's Caracol city-state occupied the region for as long as 60 years. Perhaps the great city's demise was due to a combination of several factors. We will likely never know the truth with any degree of certainty.

A few Maya probably continued to inhabit Tikal during the centuries immediately preceding the 1697 Spanish conquest. Eventually, however, the site was swallowed by the forest and apparently forgotten by all but a handful of local hunters and farmers until the mid-19th century. Today it truly lives up to its Maya name, "the place where spirit voices are heard."

Getting There

Vans and minibuses ply the highway between Tikal and Flores frequently during the morning hours, charging between $5 and $10 each way. Buses return to Flores and the Santa Elena airport at about 6 a.m., noon, 2:00 p.m., and 4:00 p.m. The Hotel San Juan operates one of the more reliable services. A public bus passes through Tikal at least twice a day, en route to the village of Uaxactún, north of the park. Inquire locally about schedules. There are many guided all-inclusive trips to Tikal from Antigua, Guatemala City, and Belize (see Chapter 4, Special Interests).

Where to Stay at Tikal National Park

Note: The three hotels in Tikal National Park have no telephones, faxes, or telexes. You can make bookings through travel agents in Flores or Guatemala City, or send a letter with a one-night deposit to the hotel in care of Tikal National Park, El Petén, Guatemala. Early reservations are advised during the high season, mid-November through mid-April.

Be advised that hotel room burglaries are a continuing problem in Tikal. Another aggravation is the necessary evil of hotel (and restaurant) power generators, which usually hum loudly until about 10 p.m., then start again at daybreak.

The Jaguar Inn, $50, hammocks $10; 926-0002. Owned and operated by Mundo Solis, formerly Tikal's Aviateca ticket agent, who speaks English and is well informed about local attractions. Accommodations consist of several rustic bungalows, some private and others dormitory style (a few have their own baths). There is a restaurant and a campsite on the premises (you can rent a tent). The food is mediocre, as it is every place in Tikal, but the staff is very friendly and eager to please. Excursions arranged here to Uaxactún, Yaxhá, and Ceibal.

The Jungle Lodge, sometimes listed as La Posada de la Selva; $60; 477-0570, in Guatemala City 476-8775, fax 476-0294, or write 29 Calle 18-01, Guatemala City. A bungalow-style with about 35 rooms in the main unit plus a less expensive wing with shared baths. A restaurant, open to the public, prepares hot meals and picnic lunches. Separate bar and gift shop. This recently updated complex, operated by a Guatemalan family, was originally built in the 1950s to provide shelter for the archaeologists and other scientists working at the nearby ruins. If you book ahead, the lodge will arrange transport from the Santa Elena airport. Currently this is by far the best hotel in Tikal, with amenities that include a swimming pool and ceiling fans, plus guided tours of the ruins.

The Tikal Inn, $55, 599-6212, fax 594-6944 (Guatemala City). The inn has three modest bungalows and about a dozen standard rooms, plus a dining hall that serves three unpretentious meals a day (some tour operators require full board if their clients stay here, at about $20 extra per day). There is also a swimming pool that is open to non-guests for a small fee. The Ortíz family, which has run the Tikal Inn for many years, is extremely knowledgeable about attractions in and around the park. Standards have slipped here in recent years. Most of the rooms are only semiprivate; open ceilings mean loud conversations and lovemaking may be shared experiences: Bring earplugs! Reservations made by sending a letter with requested dates, then full payment *after* receipt of confirmation. Write: Tikal Inn, Tikal National Park, El Petén, Guatemala.

Other Options

Tikal Campground, opposite the old airstrip from the Tikal Inn. The park's only official campground, it is clean and well maintained, with about a dozen tent sites and hammock spaces available on a first-come, first-served basis. The daily use fee is about $5.50 per camper. Hammocks and mosquito nets can be rented for about $1.80 each, tents for $3.50. There are flush toilets, cold showers, and a wash area, although water is sometimes unavailable. Recreational vehicles are allowed to park overnight in the main parking lot near the campground for the same price. A (Spanish-speaking) ranger is on-site at all times.

Where to Eat in Tikal

Remember, most restaurants at Tikal are closed on Sundays, so you'll either have to go hungry, dip into your own larder, or eat at one of the three hotels (**Jaguar Inn** is your best bet).

Café Restaurant del Parque, at the visitors center. Besides the dining rooms of the three hotels, Tikal has one expensive restaurant: this one.

Comedor Imperio Maya. Better than the Comedor Tikal, with friendly people, decent fried chicken, sweet plantains, the ubiquitous beans-and-rice, and ice-cold beer.

Comedor Tikal, nearest the entrance, has adequate, moderately priced food and service. It is run by José María López, who has worked at Tikal since 1960 and is the author of a Spanish-language guide to the ruins.

A Brief Tour of the Tikal Ruins

The Great Plaza

The Great Plaza (or Plaza Mayor) was the center of the great city of Tikal and, for perhaps hundreds of years, the entire Maya civilization. It encompasses almost 3 acres of artificially flattened land surrounded by stone monuments, temples, and other constructions. Along each side of the plaza are about 70 carved stelae and sacrificial altars, some restored and all now protected by thatch-roofed shelters. Most of the stelae date from the Pre-Classic and Classic era and were originally painted red. They are believed to have told the dynastic history of Tikal through its various cultural epochs. (No stelae were erected in the Post-Classic period.)

The Great Plaza Ball Court

This area, between Temple I and the Central Acropolis, was built during the Late Classic period and has been only partially excavated. It can be identified by the two walls that run parallel to both sides of a grassy area, where ball games were played before royal audiences who sat on the stairways at the ends of the field. The sport was a cross between basketball and soccer: Rubber balls were thrown toward a hoop by members of opposing teams of four men, but their hands could never touch the sphere. Participants were sometimes sacrificed to the gods at the end of the game.

The North and Central Acropolis

These are palace-like structures situated north and south of the Great Plaza. The mortal remains of some of the ruling families of Tikal have been found beneath these buildings, which are believed to have served a combination of residential, administrative, and ceremonial functions.

The North Acropolis, once painted bright red, contains some interesting mask carvings and stone monuments believed to pay homage to the Maya's ancient ancestors. The Central Acropolis, a warren of windowless rooms, narrow passageways, raised courtyards, and fragmented stairways, is bordered on its southern boundary by the Palace Reservoir. These structures were built over a 500-year period beginning about A.D. 200.

The East Plaza

The Méndez and Maler causeways (ancient pathways that, along with sloped plazas, once directed rainwater to reservoirs) lead to this conglomeration, north of the Great Plaza, where Temple 5D-38 and the sloping terraces of Structure 5D-43 can be found. There is also a market area and a ball court, neither restored. In fact, much of this area is now overgrown with tall trees and thick shrubbery.

The West Plaza

This grassy plaza contains several stelae and smooth altar stones but no restored buildings. A restroom and a refreshment stand, however, can be found here under tall shade trees.

Temple I

This famous pyramid rises a dramatic 145 feet above the east end of the Great Plaza and faces Temple II directly to the west. Also called the Temple of the Giant Jaguar, it is capped by an ornamental roof comb that sits majestically atop a three-room structure, which in turn rests on an immense nine-level limestone base. At the very top of the temple is the badly eroded image of a seated priest-king, surrounded by ornately

304

Bob Mahler

Temple I rises 145 feet above Tikal's main plaza.

carved scrolls and snakes. This statue was originally painted vivid red and white. Deep inside the bottom of the temple is a burial tomb, from which archaeologists extracted the remains of the royal ruler Ah Cacaw (Lord Cacao), adorned with precious jewels and other artifacts. Some of these are on display at the park's museum, which has re-created the tomb as it was originally discovered. Experts believe this and the facing temple were built around A.D. 700.

If you look at the doorway to the middle chamber of the temple, you will see one of only two ornately carved lintels at Tikal that has survived looters, archaeologists, and the elements. (The other is atop Temple III.)

In the past it has been possible to climb the steep stairway to the sacred altar on top of Temple I, but access to the structure is now prohibited, due to restoration.

The acoustics between the temples of the Great Plaza are uncanny. When the plaza is quiet, two people speaking in normal voices can easily converse between Temples I and II, across several hundred yards of open space. This design was deliberate, so that Maya priests could easily be heard by the masses gathered below.

Temple II

Directly opposite Temple I on the Great Plaza, Temple II is perhaps the most photographed of Tikal's buildings at Tikal. The Temple of the Masks, as it is otherwise known, is 125 feet tall and is believed to be a burial monument to the wife of Ah Cacaw, the ruler found beneath Temple I. No tomb has yet been discovered beneath Temple II, however. The temple takes its name from the two large masks on either side of the stairway at the third terrace, believed to have been a royal reviewing stand.

A ceremonial structure tops the three-level pyramid, and at one time the temple was crowned with a roof comb, now mostly eroded. The interior walls of the small ceremonial building were originally covered with friezes, but these have been chipped away or covered with graffiti.

This pyramid is much easier to climb than Temple I, which originally had a similarly broad stairway that has almost disappeared over the centuries. Temple II's wide block steps were used by Maya dignitaries as they ascended the temple to perform sacrifices and other sacred rituals, while lesser mortals watched from far below.

Temple III

Located some distance from Temples I and II, this 180-foot pyramid is across the Tozzer Causeway from the West Plaza. The steep base of this Temple of the Jaguar Priest has not been fully excavated or restored, and you will need to grab onto tree roots and hanging vines to pull yourself up to the high platform that supports a two-room ceremonial building. Your reward is not only a splendid view of the surrounding jungle but a look at one of the two carved lintels at Tikal that remains relatively intact and in its original position. The carving shows a rotund holy man (probably a ruler) dressed in a jaguar skin; thus the temple's name. Temple III was built around A.D. 810, the last great pyramid constructed at Tikal.

Temple IV

The highest human-built structure in the Tikal ruins is the 212-foot Temple of the Double-Headed Serpent. This pyramid is located several hundred yards north of the Great Plaza and, like Temple III, is unexcavated at its base. Fortunately, there is a sturdy wooden ladder built into the sides of the steep, soil-covered platform beneath the monument itself, which rests on an amazing 250,000 cubic yards of building material. A partly restored ceremonial building sits at the top of the platform, which overlooks an uninterrupted sea of green forest. The rock walls of these three rooms are up to 40 feet thick. Dating tests have pinpointed the time of their construction to A.D. 741, under the reign of Yaxkin Caan Chac.

An even better view—in fact, the best in Tikal—is obtained by climbing a narrow vertical metal ladder up one side of the structure to the base of the large roof comb crowning the temple. Its namesake, the double-headed serpent, is not in evidence, however; the carved lintel containing this image and a similar one on Temple I were removed in 1877 and are now on display in Switzerland's Basel Archaeology Museum, along with four other Tikal lintels. This was the highest known human-made point in the Western Hemisphere until the first skyscrapers went up in Manhattan in the 19th century. Archaeologists have recently determined that a temple at the El Mirador site, northwest of Tikal, is about 10 feet taller than Temple IV.

(Note that the climb up Temple IV is rigorous: The ladder is not continuous and very slippery when wet. The climb to the top of this temple is not recommended for those with a fear of heights, a heart condition, or a poor sense of balance. Park officials may have closed this route for safety and archaeological preservation reasons by the time of your visit.)

You can drive to the base of Temple IV by way of an access road. There is a parking lot and a

The temples of Tikal were built from enormous limestone blocks, carved by the Maya without the benefit of metal tools.

restroom, plus a large shaded platform with picnic tables. Nearby you can buy snacks and cold drinks from vendors.

The best times of day to visit Temple IV are at sunrise (remember the scene filmed here for use in the movie *Star Wars*?), when the din of bird calls and insects can be almost deafening, and at sunset, when the eerie grunts and groans of howler monkeys often fill the air.

Temple V

Located adjacent to the South Acropolis and El Mundo Perdido along the Palace Reservoir, this pyramid is 172 feet high and was built around A.D. 750. It has been seriously eroded by weather and vegetation and appears more like a steep hillside than a temple. There are no ladders or stairways, but the many trees and roots available to grip make this a fairly easy climb.

Temple VI

Located at the southern end of the Méndez Causeway, this structure takes its nickname, Temple of Inscriptions, from a long hieroglyphic text found here, which refers to the date A.D. 766 and mentions rulers dating back to Olmec times. It is believed that the temple was built by Yaxkin Caan Chac and that the glyph inscription, the longest in Tikal, was added by a ruler named Chitam. The fine stela and altar in front of this building relate to blood sacrifices.

The South Acropolis
This pyramid-like cluster of ceremonial buildings is located between Temple V and the plaza of El Mundo Perdido. It has not yet been fully investigated and to the casual observer seems to be nothing more than a hill in the jungle—a sort of mezzanine of trees.

Palace of the Windows
Also known as the Bat Palace, this is a group of structures west of Temple III. The partially restored building that gives its name to the group has many interconnecting rooms and passageways, some of them very dark and inhabited by bats and spiders. The function of this complex is unknown, but the common assumption is that priests and royal family members lived here and/or performed certain ceremonies in some of the rooms.

El Mundo Perdido
Also known as the Plaza of the Great Pyramid, El Mundo Perdido is located about 300 yards southwest of the Great Plaza. Its name—Spanish for "the lost world"—refers to a 116-foot temple here (Structure 5C-54) which is believed to be the oldest of Tikal's excavated buildings, built sometime before A.D. 300. This pyramid, with its surrounding ceremonial structures, forms part of an astronomical observatory. A short distance to the north is Temple 5C-49, a pyramid that collapsed in 1980 after a series of violent rainstorms. The El Mundo Perdido area is a good place to see birds.

Plaza of the Seven Temples
East of El Mundo Perdido, this serene plaza is surrounded by several ceremonial buildings from the Late Classic period, as well as a triple ball court and an Early Classic–era palace that dates from before the birth of Christ. Rising majestically from the thick jungle are two enormous pyramids, one with four staircases framed by remnants of huge masks.

Palace Reservoir
Located just south of the Central Acropolis, this reservoir was created by damming a ravine and lining the underlying limestone bedrock with

impervious clay. Causeways were built along adjacent slopes to funnel rainwater into the impoundment area.

THE MAYA BIOSPHERE RESERVE

In theory, all of Guatemala lying north of the 17th parallel is under the protective jurisdiction of the Maya Biosphere Reserve, created by the government in 1990 as part of a master plan for studying and conserving the area's phenomenal natural resources. In actual practice, however, only a fraction of these lands enjoy any measure of enforced protection from overzealous *chicleros*, *xateros*, hunters, drug lords, farmers, looters, and timber harvesters. Much of the reserve is explicitly intended for controlled extraction, which means that local residents are allowed to carry out limited hunting, farming, and harvesting of native plants. Only parts of the biosphere officially designated as biotopes and national parks are supposed to be kept free of human habitation. The multiple-use areas and buffer zones around these protected regions are relatively well populated.

The problem of resource protection is complex and should be familiar to anyone who has spent time in Central America or other "developing" parts of the subtropics. Those interested in saving Guatemala's forest ecosystems and archaeological sites are competing with a much larger number of powerful individuals (including some government officials), companies, and institutions with economic interests in exploiting its timber, wildlife, ancient artifacts, and raw land. Widespread corruption, violent crime, drug trafficking, military abuses, and poverty exacerbate these conflicting interests in the Petén.

On the positive side, Guatemala's National Protected Areas Council is working closely with local and overseas conservationists on preservation designs and management plans for protection of the Maya Biosphere. With support funds from the U.S. government's Agency for International Development, the nonprofit Conservation International has undertaken extensive training of local Guatemalans in park management techniques and sustainable harvesting of wild trees and plants. Scientists and other conservation groups are conducting an exhaustive (and overdue) inventory of the region's flora and fauna.

Several distinct ecologically and/or archaeologically sensitive areas within the boundaries of the Maya Biosphere currently enjoy a special measure of official protection. In addition, the Austrian government funds a private biosphere, the Bio-Itzá Ecological Reserve, about 20 minutes by car northeast of San Andrés, near Lake Petén-Itzá. This reserve is managed by local people and open to visitors. Inquire locally about access; you'll enjoy a terrific view of Lake Petén Itzá.

For more information, contact the INGUAT office in Guatemala City (331-1333, fax 331-4416) or at the airport in Santa Elena; you can also inquire locally among adventure travel outfitters and eco-friendly hotels.

Getting There
Local outfitters and travel agencies arrange trips (see Chapter 4). Public transportation is limited to a few public bus routes.

Where to Stay and Eat Within the Maya Biosphere Reserve
The area is mostly wilderness and there are few lodges or restaurants. Most visitation requires camping and meal preparation. Where appropriate, recommended facilities are mentioned in the text that follows.

CERRO CAHUÍ BIOTOPE
Location: Near the village of El Remate, on the road between Flores (20 miles) and Tikal (18 miles) at the eastern tip of Lake Petén Itzá.
Hours: Trails are open 7:00 a.m. to 5:00 p.m. daily; no admission charge.
Services: Guards are on duty during most daylight hours and guides can be hired for nature tours. Several hotels are located near the reserve. The villages of El Remate and Jobompiche provide basic services and boat rentals.
For More Information: Contact tour operators (see Chapter 4: Special Interests) or inquire locally in El Remate and Jobompiche.

Near the village of El Remate, the 1,600-acre Cerro Cahuí Biotope is a nature reserve set up specifically to protect the Petén (or ocellated) turkey, the howler monkey, and several species of waterfowl. The park has several footpaths, a spectacular lookout point above the lake, and a camping area.

The protected area encompasses about 1,600 acres of hot and rainy subtropical forest. Preservation of this broadleaf jungle is partly calculated to maintain the quality of water entering Lake Petén Itzá. Elimination of trees around other parts of the lake has accelerated erosion, which threatens to change the aquatic ecosystem. The varied plant life in the reserve includes many species of orchids and bromeliads, along with mahogany, cedar, ramón, sapodilla, and marmalade fruit trees.

Dozens of mammals have been recorded at Cerro Cahuí, including ocelot, jaguar, raccoon, armadillo, and white-tailed deer. Several kinds of primates and reptiles are also found here.

The Petén turkey is fully protected in the park, one of the few places where the once-common bird still thrives, although it is now in greater evidence in Tikal National Park. Sharp-eyed visitors can also expect to see parrots, toucans, hook-beaked hawks, kingfishers, grey herons, purple herons, ducks, woodpeckers, and, during winter months, many migratory birds.

Getting There
The biotope is accessible by private car, taxi, or the Jobompiche–El Remate public microbus, which departs from the Santa Elena market each day at about 11:00 a.m.

This huge ceiba tree looms over Tikal's partially excavated Mundo Perdido.

UAXACTÚN ARCHAEOLOGICAL PARK
Location: Directly north of Tikal, reached by 14 miles of dirt road.

Services: Government-certified guides are available for day or overnight trips to the Uaxactún ruins as well as the Maya sites of Río Azul, El Mirador, El Totz, and Xultún. Be advised that the archaeological knowledge of most guides is unreliable.

For More Information: Contact tour specialists such as Ecotourism & Adventure Specialists (Guatemala City), Monkey Eco Tours (San Andrés), and ProPetén-Conservation International (Flores). (See Chapter 4: Special Interests for details.)

Directly north of Tikal is the largely unrestored (except for its plazas) Maya ruin of Uaxactún, built and rebuilt during roughly the same era as its famous and larger neighbor. A tour of the site can be disappointing after a visit to Tikal, which Uaxactún resembles on a much smaller scale. The tallest temple pyramid here rises to only 27 feet, for example, and most of the stelae have been either removed or eroded beyond recognition.

The site is best known for its massive astronomical "observatory." A set of three temples known as Group E are oriented so that when viewed from the middle structure (with its two large stucco faces flanking the stairway), the sun passes directly over the northernmost pyramid on the summer solstice and over the southernmost pyramid on the winter solstice. This distinctive Maya architectural pattern was first discovered here and later turned up at similar observatories at other ancient sites.

Fieldwork at Uaxactún, as at Tikal, was clumsy in its earliest phase.

Dynamite was reportedly used to remove some of the friezes, stelae were carted off to overseas collections, and buildings were crudely cut open to look for burial tombs. The explorations turned up some interesting painted murals, however, and evidence that portions of the temple pyramids may have been originally covered with wooden, thatch-roofed shelters. A copy of a magnificent Uaxactún fresco is displayed at the National Museum of Archaeology and Ethnography in Guatemala City.

The ruins are in eight groups of structures, bisected by a dirt airstrip. Once used to transport balls of rubber and chicle, the runway now serves as a combination soccer field, plaza, and pasture for the village of Uaxactún, home to about 950 people. The largest cluster of buildings is on the west side of the airport and includes a wooden observation platform that is now in disrepair. Be sure to check out the **Museo Juan Antonio Valdés**, next to the airstrip, which holds a large collection of Maya ceramics. No admission charge.

The name Uaxactún means "eight stone" and is derived from a piece of limestone found here with an inscription that begins with that number, apparently an early date on the Maya historical time line. Some archaeologists theorize that Uaxactún may have been occupied longer than any other Maya city. This may well be, therefore, the place where the culture was consolidated, the writing system perfected, and the calendar started. Artifacts found here provide an unusual record of how Maya ceramics evolved over the centuries. A number of exquisite jade pieces have been recovered at Uaxactún, and beneath one temple is a building dating back to 2000 B.C., one of the oldest structures found in the Petén.

An examination of local soil history found evidence of extreme erosion here toward the end of the Classic era, apparently due to overuse of the land. Much of the forest was denuded and topsoil was washed away, bolstering one theory about the cause of the Maya's decline. Skeletons found at nearby Tikal show signs of malnutrition among the lower classes during the same period.

Getting There

The road to Uaxactún begins at the inspection station for the Tikal ruins. The route takes about 30 to 45 minutes by car, or you can walk the distance in about 4 hours. Public buses run daily between Uaxactún (stopping at Tikal) and Santa Elena's main market, departing the village around 5:30 a.m. and starting its return from Santa Elena at about 1:30 p.m. The trip is about 3½ hours in either direction. Some Tikal-based tour guides will make the trip to Uaxactún for a reasonable fee (about $40).

The small unrestored ruin of **Xultún** is at the end of a very poor track that branches off the Uaxactún road about 9 miles north of Tikal. There is not much to see here, and the road is not recommended except for four-wheel-drive vehicles traveling in dry weather.

Where to Stay and Eat at Uaxactún
After checking in at the security office, you can camp in the park. A villager rents tent and hammock spaces, plus a couple of bungalows for $4 each; inquire locally. Simple meals are available at several comedores and there are a number of tiendas selling food supplies.

Hotel Campamesto Chiclero (El Chiclero Camp), in the village next to airstrip; $9; no phone, ecoadventure@mail2.guate.net. Offers six rustic bungalows; owned by one of the area's leading chicle-extracting families. Jungle trees, horseback riding, camping, birding, and visits to remote ruins.

EL ZOTZ–SAN MIGUEL LA PALOTADA BIOTOPE
Location: Within the Maya Biosphere Reserve, northeast of San Miguel and southwest of Uaxactún.
Services: Camping is permitted, but there are no services of any kind.
For More Information: Tours are arranged by Epiphyte Adventures in Flores and Monkey Eco Tours in San Andrés. (See Chapter 4: Special Interests.) Recommended local guides include Alfredo Caal and Ramiro Cho.

This tract of forest and savanna runs the exact length of Tikal National Park's 16-mile western border and continues west for about 10 miles. It serves as a buffer zone where limited exploitation of the forest is allowed without jeopardizing the integrity of its ecosystems or those of neighboring Tikal.

The small Maya ruin of **El Zotz** is located within the borders of this reserve on a dirt road that runs between the village of San Miguel and Uaxactún. The site (its name is Maya for "bat") consists of four unrestored temple pyramids and several other structures, plus a cluster of unexcavated mounds. Climb El Diablo temple for an outstanding view of the forest, with Tikal's highest temples visible in the distance. At dawn and dusk you'll see thousands of bats beginning or ending their evening flights (El Zotz is a designated bat refuge, as well as haven for the southern river otter).

Getting There
El Zotz is 12 miles (1 hour by car) northeast of San Miguel (also called El Cruce, it is 13 miles north of Lake Petén Itzá) and 20 miles (2 hours) south-

west of Uaxactún. The dirt road that runs from the village of San Miguel to the ruins may be impassable during the wet season. Allow about 3 hours for a trek or horseback ride from San Miguel/El Cruce.

Several tour operators now include El Zotz on their itineraries, including Ecotourism & Adventure Specialists.

NAACHTÚN–DOS LAGUNAS BIOTOPE AND RÍO AZUL NATIONAL PARK

Location: About 55 miles north of Uaxactún.

Services: There are resident guards at the Río Azul site and occasional researchers, but no services, food, or water. It takes a small expedition to get here, and there is real danger from looters. It is recommended that trips to Río Azul be arranged with the help of an experienced guide or tour operator. Advance permission may be required by local authorities and Guatemala's Department of Archaeology.

For More Information: Contact the INGUAT office at the airport in Santa Elena or Maya travel specialists for assistance (see Chapter 4: Special Interests); Servicios Turísticos de Petén and Maya Expeditions are recommended. One of the more reliable tour operators for Río Azul is Manuel Zotz in Flores.

A large rectangle of land extending directly south of Guatemala's northern border with Mexico, contiguous with Mexico's 1.8-million acre Calakmul Biosphere Reserve, the Naachtún–Dos Lagunas Biotope and Río Azul National Park encompass a rugged and mostly unpopulated tract of primary forest and wetland, a breeding refuge for jaguars and other large animals.

Your reward at the end of the difficult journey you'll take to get here is a large collection of Classic-era ruins spread over about 750 acres. A good overview can be obtained by climbing to the top of Río Azul's 155-foot temple. Scattered in the distance are the remains of an intricate network of dams, aqueducts, and causeways, as well as the usual pyramids, ball courts, residential buildings, and monuments. It is believed that Río Azul served as a kind of frontier buffer for Tikal, fending off would-be invaders from the north. There is also evidence of Mexican influence at the site, probably late in Río Azul's pre-Columbian history.

Although much of this remote site has been badly looted since its 1962 discovery by Shell Oil geologists, archaeologist R. E. W. Adams managed to uncover a pristine, brightly painted burial chamber dating from about A.D. 400. Another discovery was a one-of-a-kind ceramic pot with an ancient screw-top lid. In addition to its archaeological riches, Río Azul is also noted for the high quality of the brightly painted murals, columns, and hieroglyphics in many of its sacred burial tombs.

Richard Mahler

Kekchí Maya xate harvesters pause after an expedition into the jungle.

Experts believe that the Río Azul area had a peak population of 5,000 and may have been founded by Stormy Sky, one of Tikal's most powerful rulers, in order to consolidate his influence in the region. This belief was enforced when one of the emperor's sons was found buried here.

South of Río Azul and just west of the Belize frontier are the minor Maya ruins of Kinal, La Honradez, Xmakabatún, and Holmul, none accessible by road. Visitors who wish to proceed to these sites by mule or helicopter must first obtain permission from local authorities.

Getting There

The dirt road that heads north from the Uaxactún airstrip deteriorates rapidly and is recommended only for dry-season travel by rugged four-wheel-drive vehicles. It is about 35 miles to the village of Dos Lagunas and another 20-odd miles to Río Azul, just below the Mexican frontier. The small and largely unexcavated Maya ruins of Naachtún and La Muralla are even more remote—some 28 miles northwest of Dos Lagunas by a nearly impassable track.

Dos Lagunas is named after two small lakes located near a minor ruin. Some *chicleros* and *xateros* live at this remote jungle intersection, where there is a biological research station, but there are no services for travelers.

From Dos Lagunas, the dirt road veers east through dense jungle. Expect to stop often to clear trees and other debris from the road, which seems to go from unimaginably bad to even worse.

The round-trip journey from Tikal usually demands a minimum of four days, camping out each night.

LAGUNA DEL TIGRE–RÍO ESCONDIDO BIOTOPE AND NATIONAL PARK

A vast freshwater wetland (among the biggest in Central America) lies north of the Río San Pedro, near the Mexican border. Most of this is part of the Laguna del Tigre–Río Escondido Biotope and National Park, encompassing about a third of the Maya Biosphere Reserve's acreage.

Laguna del Tigre theoretically enjoys strict environmental protection by the Guatemalan government, but the reality of the current situation is grim. Representatives of U.S. and Guatemalan conservation agencies established a scientific research station on the Laguna del Tigre in the early 1990s only to be burned out by disgruntled locals who felt the presence of outsiders inhibited their own activities. It seems that this biologically sensitive area is also the domain of a motley assortment of oil prospectors, timber rustlers, drug dealers, and wildlife poachers. Environmentalists, who have received death threats here, are keeping a low profile in this part of the Petén until things settle down. So should you.

SIERRA DEL LACANDÓN NATIONAL PARK

This park preserves a vast, little-explored wilderness area in the remote Lacandón Mountains. Its boundaries extend along the east side of the Usumacinta River for about 50 miles, starting a few miles north of Frontera Corozal, Mexico. The park has no services or roads and is primarily being protected as an important watershed, nature preserve, and wildlife habitat.

THE YAXHÁ-NAKUM-NARANJO TRIANGLE

This triangular chunk of the eastern Petén wilderness butts against Tikal National Park on the west, Río Azul National Park on the north, and the Belize frontier on the east. Besides relatively undisturbed wetlands and subtropical forest, the reserve protects several major and many minor archaeological sites.

YAXHÁ

Location: On the shoreline of a lake of the same name, about 20 miles southeast of Tikal.

For More Information: Tikal-based tour operators arrange horseback trips in this area, including journeys from Yaxhá to Tikal via an ancient, 20-mile-long trail through thick lowland forest. This is a strenuous trip recommended for experienced equestrians. Inquire at the INGUAT office at the airport in Santa Elena. Many local operators now provide easy automobile access to Yaxhá.

Steele Wotkyns

A tour guide takes a group of visitors through Tikal's main plaza area.

Discovered by Europeans in 1904, Yaxhá is believed to be the third-largest Classic-era Maya ceremonial center in Guatemala. Unlike other communities from that period, two sectors of Yaxhá adopted a grid system much like modern cities. You can still see how the streets were lined with buildings in block-like, high density quadrangles. Archaeologists suspect that since the site shows Teotihuacán influence in its stelae and architecture, this contemporary urban layout was adopted from the Mexican migrants. There is an interpretive center and bird release/observation tower at the site, one of the most beautiful in the Petén. This is considered to be one of the best birding locations in Guatemala.

Topoxté, a small, separate site, is located on an island in Yaxhá Lagoon. You can usually walk to it during the dry season. A joint Guatemalan-German team is doing excavation work at Topoxté, a city unusual among Maya sites because it flourished between the 12th and 14th centuries, long after most other Post-Classic communities of the Petén had been abandoned. Several smaller Maya ruins have been found along the lagoon's western shoreline and on La Naya Island in nearby Macanche Lagoon. The site is comprised of the peninsula and several small islands in the lagoon.

Getting There

There is a horse trail through thick jungle from Tikal to Yaxhá, but the recommended route for visitors is via a rough dirt road that cuts north from the Belize Highway west of Melchor de Mencos, about an hour east. The trip from Flores takes about 1½ hours (dry season only). The 8 miles from the highway can be covered in about 30 minutes by four-wheel-drive vehicle, or you can walk there in 2 or 3 hours.

Where to Stay and to Eat near Yaxhá

El Sombrero EcoLodge, near the Yaxhá ruin, $10 or less; 926-5229, fax 926-5198. The *Petenero* owner is very knowledgeable about the area and will arrange horseback tours or treks to Tikal, Nakum, and some of the more remote attractions. The nine-room ecolodge also provides windsurfing, fishing, birding, trekking, and boating services at their lakeside hotel, in addition to offering complete meal service. Camping is permitted along the lake near the ruins for a minimal charge. Recommended. Owner Gabriela de la Hoz can arrange transportation to the lodge, for a fee.

NAKUM

Location: About 12 miles (1 hour) north of Yaxhá.
Services: Camping is allowed at both Nakum and La Ponchitoca (see below), but there are no services.

A Late-Classic Maya city north of Yaxhá, Nakum is noted more for its size than its buildings and monuments, although several structures are still standing. It is believed that Nakum was founded shortly before the end of the Classic era and occupied through at least A.D. 850. It was an important trade center, and 15 well-preserved stelae have been found here. The foliage-covered pyramids are slated for eventual excavation.

Getting There

Nakum can be reached by a poor road on foot, on horseback, or by four-wheel-drive vehicle during the dry season. You may have to walk the last few miles to the site. You will pass a small Maya site, **La Ponchitoca**, on the right side of the road about 4 miles south of Nakum. Mayan Expeditions (Guatemala City) is a popular outfitter for trips to Yaxhá and nearby ruins.

EL NARANJO (EAST)

Location: 14 miles northwest of the Guatemalan border town of Melchor de Mencos.
Services: Camping is permitted; there are no other accommodations.

Not to be confused with the ruin and village of El Naranjo much farther west, Naranjo is an unexcavated Late-Classic site believed to have been a satellite city of Tikal and Xunantunich (in Belize). There is little to see here beyond mounds, an overgrown plaza, and some structural artifacts, such as a Maya ball court with an intact stone ring, one of the few such artifacts in Guatemala. A crumbling stela tells of a marriage alliance between a woman, probably the sister of the king of Dos Pilas, and the ruler of Naranjo.

Getting There

From Melchor de Mencos, head 14 miles northwest (3 hours of poor road) by horseback, private vehicle (four-wheel-drive recommended), or chartered plane (check airstrip conditions first).

EL PILAR

On the eastern border of Guatemala, a few miles north of Melchor de Mencos, is El Pilar, a medium-sized site that lies mostly on the Belize side of the frontier. Efforts are underway by the University of California–Santa Barbara and local residents to make El Pilar an international archaeological park, with an emphasis on preserving ecological as well as archaeological treasures. Inquire at Eva's Restaurant in San Ignacio, Belize, about the current status of this project. The main part of the ruin is accessible by dirt road from the village of Bullet Tree Falls, Belize, a few miles east of the border.

OTHER MAYA SITES IN THE PETÉN

EL NARANJO (WEST)

Location: About 100 miles (5 hours or more) west of Flores at the end of a poorly maintained dirt road.

Services: There is a Guatemalan immigration station in El Naranjo and a Mexican border crossing downriver. Boats can be hired in El Naranjo for trips up the Río San Pedro to the nearby Mayanruins of Mactún, Paso Caballos, and El Perú. Services are very limited in the village; the inexpensive ($5) Posada San Pedro is your best bet for food and lodging.

For More Information: The best tour specialists for this and other parts of the Maya Biosphere are Epiphyte Adventures (Flores), Monkey Eco Tours (San Andrés), Ecotourism & Adventure Specialists (Guatemala City), and ProPetén-Conservation International (Flores).

The small Maya ruin of El Naranjo is on the banks of the Río San Pedro near the village of the same name. The archaeological site itself is not very

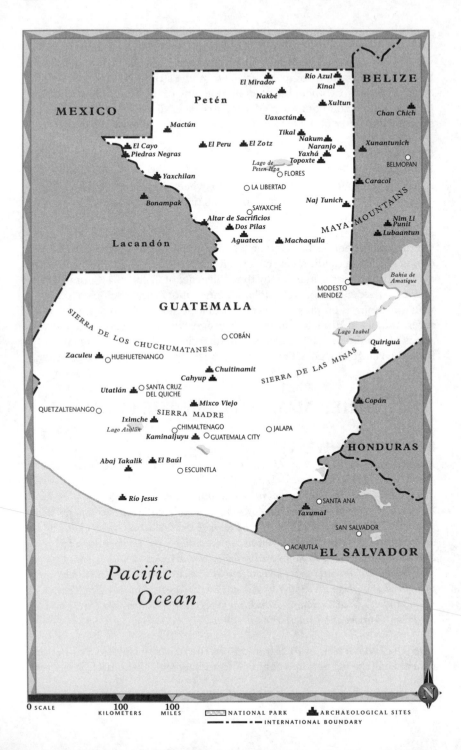

MEXICO

BELIZE

Petén

El Mirador
Nakbé
Río Azul
Kinal
Xultun
Chan Chich

Mactún
Uaxactún

El Cayo
Piedras Negras
El Peru
El Zotz
Tikal
Nakum
Naranjo
Yaxhá
Topoxte
Xunantunich
BELMOPAN

Yaxchilan
Lago de
Peten Itza
FLORES
Caracol

LA LIBERTAD

Bonampak
SAYAXCHÉ
Naj Tunich
Nim Li
Punit
Lubaantun

Altar de Sacrificios
Dos Pilas
Aguateca
Machaquila
MAYA MOUNTAINS

Lacandón

Bahía de
Amatique

MODESTO
MENDEZ

GUATEMALA

SIERRA DE LOS CHUCHUMATANES
COBÁN
Lago Izabel
Quiriguá

Zaculeu
HUEHUETENANGO
Chuitinamit
Cahyup
SIERRA DE LAS MINAS

Utatlán
SANTA CRUZ
DEL QUICHE
Mixco Viejo
Copán

QUETZALTENANGO
SIERRA MADRE

Iximche
Lago Atitlán
CHIMALTENAGO
Kaminaljuyu
GUATEMALA CITY
JALAPA

HONDURAS

Abaj Takalik
El Baúl
ESCUINTLA

Río Jesus

SANTA ANA
Taxumal
SAN SALVADOR

ACAJUTLA
EL SALVADOR

*Pacific
Ocean*

0 SCALE   100 KILOMETERS   100 MILES   NATIONAL PARK   ARCHAEOLOGICAL SITES
INTERNATIONAL BOUNDARY

N

important, but its beautiful location in lush jungle makes it worth a visit. In fact, El Naranjo is on the same transportation route used by the ancient Maya, who traveled up and down the Río San Pedro from Palenque to this and other ceremonial centers. You can make the same trip by boat today; it takes about 4 or 5 hours to reach the Mexican border post of La Palma from El Naranjo and another half-day to reach the much larger town of Tenosique, from which there are buses to the Maya ruins of **Palenque** and trains to Mérida.

Getting There
You can take a public bus or charter a plane between El Naranjo and Flores. Buses leave Santa Elena daily at 5:00 a.m. and 12:30 p.m.; it's a five-hour trip.

EL MIRADOR
Location: A few miles south of the Mexican border.
Services: On-site guards (and sometimes researchers) will let you camp here. Bring your own food, water, mosquito net, and other gear.
For More Information: Escorts with pack horses or mules can be hired in Carmelita for the four- to six-day round-trip to the ruins. The Nature Conservancy and a community cooperative also provide tour assistance, but probably the best way to see El Mirador is on one of the archaeologist-led tours offered by Far Horizons Expeditions, and Maya Expeditions, which generally combines the trip with Nakbé. Local guides in Carmelita who have been recommended include Luis Morales, Carlos Catalán, Mariano Catalán, José Cárdenas, and Oswaldo Catalán. Also recommended is Ecoourism & Adventure Specialists (Guatemala City and Flores).

Only a few miles south of the Mexican border, smack in the middle of the Petén wilderness, El Mirador (The Vantage Point) is currently being excavated. Archaeologists have already determined that the site (part of the much larger El Mirador National Park) contains some of the most massive constructions in the Maya world, found in unusually concentrated numbers and built beginning around 200 B.C., before Tikal. Unfortunately, many of the structures are overgrown and the painted murals are in a degraded condition, partly because of the swampy environment.

First explored by Westerners in 1926, El Mirador is best known for its massive pyramid structures, which rise in a series of platforms as high as 220 feet above the jungle floor, now considered to be the tallest known Mayan structure. There are five temples that rise beyond the forest canopy, a half-dozen smaller pyramids, and over 200 other buildings.

At 16 square kilometers, not as large in area as several other Maya cities, it appears that El Mirador was nevertheless a very important ceremonial site during the Pre-Classic era, reaching its zenith several centuries before Tikal. Not much is yet known about the history of this city, pending further archaeological work. It is suspected, however, that village populations that had been stable for hundreds of years were moved to this central location to drain swamps and erect huge structures. Somehow the Maya elite were able to create a social system whereby such mammoth architectural projects became possible.

Wildlife here is abundant. You're likely to see (or at least hear) howler and spider monkeys, parrots, toucans, and motmots. Bring binoculars!

Getting There

The remoteness of the locale makes it difficult to visit El Mirador except by helicopter or a two-day mule trek from Carmelita, 22 miles southwest by a barely passable (or visible) track. The village is a tiny chicle and xate center about 40 miles north of Flores that can be reached via public bus or private vehicle in about 6 or 7 hours. As in the rest of the Petén, the route is likely to be impassable during the rainy season.

NAKBÉ

Location: About 14 miles southeast of El Mirador and often included in treks to that site.

Services: There are no services, and the nearest potable water is 3 hours away.

For More Information: Some adventure-tour operators, including Expedición Panamundo and Far Horizons, arrange mule and helicopter trips to Nakbé. You can camp en route to the site at the tiny settlement of Ramonal. Current information should be available at CINCAP, the nature and culture tourism center located in the old Flores jail, at Monkey Eco Tours in San Andrés, of El Sombrero Ecolodge at Yaxhá.

This hard-to-reach site, also called Zacatal, made headlines in 1992 after the oldest and largest Maya religious sculpture was discovered here by archaeologist Richard Hansen of the University of California–Los Angeles. Finding the massive Olmec-style head of the bird god Itzam Ye was considered particularly significant because it suggests religion was the final major catalyst that pushed the ancient Maya culture into blossoming as a full-blown civilization. The stone sculpture, 34 feet wide by 16 feet high, dates from 300 B.C., about two centuries earlier than most known examples of similar sculpture, an era scientists previously believed was dominated by very simple village life. The stucco-covered carving was placed on the outside of one of Nakbé's oldest pyramids, then inexplicably covered over with rocks and earth.

Besides the massive Itzam Ye sculpture, archaeologists have found evidence of at least 100 temples and other buildings at Nakbé. Other excavations revealed a large number of tombs and stone monuments, including a carved limestone frieze that depicts a mysterious historical event. Remnants of an even older community beneath the pre-Classic ruins were found under Nakbé by Hansen, now project director of the Regional Archaeological Investigation of the Northern Petén. The site is currently being studied by a large scientific team; permission to visit must be obtained from the Petén government.

Getting There
Nakbé is a two-day trek (each way) by mule or horse from Carmelita, the nearest roadhead. You may see deer, monkeys, and scarlet macaws along the trail. Try Monkey EcoTours or El Sombrero Ecolodge for guided tours.

CEIBAL
Location: 12 miles east of the town of Sayaxchá (roughly 60 miles southwest of Flores).
Services: Guards stationed at Ceibal will allow you to camp there. You must be sure to bring your own food, water, mosquito nets, and other supplies (beware of biting ants). Next to the caretaker's hut is a small museum. Ceibal is targeted for development by the Guatemalan government as a major Petén tourist attraction and things may have changed by the time you visit.

Sometimes referred to as "the Maya art gallery" because of the fine, well-preserved Late-Classic sculpture found here, Ceibal is located east of the town of Sayaxché, in a forest with many ceiba trees—thus the name, which is occasionally spelled Seibal. After Tikal, this is the most accessible Maya ruin of any size in the Petén. Ceibal is now believed to be one of at least seven ancient cities that formed an interlocking society around Lake Petexbatún and Río de la Pasión, once a major Maya trade route for the shipment of quetzal feathers, chert tools, jaguar skins, jade cobbles, and fine pottery. Internecine warfare between factional leaders was largely responsible for a breakdown of these alliances during the Late Classic era.

Much of the ruin is still unexcavated, but a couple of plazas and several buildings are visible, along with some unusually finely carved stelae, which proclaim domination by tenth-century invaders. The carved monuments tell how Lord Nine Stones was put into power by the king of Ucanal.

The basic culture sequence of the site is illustrated by its ceramics, particularly the male and female figurines that are remarkably similar to those made by highland Maya during the same period.

The low ruins of **Complex A** include some unusually well-preserved stelae depicting in sharp relief various warriors, gods, ballplayers, priests, and other important figures. Some are still pastel-colored, others are snow-white. Many bear resemblance to sculptures found in the Yucatán and Campeche, Mexico, dating from the mid-eighth century. Pieces of stucco found here indicate that Ceibal's ceremonial platforms were originally decorated with brilliantly painted friezes, of which only a few fragments remain.

Getting There
The site can be reached in about 45 minutes by four-wheel-drive vehicle via a bumpy dirt road from Sayaxché. Be warned: This route may be impassable during the wet season. A boat trip up the Río de la Pasión takes 2 hours, followed by a half-hour trek through the jungle. Many miles farther upstream is the unexcavated Maya site of Cancuen, believed to have been an outlier community of the same Petexbatún complex that Ceibal was once a part of. Private boat transportation upriver can be arranged easily at Sayaxché, Flores, or Lake Petexbatún. Maya Expeditions in Guatemala City aranges tours of all major ruins in this area.

AGUATECA AND LAKE PETEXBATÚN
Location: *15 miles south of Sayaxché.*
For More Information: *Contact tour operator Expedición Panamundo in Guatemala City (see below) or John Schmidt at Posada San Mateo (see below).*

The fortress-like ruins of Aguateca, discovered by outsiders in 1957, are about 15 miles south of Sayaxché, up a small stream that runs into Lake Petexbatún (also referred to as a *laguna*, or lagoon) and then across a natural bridge over a deep chasm. Eons ago a huge fissure split the underlying bedrock and created a naturally defensible plateau. The site is now accessible only by boat.

There are no towering temples at this site, but several of the finely carved Late-Classic stelae here are magnificent, particularly Stela 2. A main plaza, pyramid, and royal stairway are discernible, and you can visit an underground passageway that connects Aguateca with the nearby lake. Excavation is currently in progress at these otherwise-unprotected ruins, and archaeologists may be present during the dry season. Experts believe Aguateca became the capital of the transplanted rulers of Dos Pilas, 14 miles to the northwest. The ruling lineage built their town along the ridge and left monuments that describe bloody power struggles among the elite.

From the top of the hill where Aguateca is located you can look down over **Lake Petexbatún**. On the shoreline nearby are some natural springs that provide a warm, soothing bath for weary hikers.

Day Trips

From Lake Petexbatún and the Río de Pasión, the adventurous traveler can arrange trips to the (relatively) nearby Maya ruins of Tamarindito, Arroyo de Piedra, Dos Pilas, Altar de los Sacrificios, and Yaxchilán (Mexico).

Getting There

Aguateca is accessible only by boat, unless water levels are low, in which case part of the distance must be walked. Allow 90 minutes of trekking time in each direction.

Where to Stay and Eat near Aguateca and Lake Petexbatún

Mahogany Lodge, on Lake Petexbatún; $60; includes meals; 331-7588, fax 331-7565 in Guatemala City. Expedición Panamundo maintains this lodge for overnight visitors to Aguateca, Dos Pilas, and other nearby attractions. The lodge provides boat transportation to nearby ruins and arranges birding, swimming, and fishing excursions around the lake. Large snook, tarpon, and other game fish have been taken in these waters, although over-exploitation has sharply reduced their numbers during the 1990s.

Posada Caribe, on Lake Petexbatún; $60; 926-0436. An alternative to Mahogany Lodge, the Caribe has rustic cabañas and campsites.

Posada del Mundo Maya, on Lake Petexbatún; $25; no phone. Rents inexpensive, basic rooms, hammock spaces, and campsites. Meals, boats, and guides are also available.

Posada San Mateo/Hotel Petén Express, on Lake Petexbatún; $156; 926-0505. The author's favorite Aguateca lodging is operated by John Schmidt and his Mexican wife. For information or to make reservation, contact Fanny's, 24a. Calle 0-78, Zone 4, Guatemala City, 232-4483. Schmidt, who speaks fluent English and offers frequent excursions up and down the Pasión and Usumacinta Rivers on his Petén Express boats, is a wealth of information about this part of Guatemala. Access is by water only to his comfortable bungalow-style lodge, which sits on the Punta de Chimino peninsula. Three deep moats (one more than 50 feet deep) dug by the Maya at the end of the eighth century turned the site into a well-protected island.

PIEDRAS NEGRAS

Location: On the hilly Guatemalan side of the Río Usumacinta, in the remote northwest corner of the Petén.

For More Information: Maya Expeditions of Guatemala City (363-4965, fax 337-4666) has an exclusive arrangement with the archaeological team working at the site for educational tours and presentations at the site. These trips can be customized for those with special interests in birding, shamanism, architecture, photography, and other subjects. Excellent documentation of the art of Piedras Negras and nearby Yaxchilán is found in Linda Schele's beautifully illustrated books, The Blood of Kings *and* The Forest of Kings.

Piedras Negras (Black Rocks) has been only partially excavated since its discovery in 1935 in the northwest corner of the Petén, and many of its pyramidal mounds have been reclaimed by the jungle, while others have been looted. Surviving are one room with a vaulted roof, a few eroded zoomorphs, and many moss-covered stelae. The high forest canopy lends them a special air of mystery, and wildlife is abundant.

One of the most notable discoveries at Piedras Negras is a complete set of "period markers" erected by the Maya to document the end of 22 successive 1,800-day sequences called *hotuns*. The carving of these dated stelae began some time after the Maya settled here and complement the political history of the Aac (Turtle) dynasty, also noted on carved stone monuments here. Such ceremonial practices were followed more consistently at Piedras Negras than at any other known Mayan site. Twenty-two successive *hotun* monuments have been found along the riverbank,

Abandoned archaeologists' tractor (ca. 1928) at Piedras Negras

Richard Mahler

marking each of the appropriate epochs between A.D. 608 and A.D. 810. These stelae, originally excavated by experts from the University of Pennsylvania, have proven invaluable in helping reconstruct the Maya's lowland history. Piedras Negras collapsed, along with much of the lowland Maya empire, around A.D. 830.

Evidence has also been found in these ruins of considerable human sacrifice. Blood spilled from the arms, legs, tongues, ears, and genitalia of chosen individuals, apparently in return for favors from the gods. Animals, fish, food, and jade were also apparently offered for sacrifice at this location.

Many of the stone monuments here are totally overgrown, but you can still make out a large carved monkey face next to the ancient ball court. Not far away, visitors will notice a network of hot-water channels used by the Maya elite to fill their bathtubs and steam rooms.

In March 1997 the first large-scale archaeological research team in 50 years began a long-term study of Piedras Negras, under the direction of experts from Pennsylvania State University, Brigham Young University, and Guatemala's San Carlos University.

Getting There
Piedras Negras can be reached only through the use of a sturdy boat and a knowledgbable outfitter, such as Maya Expeditions. An airstrip a few miles away in the village of Lacandón has fallen into disuse. Allow two to three days for a boat trip downriver from Betél. There has been considerable banditry and violence in this region in recent years, and caution is advised.

NAVIGABLE RIVERS OF THE PETÉN

Río de la Pasión
A southeast tributary of the Río Usumacinta, this river has long been an important transportation link between the southern Petén and the outside world. Boats regularly travel up the Pasión as far as Raxrujá and Sebol in Alta Verapaz and south via the Usumacinta into Mexico. A number of adventure-oriented tour operators in the U.S., Canada, and Guatemala arrange trips along the Río de la Pasión that combine archaeology, natural history, camping, trekking, birding, fishing, and other activities (see Chapter 4).

Río Usumacinta
The Río Usumacinta forms about one-third of the border between Guatemala and Mexico, along more than 100 miles of the Petén's western

frontier, through some of the most unspoiled tropical forest in North or Central America.

Although the region has few inhabitants today, it was at one time a major population center for the ancient Maya, who flourished along the Usumacinta from around A.D. 200 to 1300. The ruins of several important Classic-era sites, including **Yaxchilán** and **Piedras Negras**, are along the river and very much worth visiting. The rapids are moderate, and you will pass through steep limestone canyons and past spectacular waterfalls en route.

Boat trips on the Usumacinta below Yaxchilán are currently not advised, with the possible exception of the Maya Expeditions archaeology float to Piedras Negras. Violence related to banditry and drug-trafficking has been reported here since 1996 when several boat passengers were injured in a particularly hair-raising incident. The most dangerous areas of the Usumacinta are reported to be the sparsely-inhabited stretch from the Budsillja Waterfall to the take-up below Cañon de San José. Attacks on foreigners have also been reported on the upper Río San Pedro, near El Naranjo, which is navigable from the village of La Palma, Mexico.

Several outfitters still float the upper Usumacinta, including its upstream feeder, the Río de la Pasión. Both rivers are considered to be relatively safe and the scenery is magnificent. Ceiba Adventures (of Flagstaff, Ariz.) offers a recommended "River of Ruins" trip that includes visits to the Maya ruins at Palenque, Bonampak, and Yaxchilán in Mexico as well as several sites on the Pasión. In the past, Far Flung Adventures (of Terlingua, Texas) has offered similar expeditions. See Chapter 4 and Appendix for details.

River travelers heading to or from Guatemala are required to clear Mexican immigration and customs in Frontera Corozal. There are Guatemalan border officials on the opposite side of the river at the village of Betél, from which there is regular bus service to Flores–Santa Elena (4 hours). A small nature-oriented lodge operates in Betél, where there is an ancient Maya *cenote* (water well) worth visiting. Conservation International is helping the village operate a cooperative devoted to sustainable development.

APPENDIX A
TRAVEL BASICS

Practicalities

For the reader's convenience, all prices in this book are listed in U.S. dollars. Based on 1999 research, they are subject to fluctuation and should be used only as general guidelines. All hotel prices are for double-occupancy and may change due to inflation, time of year, and management whim.

Guatemala is on Mayan Standard Time, equivalent to the Central Time Zone of the United States (two hours ahead of Los Angeles, one hour behind New York). There is no "daylight savings" time, since this subtropical latitude provides roughly 12 hours of daylight each day throughout the year.

Almost all electrical outlets are 110 volts, alternating current (A.C.). Standard U.S. plugs and appliances can be used everywhere except a few remote areas where higher voltages are required or power supplies are erratic. If you have doubts, ask the building's owner or manager before plugging in. Black-outs occur regularly due to a chronic national power shortage.

At the Airport

The point of entry for most visitors is **La Aurora International Airport**, near downtown Guatemala City in Zone 13. As you exit your plane and are funneled past *migración* (immigration), an office of the Guatemalan government's tourism agency (INGUAT) will be on the right, open from 6:00 a.m. to 9:00 p.m. daily. This is an excellent place to obtain information about popular destinations and have your travel questions answered. INGUAT also books hotels and arranges transportation for visitors. Staff members are friendly and most speak excellent English as well as other major languages.

Immigration and *aduana* (customs) formalities are handled quickly and efficiently. There is no health check or airport entry tax. You can immediately change money at bank counters near the baggage-claim area and on the upper level. Official rates are nearly the same at all of the country's banks and it is advisable to obtain at least some local currency here.

The glass doors beyond the customs counters open directly onto the busy road that passes in front of the terminal, where you can find a hotel courtesy van, taxi, or shuttle van. Some car rental agencies are across the street; most others are nearby on Avenida de la Reforma (Guatemala City's main thoroughfare). Cheaper cabs park on the streets away from the terminal and are often both cleaner and newer.

Taxis rarely have meters, so be sure to establish a fare before getting in. A registered taxi can always be identified by the letter "A" at the beginning of its license plate number. In 1999, it cost no more than $10 (more at night) for a ride to Zones 1 and 4, less than that to Zones 9 and 10 (one person, two bags). Beware of freelance porters who may try to grab your luggage and steer you toward a particular cab. They will expect a tip in return for their help, whether or not it has been requested.

Shuttle vans to Antigua, Panajahel, and other popular destinations meet every international flight; look for them near the taxis. Rates are set and drivers do not bargain: In 1999 the fare was $10 to $15 to Antigua.

Public buses, which are invariably crowded but cost only a few cents, stop outside the airport terminal's upper-level parking lot during the day and next to the taxi stand at night. Bus routes numbered 5, 6, 20, and 83 ran to the city center during 1999, but routes and schedules change often: Be sure to double-check locally before proceeding on any bus.

La Aurora airport can be a confusing place when you are leaving the country. Check-in stations are on the upper level, departure lounges in the basement. The airport's few restrooms are dirty and well hidden. Restaurants are overpriced and uninteresting. Newsstands may be closed on Sundays and holidays, so make sure you come with something to read. Some airlines serve complimentary juice, coffee, and pastries in their boarding lounges.

There is an $8.50 mandatory exit tax, payable only in U.S. dollars or Guatemalan quetzales. You may pay this tax to airline personnel as you check in for your departure, receiving a stamped debarkation card in return. On your way to the boarding gate you will go through several x-ray security gates; have your passport and boarding pass ready at all times.

Check in at least 2 hours before any departing international flight. Reconfirmation of ticketed reservations is advised at least 72 hours before departure.

A growing number of flights serve the **Santa Elena/Flores International Airport** in the Petén (gateway to Tikal). Formalities are simple here, and all essential services are available, including a bank and an INGUAT office.

Travel Advisories

In 1996, the U.S. State Department lifted all formal travel advisories for Guatemala. However, in recent years the United States and several other countries have urged their citizens to take precautions when traveling in specific areas of Guatemala, particularly in the northwest highlands of Quiché, San Marcos, and Huehuetenango, as well as remote parts of Alta Verapaz and the Petén (especially between Tikal and the Belize border). The most recent

Highway Bandidos

One of the unfortunate realities of post-war Guatemala is an increase in hold-ups on the nation's roads. When military forces were withdrawn from many areas, outlaws moved in. Robberies are most common on lonely stretches of highway (especially in the Petén), but they also occur on city streets that are filled with people and traffic. They usually involve private cars, but public buses and shuttle vans have also fallen victim. The bandits work as a team, with one or two members flagging down the vehicle while his companions steal money, jewelry, and other valuables from the driver and passengers. Because the robbers are armed and dangerous, the best advice is to comply with their requests and keep a low profile. The prudent course is to travel with a minimum of valuables or to conceal anything that might be attractive to a robber. Remember to ask locally about bandido incidents in the area you'll be traveling through, and to report any crimes to local authorities and the U.S. Embassy.

State Department memorandum for Guatemala warned about violent crime, bus robberies, pickpockets, and roadblocks set up by bandits. When going to remote, non-touristed areas it may be prudent for U.S. citizens to register with the U.S. Embassy before departure, and to avoid travel at night.

Although Guatemala's most popular destinations—including Antigua, Tikal, and Lake Atitlán—are probably as safe as any comparable attraction in Europe or the U.S., you may wish to check with your travel agent about advisories that may be in force at the time of your trip. Contact the U.S. State Department's **Citizens' Emergency Center** "hotline" at (202) 647-3712 or via its World Wide Web site at travel.state.gov/travel_warnings. In Guatemala City, contact the information officer at the **U.S. Embassy** at 331-1541, or 7-01 Avenida de la Reforma, Zone 10. The **Guatemala Tourist Commission** (800/INGUAT1) also issues security information to tourists. Incidents in 1997 and 1998 resulted in beefed-up security at all tourist sites, including markets, colonial districts, and Maya ruins.

Travel Documents

Foreign citizens must have valid passports to enter Guatemala. The long-standing tourist card requirement was lifted in 1996. A visa is required for some nationalities, including a few British commonwealth countries such as New Zealand. Passport stamps are good for 30 days and can be renewed for consecutive periods totaling no more than 90 days.

Information can be obtained from any of Guatemala's embassies and consulates (see Appendix B). Visas can be obtained by mail upon inclusion of a passport, 2-by-2-inch photograph, application form, and self-addressed, stamped envelope, plus $10. Visas are usually (but not always) available at land borders and can be renewed for an additional $10 fee. If you wish to stay longer than 90 days, you must either exit and re-enter Guatemala (after a minimum departure of 72 hours) or have a Guatemalan citizen vouch for your financial integrity. Visitation extensions may be obtained at the **Immigration Office** in Guatemala City at 8a. Avenida at 12a. Calle, Zone 1 (471-4670 or 471-4682). It is illegal for tourists to engage in moneymaking activities in the country without prior governmental permission.

Corruption is a serious problem at land borders in Guatemala. Some underpaid officials overcharge for visas and for non-existent exit and entry taxes. Others may ask for bribes or demand documents that are unnecessary. Officials may neglect to properly stamp documents, knowing that the visitor will later have to pay a fine or bribe in order to legally exit the country. The government is trying to eliminate these abuses and encourages tourists not to give in to such practices. Resistance is not always practical—or even feasible—but you should always try to have your papers properly stamped.

Language

The official language is Spanish. English is not widely spoken, especially in small towns and rural areas. Those who don't speak Spanish are advised to take at least an introductory Spanish class before they depart and to consider getting additional instruction while in Guatemala (tutors and classes are widely available and very inexpensive). Barring that, make sure you bring a phrase book and a Spanish-English dictionary.

About half of the population is of Maya descent, and an estimated 85 percent of these *indigena* speak one of 23 local languages (and very little Spanish). Despite these linguistic barriers, important information always seems to get communicated through gestures, facial expressions, and commonly understood words.

The Spanish spoken in Guatemala is typified by its relative slowness and formality, with an emphasis on politeness and respect. Those familiar with more modern forms of the language at times may find it rather archaic. For example, Guatemalans sometimes use the old pronoun *vos* instead of *tu* as the familiar form of the singular "you."

Guatemalan speech is usually carefully enunciated, rarely slurred as is often the case in neighboring Mexico or the Caribbean islands. Guatemalan Spanish contains some words of native origin, particularly place names, that incorporate the Mayan *x* (pronounced *zsh*) and *j* (which is vocalized as in English instead of remaining silent as in standard Spanish). You may notice that many Guatemalans occasionally add the word *va* at the end of a statement. This is a regionalism used for emphasis.

Guatemala Online

A wealth of information about Guatemala is now available via e-mail and the Internet. Many hotels, schools, and tour operators maintain Web sites and it's possible to book hotel rooms, Spanish classes, and airplane connections directly via the Internet. The **Guatemala Tourist Commission (INGUAT)** site contains useful general information at www.guatemala .travelcom. You also can reach INGUAT at inguat@geo2.poptel.org.uk.

Other good sources of background materials include **Green Arrow Guide to Central America** (www.greenarrow.com), and **Guatemalan Tourism** (www.webpres.com/quetzalnet/). For a guide to travel agencies, check out www.travelhub.com, and for other tourism businesses, try www.pronet.net.gt. Tradepoint Guatemala—www.tradepoint. org.gt—provides access to more than 1400 Guatemalan home pages, including those of many tourist businesses. Also recommended for general tourist information: www.inforia.com and www.infoguate.com.

For those with an interest in natural history tourism, I recommend the Internet clearinghouse of environmental travel information maintained by Ron Mader (author of Adventures in Nature books on Mexico and Honduras). Mader's **Eco Travels** Web site is at www.planeta.com. The site also archives a fine "green travel" newsletter, *El Planeta Platica*, available from ron@greenbuilder.com. The most popular Guatemalan newspapers, *Prensa Libre* and *Siglo XX!*, are also available (in Spanish) on-line.

Direct access to the Internet and e-mail services are provided by a growing number of companies. In Guatemala City, try **Guatemala Online** (334-7490) at 11a. Calle 3-23, Zone 9; in Antigua, **Conexión** (832-2676, conex@ibm.net), at 4a. Calle Oriente 14; and in Panajachel, **Panajachel Tourist Services** (762-2112, panamail@guate.net), on Calle Santander. For a list of cybercafés in the region, check out www2.planeta.com/ mader/ ecotravel/coffeeas/cybercafe.

The Guatemalan phone system converted from six- to seven-digit numbers in August 1996. For listings of older numbers, you may want to refer to the online conversion table maintained by Telgua, the telephone monopoly, on INGUAT's World Wide Web page (see above).

Health

No vaccinations are required to visit Guatemala, but it is advised that visitors be up to date on immunizations for tetanus and typhoid. Your local public health agency will usually have a current list of immunization recommendations, or call the **Centers for Disease Control and Prevention** at (404) 332-4559. The CDC's Web site is at www.cdc.gov.

If you are spending more than a few days in the jungle, coastal lowlands, or Tikal National Park, antimalarial drugs such as chloroquine or mefloquine are a reasonable precaution. Begin taking them one week *before* and continue for a month *after* visiting a malaria-infested region. For information and advice, call the CDC's **Malaria Hotline** at (404) 332-4555. If left untreated, malaria can be lethal. As of 1999, no chloroquine-resistant strains of the disease had been reported in Guatemala. Mosquito-borne dengue fever is also a problem in some low-lying areas.

As protection against hepatitis, many travelers also obtain an immunization specific to hepatits A and B, which must begin at least four weeks before departure and requires a booster after six months. Also, you will need a yellow fever certificate to enter Guatemala if, within the previous six months, you have been to a country where the disease has been present.

Cholera, transmitted through contaminated water, sewage, and such raw-food dishes as *ceviche*, is a serious health problem here and caution is advised in eating and sanitation habits. Preventive inoculations are available, in a two-step procedure, but these provide only marginal protection.

If you feel ill on your return, make sure your doctor is aware of your trip. Many physicians in industrialized countries are unfamiliar with the characteristics and treatments of tropical diseases and can sometimes misinterpret their symptoms as influenza or other illnesses.

Iodine tablets, Halazone, or simple laundry bleach (administered at the rate of two drops per liter and allowed to stand for 30 minutes) can be used to purify tap water, which is chemically treated only in Guatemala City and Antigua. Many local residents advise against drinking *any* tap water in Guatemala. Boiling water vigorously for 3 minutes is also effective. Bottled water is widely available except in small towns or villages. Some hotels have their own purification systems, and many supply bottled water free of charge. Bottled beer and soft drinks are safe; do not, however, add or accept ice in any drink unless you know it is purified. Remember not to brush your teeth with questionable water.

Travelers' Stomach (A.K.A. Turista)

Carelessness in the consumption of untreated water or milk, as well as uncooked vegetables, peeled fruits, and lightly cooked meat, can easily lead to diarrhea, intestinal parasites, or amoebic dysentery, which is endemic throughout Guatemala. When you first have symptoms of diarrhea, you may wish to wait a few hours in case it is simply a reaction to a food your body didn't like. Beyond that, take action!

A good treatment for common diarrhea is bismuth, found in Pepto-Bismol, as well as Bactrim, Cipro, and Doxycycline. You might also try Imodium or the natural bacteria called lacto bacillus acidophilus. If symptoms do not diminish or disappear within a few days, see a pharmacist, nurse, or physician. Nearly every community of any size in Guatemala has a clinic or public health practitioner. Diarrhea and dysentery can quickly lead to severe dehydration, which may be fatal if untreated.

Some travelers carry portable water-filtering systems that eliminate many (but not necessarily all) water-borne parasites and other hazards. Others carry enough bleach or iodine to enable them to soak the fruits and vegetables they buy at public markets, which may be tainted with germs or pesticides. Milk and cheese are unlikely to be pasteurized except in the best hotels and restaurants.

The sun is very intense at Guatemalan latitudes; a wide-brimmed hat, sunglasses, and sunscreen (SPF 15 or stronger) are advised for northerners, especially those with fair complexions. Altitude sickness may also be a problem if you are volcano climbing.

Mosquitoes, flies, and biting insects are a problem in lowland areas and to some degree the highlands, especially during rainy periods. Bring along strong insect repellents (look for those containing a 15 percent or more concentration of DEET, an acronym for diethylmetaoluamide) and lightweight, natural-fiber clothing that will cover your arms and legs. Some people carry musk oil, citronella oil, or Avon Skin-So-Soft lotion as a deterrent against no-see-ums, sand fleas, and other pesky insects. Eating lots of garlic seems to help some people. Portable thin-mesh mosquito nets and nontoxic mosquito coils are helpful for those spending extended periods in malaria-infested areas. Certain species of biting flies carry parasites and diseases, some of them dangerous to humans. Permethrin may be applied to clothes and netting for protection against all kinds of biting insects.

Getting There

By Air

Guatemala is served by a number of direct flights from the United States, Mexico, and Central America. Carriers from Europe generally transfer passengers in Miami, Mexico, or the Caribbean. The privately owned national airline is Aviateca. In 1997, an "open skies" policy was adopted, aimed at increasing the number of U.S. airlines serving Guatemala.

Guatemala City's **La Aurora International Airport** is the arrival and departure point for most foreigners traveling by air. The only other international airports are at Santa Elena, near Flores, which has scheduled flights to Belize and Mexico, and at Puerto Barrios, for flights to Belize. There are no other commercial air routes within Guatemala, although domestic charters can be arranged and tourist flights to Copán, Honduras, are common.

From the U.S., you can depart directly for Guatemala from Miami (via TACA, Iberia, Aviateca, and American), Houston (via TACA, Aviateca, and Continental), New Orleans (via TACA and Aviateca), San Francisco (via Lacsa), Los Angeles (via TACA, United, and Aviateca), Washington (via TACA), and New York (via TACA).

From Canada, Canadian Airlines offers daily round-trip flights from Toronto to Guatemala City (via San Salvador).

From Europe, the airlines originating direct flights to Guatemala are KLM (from Amsterdam, with a stop in Mexico City) and Iberia (starting in Madrid and continuing via Miami).

Many carriers serve Guatemala from Latin America and the Caribbean, including Aeronica, American, Continental, Mexicana, LACSA, TACA, Aviateca, Aerovías, Maya World, SAM, United, and COPA. Connecting airports include Mexico City, Cancún, Belize City, San Salvador, Tegucigalpa, Kingston, San Pedro Sula, Managua, San Andrés, San José, and Panama City. The easiest connections to or from South America are through LACSA (via San José, Costa Rica), TACA (via San José and Panama City), COPA, and Iberia (both via Panama City).

From Mexico, the easiest connections are by Mexicana, Aviateca, and

TACA (all via Mexico City). From Belize, direct flights are offered by Aviateca, Tropic, and TACA (via Belize City).

Many airlines now provide schedules, ticketing, and even discount fare offers via the Web. The "webport" of the five major Central American airlines lists weekly bargain flights to selected countries (http://www.flylatinamerica .com). For a rundown on discount fares to Guatemala, visit www. guatemalaweb.com and click on the Guatemala Web Airfare Reservation Center.

By Land

Guatemala is at least a three-day drive (about 2,000 miles) from the southeast Texas border via the **Pan American Highway** (Route CA-1), which enters the country from Mexico at La Mesilla and from El Salvador at San Cristóbal. Up-to-date vehicle registration and title documents are required. Valid driver's licenses and International Operator's Permits (issued by the American Automobile Association) are both honored while driving in Guatemala, but auto insurance policies issued in the U.S. or Mexico are not.

Other main points of entry include Tecún Umán on the Mexican frontier via the Coastal Highway (Route CA-2), which enters El Salvador at Ciudad Pedro de Alvarado. Valle Nuevo, on Route CA-8, and Montecristo, on Route CA-12, are the other main Salvadoran frontiers. The two principal border crossings into Honduras are at El Florido, near that country's Copán ruins, and Agua Caliente, farther south near Esquipulas. The only road crossing into Belize is at Melchor de Mencos on Route CA-13, which continues as Belize's Western Highway all the way to the Caribbean.

If you are crossing the border by bus or taxi, be sure to have your passport and, if required for your nationality, a Guatemalan visa.

By Sea

The only regularly scheduled seagoing public transportation to Guatemala are the daily powerboats between Punta Gorda, Belize, and Puerto Barrios, Guatemala. Boats leaves the Puerto Barrios municipal wharf at about noon. The trip takes about 1½ hours and costs about $15 one-way. You must clear immigration before you can buy a ticket and board the boat.

An inland waterway, the Río San Pedro, has daily service between El Naranjo in the Petén to villages along the river in Mexico and the town of La Palma. Daily buses connect La Palma with Emiliano Zapata, Palenque, and San Cristóbal de las Casas. El Naranjo has bus connections to Flores and, from there, Guatemala City and Belize. Small boats also cross the international frontier between Betél, Guatemala, and Frontera Corozal, Mexico, on the Río Usumacinta. There are immigration posts in both communities where you can have your passport stamped.

Small private boats also make regularly scheduled trips between Puerto Barrios and various towns in Honduras and Belize. Be sure to check with border officials on both sides of the frontier before departing.

Several cruise ships and passenger-carrying freighters dock occasionally on Guatemala's Pacific and Caribbean coasts.

Climate

Many first-time visitors are pleasantly surprised by Guatemala's year-round spring-like weather. They often come expecting hot, humid, subtropical conditions, when in fact much of the country is temperate. This "Land of Eternal Spring," as many Guatemalans refer to their country, enjoys an annual mean temperature of 75 degrees Fahrenheit. (A spring climate also means allergies for some people, so bring appropriate medications.)

Cool nights and warm days are the norm in Guatemala's highlands, with lows generally in the 40s and 50s and highs in the 70s and 80s. Climatic extremes are greatest during the dry season, December through April, when the very highest elevations can be cold enough to have snow at night and lower levels can be sweltering during late afternoon. Pack a jacket or sweater if you visit between December and February.

Quetzaltenango is the coolest major city, with overnight lows consistently in the 40s (even colder during January). Temperatures are slightly warmer in Guatemala City, Antigua, and Panajachel—each around 5,000 feet in elevation—rising to 90 degrees in March or April but invariably dropping to the 50s or 60s at night. Even during the wet season, rain in the highlands usually falls only for brief, intense periods in the late afternoon, although 20-day monsoons sometimes occur.

Along the Pacific and Caribbean coasts and in the Petén, the climate is much wetter and warmer. Expect lows in the 60s and 70s, highs in the 80s and 90s—or more—at any time of the year. Rains can be steady and torrential May through November, with periodic thunderstorms during other times.

Throughout the country, the warmest temperatures are experienced in March and April, and the rainiest months are June through October, although rain can fall any day of the year. Packing an umbrella, rain parka, or poncho is prudent. March and April are the driest months.

What to Bring

A good money belt that can be concealed underneath clothing is essential for travel in Guatemala, as in most parts of the world. Some travelers prefer packs or belts that are worn externally, but these are both visible and accessible to criminals. Whichever you choose, be sure to carry photocopies of the front pages of your passport and other important papers (such as traveler's check numbers) in a separate place in case the money belt or pack is lost or stolen. Another good idea is to leave a copy of the front pages of your passport with a friend or relative at home. (Under Guatemalan law, foreigners are required to carry their passport at all times.)

Many people insist on carrying traveler's checks whenever they go abroad. In the smaller towns and villages of Guatemala, however, changing traveler's checks may be impossible, and if they are stolen it may be extremely difficult to replace them or obtain a refund. You may be better off carrying cash that is strategically and discreetly hidden in various pockets.

A small knapsack or fanny pack is useful for carrying cameras, lenses, and film. Earplugs are handy for light sleepers and those not used to the constant din of Guatemalan roosters, radios, buses, and traffic jams. You may wish to bring a Walkman-style tape player for the same reason. Women may want to carry mace or pepper spray if traveling alone.

Pants are acceptable for women, but shorts, halter tops, and scanty attire are discouraged for both sexes except at beaches, resort areas, and in the Petén. Guatemala is a country where religious feelings run deep and revealing dress is considered offensive. For the same reason, nude swimming is discouraged unless you are away from inhabited areas.

Major brands of toiletries, contact lens materials, tampons, and cosmetics are widely available in Guatemalan cities at reasonable prices. It is not necessary to bring extra supplies unless you will be spending most of your time in the hinterlands. You also do not need to carry candles, towels, sheets, or purified water except in remote areas or if you will be staying in the most budget-priced hotels. It's always wise to carry toilet paper (a relative rarity) and remember that used toilet paper goes in the basket next to the toilet. Flushed toilet paper cannot be handled by most Guatemalan sewage systems.

It is always a good idea to make a list of everything in your luggage (including serial numbers) so that if it is lost or stolen you will know exactly what is missing. Copies of prescriptions for medications carried are also useful, as is an extra pair of any prescription eyeglasses worn.

Reservations

Advance reservations are recommended during Guatemala's high season, December through Easter, and are increasingly advisable during the rest of the year. Beach and lake resorts, for example, are often crowded with domestic visitors on weekends and holidays, especially during March and April. The two weeks before Easter are a summer holiday for public school students, and the week immediately prior to Easter, *Semana Santa* (Holy Week), is a vacation time for everyone. Reservations should be made in advance for such popular Semana Santa destinations as Antigua and beach resorts, where choice hotel rooms are secured as much as a year ahead.

Bookings should also be considered for lodging at national parks and nature reserves, such as Tikal, where space is at a premium. Remember that you are more likely to find discounts on room rates, particularly for extended stays, during the low season. The months with fewest foreign visitors are May and September.

Maps and Tourist Information

Good background materials, including a detailed "tourist map," gas station map, and brochures, are available from the various Guatemalan consulates in the U.S. and other countries. You may also try the **Guatemala Tourist Commission (INGUAT)** through Guatemala's overseas embassies and consulates. The main office of INGUAT is at 7a. Avenida 1-17, Centro Cívico, Zone 4, Guatemala City (331-1333); a multilingual information desk on the ground floor is open 8:00 a.m. to 4:30 p.m. weekdays, 8:00 a.m. to 1:00 p.m. Saturdays. Maps are sold here for about 15 cents each and brochures are free.

INGUAT offices are also in Antigua, Quetzaltenango, Panajachel, the Santa Elena airport, and the Guatemala City airport, and at major border crossings. Information and services vary at different offices, but there is usually at least one knowledgeable person on duty who speaks English.

The author's favorite general map of Guatemala is made by **International Travel Map Productions** (Box 2290, Vancouver, B.C. V6B 3W5, Canada) and sold widely at better bookstores throughout the U.S. and Canada. The **Instituto Geográfico Nacional** has good topographic maps. The office is open from 8:00 a.m. to 4:00 p.m. weekdays at 5-76 Avenida de las Américas, Zone 13, Guatemala City.

Money Matters

Experienced travelers often bring a mix of U.S. currency and traveler's checks to Guatemala. The latter usually can be replaced if lost or stolen but can be difficult to cash in some areas. American Express traveler's checks are particularly hard to cash outside Antigua and Guatemala City. Make sure your U.S. currency is not tattered, torn, or marked: Such bills are sometimes not accepted. It's a good idea to change some money as soon as you enter the country, since banks throughout Guatemala have similar exchange rates. Some banks will allow you to draw cash against your credit card (bring passport) and larger cities have ATMs. If you haven't memorized it, bring your PIN!

Guatemala's monetary unit, the *quetzal*, has historically been one of the most stable currencies in Central America. In early 1999, with the annual inflation rate running at about 10 percent, the quetzal was being exchanged at slightly more than six to the U.S. dollar, or about 15¢ each. Because the rate of exchange is in constant flux, all prices in this book are quoted in dollars, not quetzales.

There are 100 centavos to a quetzal, which is symbolized by the letter *Q*. Named for Guatemala's national bird, the quetzal comes in notes of 1 to 100 in several denominations. The two largest bills, 50 and 100, can be very difficult to change in markets, small shops, and outlying communities. Coins are issued in 1-, 5-, 10-, and 25-centavo pieces but are almost never seen. The green and invariably grimy 1-quetzal note, sometimes called a billete, is the most common currency in circulation and is particularly handy on buses and in public markets.

The government-owned **Banco de Guatemala** will exchange most international currencies. Other banks are more likely to change dollars and major European currencies only. You are better off changing money in large cities, because many parts of the country have no facilities for exchanging currency.

Banking hours are generally 8:30 a.m. to 3:00 p.m., Monday through Friday, with an extra 30 minutes on Friday afternoons. In bigger towns some banks stay open later on weekdays and are also open on Saturday mornings. All are closed on holidays, including Wednesday through Friday of Semana Santa.

Most banks, with the notable exception of those in the Guatemala City airport, Panajachel, Lívingston, and Antigua, are so bureaucratic that changing money is a laborious process involving much paperwork. Be sure that you are standing in the correct line (this is usually unmarked, so you will need to ask someone) and that, as always, you have your passport with you.

Cashing a traveler's check in a bank usually requires one or more signatures from a bank officer, which can make the process even lengthier than changing foreign currency. There are Thomas Cook, Barclay's, and American Express offices in Guatemala City if you need to replace stolen checks. The **Banco de Café** in Zone 9 and Clark Tours in Zone 4 are also American Express agents. Be sure to keep your checks and a list of their serial numbers safe and separate.

Credit cards are accepted by major hotels and tour companies, plus a growing number of restaurants. The most widely accepted are American Express and Visa. A processing fee of about 3 percent is usually added when credit cards are used, even when drawing on a Guatemalan bank. ATMs usually draw on Visa accounts (less often MasterCard) and are common in big cities.

Personal checks drawn on foreign banks are rarely accepted in Guatemala, although there are a few branch offices of some international banks where you can cash a check, including Lloyds and Barclay's.

There is a 7 percent value-added tax, referred to by the acronym IVA, on virtually all goods and services in Guatemala. Some exemptions are taxi and bus tickets and merchandise bought in public markets. Hotel rooms carry a separate 10 percent tax.

Telephones

If you are calling Guatemala from the U.S., first dial 011 for an international circuit, then Guatemala's country code, 502. Dialing Guatemala direct is very easy from overseas telephones, and most hotels are happy to take reservations by fax or phone. Note that in August 1996 the entire country switched from 6-digit to 7-digit phone numbers; a table of conversions is available free of charge from Guatel (the phone monopoly) in Guatemala and from major long-distance companies in the U.S.

Local calls are inexpensive, but outside of the capital there are very few coin-operated public phones and many of them don't work. All sizable towns have a Guatel office where local and long-distance calls can be made between 7:00 a.m. and 10:00 p.m. The procedure involves standing in line and giving an operator the number you wish to ring, then waiting for your name to be called. You will be directed to a booth when your party has been reached. Collect calls can be made on long-distance and some international connections, including the U.S. A few hotels have direct-dial telephones, but they are rather expensive. There are direct-dial public phones with international operators at the Guatemala City airport on the second floor. Making calls within the country is often more difficult than calling Guatemala from abroad because switching equipment is inadequate. If you receive a busy signal—or nothing at all—keep trying; you should eventually get through.

Post Offices

All post offices (*correos*) are open from 8:00 a.m. to 4:00 p.m., with the exception of the main branch in Guatemala City, which opens at 9:00 a.m. and closes at 5:30 p.m. The office in Tikal maintains irregular hours.

Postage rates are one of the many great bargains in Guatemala, and, thankfully, the postal system is fairly efficient in its handling of postcards and letters. Packages are another story. There are complicated regulations concerning how parcels may be wrapped, and anything sent overseas must be inspected by postal officials before it is sealed. For faster service, try UPS, DHL, Federal Express, or a local shipping specialist, such as Get Guated Out in Panajachel or Conexión in Antigua.

First-class airmail between Guatemala and the United States or Europe typically takes about ten days to reach its destination. Postcards are delivered within three to six weeks. International postal rates are inexpensive.

Media

The most popular daily newspapers are *Prensa Libre, Siglo XXI,* and *El*

Gráfico, published in the capital and available in most parts of the nation. Local English-language publications appear from time to time in Antigua and Guatemala City. The best in recent years have been *This Week in Central America*, an irreverent and opinionated regional report on business and politics based in Guatemala City, and *The Revue*, an Antigua weekly catering to expatriates. Also helpful (and free) is *The Siglo XXI News*, published in Guatemala City on the Web.

Taxes and Tipping

Moderate tips of about 10 percent are customary in Guatemala when paying for restaurant meals. Tipping is also expected for hotel porters, maids, doormen, tour guides, and others who provide personal services. Tipping taxi drivers is not a Guatemala tradition, but the practice is becoming more common with the influx of foreign visitors.

In major hotels, tips to bellboys, skycaps, and porters for check-in and check-out assistance averages $1 per bag. Hotel maids are generally tipped 50 cents per person per night and doormen $1 for hailing taxis.

There is an automatic value-added tax of 7 percent on restaurant food and beverages and an additional 10 percent on lodging.

Business Hours

Most businesses are open Monday through Friday from 8:00 a.m. or 9:00 a.m. to 6:00 p.m. or 7:00 p.m., with an *almuerzo/siesta* break from noon to 1:00 p.m. or 2:00 p.m. Retail stores and some other businesses are open Saturday mornings. Shopping centers are usually open from 9:00 a.m. to 8:00 p.m., Monday through Saturday.

Government and professional offices are generally open continuously from 9:00 a.m. to 5:00 p.m. weekdays. Banks are usually open from 8:30 a.m. or 9:00 a.m. to 2:30 p.m. or 3:00 p.m. Museums and art galleries generally are open from 9:00 a.m. to noon and 2:00 p.m. to 5:00 p.m., closing Monday or Wednesday. Archaeological sites are open every day except principal holidays, from 8:00 a.m. to 5:00 p.m.

Native Food and Drink

Guatemala is not known as a gastronomical paradise—for good reason. The native food, differing only slightly from indígena to Ladino to Caribbean regions, is usually simple and bland. The emphasis is on corn tortillas, white rice, black beans, *plátanos* (fried bananas), squash, and the occasional piece of fried, roasted, or stewed chicken. Although onions, pepper, chile, garlic, and achiote spice are added to Guatemalan dishes with some regularity, there is nothing incendiary on the typical menu. Traditional meat dishes, such as *pepián* and *carne guisada*, are often served with a red or dark sauce, but these tend to be mildly flavored. Guacamole (avocado salsa) and *chirmol* (a red pepper sauce) are sometimes served as side dishes. They are a welcome complement to the *tamales* (cornmeal-wrapped meat pies) and *chile rellenos* (stuffed peppers) that are part of native Guatemalan cuisine.

Rum is delicious and downright cheap. Locally produced alcoholic beverages include *caldo*, a fruit punch, and *rompopo*, a concoction made with rum, eggs, and sugar. *Horchata*, the milky rice drink popular in southern Mexico, is also available here, as is *aguardiente*, a high-octane sugarcane brew popular at fiesta time. In lowland areas you may also be offered home-brew cashew wine.

As in most of Latin America, lunch (*almuerzo*) is frequently the biggest meal of the day. Many businesses and offices shut down between noon and 2:00 p.m. to accommodate this custom. Dinner (*cena*) begins around 7:00 p.m. or 8:00 p.m. and may continue as late as midnight. Breakfast (*desayuno*) is typically light fare, such as toast, coffee, eggs, and/or fruit. Guatemalans have a sweet tooth, and bakeries and candy vendors can be found throughout the country. Despite Guatemala's status as one of the world's premier coffee exporters, it is difficult to find a good cup of coffee. Almost all of the best beans are exported, and restaurant patrons are often served a lukewarm liquid flavored by dehydrated coffee crystals or powdered Nescafé.

Fresh fruit and salad are available in many restaurants, but exercise caution whenever you are uncertain about cleanliness in storage and preparation. Hepatitis, cholera, and other infectious diseases are easily transmitted through careless handling and washing of these foods. The same applies to *ceviche*, the marinated raw-fish salad popular here and in other parts of Latin America.

In Guatemala City and Antigua, and to a lesser extent Panajachel and Quetzaltenango, are many restaurants serving international cuisines from Chinese to German to Brazilian, as well as fast-food outlets such as McDonald's, Pizza Hut, Taco Bell, Wendy's, and Burger King. The Guatemalans are fond of fried chicken, and local chain stores such as Pollo Campero do a brisk business.

Holidays, Feast Days, and Festivals

Guatemala's legal national holidays are January 1, Semana Santa (dates vary), May 1 (Labor Day), June 30 (Army Day), September 15 (Independence Day), October 20 (Revolution Day), November 1 (All Saints' Day), December 24, December 25, and December 31. Many people also take Friday afternoons off during the Lenten season and/or on Corpus Cristi Day (in early June, date varies).

INGUAT publishes an invaluable directory of fiestas that is available from any of its offices as well as from Guatemalan embassies and consulates. Ask for the **Directorio de Fiestas**.

APPENDIX B
INSIDE GUATEMALA

Transportation

Airlines
Note: Airline service to and from Guatemala is subject to frequent change. The following carriers were serving Guatemala to and from the following destinations as of 1999. All phone numbers are in Guatemala City unless otherwise indicated.

AeroCaribe, Flores, Chetumal, Cancún, Mérida, Tuxtla Gutierrez, Oaxaca, 333-6001

Aeronica, Mexico City, Managua, San José, Panama City, Toronto 332-5541

Aeroquetzal, Flores, Cancún, 331-1173

Aerovías, Flores, Belize City, Chetumal,Cancún, 334-5386

American Airlines, Miami, 334-1716; in U.S. (800) 433-7300

Aviateca, Flores, Miami, New Orleans, Los Angeles, Mexico City, Cancún, Managua, San José, 331-8222 in Guatemala City; 926-1337 in Flores; in U.S. (800) 327-9832

Canadian Airlines, Toronto, San Salvador, in U.S. (800) 426-7000

Continental, Houston, 335-3330; in U.S. (800) 525-0280

COPA, Miami, San Salvador, Managua, San José, Panama City, 331-6813

Iberia, Santo Domingo, Madrid, Panama City, Miami, 331-1012; in U.S. (800) 772-4642

Jungle Flying, Tikal, Copán, Guatemala City, 360-4920, jungleflying@guate.net

KLM, Curaçao, Lisbon, Amsterdam, Mexico City, 337-0222; in U.S. (800) 777-5553

LACSA, San Francisco, Mexico City, San José, San Salvador, Panama City, San Pedro Sula, 331-8222, ext. 1310; in U.S. (800) 225-2272

Mayan World Airlines, Guatemala City, Flores, Cancún, Managua, Tegucigalpa, San Pedro Sula, 339-1519 or 334-2067, Petén 926-0370

Mexicana, Los Angeles, Mexico City, San José, 333-6011; in U.S. (800) 531-7921

SAM, San José, San Andrés, Bogotá, 334-6797
TACA, Los Angeles, Washington, Houston, New York, Miami, Belize
City, San Salvador, 332-2360; in U.S. (800) 535-8780; in Canada
(800) 387-6209
Tapsa, Flores, 331-4860
Tikal Jets, Flores, 926-0386
Tropic Air, Flores, from Belize City and Ambergris Caye; U.S. (800)
422-3435; Texas (713) 440-1867
United Airlines, Los Angeles, 334-5285; in U.S. (800) 241-6522

Boats
To and from Punta Gorda, Belize, to Puerto Barrios, Guatemala (daily).
To and from La Palma, Mexico, and El Naranjo, Guatemala (daily). Water
taxis also make shuttles between Puerto Barrios, Lívingston, and towns in
Honduras. Puerto Quetzal on the Pacific and Puerto Santo Tomás on the
Caribbean are served by about a dozen cruise ships per year.

Buses
Check with local hotels or travel agencies for international bus companies
serving the Guatemalan land border crossings at Talismán and Tecún
Umán, Mexico; Benque Viejo, Belize; El Florido and Agua Caliente,
Honduras; and Ciudad Pedro de Alvarado and San Cristóbal Frontera, El
Salvador. Major bus companies (all based in Guatemala City unless oth-
erwise indicated) are listed below.

Fuente del Norte (second-class), 9a. Calle at 17a. Calle, Zone 1
238-3894 - Guatemala City/Petén
Galgos (first- and second-class), 7a. Avenida 19-44, Zone 1, 253-9943 -
Guatemala City/Coatepeque/Quetzaltenango/Mexican border
Línea América (first- and second-class), 2a. Avenida 18-47, Zone 1,
232-1432 - Guatemala City/Quetzaltenango
Litegua (first- and second-class), 15a. Calle 10-42, Zone 1, 253-8169 -
Guatemala City/Puerto Barrios
Los Halcones (first- and second-class), 7a. Avenida 3-62, Zone 1,
Huehuetenango, or 7a. Avenida 15 27-29, Zone 1, Guatemala City,
253-8169 - Huehuetanango/Guatemala City
Maya/Tikal Express(first- and second-class express). 17a. Calle 9-36,
Zone 1, 253-9325 - Guatemala City/Petén
Rápidos del Sur (first- and second-class), 20a. Calle 8-55, Zone 1,
251-6678 - Guatemala City/Mexico/El Salvador/Honduras borders

Rosita (second-class),15a. Calle 9-66, Zone 1, 251-7351- Flores/Belize
City/Guatemala City
San Juan Travel (first-class), Hotel San Juan, Santa Elena, Petén,
926-0041 - Flores/Sayaxché/Belize City/Chetumal
Tica (first-class), 11a. Calle 2-72, Zone 1, 331-7705 - Guatemala
City/El Salvador/Honduras/Nicaragua/Costa Rica
Transportes Melva, 3a. Avenida 1-38, Zone 9, 331-0874 - Guatemala
City/San Salvador

Auto Rental
Aventuras sin Límite, Hotel Melchor Palace, Melchor de Mencos,
926-5196. Specialists in Petén and Belize car rentals.
Avis, 12a. Calle 2-73, Zone 9, 331-2734, fax 332-1263; 5a. Avenida
Norte No. 22, Antigua, 832-2692
Dollar, Avenida de la Reforma 6-14, Zone 9, Guatemala City,
334-8285, fax 332-6745
Hertz, 7a. Avenida 14-76, Zone 9, Guatemala City, 332-2242, fax
331-7924
National, 14a. Calle 1-42, Zone 10, Guatemala City, 368-0175, fax
337-0221
Optima, 3a. Avenida 3-63, Zone 13, Guatemala City, 472-3180, fax
472-3195; also at the airport and Antigua.
San Juan Auto Rental, Hotel San Juan, Santa Elena, Petén,
926-0042, fax 926-0041. Specialist in Petén car rentals.
Tabarini, 2a. Calle A 7-30, Zone 10, Guatemala City, 331-6108, fax
334-192, and 2a. Calle Poniente 19 "A", Antigua, 832-3091
Tikal Rent A Car, 2a. Calle 6-56, Zone 10, Guatemala City, 336-
7832. Arranges for cars to be picked up in Flores and Santa Elena.

Travel Information

U.S. State Department Travelers' Advisory Service
(202) 647-3712 (Washington, D.C.)

Centers for Disease Control and Prevention
Travelers' Advisory Service, (404) 332-4559 (Atlanta, Ga.)

Institución Guatemalteco de Turismo (INGUAT)
7a. Avenida 1-17, Centro Cívico, Zona 4, Guatemala City, 331-1333,
fax 331-4416

Recommended Tour Guides and Travel Agencies

Guatemala City

Clark Tours/Guatemala Travel Advisors, Edificio El Triangulo, Nivel 2, 7a. Avenida 6-53, Zone 4, 331-0213, fax 331-5919 Traditional tours of highlands, cities, and Tikal. Recommended.

Ecotourism & Adventure Travel Specialists, Avenida Reforma 8-60, #105, Zone 9, 361-3104, fax 334-0453, ecoadventure@ mail2.guate.net, www.ecotourism-adventure.com. Petén office: Casa Roja, El Remate, 204-8826. Specializes in natural history tours and adventure travel throughout Guatemala as well as Belize, Mexico, Honduras, and the Dominican Republic. English spoken. Highly recommended.

Exclusive Travel, 16a. Calle 7-29, Zone 9, 334-3854, fax 334-3901. Traditional and Spanish-language instruction tours of highlands, major cities, and Tikal.

Excursiones Spross, 2a. Avenida 3-25, Zone 9, 336-6594, Tours of Lake Izabal, Río Dulce, and Belize cayes.

First Discount Travel, Boulevard Liberación 6-31, Zone 9, 339-3601, fax 339-3608. Specializies in highland tours; good prices on airfares.

Turansa, Centro Comercial El Molino, Km. 15, Carretera Roosevelt 590-3574, fax 590-4688. Traditional circuit: Tikal, other Mayan sites.

Unitours, 7a. Avenida 7-91, Zone 4, 331-4151, fax 334-2001, unitours@infovia.com.gt. Traditional circuit plus archaeology, adventure, and nature-oriented tours.

Viajes International, Edificio Villa Vistana 110, Avenida las Americas 34-42, Zone 13, 333-3456. Cultural and Spanish-language instruction tours, in conjunction with Backroads International of New Orleans.

Antigua

Antigua Tours, (Casa Santa Domingo Hotel, 3a. Calle Oriente 28 832-0228, elizbell@guate.net. Guided walking tours of Antigua by Elizabeth Bell, resident historian and bilingual co-author of an excellent guidebook on the city; slide lectures. Highly recommended.

El Club de los Viajeros, 1a. Calle Poniente 14C and 6a. Calle Poniente 14, 633-3408, fax 832-3408. Organized tours throughout Guatemala, including Tikal, Lívingston, Lake Atitlán, and Chichicastenango; shuttle service.

Servicios Turisticos, Atitlán, 6a. Avenida Sur 7, 832-0648. Shuttle transportation to Panajachel, tours of Lake Atitlán area.

Turansa (Radisson Villa Antigua), 9a. Calle Final, 832-2928 5a Avenida Norte 22. 832-2664, fax 832-2928. Traditional tours of Antigua and the highlands, as well as Tikal, Copán, and other Mayan ruins.

Viajes Tivoli, 4a. Avenida No. 10, 832-4274 or 832-0892. Traditional tours of Antigua and the highlands.

Quetzaltenango

Guatemala Unlimited, 12a. Avenida C-35, Zone 1, 761-6043. Traditional circuit, plus auto, horse, and bicycle rentals.

SAB de Guatemala, 1a. Calle 12-35, Zone 1, 761-6402, fax 761-8878. Traditional tours of Quetzaltenango and the western highlands.

Panajachel

Panajachel Tourist Services, Edificio Rincon Sai,Calle Santander 1-30, 762-2333. In U.S. Box 520922, Miami, FL 33152. Horseback riding, nature walks, and biking tours.

Servicios Turisticos Atitlán, Calle Santander 3-47. 762-2246. Shuttle transportation to Antigua, tours of Lake Atitlán area.

El Petén

Aventuras sin Límites, Hotel Melchor Palace, Melchor de Mencos, 4a. Calle 8-15, Santa Elena, 926-5196. Maya sites, river trips, auto rental, hotel, and restaurant.

Hotel San Juan Travel Agency, Santa Elena, 926-0041, fax 926-0041. Maya sites, including Tikal. Auto rental, hotel, bus service, plane tickets.

☷ GUATEMALA

Based Outside Guatemala

Exito Latin American Travel Specialists,5699 Miles Avenue, Oakland, CA 94618, (800) 655-4053 exito@wonderlink.com. Full-service, Latin America-only, discount travel agency specializing in cut-rate fares, student tickets, land packages, and tours.

Conservation Groups
(partial list)

Asociación Amigos del Bosque, 9a. Calle 2-23, Zone 1, Guatemala City, 338-3486

Comisión Nacional del Medio Ambiente (CONAMA), 5a. Avenida 8-07, Zone 10, Guatemala City, 334-1708, fax 332-7174

Consejo Nacional de Areas Protegidas (CONAP), 3a. Calle 6-28, Zone 1, Guatemala City. 250-0454, fax 253-7061

Defensores de la Naturaleza, Avenida las Américas 20-21, Zone 14, Guatemala City, 337-3897, fax 368-2648, defensores@pronet.net.gt

Proyecto Petenero para un BosqueSostenible (PROPETEN), Flores, Petén. 250-1370, fax 250-1370

Proyecto Ecológico Quetzal, 2a. Calle 14-36, Zone 1, Cobán, 952-1047, bidaspeq@guate.net

Based Outside Guatemala

Audubon Society, 950 Third Avenue, New York, NY 10022, (212) 832-3200. Guatemala City office: 10a. Avenida 2-44, Zone 14, 333-7491, fax 448-7490.

Conservation International, 2501 M Street NW, Suite 200, Washington, DC 2003, (202) 429-5660, fax (202) 887-5188. Guatemala office: ProPetén, Flores, Petén, 926-1370, fax 926-0495.

Ecologic Development Fund, Box 383405, Cambridge, MA 02238 (617) 441-6307 spaul@ecologic.org

Greenpeace International, 1436 U Street NW, Washington, DC 20009. Guatemala City Office: 10a. Calle 3-15, Zone 1, 251-7608, fax 253-4206

The Peregrine Fund/ World Center, for Birds of Prey, 5666 West Flying Hawk Lane, Boise, ID 83709, (208) 362-3716,fax (208) 362-2376. Guatemala office: Parque Nacional Tikal, Petén

U.S. Agency for International Development, Guatemala Conservation Project, 1a. Calle 7-66, Zone 9, Guatemala City, 332-0202, fax 331-1151

Wildlife Conservation Society, 4424 NW 13th Street #A-2, Gainesville, FL 32609, (352) 371-1713, wcsf1@afn.org. Guatemala office: Flores, Petén, 926-0569, wcspeten@guate.net

Guatemalan Embassies and Consulates in the U.S.

Guatemalan Embassy, 2220 R Street NW, Washington, DC 20008, (202) 745-4952
Guatemalan Consulates
• 57 Park Avenue, New York, NY 10016, (212) 686-3837
• 548 S. Spring Street, Suite 1030, Los Angeles, CA 90013, (213) 489-1891
• 9700 Raymond Avenue, Suite 218, Houston, TX 77042, (713) 953-9531
• 300 Sevilla Avenue, Coral Gables, FL 33134, (305) 443-4828

Some Foreign Diplomatic Missions in Guatemala City

Belize - Avenida la Reforma 13-70, Zone 9, 334-5531, fax 334-5536
Canada - Edificio Edyma, Nivel 8vo., 13 Calle 8-44, Zone 10, 363-4348
El Salvador - 12 Calle 5-43, Zone 9, 332-5848, fax 334-3942
Honduras - 16a. Calle 8-27, Zone 10, 337-3921, fax 333-4629
Mexico - 13 Calle 7-30, Zone 9, 333-7258
United States - Avenida de la Reforma 7-01, Zone 10, 331-1541, fax 331-8885

Suggested Reading

History
Galeano, Eduardo. *Guatemala: Occupied Country*. Translated by Cedric Belfrage. New York: Monthly Review Press, 1967.
An excellent and creative glimpse into Guatemala's civil history.

Handy, Jim. *Gift of the Devil: A History of Guatemala*. Toronto: Dumont/South End Press, 1984.
A thorough history of Guatemala from the colonial period through 1983, with an emphasis on economic conditions and peasant uprisings.

Maya Civilization
Coe, William R. *Tikal: A Handbook of the Ancient Maya Ruins*. Philadelphia: University of Pennsylvania Press, 1967.
The best description and maps of Tikal, written by a supervising, on-scene archaeologist. Available in Spanish and English editions.

Everton, Macduff. *The Modern Maya: A Culture in Tradition*. Albuquerque: University of New Mexico Press, 1991.
Excellent photos of the contemporary Maya, accompanied by anthropological essays. Ideally read in tandem with Ronald Wright's book listed below.

Kelly, Joyce. *The Complete Visitor's Guide to Mesoamerican Ruins*. Norman: University of Oklahoma Press, 1982.
A recommended travel companion for the amateur Mayanist.

Prechtel, Martín, *Secrets of the Jaguar: A Mayan Shaman's Journey to the Heart of the Indigenous Soul*. Tarcher/Putnam, 1998.
A Swiss-Native American artist describes his apprenticeship to a traditional Tzutujil shaman in Santiago de Atitlán.

Schele, Linda, and David Freidel. *The Forest of Kings: The Untold Story of the Ancient Maya*. New York: Morrow, 1990.
A gripping story of how secrets of the Maya have recently been unlocked.

Tedlock, Dennis, trans. *The Popol-Vuh: The Maya Book of Wise Council*. New York: Simon & Schuster, 1986.
Several other translations of this unique and sacred book of the Quiché Maya are available.

Wright, Ronald. *Time Among the Maya.* New York: Weidenfield
& Nicolson, 1989.
Entertaining and insightful contrasts between the ancient and modern Maya,
including a good summary of post-conquest history.

Human Rights and Politics

Amnesty International. *Guatemala: Human Rights Violations Under the*
Civilian Government. London: Amnesty International, 1990.
A dispassionate and accurate summary of a horrific history.

Barry, Tom. *Guatemala: A Country Guide.* 2nd ed. Albuquerque: Inter-
Hemispheric Education Resource Center, 1990.
Excellent overview of Guatemala's contemporary history

Daniels, Antony. *Sweet Waist of America: Journeys around Guatemala.*
London: Random Century Press, 1990.
One of the best books on the country written in recent years.

Schlesinger, Stephen, and Stephen Kinzer. *Bitter Fruit: The Untold Story*
of the American Coup in Guatemala. New York: Doubleday, 1979.
A good primer on the CIA-backed coup of the early 1950s.

Simon, Jean-Marie. *Guatemala: Eternal Spring/Eternal Tyranny.*
New York: W. W. Norton, 1987.
Amazing beauty portrayed against a backdrop of terrible poverty and
injustice.

Conservation and the Environment

Beavers, R. A. *The Birds of Tikal.* Houston: Texas A&M Press, 1992.
Available in Spanish and English editions.

Beletsky, Les. *Belize and Northern Guatemala: The Ecotravellers' Wildlife*
Guide. Orlando, Fla: Academic Press, 1998.

Chickering, Carol. *Flowers of Guatemala.* Norman: University of Oklahoma Press, 1973.
Best guide for flower fans.

Correll, Donovan Stewart, and Oakes Ames. *Orchids of Guatemala &*
Belize. New York: Dover, 1985.
Details on the hundreds of orchid species endemic to the region.

Emmons, L. H. *Neotropical Rainforest Mammals: A Field Guide*. Chicago: University of Chicago Press, 1997.
Up-to-date and packed with fascinating facts.

Howell, S. N. G. and Webb, S., *A Guide to the Birds of Mexico and Northern Central America*. 1995.
One of the most comprehensive regional guides for the serious birder.

Kricher, John C. *A Neotropical Companion: An Introduction to the Animals, Plants and Ecosystems of the New World Tropics*. Princeton: Princeton University Press, 1980.
Researched primarily in Central America, this book provides a good overview of nature in the subtropics.

Peterson, Roger Tory, and Edward L. Chalif. *Field Guide to Mexican Birds*. Boston: Houghton Mifflin, 1973.
One of the best birders' field guides for Guatemala, since many of the same species are found in Mexico.

Travel Literature
Canby, Peter. *The Heart of the Sky: Travels Among the Maya*. New York: Harper Collins, 1992.
A real pleasure.

Huxley, Aldous. *Beyond the Mexique Bay*. New York: Harper, 1934.
Impressions by the British novelist.

Maslow, Jonathan Evan. *Bird of Life, Bird of Death: In Search of the Quetzal*. New York: Dell, 1980.
Powerful stuff, a modern classic.

Perera, Victor. *Rites: A Guatemalan Boyhood*. New York: Harcourt Brace Jovanovich, 1986.
Perera is a Sephardic Jew who left Guatemala as a teenager to live in the U.S. but has been back many times since, writing wonderful books about his homeland and neighboring Chiapas.

Stephens, John Lloyd. *Incidents of Travel in Central America, Chiapas, and Yucatán*. 2 vols. New York: Dover, 1969.
One of the best travelogues ever written.

Newspapers and Magazines
AMNESTY BULLETIN
Amnesty International, 322 Eighth Avenue, New York, NY 10001
(212) 807-8400. *Updates on human rights issues in Guatemala.*

THE GUATEMALA BUS TRAVELER'S LITTLE HELPER
Ediciónes Guatejano, 4a. Calle 14, Antigua, 322-1076. *An invaluable English-language guide to the bus routes, schedules, and prices of Guatemala, with additional information on hotels, updated periodically.*

LA PLANETA PLATICA/ECOTRAVELS WEB SITE
ron@greenbuilder.com, www.planeta.com. *Quarterly newsletter devoted to Latin American environmental news, travel information, and cultural resources. $10/year, or free via e-mail and the Web.*

THE REVUE
4a. Calle Oriente 23 or P. O. Box 262, Antigua, Guatemala, 832-0767, Revue@conexion.com.gt, www.revue.connexion.com. *Published weekly in Antigua, a lively compendium of articles, opinion, reviews, and advertising relating to all of Guatemala; available on the Web.*

THE SIGLO NEWS
11a. Calle O-65, Zona 10, Edificio Vizcaya, Guatemala City, 332-8101, fax 332-8119, editors@sigloxxi.com. *Weekly newspaper containing Guatemalan news and features.*

TIMES OF THE AMERICAS
1001 Connecticut Avenue NW, Washington, DC 20036. *Biweekly newspaper concentrating exclusively on news of Latin America.*

TRANSITIONS ABROAD MAGAZINE
P.O. Box 344-6330, Amherst, MA 01004. *Helps place volunteers with nonprofit organizations working for social change in Guatemala and other countries.*

MAYA MESSENGER
Adopt-A-Village, 206 Sixth Street, Bonita Springs, FL 34134, (941) 495-7222, fax (941) 992-7378. *Nonprofit group that sponsors reforestation, education, health care, and economic development programs in Mayan villages of Guatemala's western highlands; participants "adopt" a village to improve the lives of indigenous people. Sells handcrafted Guatemalan gifts to raise funds for its projects.*

INDEX

✸ GUATEMALA

ABOUT THE AUTHOR

Richard Mahler is a writer and broadcast journalist who has reported on conservation and nature topics for more than 25 years. The author of five published books, he has written for more than 100 magazines and newspapers, includ-ing the *Los Angeles Times, Christian Science Monitor, Miami Herald, Out-side, Great Expeditions, Belize First, Mother Jones,* and *New West.* He has been a freelance correspondent for National Public Radio since 1973 and covers environmental matters for the public radio series *Living on Earth,* reporting on such issues as rain forest destruction and preserva-tion of Native American sacred sites.

Mahler's writing and radio pro-ductions have received awards from the Associated Press, PEN USA, the Society of American Travel Writers, and the Radio-TV News Directors Association. As an advocate of natural history tourism and conserva-tion activism, he has worked on behalf of numerous environmental organizations in the American West and Latin America. A longtime resident of New Mexico, Mahler is based in Santa Fe.

The resplendent quetzal, Guatemala's national bird and symbol (Kevin Schafer)

▲ The afternoon ferry unloads at San Pedro on Lake Atitlán.
(Richard Mahler)

▼ Fishing on Lake Atitlán (INGUAT)

Carved stela in the Mayan ruins of Tikal (J.W. Smith)

▲ Dormant volcanoes pierce the morning mists of highland Guatemala. (J.W. Smith)

▼ The "hot lips" plant is used as a natural contraceptive. (Kevin Schafer and Martha Hi

▲ A happy group of highland Maya women and children (Don Usner)

▼ Colonial-era church in the highland town of Zunil (INGUAT)

The roof comb of an ancient Maya temple looms above the jungle at Tikal.
(Kevin Schafer)

Modern Maya are direct descendants of Guatemala's indigenous people. (J.W. Smith)

▲ A tight weave and bright colors characterize traditional Guatemalan toys and textiles. (Richard Mahler)

▼ A Quiché Maya woman sells handwoven clothing in a public market. (J.W. Smith)